SCARLETT'S SISTERS

SCARLETT'S SISTERS

YOUNG WOMEN IN THE OLD SOUTH

ANYA JABOUR

The University of North Carolina Press   Chapel Hill

© 2007 The University of North Carolina Press
All rights reserved
Manufactured in the United States of America

Designed by Kimberly Bryant
Set in Quadraat by Tseng Information Systems, Inc.

The paper in this book meets the guidelines for permanence and
durability of the Committee on Production Guidelines for Book
Longevity of the Council on Library Resources.

Library of Congress Cataloging-in-Publication Data
Jabour, Anya.
Scarlett's sisters : young women in the Old South / Anya Jabour.
p. cm.
Includes bibliographical references and index.
ISBN-13: 978-0-8078-3101-4 (cloth : alk. paper)
1. Young women—Southern States—Social conditions—19th
century. 2. Sex role—Southern States—History—19th century.
3. Southern States—Social conditions—19th century. 4. United
States—History—Civil War, 1861–1865—Social aspects. I. Title.
HQ1438.S63J33 2007
305.242'2097509034—dc22

                                                    2006028929

11 10 09 08 07   5 4 3 2 1

Portions of Chapter 2 appeared previously in "'College Girls':
Community and Identity in the Antebellum South," in "Lives Full
of Struggle and Triumph": Southern Women, Their Institutions and Their
Communities, ed. John Salmond and Bruce Clayton (Gainsville:
University Press of Florida, 2003), 74–92. Portions of Chapter 3
appeared in "'It Will Never Do for Me to Be Married': The Life
of Laura Wirt Randall, 1803–1834," Journal of the Early Republic 17
(Summer 1997): 193–236, and "Resisting the Altar: A Case Study
of Conversion and Courtship in the Antebellum South," Maryland
Historical Magazine 96, no. 1 (Spring 2001): 29–51. Portions of
Chapters 2 and 6 appeared in "Albums of Affection: Female
Friendship and Coming of Age in Antebellum Virginia," Virginia
Magazine of History and Biography 107 (Spring 1999): 125–58. All
are reprinted with permission of the publishers.

CONTENTS

ILLUSTRATIONS

ACKNOWLEDGMENTS

This book has been more than ten years in the making, and I have accumulated professional and personal debts that can never be repaid but must be acknowledged. I am grateful to the helpful and knowledgeable staff at the Southern Historical Collection, the Maryland Historical Society, the Virginia Historical Society, the South Carolina Historical Society, the Center for American History, Emory University, the Special Collections Library at Duke University, and the Interlibrary Loan Department at the University of Montana for their invaluable assistance. A Mellon Research Fellowship from the Virginia Historical Society and a Women's Studies Research Grant from Duke University helped to defray the expenses of research in their archives; several grants from the Department of History and the University Grant Program at the University of Montana made it possible to purchase several valuable collections on microfilm, as well as to conduct research at the Southern Historical Collection, Emory University, and the South Carolina Historical Society.

Meeting fellow travelers is one of the greatest pleasures of conducting research in far-flung archives. I would like to express my appreciation for the many people who showed an interest in my work and guided me to relevant sources, including Dwayne Cox, who provided me with photocopies of the Whitfield Family Papers at Auburn University; Mary Carroll Johansen, who introduced me to the Carrington Papers at the Virginia Historical Society; Gitte Nielsen, who photocopied Sarah Lois Wadley's diary for me; and Tammy Whitlock, who gave me an undated essay titled "Womanhood," salvaged from an estate sale and a "Little Southern Belle" paper doll for inspiration.

At professional conferences sponsored by the Southern Historical Association, the Society for Historians of the Early American Republic, the Southern Association for Women Historians, and the Society for the History of Children and Youth, I have benefited from the encouragement, insight, and criticism of other scholars working on related topics. I would like to acknowledge helpful exchanges with Emily Bingham, Joan Cashin, Catherine Clinton, Cita Cook, Dan Kilbride, Charlene Boyer Lewis, Jan Lewis, James Marten, Lucia McMahon, Victoria Ott, Anne Firor Scott, Elizabeth Varon, and Tammy Whitlock. Charlene Boyer Lewis and Jane Turner Censer gave especially generously of their time and knowledge by reading the entire manuscript. I am immensely grateful to them for their comments and suggestions, as well as to the three anonymous readers who reviewed the work for the University of North Carolina Press.

Closer to home, I am grateful for the support and insights of my colleagues in the Department of History, especially Richard Drake, Linda Frey, Paul Lauren, Kenneth Lockridge, Jody Pavilack, Fred Skinner, Pamela Voekel, and Jeff Wiltse; and in the Women's Studies Program, especially Jill Bergman, Sara Hayden, and Rita Sommers-Flanagan. I also owe a debt of gratitude to my students; I am glad to say that the young women I teach have greater opportunities to enact their resistance than the young women I study. My students' academic and activist achievements are a constant source of inspiration for me.

Katherine Beckley has not read a single word of this manuscript, but her influence is evident in these pages nonetheless. She has accompanied and assisted me on research trips, accommodated my writing schedule, become acquainted with the women who inhabit this book, and provided unstinting and ever-enthusiastic support throughout the process of writing it. Her presence in my life serves as a constant reminder of the continuing importance of women's relationships in contemporary America.

I can think of no more appropriate introduction to this book than to dedicate it to the women who reside in its pages. Young women in the Old South were not always admirable (or even likable) characters, but they did their best with what they had, and in the process, they left a poignant record of possibilities unexplored, alternatives foreclosed, and resistance suppressed. I hope that this story of the women who came before me will help the women who come after me to write—and live—a different story.

SCARLETT AND HER SISTERS:
YOUNG WOMEN IN THE OLD SOUTH

In my office in the Department of History at the University of Montana, a "Gone With the Wind" mouse pad has been my constant companion for the past decade. Now curling and dingy, this usually pedestrian object is enlivened by a Technicolor image of a swooning Scarlett O'Hara supported by the handsome Rhett Butler against a background of the flames that consumed Atlanta near the end of the Civil War.

I purchased this item when I first came to Montana as a whimsical commentary on my field of study—southern women's history—which seemed somehow anomalous in a western state that granted women the right to vote in 1914 (six years before the ratification of the Susan B. Anthony Amendment) and gave the nation its first congresswoman, Jeannette Rankin, three years later. Yet over the years, countless people have been captivated by the image; a stunning number of my northern-born-and-bred visitors exclaim, "*Gone with the Wind* is my favorite movie (or book)!" These comments gradually taught (or reminded) me of a fundamental truth that scholars of the South sometimes prefer to ignore (or forget): Americans' ideas about the South—and particularly about southern women—continue to be shaped by Margaret Mitchell's Depression-era account of the Civil War South and by David Selznek's tremendously popular film adaptation of the novel.[1]

For all of historians' efforts over the past three decades to dispel the myth of the southern lady—Laura Edwards's recent synthetic account, *Scarlett Doesn't Live Here Anymore*, might well be subtitled *And She Never Did*—the image of Scarlett O'Hara, the quintessential southern belle, continues to dominate the popular imagination. Given the focus of most histories of southern women, this is not surprising. Although scholars have recently —and rightly—expanded their definition of "southern women" to include nonslaveholding white women, free black women, and enslaved African American women, as well as elite plantation mistresses, they have not yet turned their attention to *young* women of any class or racial background. Indeed, while southern historians of gender have begun to investigate elite white men's coming-of-age experiences and northern women's historians have recently undertaken scholarship on northern girls and adolescents, remarkably few scholars have addressed the subject of young white women in the nineteenth-century South. (By contrast, slave children, both boys and girls, have drawn more scholarly interest, as the notes and bibliography in this book attest.) The few extant book-length studies of white girls and young women in the antebellum South perpetuate, rather than investigate, the mystique of the southern belle by using the word "belle" in their titles. In short, historians have not yet produced the sort of in-depth analyses of young white women in the Old South that might challenge or complicate the popular image of this group as giddy girls, fickle flirts, and husband-seeking hussies.[2]

Yet probing the experiences and identities of young women in the Old South is tremendously important to our understanding of the American South, the Civil War, and gender identity more generally. After all, it was young white women of the slaveholding class, more than any other group, who epitomized the grace, leisure, and beauty of the mythical southern lady. Thus, understanding southern (white) womanhood requires more than exploding the moonlight-and-magnolias mythology of the southern lady, as Anne Firor Scott did in her pioneering study, *The Southern Lady*; it demands probing beneath the surface of the romanticized image of the southern belle. A full understanding of southern white womanhood necessitates investigating the experiences and identities of young women in the Old South. This study of young women in the Old South—a group I refer to as "Scarlett's sisters"—introduces a new category, age, to the study of white women in the antebellum South. In doing so, it demonstrates that age is as definitive a social category, both on its own and in combination with others, as the classic triumvirate of race, class, and gender that have concerned most historians of the American South.[3]

Scarlett's Sisters brings together the history of the American South and the emerging study of female coming-of-age in the Anglo-American world. What Joseph Hawes termed "the strange history of female adolescence" in a 1985 article has at last, two decades later, begun to receive due scholarly attention. In his pioneering study of adolescence in the United States, Joseph Kett commented that, as the first group to experience a prolonged period of physical maturity without work responsibility, (elite) "girls were the first adolescents." Yet despite this insight, Kett, who published his study shortly before a new wave of feminist scholarship called attention to the importance of women's history, neglected girls to focus on boys' development. Until recently, many historians—including women's historians—have accepted the notion that girls experienced a relatively smooth transition from childhood to adulthood, seamlessly shifting from dependence on their parents to dependence on their husbands rather than wrestling with a prolonged period of "semidependence," the heady and confusing mix of independence and dependence that Kett attributed to young males grappling with the changing possibilities of an urbanizing, industrializing, democratizing nation. New scholarly studies challenge this presumption, revealing that the transformation from girl to woman was a significant—and often contested—process on both sides of the Atlantic Ocean, beginning prior to the nineteenth century and continuing to the present. Yet while the new study of female coming-of-age has been attuned to national differences, it has not addressed regional variations, instead presenting the American Northeast as the normative path of development for the entire United States.[4] In this book, I hope to address this oversight by combining sensitivity to regional variations with awareness of age as a category of analysis.

I also intervene in an ongoing debate over the definition and meaning of youth and adolescence. Nineteenth-century Americans generally understood the life stage of "youth" as beginning in the teens and lasting well into the twenties. Yet, much like contemporary historians, the writers and reformers who concerned themselves with young people in nineteenth-century America usually included only males in their definition of youth. Although the rise of women's history has challenged the historical invisibility of girls and young women, most scholarly studies of female youth focus on the problematic category of adolescence. Both the meaning and the nomenclature of female coming-of-age were in flux in the nineteenth century, as the title of Jane Hunter's recent study of Victorian girlhood in the United States, How Young Ladies Became Girls, suggests. Historians have rightly noted that the concept of "adolescence" is historically and socially constructed, yet in their attempts to define "girls" and "girlhood," they propose arbitrary definitions (females under the age of twenty, unmarried, and unemployed; the period between menarche and marriage) that say more about contemporary understandings of coming-of-age in the present than they do about the realities faced by girls and young women in the past.[5] In short, the terminology in use inadequately conveys the challenge that confronted girls in the process of becoming women: a lengthy process of transformation that encompassed multiple stages of life, each marked by distinctive rites of passage.

In this book, I have chosen to accept this ambiguity and to highlight the nebulousness of coming-of-age by using both the term "girls" and the phrase "young women" to refer to my subjects. Like my subjects, however, I

Nineteenth-century Americans regarded women's destiny as inevitable. "The Life & Age of Woman" depicts the "stages of woman's life from the cradle to the grave," from a "smiling infant . . . unconscious of her future days" to the pinnacle of mature womanhood, enclosed in "a husband's arms," full of "a mother's anxious love and care," and "absorbed in household duties." Southern girls revealed female coming-of-age as a contested process, however. Prolonging the unnamed stage of "ripened beauty" between "girlish pastimes" and "a husband's arms," they resisted assuming "the cares which woman's life must know." (Library of Congress)

alter my use of these signifiers as girls-becoming-women gained in age and experience. For instance, I almost always refer to female students as girls—or, more often, as they did, as "schoolgirls"—but I use the phrase "young women" to refer to newlyweds, inexperienced matrons, and young mothers, reflecting these women's own understanding of their changing status. By using shifting language to refer to my subjects, I wish to remind my readers of the changing meanings attached to age and gender. I also wish to call attention to the betwixt-and-between nature of these southern ladies-in-the-making, for it was this very life stage—this liminal position on the borders of girlhood and womanhood, this age and gender limbo—that made "Scarlett's sisters" so attuned to the liabilities of their culture's definition of femininity. Young women in the Old South were both critical to and critical of their culture and their place in it. Their unique situation gave them the ability and the desire to comment upon, to challenge, and, ultimately, to change the American South's narrow definition of southern womanhood.

In this book, I use the personal writings of young women in the Old South to explore the meaning of southern womanhood from the vantage point of a group poised to become their society's feminine ideal: young, elite, white women. Although at times I will call attention to experiences that were specific to this group's regional identity, their class standing, and their racial privilege, Scarlett's Sisters is not a comparative study; I refer readers interested in learning more about northern, working-class, or enslaved children to the notes and the bibliography. While the subjects of this study are generally between the ages of fifteen and twenty-five, I am more interested in their life cycle than in their chronological age. I define "girls" and "young women" as individuals engaged in the process of coming-of-age—of becoming adult women. As the table of contents suggests, this was by no means a simple or quick process. Rather, young women in the Old South experienced—and helped to shape—coming-of-age as a prolonged and contested set of experiences that spanned a decade or more of their lives. Moreover, this set of experiences was shaped by the time and place in which it occurred, as well as by the group for whom it occurred. By focusing on young, white, female southerners, I present coming-of-age as a self-fashioning process that involves adopting—and adapting—racial, regional, and gender identities within a particular historical context: the mid-nineteenth-century South.[6]

Turning our attention to young women in the Old South sheds new light on southern womanhood, as well as female coming-of-age. No group of southerners lavished more attention on the meaning of southern femininity than the individuals expected to epitomize it; nobody reflected more seriously on what it meant to be an elite, white, southern woman than southern ladies-in-the-making. Training the spotlight on ladies-in-training thus illuminates the identity of the South (and, thus, by extension, regionalism). Focusing on young women in the Old South exposes the meaning of womanhood (and thus, by extension, gender). Finally, studying "Scarlett's sisters" also makes possible a new interpretation of this country's greatest internal conflict: the Civil War.

While historians have long recognized the ways in which the war served as a national coming-of-age, they have yet to probe how individuals came of age during the United States' own bildungsroman. Although the most recent and accomplished study of elite women in the Confederate South, Drew Gilpin Faust's Mothers of Invention, includes young women, Faust does not differentiate between their actions and attitudes and those of older women.

And, as her title suggests, she is more interested in adult women than in girls and adolescents. But for young women in the Old South, the Civil War represented not only a political crisis but a personal one, as they measured the lessons they had learned about womanhood against the exigencies of war—and found them wanting. It was southern girls and young women—"Scarlett's sisters"—who would challenge conventional gender roles and contribute to what Jane Turner Censer has dubbed "the reconstruction of white southern womanhood" in the postwar era.[7]

Scarlett's Sisters, like Gone With the Wind, is a story that understands southern girls' experiences as inextricably intertwined with southern history, particularly the Civil War, which divided not only North from South but also the Old South from the New. But unlike Gone With the Wind, it is a story based in fact, not fiction; it is the story of the fictional Scarlett's flesh-and-blood counterparts, her historical "sisters," not the story of Margaret Mitchell's green-eyed vixen. But for all that, it is no less a story, and it is as full of romance and passion, grief and heartache, drama and pathos, as the story from which it borrows its title.

In an effort to capture the personal dimensions of this story, I have begun each chapter with a "cameo": a brief review of the life of one young woman whose experiences encapsulated the stage of life, or rite of passage, detailed in the chapter itself. It is my hope that this approach will allow readers of Scarlett's Sisters to become personally acquainted with a few of the individuals whose lives and writings compose the basis of this book.

Meet Lizzie Kimberly, who spent a wintry afternoon in Raleigh, North Carolina, building a "snow lady," complete with "laced bodies and large hoops." Follow Margaret Graham, a shy schoolgirl from rural Georgia, to the "perfect paradise" of Wesleyan Female College, where she reveled in her newfound identity as "a college girl." Probe the thoughts of Washington, D.C., resident Laura Wirt, who, declaring, "it will never do for me to be married," tutored her younger siblings and dreamed of establishing a "charming happy hall" for single women with her cousin, Louisa Cabell. Become acquainted with Virginia belle Ella Noland, who enjoyed "a most delightful winter" with her female friends and male admirers in the capital city, Richmond, prior to her engagement. Eavesdrop on the private musings of Texas bride Lizzie Scott, who, pondering the meaning of marriage in her journal, predicted, "My life will be entirely changed." Trace the transformations experienced by Loula Kendall Rogers, an incurable romantic who bewailed the exchange of sanctified love for "lard and sausages" in the rural Georgia home she shared with her husband. Experience the trials of southwestern migrant Martha Hunter Hitchcock, who, after several miscarriages, at last gave birth to a sickly child named Lily who made Hitchcock "a perfect slave" to her care. Finally, enter into the world of Sarah Morgan, who witnessed the destruction of the Civil War firsthand in the occupied city of Baton Rouge, Louisiana, and longed to don her brother's Confederate uniform but turned aside at the last moment for fear of being witnessed in male garb—by her pet parakeet! These are just a few of the many nineteenth-century southern girls and young women whose voices demand an audience in this book.

I have used the personal writings of more than three hundred southern girls and young women in the preparation of this volume. The sources range widely in time period, geographical area, and type. The earliest documents date from the last decade of the eighteenth century; the latest documents date from the closing decade of the nineteenth, although the greatest bulk of materials date from the mid-nineteenth century. My subjects hail from the Upper South, the Deep South, and the Old Southwest; they lived in large cities, in small towns, and in the countryside. In selecting materials, I was primarily interested in how revealing the sources were—in how much they had to say about girls' own experiences and emerging identities—and thus I have defined personal writings broadly to include letters, diaries, notebooks, scrapbooks, autograph albums, and memoirs. While a few are published, most are handwritten documents held in university archives and state historical societies located throughout the South; interested readers may consult the bibliography at the end of this volume for a complete list.

Each type of source illuminates a different aspect of southern women's coming-of-age experiences. Personal correspondence is perhaps the single richest source; extensive collections of letters between friends and family members comment on a wide range of topics, including school, single life, courtship, marriage, and motherhood. Autograph albums highlight particular rites of passage, including commencement and marriage; albums also draw attention to the significance of female friendship, since signatories were, almost without exception until the Civil War, overwhelmingly female. Diaries offer in-depth speculations on personal identity at nearly every stage of life, from girlhood through adulthood. Notebooks and scrapbooks contain information on both southern girls' formal education and their recreational reading. Memoirs help to fill in the gaps left in other materials and are especially useful in illuminating the years prior to adolescence, when few girls kept diaries or corresponded with friends.[8]

I have augmented these sources with a variety of illustrations. Many are drawn from the personal papers of my subjects. Diary entries, sketches, and report cards not only illustrate important themes but also convey the delightful sense of discovery that every researcher finds endlessly fascinating.

I also analyze images of young women from popular print. Because images of southern women before the Civil War are few and far between, I turned to national periodicals to illustrate certain aspects of female coming-of-age. While such images usually were produced in the North, those chosen for inclusion here reflect themes and activities prominent in the lives of my southern subjects; they also appeared in magazines marketed throughout the United States and mentioned in the writings of southern girls and young women, such as *Godey's Lady's Book*. Including these images alongside the text underscores the importance of national trends as well as the persistence of regional variations. Finally, whenever possible, I have included photographs of the young women featured in this book and of unknown southern girls like them. I hope that all these images will complement—and complicate—the more familiar image of southern womanhood depicted in *Gone With the Wind*.

While my subjects exhibit considerable variation in place of residence, they can all be classified, broadly speaking, as elite: white, well-to-do, and educated. Although the majority of women included in this study came from slaveholding families, not all were members of the planter class; many were the daughters of small farmers, professionals, merchants, and artisans. As a group, the girls and young women who inhabit this study came from the South's mercantile and planting elite and those who aspired to that status. The socioeconomic standing they held (or were in the process of achieving) inspired—and in some instances required—them to reflect carefully on the meaning of becoming a southern lady.

This wide-ranging set of sources reveals a strikingly consistent composite of southern ladies-in-the-making. As the chapter titles suggest, time of life proved a more useful interpretive distinction than comparisons between rural and urban, planter and professional, or Upper South and Lower South. Without discounting the very real differences among well-to-do white southern women, I argue that the process of coming-of-age was, while not a universal experience, certainly a meaningful experience that was shared by a broad cross-section of elite white women. I also contend that southern girls' coming-of-age experiences remained remarkably similar throughout the antebellum era, differing more in detail than in substance until the onset of the Civil War. The democratizing impulses set in motion by the American Revolution and the rise of evangelical Christianity, as well as the market revolution driven by the industrial revolution and a nascent consumer society—both commonly identified with the decline of patriarchal authority and the rise of youthful rebellion—were stalled by the South's reliance on slavery as both a source of labor and a building block of society. In the antebellum South, then, challenges to both male and parental authority were blunted by the presence of slavery; one result was a marked pattern of continuity in the life experiences of elite white girls and young women prior to the upheavals that accompanied the Civil War.[9]

Girls' personal documents have shaped the form of this book, as well as providing its content, for I have taken my cue from my subjects in determining what exactly constituted coming-of-age in the antebellum South. In choosing what topics to treat, I have followed my subjects' lead, focusing on issues that they discussed in depth and at length. Each chapter takes up a life stage that young women in the Old South regarded as an important aspect of the lengthy process of becoming a southern woman. Thus, while some expected topics are treated here—such as southern debutantes' "coming out" balls—many unexpected topics are included as well, such as religious conversion, academic competition, and single life. Although I originally anticipated concluding this study with marriage (as most studies of "girls" do), my reading of the sources convinced me that this would misrepresent young women's own experiences. Adjusting to married life, learning to keep house, and assuming the responsibilities of motherhood, my informants told me in no uncertain terms, were important aspects of coming-of-age. Not until all these phases had been completed did a young female achieve full status (and accept total subordination) as a southern woman. In short, I allowed my subjects to guide my selection and organization (although not my interpretation) of topics. When they wrote about a given experience, "I am a woman now," I paid attention.

I also paid attention—at first reluctantly, then with growing enthusiasm —to the changes ushered in by secession, war, and defeat. While the remarkable consistency of girls' emphasis on particular portions of the life cycle initially drew me toward a study of the constant features of coming-of-age in the nineteenth-century South, I gradually became convinced that the Civil War was just as important an era for southern *girls* as many scholars have contended it was for southern *women*. The Civil War and its aftermath not only reshaped the rituals that defined southern womanhood but became a set of experiences that redefined what it meant to be a southern woman. Most importantly, the Civil War allowed the latent—or suppressed—rebelliousness of young southern women to emerge for the first time. If the story of young women in the Old South might be described as "how young women were kept in line," the story of young women in the Confederate South might be called "how young women re-drew the lines."[10]

Ultimately, I contend that the South's young women—those who had not yet been fully socialized into compliance with the status quo—held and wielded the most power to disrupt that status quo, at least relative to their adult counterparts. While southern historians have called attention to the subtle resistance and outright rebellion of poor whites and enslaved blacks, when they address elite women, they usually conclude that these women changed—when they changed at all—with tremendous reluctance. Indeed, in the introduction to her recent collection of southern women's documents, Joan E. Cashin has proposed that elite women in the Old South participated in what she terms a "culture of resignation": a shared conviction that "women should accept inequity, not resist it."[11] The fundamental conservatism of the older women who inhabit most studies of southern women offers a striking contrast to the young women who are the subjects of this book, who positively ached for—and ultimately helped to create—change. Young women in the Old South participated not in the culture of resignation that Cashin describes but rather in what I describe as a culture of resistance.

In using the word "resistance" to describe the actions of my subjects, I am drawing upon the work of revisionist scholars of slavery who revolutionized the study of the South's "peculiar institution" beginning in the 1960s and 1970s. Rejecting the viewpoint of the so-called Dunning school, which held that since American slaves held few large-scale slave rebellions and established few runaway slave communities, they accepted their enslaved status, revisionist historians argued that the behavior of American slaves fell along a continuum of resistance, with absolute quiescence (the child-like "Sambo") at one end and total rebellion (the vengeful "Nat Turner") at the other. The vast majority of slaves fell somewhere in between, using what James Scott has termed the "weapons of the weak" to engage in "everyday forms of resistance"—breaking tools, feigning illness, forging friendships, creating families, practicing religion—that helped them to maintain their own humanity and identity (and thus resist the worst aspects of enslavement) without drawing notice (and punishment) from their masters.[12]

From the mid-nineteenth century forward, observers have commented upon certain similarities between the status of women in antebellum America and the position of slaves in the Old South. From different ends of the political spectrum, South Carolina slaveholder Mary Chesnut, with her famous pronouncement, "Poor women! Poor slaves!" and New York abolitionist-feminist Elizabeth Cady Stanton, who declared that "the wife . . . holds about the same legal position that does the slave," antebellum women in particular drew comparisons between white wives and black slaves, both of whom were deprived of the fruits of their labor, their legal identity, control of their sexuality, and rights to their children.[13]

Early scholarship in southern (white) women's history often echoed these comparisons. Pioneering southern women's historian Anne Firor Scott argued that the control of both white women and enslaved blacks was essential to the theory and the practice of the South's agricultural economy, based on a "peculiar institution" of racial bondage. While the dominant ideology of southern womanhood that placed white women under the control and protection of white men—the myth of the southern lady—was distinct from the dominant ideology of white supremacy that sanctioned the enslavement of people of African descent, these ideologies were both interlocking and mutually reinforcing. In her provocative study *The Plantation Mistress*, Catherine Clinton argued that there were important parallels between the position of women and the position of slaves in the antebellum South. Both groups, Clinton contended, were under white male control, and both were treated as "reproductive units, replaceable if necessary." [14]

In the wake of a more recent wave of scholarship focused on African American and non-elite white women in the South, southern historians have become increasingly attuned to the benefits that accrued to slaveholding white women, as well as the disabilities under which they suffered. In her comprehensive study of southern women (both black and white), Elizabeth Fox-Genovese persuasively argued that many (perhaps most) elite white women, aware of the advantages of race and class that they enjoyed in slaveholding society, allied themselves with their husbands, fathers, and sons rather than identifying with their slaves. As southern women's history matured, historians became increasingly convinced that elite white women enjoyed significantly more power and freedom than enslaved African Americans—and they knew it. Yet even as they wielded (and sometimes abused) power relative to nonslaveholding whites and black slaves, elite white women remained subordinate to men of their own class and race. As Drew Gilpin Faust has recently and perceptively argued, slaveholding women in the Old South were simultaneously privileged and oppressed.[15]

Awareness of the important distinctions between African American slaves and the white women who called themselves their mistresses, then, should not obscure the equally important parallels between these two groups, who were oppressed similarly, although not equally. Given the similarities between the status of women and slaves in the Old South—indeed, given the similarities between all forms of oppression—it should come as no surprise that young women resisted the status quo in ways very similar to those practiced by black slaves—that is, by engaging in covert resistance rather than in overt rebellion.[16]

Just as the majority of American slaves did not engage in armed warfare, the majority of southern white women did not join the women's rights movement that emerged in the antebellum North and that was closely tied to the growing abolitionist movement. But this does not mean that southern women unquestioningly accepted the South's social order and their place in it, any more than the lack of large-scale armed rebellions among American slaves indicates that black people accepted their enslavement. Young women, in particular, showed themselves willing and able to resist the status quo. Much like enslaved African Americans, they did so by practicing subtle arts of resistance rather than engaging in overt acts of rebellion. Unlike black slaves, they were able to make use of their relative advantages—including higher education, financial security, and leisure time—to develop a critique of the very society that gave them those advantages. Thus, the resistance evinced by "Scarlett's sisters" reflects both the similarities and the differences between white women and black slaves in the antebellum South.

My research in the personal writings of young women in the Old South reveals the existence of a vibrant subculture that sanctioned and encouraged resistance to prevailing models of southern womanhood. As historians of southern women—who generally focus on mature women—have pointed out, adult southern women tended to lead isolated lives on remote plantations. In addition, because of the relative lack of separation between men's and women's "spheres" of home and work, older women who led their lives "within the plantation household" had relatively few shared and sequestered spaces in which to safely develop a critique of the status quo. Yet southern girls and young women, who enjoyed the opportunity to congregate in peer groups at female academies, fostered and maintained a sense of community through ritual visits, autograph albums, and extensive correspondence. Female friendship networks in the Old South allowed young women to explore and express their dissatisfaction with the future that awaited them. Young women in the Old South thus constituted a dissident subculture that resisted the dominant culture's definition of femininity.[17]

Young women in the Old South created and maintained a significant southern subculture: a female youth culture of resistance. Recent scholarship has revealed young people and single women participating in southern subcultures—whether in urban centers or at spa resorts—that sanctioned unconventional female behavior, if only temporarily or in the name of familial duty. In Scarlett's Sisters, I suggest that young, well-to-do, white, southern women not only individually critiqued prevailing models of southern womanhood; they also collectively (if not fully consciously) created a female youth culture that undermined male dominance and promoted female agency. While this culture of resistance was, in some sense, futile— young white women did not, after all, build a women's movement or create feminist institutions—it was nonetheless significant, both for southern girls' identities and experiences in the Old South and, in the Civil War era, to lay the groundwork for the reconstruction of southern white womanhood.[18]

Southern girls' remarkable and widespread reluctance to come of age—to become southern ladies—both illustrates the ambivalence with which they viewed their assigned roles and demonstrates their ability to resist adopting those roles. Young women in the Old South proved stubbornly resistant to cultural imperatives that would usher them smoothly and quickly from the status of dependent daughters to that of submissive wives. They both prolonged each life stage as long as possible and relished the opportunity to develop certain life stages—school attendance and single life in particular—that, at least temporarily, opened up alternative female identities and thereby new visions of southern womanhood. Prior to the Civil War, the extended and contested process of coming-of-age, which indicated girls' reluctance to accept socialization into their assigned roles, was the chief way in which "Scarlett's sisters" expressed their resistance.

Young women in the Old South resisted their subordinate status and assigned role by manipulating the privileges they possessed without endangering their privileged status. Like the quiet revolutionaries in James Scott's analysis, referenced above, southern girls exhibited a "prudent awareness of the balance of power" in their words and actions. Thus, young southern women did not reject marriage, housekeeping, and motherhood, but they did resist these roles, waging a form of ideological—if safely invisible—warfare by prolonging each life stage and thereby postponing adult female responsibilities. They did not produce a coherent argument in favor of equal rights, but they did develop a piecemeal critique of male dominance by complaining about their constricted opportunities. Finally, during the Civil War, they translated what Scott terms "the infrapolitics of subordinate groups"—in this instance, a female youth culture of resistance—into a politics of rebellion.[19]

Although southern girls and young women resisted male dominance and exerted female agency throughout the process of coming-of-age, some stages of the female life cycle—and some periods of southern history—offered more opportunities for resistance than others. As girls and adolescents in the antebellum South, "Scarlett's sisters" observed firsthand both the liberties to be lost and the privileges to be gained by exchanging the identity of a little girl for that of a young lady. Sequestered in private homes and subject to parental rules, however, southern teenagers had few opportunities either to envision or to enact alternatives to the status quo.

Attending school was a pivotal experience for many young women in the Old South. The female academy gave young southern women the necessary tools to create a female youth culture of resistance: supportive friendships with other women and an alternative vision of womanhood. Southern schoolgirls reveled in the company of their peers and in the opportunity to improve their minds. Even after leaving school, young single women relied on a community of their peers to support them in their efforts to exert control over their lives and their futures, whether as dutiful daughters or as fascinating belles.

The life stage of engagement would prove to be another pivotal moment in young women's lives. By agreeing to subject themselves to the constraints of marriage, young women in the Old South moved away from a culture of resistance and toward a culture of resignation. Southern brides-to-be grudgingly accepted the harsh reality that attaining romantic love required them to submit to male dominance. Married life, which once again subjected women to male guidance and limited them to the family circle, offered little scope for resistance. Nonetheless, new wives and young matrons continued to depend on their female friends for emotional and practical support as they assumed their adult roles. While some women found romantic love and domestic authority to be sufficient exchange for female friendship and intellectual challenges, others were deeply dissatisfied; their outspoken unhappiness contrasted sharply with popular prescriptions of cheerful submission. Externally compliant, these young women were far from complacent. Their ability to enact their resistance was reduced, but their desire to exert agency over their own lives remained intact.

It was not until after having children that young women in the Old South discovered an identity that was both compelling and rewarding enough to compensate them for their lost youth and reconcile them to their assigned role: motherhood. Unlike the life stages that preceded marriage, motherhood was permanent rather than temporary; unlike marriage, it offered women both companionship and purpose. Maternity quickly became central to female identity in the Old South. As mothers, young women rested their hopes on their children's future rather than their own.

That future proved to be different for girls who came of age during the Civil War. Young women's resistance escalated into rebellion during, and in response to, the Civil War. The war upset the social order that had both granted these women their privileged status and ensured their oppression. With many of their privileges of race and class already reduced because of war and emancipation, the delicate prewar balance—resisting oppression without endangering privilege—was no longer tenable. The balance tipped toward rebellion as southern girls, inspired not by northern feminists' assertions of natural rights but by Confederate mottoes of independence, challenged the oppression of gender.

In *Scarlett's Sisters*, I argue that young women in the Old South resisted their culture's imperatives at the same time that they embodied its ideals. Much as they objected to certain aspects of the Old South's patriarchal society based on the "peculiar institution" of slavery, southern girls also regarded both coming-of-age as southern ladies and the presence of enslaved African Americans as inevitable and unchangeable. Thus, they expressed their doubts about the status quo in covert ways, such as prolonging each stage of life and avoiding the next, rather than in overt ways, such as joining the fledgling women's rights movement that burgeoned in the mid-nineteenth-century North. The outbreak of civil war offered young women an opportunity and an ideology to translate their long-standing resistance into outright rebellion. When the Civil War challenged the accepted institution of race-based slavery, young women also challenged the conventional definition of southern womanhood, casting accepted understandings of southern femininity aside along with their former dependence on male guidance and slave labor. Because of their actions, the southern lady was truly "gone with the wind," even as the image endured.

"THE LADY YOU WOULD HAVE ME BE":
LIZZIE KIMBERLY

When Lizzie Kimberly, the daughter of University of North Carolina professor John Kimberly, left her home in Chapel Hill, North Carolina, to attend St. Mary's School in Raleigh in 1856, she was thirteen years old and rapidly approaching adulthood. As her aunt remarked, "Lizzie grows so fast she will be a Young Lady in size before she is one in mind unless she applys [sic] herself closely to her studies." While Lizzie did indeed apply herself to her studies, she devoted even more attention to another task: becoming a young lady. Over the next three years, Lizzie became increasingly aware of what it meant to become a southern lady and increasingly anxious to adhere to the standards of ladylike conduct. Her correspondence with her father from 1856 to 1859 illuminates the teen years as a period of transition from childhood to adulthood—and the transformation of a girl into a lady.[1]

At age fourteen, Lizzie still considered herself a "little girl" and enjoyed boisterous outdoor play. In November 1857, she reported to her father that she and the other "little girls" liked to "run out in the woods and play and ride on the branches of the tall pine trees." Lizzie was unconcerned with propriety; pleasure was her aim. "We have fun," she pronounced emphatically.[2]

Soon, however, the girls' "fun" began to foreshadow their future. Later that same winter, in February 1858, Lizzie and her schoolmates built "a snow lady" in the center of the schoolyard. "It has a *very large hoop* and a *very small waist*," she explained, and was "made to imitate some of the fashionable young ladies" at school, complete with "laced bodies and large hoops."[3] Although Lizzie and her playmates may have been poking fun at the airs that the "fashionable young ladies" put on, they were no doubt also aware that they too would soon don corsets and hoopskirts.

While Lizzie was surely not wearing either a corset or a hoopskirt when she engaged in such vigorous activities, by the following summer, she needed a new wardrobe; "all my dresses was [sic] too small," she explained to her father, despite her attempts to let out tucks and hems to prolong their life, and she had outgrown her underclothes as well. In her fifteenth year, Lizzie lengthened her skirts, exchanged the loose-fitting chemise of girlhood for the form-fitting corset of womanhood, and joined the ranks of "the fashionable young ladies" at her school.[4]

The restrictive clothing in vogue in the mid-nineteenth-century South both represented and required a new concern with proper behavior rather than with boisterous play. Lizzie soon adopted a more dignified manner that befitted her standing (and her clothing) as "a grown lady." After her fifteenth birthday in March 1858, much to her younger sister Emma's evident disgust, Lizzie preferred "to sit up like a young lady and talk, and laugh," rather than play outdoors.[5]

Lizzie's transformation from little girl to young lady was not only external. As she approached her fifteenth birthday, she wrote to her father to ask permission to join the Episcopal Church. "I am old enough," she argued, "and I wish to lead a christain [sic] life." When John Kimberly responded favorably, Lizzie was delighted. Confirmation would transform her not only from an unbeliever to a Christian but also from a child to an adult—and, equally importantly, from a girl to a woman: "I am so glad that you like for me to be a true christain [sic] woman," she wrote to her father.[6]

Being "a true christain woman" meant, among other things, repressing anger. With her natural high spirits, Lizzie evidently found it difficult to adhere to codes of conduct that viewed anger as both sinful and unladylike. In April 1858, Emma tattled that Lizzie had "been angry several times since confirmation." Such displays of temper threatened to negate both Lizzie's claim to Christianity and her standing as a well-behaved young lady. Although she found the task difficult, Lizzie did her best to subdue her passions and govern her temper. "It is so hard Father to be meek submitting and unmindful of self," she confessed in November 1858.[7]

Learning to be "meek submitting and unmindful of self," like wearing cumbersome clothing and making polite conversation, was part and parcel of becoming a lady, however, and Lizzie was determined to lead "a young lady's life." In spring 1858, she began calling herself "Lilly," a nickname that called attention to her new, adult identity. People outside of the family also recognized Lizzie's new status; during a summer trip to a fashionable retreat in the North Carolina countryside in July 1858, Lizzie was delighted to be addressed as "Miss Kimberly," a title that signified her standing as a young lady rather than a little girl.[8]

Although she continued to struggle with her temper, by 1859, Lizzie could with some justification claim to be a young lady in both body and mind. On the day that made her "sweet sixteen," she boasted to her father that she was no longer "awkward" but had heard "a good many persons say how lady like and graceful [she] was." Lizzie did her best to be ladylike in attitude, as well as appearance: "I hope I may . . . learn to conquer all my passions," she vowed, and become "the lady you would have me be."[9]

Three years of intense self-scrutiny and intentional self-fashioning had transformed Lizzie Kimberly from a hoydenish tomboy into a sedate young lady. Like young Lizzie, many southern girls expressed a desire to adopt lady-like behavior when they entered their teens. Also like Lizzie, other southern girls found that becoming a lady was a complicated and lengthy process. Becoming a lady meant giving up childish play for adult pursuits—and adopting new clothing that both symbolized and enforced the decorum expected of young ladies. It also meant adopting a gentle, agreeable manner—and, hopefully, the morality that reinforced and made genuine the display of amiability required of southern ladies. Ultimately, however, becoming a lady meant learning to please others; whether inspired by Christian principles or social pressures, girls like Lizzie Kimberly learned to tailor their behavior to others' desires and to become the ladies that others would have them be. The teen years thus suggest what was at stake for southern girls-becoming-women: what privileges they stood to gain, and what liberties they stood to lose.[10]

"I DID AS I PLEASED": GIRLHOOD

Before they entered their teens, southern girls experienced significant license in their daily activities. The reminiscences of Virginian Nell Grey illuminate the relative freedom of the preteen years. Commenting on antebellum life from the vantage point of the early twentieth century, Grey contrasted the "reserve of the American girl" in her teens with "the freedom with which Southern children entered into the social life."[11]

Grey's use of the term "children," rather than "girls," was significant, for in the antebellum South, girls' and boys' lives were not sharply demarcated prior to adolescence. Southern women's reminiscences are full of fond recollections of friends of both sexes. Although some girls were educated privately at home or attended all-girl schools, boys and girls often attended school together. Boys and girls also played together. Without regard to gender (or race, according to some accounts), southern children engaged in many vigorous outdoor activities: snowball fights, sliding on the ice, and sledding in the winter; "running games," fishing, swimming, and wading in brooks, and sliding down grassy hillsides on planks in the summer.[12]

Girls' play with each other was similarly active. Gay Robertson Blackford, who grew up at The Meadows, a plantation in Washington County, Virginia, before the Civil War, described a particularly rowdy game of blindman's bluff (a popular game in which a blindfolded child fumbles about in search of the other players, who dance just beyond reach) in her postwar reminiscences. While she and her sister Lizzie were playing in the "nursery" upstairs, their running and jumping caused the plaster of the ceiling of the room below to crack.[13]

Outdoor activities were still more lively. Anna Rosalie Quitman, the daughter of a wealthy sugar planter in the Natchez, Mississippi, area, attended a neighborhood school where she joined a group of high-spirited girls who enjoyed vigorous outdoor play during midday recess. Quitman's journal, which she began keeping when she was ten years old, suggested that she and her playmates enjoyed freedom to roam around the schoolyard and surrounding woods, where they found numerous ways of entertaining themselves and each other. On one occasion, when one enterprising girl brought a dead crow to school, the entire gang took turns kicking the feathered carcass down to the bay. Other pastimes were more organized, though no less active. An especially popular game was one that Quitman simply called "Bear." Although the details of this game are unclear, "Bear" was evidently an active game, as on one occasion, Quitman tripped over a stump and hurt herself while playing.[14]

Georgia resident Ella Anderson Clark also enjoyed outdoor play. In her postwar memoirs, she described the "great fun" that she and her female classmates had damming up a stream near her neighborhood school. The girls hurried to remove their high shoes and woolen stockings, roll up their pantalets, and hold up their petticoats to wade in the resulting "pond" before the dam broke. When it did, joyous panic ensued: " 'There goes the dam' someone screamed and amid peals of laughter each one hopelessly tried to stop the break," recalled Clark, adding, "Oh the carefreeness of that country life! I can hear the screams and merry laughter after all these years!"[15] Such wistful recollections indicate that as children, white girls in the antebellum

South enjoyed the opportunity to engage in raucous romps with each other, with boys, and, sometimes, with slave playmates.

Girls combined such spirited play with more sedate pursuits, such as

reading novels and "fairy tales," holding tea parties, picking flowers, drawing or painting, and playing with dolls. Such activities set elite girls apart not only from boys, who avoided such feminine play, but also from slaves, who lacked the education and the tools to engage in these types of leisure activities. Unlike outdoor play, indoor play segregated children by both gender and race. Much as they enjoyed running and yelling outside, girls also appreciated the quieter indoor activities that indicated the racial privilege and gender role they would assume as adults. Georgian Loula Kendall Rogers pronounced that she "had always rather read than do any thing else" and recalled with pleasure the "plays" that she and her girlfriends wrote, directed, and acted out based on their favorite novels.[16]

Playing with dolls was another favorite pastime. When South Carolinian Rose Ravenel's dolls were lost during the early days of the Civil War, her governess cut out paper dolls as a substitute. Ravenel and her siblings also enjoyed playing with "flower dolls," which they constructed from inverted flowers, using straw or grass for arms and legs (the petals were the dolls' dresses, and "dolls had narrow skirts or wide skirts as each flower came in season"). These makeshift dolls afforded Ravenel and her sister, Lizzie, many hours of pleasure. "We amused ourselves by telling their histories," she recalled, explaining, "they had many adventures[;] I would bring a large family of snowdrops to visit Lizzie's Periwencle's [sic]." Before the Civil War, southern girls had more elaborate dolls, like the "pretty wax doll" that Anna Rosalie Quitman's sister received as a gift from her father in 1852.[17]

Whether they were elaborate or simple, dolls were important to southern girls. What eleven-year-old Virginian Katie Darling Wallace called "playing babies" encouraged girls to practice their adult roles. Girls sewed clothing for their dolls, nursed them when they were sick, and even said bedtime prayers for them. Such activities were clearly modeled on their mothers' behavior and foreshadowed girls' responsibilities to their own families in the future. Doll play could teach lessons about race and class, as well as about gender. Rose Ravenel remembered that she and her sister had "hickory nut dolls as mammers [i.e., mammies] for our flower dolls." Even in the realm of imagination, southern girls understood that enslaved black people served privileged white ones.[18]

Dolls enabled girls to play at courtship and married life, as well as at motherhood and housekeeping. Mississippian Anna Rosalie Quitman had an extensive collection of dolls that included both "gentlemen" and "Ladies." In addition to sewing clothing and holding tea parties for her dolls, Quitman acted as her dolls' scribe, recording "all my dolls letters" to each other. Clearly modeled on letters that Quitman's mother and sisters received from female relatives and read aloud to the family, these letters suggest Quitman's awareness of southern women's adult roles. The letters begin with an exchange between "Mansfield Lowell" and his fiancée "Josephine." Lowell was extremely anxious for the wedding to take place. "O my darling dont you wish that the wedding night would make hast [sic] and come[?]" he demanded. The "letters" also included correspondence between "cousins" regarding family news, between female friends about "beaus," and even one from a "married" woman complaining about her loneliness in the absence of her "husband," to whom she referred as her "Lord & Master." Even before entering her teens, then, Quitman understood that in the Old South, marriage was expected and men were in charge.[19]

Some of girls' play-acting games with each other also imitated adult roles. One of the favorite games of Anna Rosalie Quitman and her schoolmates was one that Quitman referred to as "Ladies go a visiting." Apparently in this game, as in "dancing school," the girls mimicked their elders' social conventions. Virginian Lily Logan Morrill played a similar game with her mother, in which mother and daughter assumed the personalities of the women who inhabited the Victorian novels both read avidly: "She would pretend to live in one room and personate there some great lady from Bookland. I would choose another room adjacent, and thus together we would 'play ladies,' going to see each other and talking in grand language borrowed from various books." In role-playing games like these, southern girls learned to balance male-female relationships with same-sex friendships. They also practiced their social position as members of the elite, with the education and leisure to engage in refined, cultured activities.[20]

Girls' play with boys also sometimes mimicked adult relationships. Georgian Ella Anderson Clark filled her reminiscences with tales about "sweethearts" at her school. To impress the girls, boys offered them gifts of chinquapins (beechnuts) or sugar cane, drew them water from the spring, or allowed them to ride their plank down the hillside. "Misfortune, but not disaster, often occurred when perchance plank and girl hit a tree, the girl going one way, and the plank going the other way," she recalled with amusement. But a vigilant boy was ready to prove his mettle: "Her sweetheart was watching for this, giving him an added opportunity to prove his devotion and gallantry," she concluded. In interactions like the ones Anderson described, boys learned to be gallant, devoted "suitors," and girls learned to graciously (and passively) accept male attention.[21] Thus, while southern girls' play offered them a glimpse of a world relatively unencumbered by the rules of racial etiquette or feminine propriety, it also reminded them that such freedom from restraint was temporary.

Girls also had household responsibilities that reminded them that they would not be playing mumblety-peg with boys for long. Mothers did their best to teach their daughters the rudiments of housewifery, even if their daughters—like Anna Rosalie Quitman—frequently escaped their supervision to observe lizards in the garden, gather chinquapins from trees, visit the stables to feed the horses, or go fishing at a nearby pond. By age ten, if not before, girls were assigned tasks such as dusting and polishing furniture, setting the table, washing dishes, caring for younger siblings, and, in some cases, supervising slaves at their work. Such activities introduced elite girls to a peculiarly southern form of Victorian domesticity: domestic authority (as slave supervisors) combined with domestic service (as household workers).[22]

The most common household task for girls was sewing. As New Orleans native Eliza Ripley succinctly expressed it: "Every woman had to sew." In the largely rural antebellum South, sewing was an essential skill to outfit homes with bedding and linens and slaves with clothing and blankets. Girls learned to sew early. When still a "little tot," Margaret Walker Weber was required to show off her skill in hemming linens to visitors at her school. Eleven-year-old Katie Darling Wallace often recorded sewing in her Civil War diary. In her memoirs, related in the third person, Gay Robertson Blackford boasted that she and her sister made all their own clothes by the time they were twelve years old. "They never tried anything on—just held it up and cut—and never made a mistake," she recalled proudly. Sixteen-year-old Tennessean Myra Inman sewed and embroidered her own underclothing. Decades later, Eliza Ripley could hear her mother's injunctions ringing in her ears: "Be careful in the stitching of that bosom; take up two and skip four."[23]

In addition to sewing, many girls learned to embroider and knit and experimented with what Margaret Walker Weber called "the culinary art," although girls' cooking was generally limited to special treats, such as popcorn balls, molasses candy (taffy), or gingerbread. Whether practical, like hemming sheets or canning fruit, or purely entertaining, like pulling taffy or baking cakes, such tasks not only taught southern girls useful skills but also acclimated them to the parlors, gardens, and kitchens for which they would soon leave the woods, streams, and fields. "Gay romping girl[s]" would not remain "ever in some mischief," as Loula Kendall described herself at age fourteen; indeed, they learned to regard such youthful freedom as a form of

As they approached their teens, southern girls were encouraged to exchange vigorous outdoor activities for more sedate indoor pursuits. Mothers and other female relatives assumed responsibility for preparing young women for a life of submissiveness and subservience. In this frequently reproduced engraving, "Heel and Toe," an older woman instructs a girl in the quintessentially domestic task of knitting socks. Enclosed by her surroundings—her grandmother's arms, the armchair, the lavishly decorated parlor—and absorbed in her task, the young girl appears not even to notice the world outside. (Library of Congress)

misbehavior. "I was really a bad little girl, a very bad little girl then," Kendall recalled from the vantage point of her seventeenth year, "but I am a little better now."[24]

Although South Carolinian Sally Elmore Taylor, who rode horseback "fearlessly" and dreamed of being a missionary to China, declared of her childhood, "I did as I pleased," her statement captured only part of the reality of southern girls' lives. Southern girls did indeed enjoy a great deal of freedom. What Eliza Ripley referred to as "little girls in pantelettes and pigtails" engaged in vigorous play both with each other and with local boys. At the same time, southern girls recognized that their future would be governed by different rules, and this awareness was reflected in their daily activities. This also was the message that Sally Elmore Taylor's mother tried to impress on her seven-year-old daughter when her uncle lifted her up to stand on the mantelpiece. "I thought my Mother's indignation was appalling," Taylor recalled. "She told him I was a lady (I was *seven* years old!)."[25] Although seven-year-old Sally may not have wished to acknowledge it, she, like other southern girls, grew up with the knowledge that, ultimately, southern ladies-in-the-making would have to exchange the freedom of childhood for the restrictions of adulthood. In the Old South, "little girls" grew up to become "young ladies."

"AT THE THRESHOLD OF WOMAN'S LIFE": ADOLESCENCE

Young women in the Old South became intensely aware of their age—and the birthdays that marked their advancing years—in their teens. When she was only fifteen years old, Mississippi resident Anna Rosalie Quitman referred to herself as a "renowned spinster of Antiquity" and composed a poem commenting on her advanced age:

> Oft am I by the people told,
> "Poor Rosalea! thou grow'st old,
> Look! how thy hairs are falling all,
> Poor Rosalea! how they fall!"[26]

Other teenaged girls likewise registered awareness of their advancing age. "You are indeed getting old," Minnie Bacot teased a friend, Charleston, South Carolina, resident Jane Allston, on her birthday. Growing older was a concern for Bacot as well: "I think I will be very aged when on the 30 of March I am sixteen," she added. Echoing Bacot's concern, North Carolinian Jennie Johnson wrote on her birthday: "Today I am seventeen years old,

A Journal containing a true account of the valorous & chivalrous exploits and hair brained adventures of that renowned spinster of Antiquity A Rosalie Quitman

Monmouth

September 11 1835

"Oft am I by the people told,
"Poor Rosalea! thou grow'st old,
Look! how thy hairs are falling all;
Poor Rosalea! how they fall!'"

Anacreon

Southern girls became intensely aware of their age during the teen years. On the frontispiece of her diary, fifteen-year-old Mississippian Anna Rosalie Quitman described herself as a "renowned spinster of Antiquity." Documents like this one offer a wealth of information about and insight into girls' coming-of-age experiences—what Quitman described as "valorous & chivalrous exploits and hair brained adventures." (Southern Historical Collection, Wilson Library, The University of North Carolina at Chapel Hill) getting old am I not?" Such comments reflected young women's awareness that a teenaged girl was poised "at the threshold of woman's life," as one woman expressed it.[27]

Perhaps because women had so few rights in antebellum society, there was no consensus on the age that marked adulthood. Southerners' private correspondence contains very few references to the idea of a young woman reaching her "majority" at age eighteen or twenty-one.[28] Yet southerners seem to have shared the assumption that in her late teens, a female crossed the threshold from girlhood to womanhood, never to return. One fond mother referred to her daughter's seventeenth birthday as "an hour so looked forward to—of sweet associations & glad hopes" and quoted the young woman herself as saying, "I shall be a *woman* then." Alice Kerr's teacher and mentor Miss Spencer quoted the French author Madame de Saussure to her on her eighteenth birthday: "At eighteen *there is no retreat*—here is womanhood in all its glory—& what increase of dignity & of duty. The child is a child no longer."[29]

In their mid- to late teens, then, young southern women began to think seriously about what it meant to reach adulthood and to assume their adult gender role—to exchange the identity of a little girl for that of a young lady. Like seventeen-year-old Maria Catherine Wiestling, who wrote in 1838, "What an awkward thing I am[!] I wish I knew how to be more lady like," southern teenagers expressed increasing anxiety about their ability to embody the ideal of southern womanhood.[30]

Susan McDowall's reflections were typical of southern adolescents. On the eve of her sixteenth birthday, she recorded a thoughtful entry in her diary that suggested the importance of the teen years as a transformative era in a young woman's life. "My last fifteenth day has passed," she mused; "with the rising sun, I will hail me sixteen, scarcely can I realize that my life has flown so quickly, it seems as yesterday, when I was a tiny babe playing around my mother's knee and in a few years I will be a young lady[.]"[31]

In their teens, southern girls like McDowall began to think seriously about the meaning of becoming young ladies. As Chapter 2 details, many girls spent these years away from home, in a setting that encouraged them to resist the demands of adulthood rather than to accept them as inevitable. Yet to understand the scope of this resistance, it is necessary first to explore southern girls' expectations of the future and their experiences of adolescence. It is against the backdrop of the seemingly non-negotiable demands of southern ladyhood that southern girls' insistence on shaping their own futures appears most clearly as the catalyst for the creation of a female youth culture of resistance.

Adolescence is a historically conditioned concept. The term was not widely used until 1904, when psychologist G. Stanley Hall published his massive two-volume study by that name and established the teen years as a period of problems and possibilities. Even after the "discovery" of adolescence, discussions of this stage of life focused on teenaged boys, for whom the contrast between childish dependence and adult independence was presumably greater than for girls, who simply moved from one form of dependence (on their parents) to another (on their husbands).[32] In the latter decades of the nineteenth century, however, Americans began to call attention to one aspect of female adolescence: puberty.

In the Victorian era, Americans regarded female puberty—the process of physical maturation that prepares girls for childbearing—with considerable anxiety. In the late nineteenth century, many parents took notice of medical tracts that warned that higher learning, by drawing vital energy from women's reproductive systems to their brains, would cause serious—and possibly permanent—health problems. By depriving the uterus and ovaries of energy at a critical time, some medical experts believed, excessive studying during puberty would create disorders in the reproductive organs, disable women for their destined roles as wives and mothers, and lead to mental illness and personal unhappiness.[33]

Antebellum southerners' health concerns, however, were more pedestrian. In a setting in which a fever might forecast malaria, a chill could bring on pneumonia, and a cough seemed to indicate the onset of consumption (the nineteenth-century term for tuberculosis), constant vigilance was required for all family members, not only for girls on the brink of womanhood.[34]

The letters of the Whitfield family of Alabama between 1839 and 1844 illustrate antebellum southerners' general concerns about the health of all members of the family. Mary Elizabeth Whitfield attended school first at Salem, North Carolina, and then at the Judson Institute in her home state of Alabama. In nearly every letter home, Mary assured her family of her continued good health. Yet in the same letters, she also anxiously inquired about the health of her parents and younger siblings.[35] Health, it would appear, was a concern shared by all family members, for all family members.

Certainly Mary's separation from her family heightened their concern for her health. Her instructors—who doubled as her boardinghouse keepers— sent regular reports home to her parents in which they took special care to assure the Whitfields that the school, the surrounding community, and

Mary herself were healthy. When Mary's cousin Rachel, who lived with the Whitfields and attended school with Mary, delayed writing home, she felt compelled to assure her relatives and guardians that ill health had not been the cause of her silence. And Betsy Whitfield's 1844 letter to her daughter was a poignant reminder of the great importance of regular updates. "I hope nothing will prevent you from writing us as often as you can if it is onely [sic] a few lines," she admonished. "You must know that we all feel very anxious about your health. Do my dear daughter take every precaution that lays in your power to preserve it."[36] But the Whitfields' concerns for their daughter's (and niece's) health appear unrelated to fears that intense study would lead to reproductive ailments. Instead, their concerns seem to have stemmed from a general concern about health, combined with the anxiety attendant upon prolonged separation in a time of poor communication.

There are some indications that southern parents in the antebellum era were showing signs of what would develop into the almost obsessive monitoring of the late nineteenth century, however. The correspondence of the Wirt family of Virginia, close contemporaries of the Whitfields, suggests that this southern family focused particular concern on the health of its six daughters: Laura, Liz, Catharine, Rosa, Ellen, and Agnes. All of the Wirt girls suffered from poor health, ranging from simple colds to scarlet fever, and several—Laura and Catharine in particular—also experienced repeated bouts of melancholy, which their parents described as "nervousness" and interpreted as "hysteria," the Victorian catch-all term for what were perceived as "female maladies" related to the all-important and ever-delicate workings of the uterus and ovaries. Moreover, the Wirts, who were generally passionate advocates of advanced learning for women, seem to have made some connection between their daughters' health problems and intense study, since they repeatedly withdrew Catharine from boarding school as a result of her illnesses and ultimately decided to educate the three younger girls exclusively at home.[37]

In this, however, the Wirts seem to have been ahead of their contemporaries, most of whom, like the Whitfields, expressed considerable concern about their daughters' health in general without exhibiting especial concern for their health as adolescent girls in particular. After the Civil War, increasing numbers of parents—especially mothers—wrote anxious letters to their daughters warning them against excessive study and appealing to them to protect their delicate health. But while southern parents in the late nineteenth century regarded close study as the cause of nervous disorders, in the first half of the century, there was not yet a consensus regarding the connection between mental exertion and physical debility. Prior to the Civil

War, most southern parents' concerns about their daughters' health—and most of girls' reported illnesses—revolved around such common ailments as headaches, toothaches, stomachaches, and coughs, chills, and fevers.[38] Puberty, then, does not seem to have inspired much concern—or even attracted much attention—in the antebellum South.

In the Old South, very few girls or their families made any references to bodily changes that accompany puberty, such as swelling breasts, the growth of coarse hairs under the armpits and in the pubic region, or the onset of menses. Before the Civil War, when young women discussed what Mary Frances Gray called "growing pains," they were more likely to be referring to gains in height and weight than they were to menstrual cramps.[39]

An exception to this rule is the Wirt family. Possibly because of the sheer volume of the Wirts' correspondence (Elizabeth, William, and their six daughters exchanged weekly—sometimes daily—letters over a thirty-year period), the collection contains several frank discussions of the girls' "periodical pains," as Elizabeth put it in 1831.[40] Concentrated in the mid- to late-1820s, when the girls were in their teens, these references to menstruation and its side effects offer a rare insight into girls' experience of menarche in the Old South.

In 1826, in a letter marked "Private" and directed to White Sulphur Springs, Elizabeth Wirt gave her oldest daughter, Laura, candid advice on how to deal with menstrual blood. "I do not expect to have any opportunity of sending the articles you mention," she apologized. "You will have to make your maid wash out your night gown, of a morning, & have it ready for you by night," she adjured. "Be sure to have it well *dried*, & *aired* . . . And the same by your *linens*."

In an era before "feminine hygiene" products were mass-produced and marketed directly to consumers, young women and their mothers consulted about the best ways to control the flow of menstrual blood. Most likely, Laura customarily used folded soft cloths to absorb her flow; caught unprepared away from home, she soiled her nightdress and her bedsheets. Her embarrassment is indicated both by her mother's caution in marking her letter "Private" and by the fact that the letter in which Laura presumably asked her mother for menstrual cloths ("the articles you mention") was marked through and made illegible.[41]

Embarrassment was only one of the unpleasant results of menstruation. The Wirts' letters contain several references to menstrual cramps. These letters suggest that this Virginia family regarded abdominal cramps, backaches, and diarrhea as normal (if painful) aspects of menstruation. While they drew a connection between abdominal distress and the onset of menses, the Wirts do not seem have associated puberty and pimples, although this connection appears obvious from their correspondence, in which references to acne and menses are closely linked.[42]

The Wirts did, however, remark upon the emotional, as well as the physical, symptoms of menstruation. In 1828, commenting about the health of his youngest daughter, Agnes, who was fourteen years old at the time, William speculated that both her excessive nervousness and her abdominal discomfort were the result of a "malady peculiarly afflicting at her time of life" and advised his wife to give special attention to her young charge: "This . . . malady ought to be well attended to," he commented. "Do you remember how it affected Laura's nerves & mind — and all the rest of them too at some time or other?"[43]

With the notable exception of the Wirts, southern girls and their parents maintained a stony silence about menstruation and its accompaniments until the Civil War. A few scattered references to menstruation began to appear after the Civil War. In the 1880s, twelve-year-old North Carolinian Edith Elmer drew cryptic symbols in her diary to indicate the onset of her menses. Bettie Crowder's mother expressed concern about Bettie's being "so sick" in 1870, referring to her "free" menstrual courses and recommending that her daughter drink milk with alum and keep "as calm & quiet" as possible. In the Old South, however, most girls did not refer, even obliquely, to menstrual cramps, as North Carolinian Eloise Whitaker did in an 1896 letter to a friend in which she referred to being visited by a "John Howard Payne."[44]

How southern girls thought about the onset of menses prior to the Civil War, then, is difficult to determine from extant sources. Their silence on such matters might indicate fear, loathing, or ignorance; it might also suggest that they simply attached less importance to menstruation (which was, after all, only visible to girls themselves and their intimates) than they did to the outward signs of maturity: dress and hair.

"LACED BODIES AND LARGE HOOPS":
DRESSING UP, GROWING UP

Dress and hair were vital concerns for young women in the Old South. In keeping with antebellum Americans' concerns about hypocrisy (and with elites' worries about social climbing), southern parents, teachers, and other advisers regularly admonished girls against a preoccupation with fashion, recommending "neatness and simplicity" without extravagance. Such advice notwithstanding, southern girls found what one exasperated father called "the single and apparently inexhaustible subject of dresses" endlessly

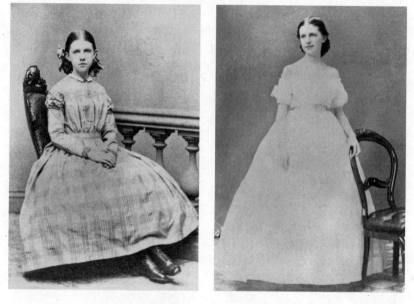

When southern girls entered adolescence, they encountered new constraints on their emotions and their behavior. The outward changes of clothing and hairstyle symbolized southern girls' transformation into young ladies. Here, Washington, D.C., resident Violet Blair is pictured before and after her official debut as a southern belle during the Civil War. Like other teenaged girls in the American South, Blair exchanged the braids and short skirts of girlhood for the elaborate coiffure and long skirts of womanhood—an exchange that both symbolized adulthood and constrained movement. (Historical Society of Washington, D.C.)

fascinating. Even young girls, like eleven-year-old Anna Rosalie Quitman, eagerly pored over fashion magazines like *Godey's Lady's Book*. When girls entered their teens, this interest intensified. Teenaged girls' letters home were filled with requests for dresses or for funds with which to purchase fabric or clothing. Emmie Johnson, a student at St. Mary's School in the 1850s, interrupted her meticulous note taking to make a list of "Dresses for Spring & Summer" in the middle of her school notebook. Girls wrote to each other to share news of the latest fashions and to trade advice about clothes and described their outfits in painstaking detail in their letters and diaries.[45]

Virginian Eliza Lavalette Barksdale was typical in her near-obsessive concern recording her ensembles for every occasion, as entries in her diary during summer 1836 demonstrate:

Rose very early to prepare for cousin Jane Gaines wedding. . . . Dressed in a white swiss muslin frock trimmed with satin, pink lustring sash &

guard, black velvet ribons [sic] inch wide going twice round my head with a small pearl buckle[.]

Dressed for dinner in my purple silk frock & belt white lawn cape & pink neck riband [sic], with the same band & buckle around my head.

Dressed myself for preaching, put on a jackonet frock blue belt & checked muslin cape ruffled all around.

Put on my calico morning gown & checked muslin cape. . . . [Later] I came up stairs to dress for preaching, put on a white jackonet trimmed with cambric in certain & edging, a yellow neck handkerchief & sash.[46]

Girls had good reason to lavish so much attention on their clothing. Despite adults' insistence that "riches and finery never make the lady," as Mary Jefferson Randolph put it in an essay titled "Dress," clothes and hair did, in some sense, "make the lady" in the Old South. At the same time that they warned against showy ostentation, affluent adults desired that their young charges be attired in "the best quality," for only good fabrics could distinguish a well-to-do (and, by definition, white) lady's clothing from that of a poor woman or a black "wench." A young woman's clothing should connote her privileged status without extravagance, as Mary Polk's father suggested when he wrote that he intended to outfit her with "every thing necessary for your comfort in a plain neat style becoming a girl of your standing in Society."[47] But fashion was more than a marker of class and racial status; it was also an indicator of age and gender. In the Old South, clothing and hairstyles functioned both as outward signs of one's status as a young lady and as effective means of enforcing ladylike behavior.

Letting down one's skirts signified girls' coming-of-age. In their teens, young women replaced the relatively short skirts of girlhood with the long, full skirts of adulthood. Many young women, recognizing the importance attached to wearing long skirts, were eager to adopt them as early as their parents would permit. Urging her mother to allow her to wear long skirts in 1847, Julia Turner appealed to prevailing practice at Floral College in Harnett County, North Carolina, to convince her: "Nearly all the girls have on long dresses," she reported, directing, "you must make my dresses long as yours."[48]

Wearing long skirts was an outward, visible sign of having achieved the status of a young lady; the long, full skirts in vogue in antebellum America also enforced the constraints on behavior considered appropriate for young women, for the cumbersome skirts reduced girls' freedom of movement. With less enthusiasm than the precocious Julia Turner, Louisianan Lucy

Scarborough recalled that adopting long skirts coincided with the enforcement of new injunctions about ladylike behavior. "At the period when the struggle to keep skirts at a proper length necessitated a constant letting out of hems and tucks," she wrote in her reminiscences, "the most continuous admonition from her elders to the Girl was not to let her knees show, not to cross her limbs, not to stand with her arms akimbo—for all these things were 'common,' and common was a thing no lady could afford to be." The worries of the "elders" about appearing "common"—that is, failing to display proper class and racial standing—are evident in Scarborough's account, but for "the Girl," what appears most bothersome is "the struggle" to abide by new rules, all of which revolved around what "not" to do.[49]

Underclothing, even more than long skirts, changed young women's appearance and limited their activities. Beginning in their teens, southern girls began to wear corsets (or "bodies"). Reinforced with stays made from steel or whalebone, corsets served to emphasize the girls' developing breasts and to exaggerate the smallness of their waists. By midcentury, hoopskirts—supported by cages of metal and buttressed by yards of tulle—helped to achieve the desired hourglass shape.[50]

Like long skirts, corsets and hoopskirts both symbolized adult status and enforced ladylike behavior. Nineteenth-century reformers railed against tight "lacing" as dangerous to women's health, but fashion continued to define women's bodies within narrow confines—as society defined their roles. Encased in corsets and enclosed in layers of heavy fabric, young women were unable to engage in vigorous outdoor activity.[51]

Changing hairstyles also signified coming-of-age. At about the same time that they let down their skirts and adopted corsets, young women also began to put up their hair and to embellish it with curls and ribbons. Just as they asked their parents for long skirts and stays, in their midteens, girls began to request hairnets, combs, and bonnets to help them to contain, confine, and cover the hair that they had previously worn loose or in braids. Like dress, hairstyles signified class status—only the well-to-do could afford the ornamentation in vogue, and only those with servants could achieve the more elaborate hairstyles—but also connoted the limitations of age and gender. While young girls' hairstyles required relatively little maintenance, wearing one's hair up involved pins, combs, and ribbons, all of which had a tendency to shift and fall out with movement. Thus, when a girl traded her childhood braids for a mature coiffure, she also experienced new restrictions on her activities.[52]

Girls' attention to changing dress and hairstyles—and their parents' willingness to finance fashion—both testify to the importance attached to these outward signs of adulthood in the antebellum South. While social commentators, then and now, have often remarked upon elite southerners' concern for appearances, these markers of class, race, gender, and age were about more than outward show. Ideally, at least, nineteenth-century Americans hoped that physical appearance reflected one's moral character: a good person would be an attractive one; a well-dressed individual would be a self-governed one. Elite southerners shared these ideas to a significant degree, although they also engaged in fashionable competitions that clearly laid more emphasis on external appearance than inner worth. Yet while fashion clearly served as a social marker, it also served other purposes. For southern girls, most importantly, it both required and reinforced a ladylike decorum and dependence that contrasted sharply with the relative freedom and independence of "little girls in pantelettes and pigtails."[53]

"A PERFECT WOMAN":
PRINCIPLES OF LADYLIKE BEHAVIOR

The strictures of young ladyhood were not limited to tight lacing, long skirts, and hairpins, however. Rather, these external controls were intended only to reflect the internalized constraints of ladylike behavior. Young women in the Old South thoroughly imbibed—and sometimes reluctantly internalized—the principles of proper feminine behavior. Many teenagers mentioned reading advice books. With titles like *Letters to a Young Lady*, such books provided a handy reference on appropriate and desirable female behavior and assured girls that becoming a lady was the route to both social acceptance and personal happiness.[54]

In April 1862, Virginian Janet Henderson wrote a composition titled "A Perfect Woman" that praised this rare creature as "one of Gods noblest works." "A perfect woman," she explained, "must be amiable kind & affectionate." Devoting herself to promoting the happiness of those in her family circle, the perfect woman never had the bad grace to feel, much less to display, bad temper: "She does not fret herself about all the petty annoyances . . . but tries to look cheerful all the time." But even this paragon of self-sacrifice was incomplete without religion. "There cannot be a perfect woman unless she fears God & loves to walk in his Holy ways," Henderson concluded. While the ultimate reward for a life of service on earth would be a place in heaven, this young author also received earthly affirmation for her successful attempt to sum up all the qualities of ideal womanhood; one of her parents wrote on the composition: "I hope my dear child that you may live to grow up to be a Perfect Woman."[55]

Like young Janet Henderson, southern girls learned to regard ladylike behavior—including cheerfulness, a gentle nature, and service to others—as a source of happiness for others and of satisfaction for oneself. Moreover, they learned that appropriate behavior would earn them not only social approval on earth but eternal life in heaven. Not surprisingly, then, acquiring the attributes of "a perfect woman" was a major preoccupation for girls on the brink of womanhood.

Eager to earn social approval, some teenaged girls sought out sources of guidance. Fannie Page Hume believed that a book titled *Advice to Young Ladies* contained "some excellent suggestions" and resolved to "preserve it as a sort of text book."[56] But southern girls did not have to take the initiative to find guidelines for proper feminine behavior. Their parents, guardians, relatives, teachers, and ministers all contributed to a virtual cacophony of rules and regulations. Parents' letters to daughters recommended certain behaviors; schoolgirls' compositions parroted approved sentiments. Throughout their teen years (and beyond), southern girls and young women were bombarded with counsel and criticism. The myth of the southern lady was defined for—not by—southern daughters in an extensive set of interlocking ideals that assumed male dominance, denied female agency, and defined womanhood in terms of self-denial and service to others.

The list of ladylike attributes was long and included cleanliness, neatness, patience, industry, kindness, cheerfulness, modesty, politeness, respect for elders, and obedience. But the qualities most frequently and forcefully demanded from "the fair sex" were amiability and piety. Most importantly, a young woman should *please others*; in all settings, a lady's responsibility was to advance others' happiness and find her own happiness in so doing.[57]

"MILD AND AMIABLE DEPORTMENT": GENTILITY AND GENTLENESS

When describing the ideal woman, southerners frequently used the words "amiable," "mild," "soft," and "gentle." Praising his student Mary Whitfield for her conduct, Salem, North Carolina, schoolmaster John Jacobson commented on her "mild & amiable deportment." Writing to her daughter Susan, a student at Mrs. Carrington's girls' school in Richmond, Virginia, Susanna McDowell prompted her twice in less than a month to be "gentle." In a short essay titled "The deportment principles and manners that constitute a lady," Virginian Mary Jefferson Randolph used the phrase "soft and gentle" no less than three times in a single page. Rachel Mordecai's father

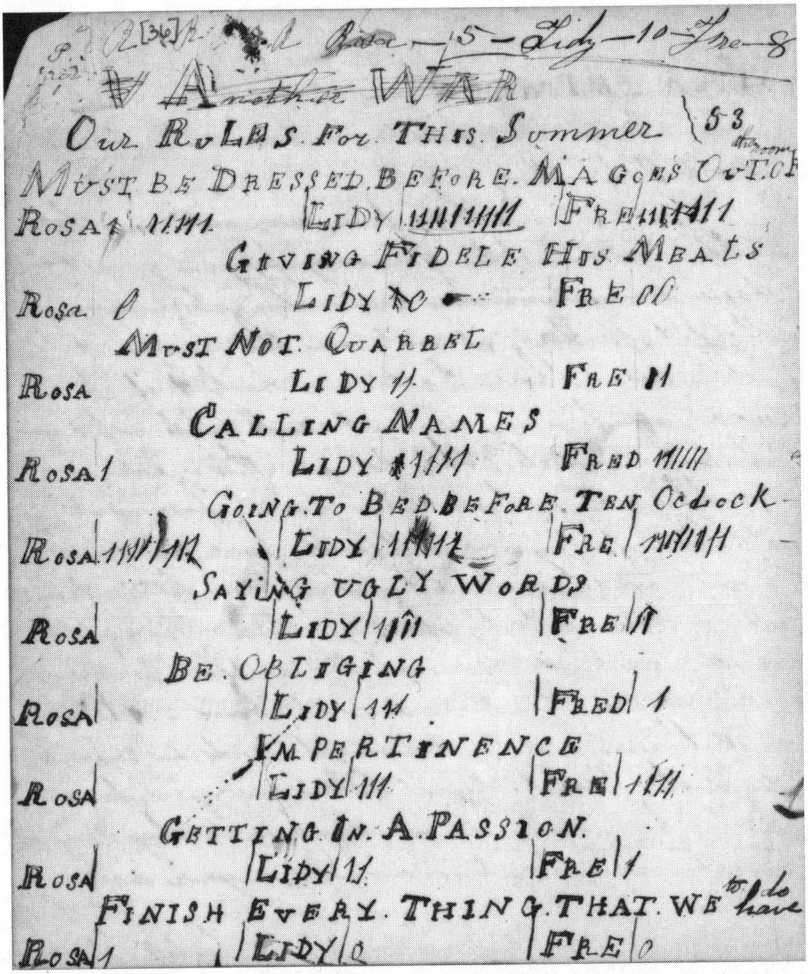

Southern ladies-in-training learned to tailor their behavior to others' expectations. In this page from her journal, titled "Our Rules for This Summer," teenager Anna Rosalie Quitman and her sisters received demerits for such behavior as quarreling, name-calling, "saying ugly words," impertinence, and "getting in a passion." The goal, always, was to "be obliging," as young women learned to earn approval by pleasing others. (Southern Historical Collection, Wilson Library, University of North Carolina at Chapel Hill)

typified prevailing sentiments when he wrote: "I wish to see you an Amiable Woman, esteem'd by your acquaintances & belov'd by your Relatives & Friends for the Gentleness of your Manners."[58]

Examined closely, the words "amiable," "mild," "soft," and "gentle" appear as code words for the suppression of self. Southerners shared with other nineteenth-century Americans the conviction that distinct emotional cultures in childhood prepared boys and girls for strictly differentiated gender roles in adulthood.[59] In the Old South, the emotional norm recommended to girls prepared them for a life of selflessness—of suppressing their own desires and regarding the comfort of others as paramount.

"The emotional work of being good," more than anything else, involved the suppression—or, when that failed, the repression—of emotions. Parents and other adults repeatedly warned young women to subdue their tempers—and their desires. "Avoid fretfulness & passion," Rachel Mordecai's father advised her. Anger "in ev'ry person is unbecoming," he admitted, "but in a female [it] is truly disgusting." Alabama student Mary Kenan's mother also drew a connection between ill temper and selfishness. "I hope you will endeavor to improve in every way & to check every thing in your disposition like obstinacy or self will," she admonished.[60]

The "Rules for This Summer" that Anna Rosalie Quitman and her sisters observed in 1852 demonstrated the concern for containing women's feelings. While the rules included such practical matters as dressing oneself in the morning, feeding the family dog, keeping belongings in order, and going to bed by ten o'clock, the majority of rules focused on keeping the girls' personal desires and passionate tempers under wraps. These included injunctions to avoid quarreling, calling names, or saying "ugly words," as well as the order to "be obliging" and its closely allied reminder to avoid "getting in a passion."[61]

South Carolinian Rose Ravenel learned the importance—and the significance—of governing her temper in an exchange with her black nursemaid, "Maum Katy." The dialogue between the young white woman and the older black woman, which Ravenel recorded in her reminiscences, indicated the class- and race-specific aspects of avoiding anger. While washing up dishes, young Rose became annoyed when she broke some glasses. The Ravenels' family retainer assumed responsibility for instructing the girl in ladylike behavior in this exchange:

MAUM KATY: "Miss Rose you ought not to get vexed"
ROSE: "Maum Katy dont you get vexed some times, every one get vexed sometimes"

MAUM KATY: "Miss Rose I get vexed, it dont hurt no one no harm for me to get vexed [but] you are old Miss daughter, a lady ought not to get vexed"[62]

"A lady ought not to get vexed"—this was a message repeated over and over in southerners' correspondence. Passionate feelings might be overlooked in a (black, lower-class) female, but they were inexcusable in a (white, elite) lady. For elite women in the Old South, avoiding anger was both a badge of femininity and proof of gentility.

If a young woman felt anger, she must never, ever display it. Teenage girls were told repeatedly to contain and conceal their feelings. James Ramsay sternly warned his daughter Margaret to repress her feelings, particularly strong, negative emotions that might cause others discomfort. A woman, he reminded her, should exert "self control, especially over her feelings, emotions, and temper." Most importantly, she should avoid "anger and vexation." "My dear child," he counseled, "you should never allow yourself to get angry . . . but if you should, you must strive not to show it, either in your looks words or actions."[63]

Strictures against anger or selfishness alone could not, of course, keep girls from feeling these strong emotions, although they might make girls ashamed of their feelings and encourage them to repress their emotions. The consequences of girls' efforts to suppress their feelings could be severe; as Chapter 3 illustrates, many young women suffered from serious depression that may have resulted, in part, from their inability or unwillingness to acknowledge their frustration with the limitations on their lives.[64] But southerners hoped that if girls embraced religion they could overcome their human frailties and achieve more than a superficial veneer of mildness and amiability. Religious conversion was thus not only a coming-of-age ritual but also indispensable to attaining the ideal of selflessness.

"PURER WHEN EMBRACED IN YOUTH": RELIGION

For many southern girls, entering one's teens coincided with a prolonged period of spiritual self-examination. As Sara Apphia Hunter expressed it in 1835: "This is my birthday[;] I am now thirteen[;] I ought to be thinking seriously of religion."[65] Belle Price's friend and former schoolmate Alice described her fifteenth birthday as a spiritual coming-of-age. "And you are fifteen, really *fifteen*," she exclaimed. "Ah! Belle, new duties, new trials, new temptations are opening before you," she expounded. "You are no longer a child and a loiterer by the way-side; you are a *woman*, and a '*soldier of the*

Cross:' . . . May God bless you, . . . make this a happy day to you, and make you a shining light in the holy church," she concluded.[66]

Writing to her daughter Susan on her fifteenth birthday, Susanna McDowell urged her to give serious consideration to the state of her soul and to seek "that pearl of great price," the assurance of everlasting life. While McDowell praised her daughter's truthfulness, amiability, intelligence, and beauty, she reminded her—in verse—that these would avail her nothing without attention to "this most important of all subjects": religious faith.

> But something is wanting—
> The picture is marred,
> By the loss of one feature—
> Ah why is it thus scarred?
> Why should not Religion
> With Heaven's own fingers
> Cast out the dark spot
> Where Satan still lingers?

When she learned that her teenaged daughter had "accept[ed] the Lord Jesus, as [her] only hope of salvation," McDowell was "moved" but remained concerned about the young convert's welfare. Urging her daughter to read the Bible and pray regularly, she pledged to assist her in her commitment to "a Christian career." At the same time, she indicated that as a believer, young Susan had also become her mother's peer; she was a fellow Christian woman, not a mere child. "May God bless and guide you," the older woman closed her letter. "Let us pray for one another, & help one another."[67]

Southerners regarded the transition from girlhood to womanhood as incomplete without a religious conversion, or spiritual rebirth. Informing his former student Mary Whitfield of a recent revival in Marion, Alabama, the schoolmaster of the Judson Institute could not refrain from urging her to follow the example of several of Judson's students and make a public declaration of faith: "I hope dear Mary that you will not suffer the precious season of Youth to pass away with out Remembering your Creator," he wrote. As Arkansas resident Elvira Boswell expressed it in a letter to her former schoolteacher, Virginian Martha Hunter, "Religion was purer when embraced in youth."[68]

Southern parents considered young women unprepared for adulthood without religion—which they usually equated with Protestant Christianity. In part, this simply reflected nineteenth-century Americans' assumption that women were incomplete without religion. Particularly in the North, where men were increasingly caught up in the mercenary, grasping world of business and industry, many social commentators regarded women as

indispensable anchors of morality in an increasingly soulless society. Not surprisingly, then, many young women in Victorian America found that a "religious quest" offered a compelling "explanatory system" to describe the "metamorphosis into adulthood."[69]

Southerners shared these prevailing ideas about ideal womanhood, but they also had practical reasons for wishing their daughters to accept the promise of eternal life before they took on the responsibilities of adult womanhood. As adults, southern women were destined to bear numerous children, a dangerous undertaking indeed in an age of high infant and maternal mortality. In addition, southerners had to contend with a hot, humid climate that fostered a disease environment in which such deadly ailments as yellow fever and malaria flourished. In an 1865 letter, James Graham Ramsay offered an instructive example and admonished his daughter Margaret on the importance of considering the state of her soul while there was still time:

We left Miss Emma Fitzhugh very sick. It is thought she will die. . . . She is frightened about her condition, thinks she will die and says she is not fit to die. She has been a wild thoughtless girl, but now she thinks[.] My daughter you should *think* while you are yet in health, before the hand of disease is laid upon you. It may then be too *late*. From this case learn the lesson that the young, healthy and beautiful may at any moment be brought to death's door, and induced in pain of disease and anguish of soul to cry upon that God they have slighted and dispised [sic], when He may not hear.[70]

Antebellum America was infused with religiosity, and the Old South was steeped in evangelicalism. Religious faith and pious behavior were important for all southerners—black and white, male and female, old and young. Yet white women's religious responsibilities attracted particular attention. As the moral guardians of society, women were expected to be religious. As members of the social elite, slaveholding women were required to exhibit piety. And as frail and dependent daughters, wives, and mothers, white women in the Old South needed faith. While they were still young and healthy, then, southern girls and young women were encouraged to take stock of their lives, repent their sins, and join the church.

Because the teen years coincided not only with a period of spiritual reflection but also, in many cases, with a spell at a female academy, many young women experienced conversion—evangelicals' term for the realization of faith—while at school. As a result, although the quest for religious conviction was an intensely private experience, it was also one that many young women experienced within a cohort of their peers.[71]

Many female academies were sites of religious revivals, in which numerous schoolgirls, responding to the emotional appeals of local preachers or academy pastors (many of whom doubled as school principals), experienced conversion. Writing to her "chum" and onetime schoolmate Mary Whitfield, a Judson Institute student informed her of one such occasion in 1844: "There has been a revival in town," she wrote, adding, "several of the girls have professed."[72]

Mary Anderson offered an unusually complete description of a revival in a letter to her friend Ella Noland in 1849. "I dont know whether you have heard before," she began, "but in case you have not I will give you an account of the great revival under which I was turned from my evil ways." So eager was Anderson to share her experience with her friend that her letter assumed a breathless tone. "It commenced last October and lasted for about a month or two in a Presbyterean [sic] chapel out in the old field during which time there were upwards of 100 young converts, immense crowds used to assemble there, unless we started very early it was impossible to get in the house," she elaborated.[73]

Recognizing conversion and baptism as markers of adult status, many girls were anxious to undergo these coming-of-age rituals. For Tennessean C. Alice Ready, confirmation (the Episcopal Church's equivalent to baptism) had been "the greatest wish of [her] life for four or five years" by the time she finally took this "most solemn step" in June 1860. Ready spent the intervening years preparing for that day by thinking, reading religious books, and searching her own soul. When at last her "most earnest desire [had] been gratified," she described herself as "so happy. and oh! so glad that I did not put it off any longer."[74]

Like Alice Ready, many young women began keeping religious diaries in their teens. Such diaries contained reflections on sermons and pious readings, self-castigation for perceived faults, and resolutions for self-improvement. Whether they focused on the hope of salvation or on self-abnegation, girls' religious diaries illustrated the importance that southerners attached to youthful conversion and allowed southern girls to evaluate their progress toward piety on earth and eternal life in heaven. If all went well, this prolonged period of self-examination ended with conversion—a private conviction of faith—and baptism—a public declaration of one's intention to "lead a christain [sic] life."[75]

In some ways, conversion and baptism reinforced dictates of feminine submissiveness. When a young woman underwent conversion, she recognized her own helplessness and depravity and a male deity's power and grace. Marylander Maria Catherine Wiestling expressed typical sentiments when she wrote in her diary: "O God I feel my weakness, on thee will I support, knowing nothing can be done without thy aid." When a woman joined the church, she submitted to a higher power. Wiestling's description of this process resonated with prescriptions of ladylike submissiveness; "subdue my stubborn heart," she pleaded. Some women found this act of total self-abnegation difficult. Mary Anderson described her reluctance to convert in language that suggested that religion was an oppressive—although ultimately irresistible—force: "I was striving against the Holy Spirit for some time before that stubborn rebellious heart would yield," she wrote, "but it must either bend or bow."[76]

But at the same time that recognizing God's ultimate power was a form of submission, conversion was also a statement of individuality that both implicitly and explicitly challenged the power of other, earthly, authorities. While adults were generally willing allies when girls joined the church, the potential remained that earthly and godly demands could be at odds someday. By making what Ann Webster Gordon called "a public profession of religion," girls made a strong statement that they would choose to follow the dictates of their consciences rather than the directives of society. Conversion, then, was simultaneously an act of submission and an act of assertion, an expression of abnegation and an expression of agency. Perhaps this was why Mary Page called baptism "the happiest hour of our lives"; it allowed southern girls to reconcile the seemingly incompatible desire for autonomy and pressure for conformity.[77]

The subversive potential of Christianity was surely not what Richard Brumby had in mind, however, when he wrote to his daughter Ann Eliza in 1858 that a true lady was "healthy in person, refined in feeling, pure in morals, & humble in religion." For Brumby, as for most southerners, religion was to reinforce, not to undermine, ladylike behavior. According to this southern father, only by keeping the precepts of proper behavior in mind could a female achieve fulfillment on earth and eternal life in heaven. "Keep this constantly in mind," he admonished his daughter. "Guided by this principle, . . . you will, I trust, become a lady,—happy, prosperous, & useful in life, & fitted by God's grace, for a blessed immortality."[78]

Although "a blessed immortality" in heaven might be the ultimate goal, southern girls knew that they had first to live life on earth, and that life was to be one of cheerful service to others. Elizabeth Lindsay summed up her notions of ideal womanhood in a letter to her dear friend Apphia Rouzee in 1811. "I cannot amagin [sic] a more pleasing picture of human perfection than that of a woman of sense and virtue ingaged [sic] in the gentle office of ministering to the happiness of those around her and by cheerfulness and good humour redoubling their joys," she pronounced, adding, "she can expect no page of history to tell the story of her worth to future times and derives her happiness from the sweet consciousness of having performed her Duty."[79]

Like Janet Henderson's vision of "A Perfect Woman," this description of ideal womanhood expected the well-bred southern lady to be gentle and virtuous, to serve others without expectation of recognition or reward, and to derive her own happiness from promoting the well-being of those around her. As Kentuckian Belle Price's parents reminded her, it was only "by cultivating those amiable traites [sic] of character" that a young woman could "secure [her] own happiness, as well as that of others."[80]

Indeed, a recurring theme in southerners' explication of ladylike behavior was the need to please others. Parents frequently referred to the need to earn others' favor, to think of how others would perceive behavior, and to use skills in the service of others. Georgian Martha Rowena Munroe captured the connection between ladylike behavior and pleasing others when she wrote home from North Carolina's Salem Female Academy to tell her guardians that she hoped that she and her sister would learn to "conduct ourselves, more like young-ladies & give you more satisfaction."[81]

Giving satisfaction to others was the ultimate yardstick of ladylike behavior. Rachel Mordecai's father's fondest wish for his daughter was that she would be "esteem'd by your acquaintances & belov'd by your Relatives & Friends." Elizabeth Noland counseled her daughter Ella to "gain the affection and good opinion of . . . all around you." Cary Whitaker reminded his daughter Anna, "I wish you, to act in such a manner, as, to deserve the friendship and esteem of every body." William Polk advised his daughter to "acquir[e] those habits & manners" that would bring "pleasure to your friends." Elizabeth McPherson's brother urged his sister to strive to be "the pride and honour of relations and friends" and "the ornament of your circle in life." Again and again, young women in the Old South learned that their chief goal was to earn the approval of others.[82]

Earning others' approval was necessary, girls on the brink of womanhood learned, because it was the only way to obtain love—the desideratum of nineteenth-century American culture, but especially important to women, who had so few other sources of satisfaction. Georgian Loula Kendall revealed the paramount importance of pleasing others and earning their love in her journal, in which she recalled her terrible fear, even at the tender age of three, that nobody would ever love her because she was cross-eyed. Although her conviction that love was the ultimate aim of life never wavered, young Loula soon learned that a beautiful appearance was less important than ladylike behavior. As a teenager, she understood the principal lesson of southern ladyhood: "To be loved I must be gentle, submissive[,] obliging, and obedient."[83]

For young women in the Old South, coming-of-age was not so much about acquiring physical maturity as it was about acquiring the appearance and the attributes of a young lady, including a pleasing demeanor and a pious disposition. As they entered their teens, southern girls adopted the outward trappings of young ladyhood, but they also learned that fine clothes and hair ribbons were not enough to earn social approval. Instead, they confronted a set of interlocking demands that required them to be cheerfully submissive, genuinely devoted to the desires of others, and satisfied to earn their reward in heaven rather than on earth. Most of all, they learned to measure their success based on their ability to please others and earn their love. North Carolinian Kate Landing expressed the ideal well in a school composition: "A true lady is loved by all."[84]

Throughout their childhood and their early teens, most southern girls seem to have accepted the precepts of southern ladyhood. They might find certain aspects of becoming "a true lady" difficult, but they also regarded the transformation from girl to lady as both inevitable and desirable. Yet as these southern ladies-in-the-making continued along the path marked out for them by society, they became increasingly reluctant to accede to their destiny. One of the most important settings in which southern girls developed a counterculture of resistance was one that they encountered during their teen years: the female academy.

"A COLLEGE GIRL": MARGARET GRAHAM

In fall 1842, Margaret Graham, the daughter of physician and planter William Graham of Newton County, Georgia, left home to attend Georgia Female College (later Wesleyan College) in Macon, Georgia. Before her matriculation, Margaret's father had conducted careful inquiries into the college's operations, writing both to the college's president, W. H. Ellison, and to a friend to determine whether the school would suit her needs. Graham's friend warned him against the college, insinuating that the school's curriculum was "more Superficial than Sollid [sic]" and warning him that the school (like most private academies of the antebellum era) was "thoroughly Sectarian"—in this instance, Presbyterian—as well as expensive. The president soothed the father's fears, however. Ellison assured him that the school offered "all that is essential to education"—English literature, the sciences, and French language classes—for $50 per term, plus an additional $10 per month for room and board. If Margaret came to his school, Ellison promised Graham, the teachers would do their best "to advance her intellectual, & moral improvement." Evidently reassured, Graham enrolled his daughter for the fall term.[1]

When Margaret Graham first left home for school, she suffered from terrible homesickness. Apart from her family for the first time in her young life, she confided, "I felt bad enough, I assure you, the first week I was here, being an entire stranger." Soon, however, Margaret had adapted to her new environment and described herself as "as happy and contented as one could

REPORT OF THE STANDING OF

Miss Margaret Graham

IN THE JUNIOR CLASS OF THE

GEORGIA FEMALE COLLEGE,

For the Quarter ending *April 1st* 1843.

Chemistry,	3
Logic,	4
Rhetoric,	4
Geometry,	3½
Composition,	3
History,	
French,	
Music,	
Writing,	3
Embroidery,	
Deportment,	4
Attendance in Recitation,	4
Absence from Church and Prayers,	12 *times*
Fault Marks,	0

BY ORDER OF THE FACULTY.

J. DARBY, *Secretary.*

EXPLANATION.—The grade of scholarship is designated by the figures 0, 1, 2, 3, 4. The lowest degree is indicated by 0, the highest by 4; and intermediate grades by intermediate figures.

Students at female academies studied a wide array of topics. This report card of Margaret Graham, who described Macon, Georgia's Female College as "a perfect paradise," suggests the parameters of higher education for young women in the Old South. Notice that courses in the sciences and the classics share time with those in music and embroidery. (Southern Historical Collection, Wilson Library, University of North Carolina at Chapel Hill)

wish." No longer a stranger, Graham rejoiced in her new standing as "a college girl." Enthusiastically recounting her studies and social life, she recognized that leaving home for school had set her apart from the younger children who remained at home. "Kiss all the children for me," she requested.[2]

Margaret's parents were no doubt pleased with her progress in her studies. As a member of the junior class, Margaret studied logic, chemistry, rhetoric, and geometry; she also was required to write a composition each week. With so many subjects to master, she told her mother, she had become "very industrious" and hardly needed the school regulations requiring students to "study hard all day" to keep her at her books. Indeed, she indicated that her desire to acquit herself well in end-of-term examinations was enough to make her apply herself to her studies. "How I do dread the examination," she wrote. "I am constantly thinking of it."[3]

Thoughts of the examination did not prevent Margaret from enjoying herself, however. She soon "became acquainted with the young ladies" at the school—more than one hundred girls—and she enjoyed the company of her schoolmates, especially of her roommate, Ophelia. The teachers, too, were "very kind and affectionate," and despite the "strict" rules monitoring students' behavior, Margaret described herself as "inexpressibly happy" at school. College, she told her mother, was "a perfect paradise."[4]

Many southern girls, like Margaret Graham, regarded boarding school as "a perfect paradise" and reveled in the opportunity to try on a new identity as "a college girl," dedicated to intellectual improvement and surrounded by congenial companions. Attending school was a significant stage of life for young women in the Old South. While many southern girls both welcomed the status of a young lady and wrestled with the constraints of that role, they generally regarded the female academy as an entirely positive experience—in large part because they found being "a college girl" more rewarding than being a proper southern lady. In the antebellum South, schooling offered elite girls a glimpse of an alternative definition of southern womanhood, one that revolved around self-improvement and female community rather than around self-sacrifice and male dominance. Although parents and educators intended school as a "preparation for pedestals," girls experienced it as an unprecedented opportunity to explore other options, including intellectual development and adult independence. Moreover, they formed lasting friendships during their schooling, friendships that would become the basis for a shared female youth culture. The boarding school experience was a pivotal moment in young women's lives. By encouraging young southern women to define and pursue their own goals, academy attendance fostered their resistance to the southern patriarchy's ideals of feminine dependence and selfless womanhood.[5]

"KISS THE CHILDREN FOR ME": LEAVING HOME

For elite girls in the Old South, attending school was an important stage of life. Antebellum Americans believed that a democratic nation demanded an informed populace. While political participation was restricted to men, women had a role to play in the new nation as the wives and mothers of male citizens. In the decades following the American Revolution, townships, churches, and individuals scrambled to establish institutions of higher learning (variously referred to as academies, seminaries, or colleges) for both women and men. Class-conscious southerners enthusiastically joined the female academy movement, first sending their offspring north to school and, later, as sectional tensions increased, building their own institutions of higher learning nearer home. Thus, what one southern schoolmaster called "a lively interest in education" encouraged many southern parents to send their daughters away from home for a period of months or years to attend school either in their home region or in the North.[6]

For southern girls, leaving home for school was a defining moment. As William Polk remarked to his daughter Mary when she left her home in Raleigh, North Carolina, to attend Mrs. Mallon's School in Philadelphia,

"You are my dear Mary about commencing a new scene in life." The female academy was, as Polk recognized, a new scene in life. During their time at school, young women moved from the family circle to a female community. Within that community, southern daughters adopted a new identity as schoolgirls. Southern schoolgirls by no means severed their connections to their parents, siblings, and kin. Indeed, most female students devoted a great deal of time to writing home. But even as they maintained their ties to their families, in their letters home, southern schoolgirls also revealed the ways in which they were redefining their community. Within the close-knit world of the female academy, southern girls created a supportive subculture that revolved around academic rigor and peer relationships.[7]

For young women in the Old South, the female academy was a unique social space, one that offered incomparable opportunities to develop a culture of resistance. Like northern girls in coeducational high schools and like college students of both sexes throughout the antebellum United States, southern schoolgirls forged a distinct campus culture. For southern girls, however, student life was an especially significant life stage. In the antebellum South, where organized feminism was stalled by antagonisms toward the allied reform of abolitionism and where dispersed settlement patterns limited women's ability to develop the networks of benevolent women so common in northern cities, the female academy emerged as one of the only sanctioned settings where a female culture might develop. In the female academy, what one scholar has termed "clusters of learned women" and "affinitive clusters" of female friendship—both preconditions for "feminist consciousness"—overlapped. While scholars of women's higher learning in the North and in England have also noted that "formal institutions [such as schools] were alternatives to the nuclear family" that empowered women to create an identity separate from the family, in the Old South, female academies proved to be one of the only "woman-controlled spaces" that would allow southern girls to develop a collective identity and create a culture of resistance.[8]

Elite girls in the antebellum South eagerly embraced the opportunities offered by the female academy, beginning with the ability to claim a new identity as schoolgirls. In 1833, Sarah Wheeler, then fourteen years old and en route to Miss Mercer's Academy in Wilmington, Delaware, wrote to her mother to assure her that her family was foremost in her mind. She promised to send "some littel [sic] presents" for "the children" who remained at home. Significantly, Wheeler did not include herself as one of "the children." Rather, she closed her letter, "Kiss all the dear littel [sic] ones for me." Wheeler's self-conscious effort to distinguish herself from the "little ones at home," even while expressing her abiding affection for them, was widely shared; in fact, this message soon became de rigueur for southern daughters-turned-schoolgirls. Nearly two decades later, Elizabeth Alexander used almost the same phrasing in her first letter home. "Kiss the children for me," she requested.[9]

For southern girls, requests that they be remembered to "the children" of the family served a dual purpose. In such formulaic messages, young southern women recognized family ties, but at the same time they rejected an identity as one of "the children" and adopted a new identity as a schoolgirl. Just as they announced their identity as young ladies in both their speech and dress, southern students used both fashion and language to proclaim their status as schoolgirls. Judson Female Institute (Alabama) students Mary Elizabeth Whitfield and her cousin Rachel Whitfield purchased gingham to make themselves "long-aprons" to wear over their dresses. "You cannot think how they improve our looks," Mary Elizabeth reported to her mother; "we look more like school girls." Greensboro College (North Carolina) alumnae Sallie S. Cotton repeatedly invoked the label "schoolgirl" in her 1897 alumnae address. " 'When I was a schoolgirl,' " she commented, "is a refrain which sounds familiar to us all." [10] Customs such as wearing schoolgirl aprons and catchphrases like "when I was a schoolgirl" alike indicated the importance that young women in the Old South attached to the time they spent away from home at school.

When they adopted a new identity as college girls, young women in the Old South also reoriented their lives. The twin themes of schoolwork and friendship dominated the writings of southern schoolgirls. While the strictures governing the lives of young ladies did not disappear, their importance dissipated as students devoted themselves to their studies and reveled in the company of their peers. When the time came to leave school, many southern girls did so reluctantly. The time southern women spent at school was important in its own right, but it also shaped the rest of southern girls' lives. Their zest for learning offered a glimpse of an alternative to domesticity; their enjoyment of their peers' company gave them a supportive network with whom to share their reluctance to acquiesce to the destiny of southern womanhood. Attending school, then, both inspired young women in the Old South to resist their assigned roles and offered them a context in which to do so. Schooling was not only an important life stage for southern girls but also an essential step toward developing a female culture of resistance.

When southern girls left home for school, they went with the advice of parents, guardians, and neighbors to apply themselves diligently to their studies. Many families made significant sacrifices—financial, practical, and emotional—to enable their daughters to attend school. Therefore, they were eager for their daughters to make the most of their opportunities. "You must exert yourself in your studies," Cary Whitaker urged his daughter Anna, reminding her, "it is for that, you are now absent from your parents, who love you so dearly." Two years later, he repeated this message, writing, "Let me again call to your recollection, and impress forcibly on your mind, the reason, why, you are seperated [sic] from us; therefore be diligent, and apply yourself closely to your studies." Other parents likewise exhorted their daughters to make the most of their time at school. William Polk advised his daughter Mary, "Gain all the information you can & in the shortest period you can." Mississippi student Elizabeth Amis's mother's parting words were typical of southern parents and guardians: "Study hard, and make good use of your time," she recommended.[11]

Despite their consensus that daughters should use their time at the academy to improve themselves, parents' emphasis on different aspects of female education varied considerably. Reflecting the inherent tensions of the female academy movement, which advocated higher education in the service of home and family, elite southerners often disagreed on the scope and purpose of educating their daughters. Some, like Alabamian Richard Brumby, insisted that "the great object of female education should be, the development of the girl into a lady"; others, like Elizabeth McPherson's brother, charged the girls to be "as studious as possible."[12]

The seemingly divergent goals of female education—academic achievement and ladylike behavior—were the result of internal contradictions in white southerners' views. Marcus Cicero Stephens indicated both popular prejudices against female education and southerners' beliefs in women's intellectual equality in an 1841 letter to his young ward, Mary Ann Primrose, then a student at the Burwell School in Hillsboro, North Carolina. Defending women against their detractors, he asserted: "Generally speaking, the Women have not been treated with Justice by the male sex. It is true the rougher walks of life have very properly been destined to man, and the knowledge necessary for such purposes is also the peculiar study of man. But if the woman be inferior to the man in bodily strength, her mind is equally vigorous as his." Stephens indicated that although women's role in life might be different from men's, their minds were by no means inferior. Indeed, he suggested, women were the victims of "a kind of conspiracy to keep the women in the background": "A prejudice has been excited against their improvement beyond a certain limit—the women have been cowed if I may so term it—for should she in her remarks on any subject of conversation show any superiority of intellect, she is instantly denounced as a bas bleu or blue stocking, and is avoided in a measure by both men and women." According to Stephens, young Mary Ann should not allow herself to be limited by such prejudices but should "store [her] mind well with useful knowledge" while at school. Moreover, he insisted, education did not end with the end of school. "Don't imagine that when you quit school, your improvement is finished," he warned. "Far from it—you then become your own instructress—the discipline of the Academy teaches you the use of the tools—points out the different routes of knowledge,—from that moment all depends on your own industry and discretion."[13] For this southern father figure, female education was not only possible but positively desirable. Knowledge, industry, and discretion, he asserted, were within women's reach while at school and would prove "useful" in later life.

Like Stephens, most well-to-do southern parents were eager for their daughters to become educated. As John Steele put it in a letter to his daughter Ann in 1800, "Knowledge is the best resource." Education, Steele firmly believed, would fit women for their future responsibilities "in the bosom of domestic retirement"; it would also provide them with a source of "consolations" in difficult times. And, although antebellum southern parents fondly hoped that their daughters would never need to put their skills to work in the marketplace, Steele admitted that a further advantage of an education was that "it makes man, or woman in a certain degree independent."[14]

The ultimate goal of female education, however, was not independence; rather, it was to procure a comfortable *dependence*—on a husband. Therefore, even as they urged their daughters to do well in their academic subjects, southern parents also encouraged them to master the feminine "accomplishments"—needlework, music, and drawing—and the social skills of conversation and letter-writing. These attainments, parents predicted, would enable southern girls to entertain and delight others while single and to occupy and divert themselves once married.[15]

While parents, guardians, and teachers recommended devoting time and energy to feminine accomplishments and social skills, they did not do so at the expense of higher learning. As Jason Gordon reminded his sister Caroline in 1843, "All other accomplishments without intelligence, are vain and transientary [sic]." Indeed, southern schools for girls steadily augmented their offerings throughout the antebellum era; while girls' schools at the opening of the nineteenth century were often little more than finishing schools, by the middle of the century, many women's schools offered curricula that rivaled those of their male counterparts.[16]

The ironic result of southerners' conflicting ideas about female education was that girls received a surprisingly thorough education. Generally speaking, girls' classes fell into three groups. First came basic education, encompassing ancient and modern history, mathematics (arithmetic, geometry, and algebra), and English (including reading, writing, grammar, composition, spelling, and "Encyclopedia"). Next came advanced studies, which could include the classics (Greek and Latin) but more often consisted of scientific study (chemistry, astronomy, botany, geology, physics) and the fields of philosophy, logic, and rhetoric. Finally came the "extras," those classes intended to fit elite southern women for their particular place in life. These classes, many of which were not included in the regular tuition but were offered at additional fees, included modern languages (German, Spanish, and French); art (drawing, watercolor, and oil painting); music (piano, guitar, harp, organ, and voice lessons); plain sewing and embroidery; and Bible. Because girls studied both traditional "classical" topics and the arts, their curriculum may actually have been superior to that offered to boys. Certainly, girls' schools offered a wider range of subjects than boys' schools did, giving girls the opportunity to receive what a later era would regard as a well-rounded, liberal arts education.[17]

The limitation was not on *what* women learned but on how they *used* their learning. Marcus Cicero Stephens revealed the complicated calculus of female education in his 1841 letter to Mary Ann Primrose. "You tell me you are taking lessons in music, drawing and French besides the usual [i.e., academic] studies," he began. "All this is very well a young woman ought to perfect herself in all the accomplishments she can, that she may in the first place render herself interesting and agreeable to others and moreover possess internal resources of pleasure and amusement in those moments of listlessness and apathy to which we are all more or less subjected," he continued. The priorities were clear in Stephens's letter to his ward; a young woman should use her education *first* to please others, and only secondarily to satisfy herself. This was true, as well, for Stephens's recommendation that his niece should apply herself to "the higher branches of education": history, geography, and philosophy. With such knowledge at her disposal, he explained, a woman would be able to converse intelligently with a suitor, rather than being limited to "insipid" topics. Consistent with the dictum that a lady's role was to please others, Stephens claimed that a student's learning was to serve others.[18]

Elite white southerners thus embraced a complicated mix of ideas about women's education. They believed in women's intellectual equality at the same time that they insisted that their role was at home. They acknowledged that education might fit women for a vocation and independence but emphasized instead that education could prepare them for marriage and motherhood. They desired—indeed, demanded—that their daughters dedicate themselves to learning but in the same breath denounced women who displayed their knowledge.

William Wirt of Virginia embodied these contradictions. A passionate advocate of higher education for women, Wirt counseled his daughters to devote themselves to intellectual improvement, but he also reminded them in no uncertain terms to avoid showing off: "The *ostentatious* display of intellect in a young lady is revolting," he pronounced. The opinions of this southern father, at once firm and inconsistent, were widely shared in the Old South. Yet the limited views and limiting directives of parents like William Wirt were not the only—or even the most important—messages to which southern schoolgirls responded.[19]

"I TRY TO BE FIRST IN MY CLASS":
REPORTS, COMPOSITIONS, AND EXAMINATIONS

During their time at school, southern girls let no opportunity for what Papa Wirt called "the ostentatious display of intellect" pass them by. Students in female academies were eager to do well in their coursework and to boast about their accomplishments, and they earned praise from their teachers, their classmates, and their parents for doing so. During their time at the female academy, southern schoolgirls disregarded ladylike modesty and displayed academic prowess. Even as they fulfilled their elders' demands that they apply themselves to their studies, then, students also developed their own agenda for their schoolwork. For southern schoolgirls, academic achievement reconciled filial duty and female agency.[20]

In the Old South, an important aspect of school culture was the grade report. Sent home weekly, monthly, or quarterly, grade reports rated students' performance in "deportment as young ladies," as well as in academic subjects. Often students were required to write a letter home to their parents to accompany each grade report. Such letters typically contained apologies (and, sometimes, excuses) for low marks, self-congratulations for high marks, and promises to do better next time. Academy students' discussions of grade reports indicate that academic achievement was a priority for southern schoolgirls.[21]

Parents clearly wanted their daughters to do well in school. Schoolgirls regularly wrote to their parents apprising them of their marks, rejoicing in their successes, and attempting to explain their failures. Emma Kimberly, writing to her father from St. Mary's School in 1857, took pains to explain the grading system to her father before commenting: "I think my report for this month is not so good as it ought to be, next month I am going to try to get a good one." Millie Birckhead, a student at Piedmont Female Academy in Virginia, was one of the fortunate ones. Apparently, even the looming prospect of secession and Civil War did not eclipse the importance of grades; in April 1861, Millie sent her report to her father with the notation, "The reports were Friday morning, and as providence happened I got perfect, and you cant imagin [sic] how happy I feel."[22] Both the practice of sending reports to parents and the letters schoolgirls wrote to accompany them indicate the importance that southern adults attached to doing well in school.

However, students also prized good grades independently of their elders. Although reports often were sent directly to parents, schoolgirls kept close tabs on their marks. Galveston, Texas, student Patricia Mercer filled her diary with a record of how many "heads" she earned each day. When she fell short of her expectations, she tried to console herself with the thought that she "had a great deal rather gain knowledge than marks," but despite such philosophical statements, Mercer's evaluation of each day's success hinged upon the number of top marks she earned. Although Mercer was aware that her "father seemed to be very anxious for [her] to learn," her careful, almost obsessive, record of her grades leaves no doubt that she herself cared deeply about her performance; when she "got down in the class," she confessed in one entry, she "had to cry like a child."[23]

Good reports were a source of status in the academy as well as a source of personal pride. Often the entire school knew each student's class standing thanks to the common practice of marks being "read out" in public. Even when grades were not publicized, students compared grades. Vicksburg, Mississippi, native Emma Shannon reported that at her school, the girls compared marks; only one "got all nines," the highest possible score. Such practices allowed — indeed encouraged — girls to compete for the highest standing. In 1858, Wesleyan Female College (Virginia) student Olin Davis boasted to her brother, "The past week I have 7 (the highest mark) on all of my studies and I hope that I will do the same through the seven weeks, or until the next reports go out." While her own report was "very good," Davis admitted that "it was not perfect" and compared her performance to "one of the girls" who "got 93," which she thought "was the highest number which any got."[24]

Southern students' almost obsessive concern with grades suggests that in the Old South's female academies, schoolgirls created a peer culture that valued academic achievement and made academic competition a central aspect of student subculture. While consistent with parents' and teachers' desires, schoolgirls' standards were their own; young women recorded, compared, and boasted about their grades independently of adults, although with their tacit approval. Intellectual ability—or at least academic achievement—thus became an essential feature of schoolgirl identity. While academics did not substitute for the accepted ladylike qualities discussed in Chapter 1, they did, at least in the minds of southern schoolgirls, eclipse them.[25]

Compositions, like grade reports, were a standard part of the academy experience. Graded on grammar and penmanship, compositions tested students' ability to parrot popular sentiments rather than encouraging original thought. Typical composition topics included domesticity, education, fashion, womanly graces, and motherhood. While students sometimes had leeway to choose their own topics, they tended to stick to such tried-and-true themes. Originality was not rewarded. When Kate Landing, a student at North Carolina's Davenport Female College, used her essay titled "The Morning of Life" to reflect on "youthful days," the teacher's only comment was "Stick to the subject."[26]

Many students remarked that they found writing compositions to be an arduous and unrewarding endeavor, perhaps in part because the assignments required schoolgirls to uphold conventional ideals of feminine selflessness at the same time that young women were discovering the rewards of female achievement. Students labored over their compositions. Writing from Wesleyan Female College in 1859, Olin Davis complained: "I have been thinking all day about my Composition and have not written the first word on it yet. Our subject is 'The Seasons of Life.' I think it is next to the hardest subject that I ever had to write on." St. Mary's School's Julie Warren expressed a typical sentiment in a letter to her mother: "I have written my Composition this morning, and of course feel quite relieved [sic], Fannie is groaning and sighing over hers."[27]

Despite their conventional content, compositions could offer southern schoolgirls an opportunity to win acclaim. Compositions were designed to be read aloud—the closest that most female students came to the study of rhetoric offered in men's colleges. While students complained about writing assigned compositions, they sought out opportunities to speak in public. Mary Virginia Early, a student at the Female Collegiate Institute in Buckingham County, Virginia, in 1840, was one of the founding members of a "Young

Ladies Lyceum" that required its members to read their "Moral Essays" aloud. Such informal exercises served as a rehearsal for final examinations, where the authors of the top essays were invited to read their compositions to the assembled audience. Such an invitation was a distinct honor; when Texan Patricia Mercer read her essay on her home state aloud at the examination, she rejoiced, "[It] did me a great deal of credit."[28] By reading compositions aloud, as well as by having good marks "read out," southern schoolgirls gained status in the student subculture of the female academy.

Another important school ritual that allowed girls to advertise their academic prowess was the end-of-term examination. Modeled after commencement exercises at male colleges, such examinations offered young women an opportunity to display their knowledge and to earn top honors in their class. Many young women eagerly vied for the post of valedictorian. Texas student Patricia Mercer wrote of little other than "the examination" in the days leading up to the event at her school in fall 1840. "It is now only a few days before our examination and the whole week will be employed in get[ting] ready for the examination," she wrote. Engaged in a competition for the top score with another student, Janette, Mercer worried that her recent poor performance would harm her standing. "If I get all my marks taken off when it is so near examination time," she agonized, "it will be a very hard time when our marks are read out. I guess there will be some very red cheeks and wet eyes at the time when the bad marks are read out to the company," she predicted, resolving "to try to learn my lessons to night." Although Mercer was pleased with her good showing over the next several days, by the time the headmaster "got the prizes for the examination and counted up our marks to see who will make number one," it was clear that Mercer would not have this distinction, and she was crushed. "It is already decided that Janette will rank one and will get the best prize in the school and that will make me feel the worst," she lamented, adding, "It will be a very bad thing for me to leave the school disgraced for ever." Much to her relief, however, Mercer managed to redeem herself by working an especially difficult geometry problem and earning "heads" in multiple classes. Ultimately, she earned two prizes at the examination.[29]

Mercer was not alone in her concern about examinations. What Winifred Faison called "those awful examinations" were a major event in students' lives. Southern schoolgirls engaged in a frenzy of preparation for exams, competed fiercely for first place in their class, and implored their families and friends to attend the event to witness their triumphs. While students' eagerness to earn good grades might be attributed simply to a desire to please their parents, their close attention to examinations appears to reflect their own aims; indeed, girls mentioned end-of-term examinations much more often, and discussed them in much more detail, than did their parents. In their intense focus on what they often referred to simply as "the examination," southern schoolgirls indicated the importance that they attached both to academic achievement and to public display—what William Wirt disparaged as "ostentatious" behavior and Marcus Cicero Stephens warned would earn a young woman opprobrium as a "blue stocking."[30] Far from shunning the spotlight as modest maidens were expected to do, southern schoolgirls coveted the distinction to be gained by public performance.

Public performance was a major part of school examinations. Busily preparing for end-of-term examinations in 1844, Judson Institute Mary Elizabeth Whitfield breathlessly informed her parents that "from the reports we hear, not only the state of Alabama, but all surrounding states will be here." Not only were examinations public, but anybody in the audience—including men—could challenge the students. For some students, the public nature of examinations was a source of anxiety. Georgia student Margaret Graham worried in a letter to her father: "How I do dread the examination in July. I am constantly thinking of it. I expect if I learn any thing before, I will be so embarrassed then, that I will forget every thing. But I will try not." Mississippi student Emma Shannon, anticipating her geometry exam, expressed similar sentiments: "The idea of having to go up to the blackboard draw the figures and recite from books, kills me nearly," she complained.[31]

Despite such lamentations, many schoolgirls prized examinations as a time to display their knowledge. They urged their parents, relatives, and friends to attend the proceedings and acknowledge their achievements. Francis Moody, a student at Davenport Female College in Lenoir, North Carolina, begged her uncle to come to school to witness her examination. "I try to be first in my class and I have been first or with the first every time the marks have [been] read out," she noted with satisfaction, adding, "The examination will be the last of this month, you must come up if you can." Martha Turner, writing from North Carolina's Floral College in 1846, filled an entire letter with news of the impending examination. Closing, she remarked, "I have not wrote any thing yet but it is so near the examination that we cannot think of any thing except the examination." For Turner, the examination was clearly a much-anticipated event; she urged her father to attend and asked her mother to make her a special dress for the occasion. Similarly, Mary Virginia Early, despite her protestations that she "expect[ed] to come up missing" at the examination, asked her mother to attend the event at the Female Collegiate Institute in Buckingham County, Virginia. Her cousin, Virginia Wilber, added a postscript in which she commented sagely:

"She has appeared the most desponding *creature*, about her studies and composition you ever saw but I hope you comprehend her meaning. She is inviting you down to witness her examination, which she as well as I know, will result in bestowing honour upon her parents and credit to herself."[32]

Although this student referred to the honor reflected on parents, most eagerly claimed "credit" for their accomplishments. Schoolgirls took great pride in the recognition they received at the end of each report term. At the end of term, schoolgirls' class standings were "read out" to the assembly and the top scores were recognized and rewarded. Mamie Normal reported from Littleton College in Warren County, North Carolina: "Last week I stood examinations all the week. I got the highest grade on Arithmetic in my class." Students carefully recorded the prizes, distinctions, and honors they received at examination time. Salem Female Academy (North Carolina) student Winifred Bryan Whitfield gleefully reported her successes in 1826: "I was distinguished in eight of my Classes, as follows, in Geography I was second with three others, and in History I was second with one other, in Musick [sic] I was second with one in one Class, and second with three in the others; in Grammar I was first with three others, in painting I was first with one other, and in writing first by my self, and I was also named among those who were distinguished for uniformly good behaviour." In less detail but with no less enthusiasm, Penelope Skinner, a student at Miss Burk's female academy in Hillsboro, North Carolina, rejoiced, "Received twenty nine honours and last time I only received nine."[33]

At some schools, the examination was part of a social event that included a concert and other celebrations. Martha Munroe, a student at North Carolina's Salem Academy in 1843, gave her aunt and uncle an especially complete description of the examination:

> The examination . . . took place on the 1st and 2nd days of June. We were examined in the Church, because the Chapel was not large enough for so many persons. On the sides of both galleries there were specimens of painting drawing, needle-work, embroidery, & work on canvas exhibited. There were also a great many persons present at the examin[ation.] Sister Hatty had a recitation to say, & also a piece on the piano . . . besides having a party in the "Botany Dialogue." I had a part in the Astronomy, Chemistry, [and] Botany Dialogues, with about 20 or 30 more girls.

All of these displays, recitations, and dialogues were in addition to the public examinations in other school subjects, suggesting that southern schoolgirls—far from hastening through examinations—welcomed the chance to show off their learning.[34]

Southern students at female academies prized academic achievement. At a time when some educators worried that examinations, honors, and prizes might foster an unfeminine competitiveness in their female scholars, and in a society in which southern women were adjured to modestly downplay, even hide, their intellect, southern schoolgirls embraced the opportunity to gain and to display their knowledge. In doing so, they experimented with an alternative model of southern femininity and resisted prevailing definitions of ladylike behavior.[35]

"I LOVE MY TEACHER DEARLY": STUDENT-TEACHER RELATIONS

The close relationships that students developed with their teachers encouraged them to excel in their classes. Women were the dominant figures in the South's female academies. Even when men participated in the operations of the schools, schoolgirls reported the most contact with their female instructors. In their letters home, schoolgirls highlighted their relationships with schoolmistresses. Emma Kimberly, a North Carolina student, was not alone in confiding to her father: "I love my teacher dearly, she is so good." Affectionate teacher-student relationships in southern academies fostered both academic achievement and female resistance.[36]

The female academy constituted a woman-centered, woman-controlled space within a male-dominated society. While parents and guardians probably hoped that a closely regulated, all-female environment would protect their young charges from undesirable male attention and prepare them for a lifetime of subordination, the women's community that developed at girls' schools proved to be an essential element in the creation of a female youth culture that encouraged women to define their own lives and to resist patriarchal control.[37]

Women teachers were the anchors of the female academy, charged with creating a homelike environment and giving motherly attention to their charges. Parents entrusted female schoolteachers and principals not only with their daughters' intellectual development but also with their physical well-being and moral purity. William Polk, whose daughter Mary attended Mrs. Mallon's School in Philadelphia, rejoiced that the schoolmistress "has provided you with every thing necessary for your comfort." Writing to Peter Hagner to assure him of his daughter's good situation at the Virginia school he ran together with his wife, James Garnett praised "Mrs G[arnett]'s plan of deriving her influence over her Pupils rather from their personal regard, than their fears" and explained that she considered herself equivalent to a parent or guardian. As such, one of her primary missions was moral instruction: "Should she succeed in rendering a portion of them sensible, virtuous Women," Garnett commented, "it will be her best reward on this side of the Grave."[38]

Southern parents admonished their daughters to pay close attention to their schoolteachers' lessons in ladylike behavior, as well as their formal instruction. Writing to her daughter Ella, a student in Leesburg, Virginia, in the 1840s, Elizabeth Noland expressed much concern that her daughter would "gain the affection and good opinion of Mrs Edwards," her school principal. "Whilst under her protection, She must be your guide," she admonished. A. M. Baker wrote to his daughters to remind them to "undertake nothing where you feel yourselves at a loss without first consulting Mrs Granbery [?] and be sure you take her advice upon all occasions."[39] Educators and guardians alike urged southern schoolgirls to regard their teachers as surrogate parents. In the process, they (probably unintentionally) sanctioned and (no doubt unknowingly) encouraged female students' tendency to shift their loyalties from the family circle to the female academy.

Older women teachers played a key role in welcoming new students and advancing their comfort. Mary Virginia Early, a student at Virginia's Female Collegiate Institute, summed up this role in her description of a teacher named Mrs. Booth. "I am becoming more & more attached daily to my dear friend Mrs Booth," she wrote in 1839. "She is indeed a mother to us all."[40] Early's comments suggest that by supplanting mothers in their students' affections, southern schoolmistresses became important mentors for their students. As in the North, "emotional bonds between student and teacher" offered a "profound challenge . . . to familial identification." In addition, in the South, where opportunities for female independence were limited, female teachers served as attractive role models for girls who regarded marriage and motherhood with distaste.[41]

While older, often married, women were important maternal figures for their students, southern schoolgirls were particularly attracted to younger, usually single, teachers, who they could regard as role models. As in northern schools, admiration bordering on schoolgirl crushes was not uncommon. Emma and Lizzie Kimberly, students at St. Mary's School in the 1850s, both developed intense attachments to their favorite teachers. Lizzie wrote several letters about her art teacher, Gertrude Bothamly. In the spring of 1859, she wrote rapturously: "It is warm here, and all the flowers are blooming, I have a good many given to me but I deny myself the pleasure of keeping them for I give them to one that I love *better* than myself, it is to one of the Teachers. . . . I have always admired the name of 'Gertrude' I love it now because the one I *love* bears that name. I guess you think I am foolish, but I do love her more than *ten thousand tongues can express*. I never loved any body so before, love for her strengthens my whole soul, my mind, my body." When another teacher, Miss Bothamly's roommate, took the art teacher's attention away from her besotted student, Lizzie was crestfallen. "She used to love me I thought but she treats me so coldly now since she has been with Miss Marin, but I love her . . . as much as ever and will always, I cannot help it."[42]

Although they did not always use such extravagant language, many southern schoolgirls expressed similar sentiments when they mentioned their favorite teachers. North Carolinian Margaret Mordecai, who attended school in Philadelphia, confided to her sister Ellen, "Miss Dagon went away yesterday I was very sorry for I loved her very much." Interestingly, such comments were almost entirely reserved for young, single, female teachers; of all the schoolgirls included in this study, only one recorded a crush on a male instructor. This pattern suggests that southern girls not only saw their women teachers as objects of affection; they also (like their counterparts in the North and in England) cast them as role models.[43]

North Carolinian Anna Cameron translated her intense attachment to her music teacher, Augusta Stevenson, into a desire to study and teach music. "I am perfectly in love with Augusta, she is *beautiful & charming*," she confided to her diary in November 1863. Subsequent diary entries revolved around the increasingly close relationship between "Gussy," as Cameron fondly referred to her teacher, and her besotted student. Cameron presented the object of her affection with gifts of popcorn and walnuts; the teacher reciprocated by abandoning the formal "Miss Cameron" for the friendly "Anna" and encouraging her student's efforts to write song lyrics. "She is one of the sweetest, most amiable girls I ever saw," Cameron gushed; "I cant help loving her *doubly*[.]" But, much to Cameron's dismay, the music teacher was engaged to be married: "She will go away & forget me & I shall continue to love her," she predicted dolefully. After an "affectionate farewell," complete with tears, hand-holding, and kisses in December, Cameron shifted her attention to her former teacher's specialty. Declaring, "Music is my *passion*," she formulated a plan to "spend the next five years of my life in Studying & perfecting myself in music." Jealous of her teacher's intended husband ("I am sure I do not thank him for depriving me of her society," she once remarked), Cameron expressed no interest in marrying but planned for an independent future. "If I succeed," she explained, "I shall then be able to make my bread by teaching" piano and voice lessons. While singlehood was evidently only a temporary phase for the erstwhile Miss Stevenson, for her student, it became a lifelong goal.[44]

Schoolgirls' close ties to their teachers not only encouraged them to do well in their classes but also inspired them to pursue a life outside the bounds of marriage and family in imitation of their favorite teachers. Contact with inspiring teachers convinced many young women that becoming a schoolteacher was both a viable and a desirable possibility, one that is explored in Chapter 3. Attending school thus introduced young southern women to one form of possible resistance to their presumed destiny as wives and mothers: teaching.

"MAIDEN'S RETREAT": BOARDING SCHOOL LIFE

Although schoolmistresses of all ages were important to them, southern students formed their most important attachments with other women of their own age. The importance of female friendships to nineteenth-century American women has been well documented. While women of all ages enjoyed close emotional ties to other women, school was an especially important time for young women to form intense relationships with one another. This was particularly true in the Old South, where both the strict rules typical of girls' schools and the physical layout of student dormitories fostered camaraderie among students. Unlike either northern high schools or southern men's colleges, southern women's educational institutions were residential campuses that required their students to live under the round-the-clock supervision of their teachers and principals—and in the constant company of their fellow female students. Academy life in the antebellum South revolved around relationships with other women.[45]

School rules limiting students' social interactions beyond the bounds of the academy encouraged young women to form relationships with their fellow students. Margaret Whitaker, a student at Chowan Female Institute in Murfreesboro, North Carolina, did not exaggerate when she informed her father, "We are all watched very closely down here." Teachers at female academies took their duties in loco parentis seriously and did their utmost to prevent their young charges from mingling with townsfolk, particularly with the male students who often attended school in the same communities where girls' schools were located. Mississippian Ann Shannon, who attended school in Burlington, New Jersey, poked fun at her school's regulations: "You would laugh to see the pains taken to keep any one from seeing inside the yard. First there is a high board fence, with all the knot holes

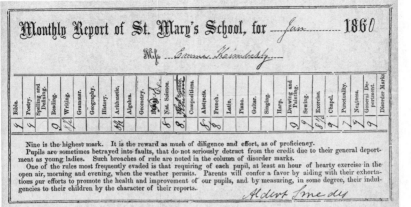

Schoolgirls' behavior was strictly monitored. As this report card from St. Mary's School in Raleigh, North Carolina, shows, "deportment as young ladies" was of great importance, and students who broke the rules ran the risk that their parents would "exhort" them if their report cards recorded "disorder marks." Parents and teachers thus were allies in enforcing feminine propriety, even as teachers sometimes supplanted parents in students' lives and provided southern girls with role models for independent womanhood. (Southern Historical Collection, Wilson Library, University of North Carolina at Chapel Hill)

nailed up with tin, and great sharp iron spikes stuck all along the top. Inside of that is a high close hedge of thorny bushes." Despite all these precautions, one fine day in May, two men breached the barrier, much to the consternation of the school's principal, a northern woman.[46]

Rules were no less strict—and may have been more so—at southern schools. Ella Anderson described Georgia's Wesleyan Female College as completely removed from the outside world. "The girls never left the college grounds except for church, or for a daily constitutional walk back and forth to the cemetery," she recalled, and even then, the students were "always accompanied by teachers, one at the front, one in the center, and another at the end of the line."[47] Such a setting not only isolated girls from the outside world; it also encouraged them to foster relationships with their (female) classmates and teachers. As Anderson explained: "One might think I rebelled under the confinement. On the contrary, my life at Wesleyan was happy and enjoyable." She "soon made friends of the girls and faculty" and became especially attached to her roommate: The two girls "lived together, slept together, [and] made our beds together," she recalled happily; "we loved each other devotedly."[48]

As Anderson's reminiscences indicate, boarding school life encouraged

[Jan 24 - 1862]

Plan of our darmatory

a alcove
b bed
c teacher's room
+ my alcove bed & trunk

At the female academies that proliferated in the antebellum South, dormitories were the focal point of student life. Here, Fannie Patton, a student at St. Mary's School in Raleigh, North Carolina, illustrates the close quarters typical of female boarding schools. Although young Fannie had an alcove to herself, most girls shared alcoves. At many schools, students shared beds as well; choosing a "bedmate" was an important ritual in schoolgirl culture. (Southern Historical Collection, Wilson Library, University of North Carolina at Chapel Hill)

sociability. Lucy Warren described the "dormitory" at St. Mary's School in Raleigh, North Carolina, in 1865; like other girls' schools, the boarding-house's quarters consisted of a long room with small alcoves "made up against the wall," where the girls slept. With two beds (or, in some cases, one double bed) to an alcove, this arrangement fostered friendships between roommates. Schoolgirls sometimes reorganized their living quarters to promote even more social interaction. Writing from Floral College in Harnett

County, North Carolina, Julie Turner described the sleeping arrangements to her mother: "The way we all sleep is that we put two of the bedsteads together and then we put one bed the side of it on the other and three of us sleep together in one bed we all have a heap of fun after studying [h]ours."[49]

Dormitories were the focal point of female students' lives. Susan Mc-Dowall, a student at Patapsco Institute in Maryland during the spring term of 1856, kept a meticulous record of room arrangements in her diary. When McDowall first arrived at the Institute in January 1856, she roomed with two girls, Annie Hoskins and Eliza. But within a week, McDowall and her roommates had a falling out and McDowall mentioned a different set of roommates: Alice, Lou, and Maggie. Alice, however, talked of "moving from our room to Lea Irwins," while Maggie, McDowall's bedfellow, abandoned her to sleep with Lou and Alice. "I really thought it unkind to leave me as cold as it was in the bed alone," McDowall commented. After a spell of several days in the "sick room," McDowall changed her room to live with Jennie Hawkins and her roommates, Lavinia and Sallie. "How pleasantly I am situated now," she reflected in mid-January, "my room-mates are so amiable, and kind, I hope I may continue pleased." She did not. McDowall's bedmate, Lavinia, left her to share a bed with another girl, Annie Roberts, in early April. "I do not relish loosing [sic] my bedfellow, at all," she commented. And after Lou Alston (possibly the same Lou mentioned earlier) left school later that month, McDowall worried that Jennie would decide to room with another girl, Lou's former roommate, Laura Baker. By the end of the term, in May, McDowall saw little of any of her roommates. "I have been in my room alone all day," she complained. "Jennie lives in Laura Bakers room almost and Lavinia in Amanda Hussons, so Sallie & I are alone most of the time, and often I am left entirely to myself." A few days later, it appeared that even Sallie would abandon ship, when her friend Mary Ligon returned to school after a prolonged absence. "Oh is there a true heart on earth!" McDowall demanded. Although McDowall's difficulties were perhaps unusual, the importance she attached to relationships with her roommates was not; many students devoted a significant portion of their diaries and correspondence to naming and describing their roommates, sometimes to the exclusion of other subjects.[50]

Mary Elizabeth Whitfield, a student at Judson Institute in the 1840s, was more fortunate than McDowall. Her description of dormitory life likewise suggests the importance that schoolgirls attached to relationships with fellow students, but with an emphasis on the satisfaction that dormitory life afforded. Whitfield dubbed the quarters she shared with three other girls "Maiden's Retreat." The foursome were "comfortably and happily situated" in "a little room on the second story," she announced with satisfaction, adding, "My room mates are three of the most agreeable young ladies in school ... we spend our time very pleasantly away from the noise and bustle of the other students."[51]

As Whitfield's reference to "the noise and bustle" of the main dormitory indicates, far from being quiet retreats for study and sleep, student dormitories were the site of a lively social life that revolved around sociability, food, and frolic. South Carolina student Mary Belle Porcher wrote home in the midst of a "hubub" in her room: "I am sure I don't know how to proceed," she complained, "as the girls are trying, with all their might, to hinder my progress. Dutch is making all manner of shadows on the wall, while Carrie Desel is making her ugliest faces over a sour orange, and Addie is singing some ridiculous song." Julie and Martha Turner, who attended college together in the 1840s, described boarding school life to their father in similar terms: "We are studying hard and frolicking every time we get up stairs," Martha wrote to her father in 1847, adding sagely, "you may know how it is when sixty three of us girls get together."[52]

In the Old South (as at many residential campuses today), food was an important element of schoolgirl socializing. Mary Belle Porcher, a student at the Female Collegiate Institute in Barhamville, South Carolina, confided to her father: "I am in a most happy state of mind at present, for you must know I am invited to partake of a box, and such thoughts, always never fail to bring a smile to the face of a Barhamville girl." A highlight of Ella Anderson's reminiscences of her years at Wesleyan Female College (Georgia) was an impromptu party inspired by her roommate's discovery of sugar cane, nuts, and apples in the bottom of her trunk. "Night after night we feasted until all were gone," she wrote.[53]

Placed in the context of boarding school regulations, Anderson's reference to evening feasts suggests that the social life of the female academy sometimes led girls to break the all-encompassing rules typical of institutions of higher learning for women. School rules attempted to limit the scope of students' interaction by instituting rules that dictated study time, lights-out, and so forth. At Sarah Wheeler's school in Wilmington, Delaware, for example, "the rules of the school" specified that dormitory residents "must not speake [sic] to any pearson [sic] but to them that you sleep with." Parents clearly expected their daughters to follow school rules. They inspected their grade reports, complete with merits and demerits for "deportment," closely, and they urged them to attend to their teachers' advice and their school's regulations. Most parents eagerly awaited—and responded favorably to—letters like the one Virginia student Sally Lucas wrote to her father in 1850. "I have one thing to tell you dear Father which I know will give you . . . much pleasure and gratification," she announced. "It is that Mrs Wilner thinks I am a young lady of very good manners."[54]

Schoolgirls' eagerness to enjoy the company of their classmates and friends, however, led even the most well-mannered young ladies to test the boundaries of authority in their schools—and thus, by extension, their parents. Despite requirements for quiet study time at North Carolina's St. Mary's School, for instance, Lucy Warren complained, "The girls are making such a noise that I can hardly write." A letter that Greensboro College student Julie Frances Lilly wrote to a friend similarly indicates that girls often disregarded school rules in their pursuit of sociability: "We were excused from recitations today and tomorrow but we have to keep the rules and study hours. You can imagine how many rules we keep and how much studying we do," she commented wryly. At St. Mary's School in North Carolina, Mary Jane Jarratt and her classmates, whom Jarratt described as "a miserably wild set," regularly held midnight picnics in the dormitories and sometimes played practical jokes on one another; Jarratt's greatest offense while at school was skipping evening prayers to remove the slats from a classmate's bed.[55]

An album kept by Marion Richardson, a student at Baltimore, Maryland's Southern Home School for Girls in the mid-1890s, offers additional insight into students' behavior. Richardson filled her album with whimsical sketches of schoolgirl life after hours. Her choice of subjects suggests that southern schoolgirls engaged in high jinks without regard for school rules, especially those directing that students should be silent and stay in their own rooms after lights-out. One drawing of "Room No 5" depicted a group of girls in nightgowns enjoying a midnight snack; another showed the sleeping occupant of "No. 2," on a "Memorable night" in 1895, having water poured on her by mischievous classmates. Yet another sketch of the occupants of room number two depicted the room's occupants in bed, feigning sleep, while an illicit visitor from another room hid under the bed to escape the vigilance of the hall monitor. "Mrs Grady is in for us," the caption read.[56]

Late-night snacks and visiting after lights-out may seem like tame violations of the rules when compared to the rowdy behavior typical of students at the South's male institutions of higher education, where young men routinely engaged in reckless and sometimes despicable behavior, ranging from playing pranks on schoolmasters, to drinking, gambling, and womanizing, to violent and even deadly rebellions against school authorities.[57] However, in the context of "the rules of the school" at female academies—invariably more strict than at their male counterparts—and in light of the emphasis

Food was an important element of schoolgirls' social life. This drawing, included in Baltimore student Marion Richardson's album, shows a group of girls in nightgowns enjoying a midnight snack. In the context of strict school rules that prohibited socializing after hours, such behavior represented a form of female rebelliousness. (Rare Book, Manuscript, and Special Collections Library, Duke University, Durham, North Carolina)

that teachers, administrators, and parents placed on southern girls' good manners, southern schoolgirls' minor infractions of rules appear as an act of defiance against both adult authority and feminine ideals. In following their parents' injunctions to make the most of their time at the female academy, southern schoolgirls sometimes acted in ways contrary to their parents' expectations of ladylike behavior.

"I AM ALMOST CRAZY TO SEE YOU DEAREST": ROMANTIC FRIENDSHIPS

The friendships that southern girls formed with each other also posed a challenge to conventional definitions of southern womanhood. Nineteenth-century Americans encouraged same-sex relationships. Because most people believed that women and men were fundamentally different, they expected them to form their closest relationships with members of the same sex. Women's friendships were especially revered. Until the late nineteenth century, most Americans regarded women as lacking sexual passion and viewed women's relationships, by definition, as asexual; at a time when many people drew a sharp distinction between "pure" friendship and "impure" passion, this view lent legitimacy to women's relationships with each other. Moreover, because women had few alternatives to marriage and motherhood, their affection for each other posed no serious threat to heterosexual relationships; indeed, many women combined traditional married life with intense female friendship. Nonetheless, as later generations would recognize, women's romantic friendships held the potential to upset traditional gender roles, for if women looked to each other for emotional fulfillment, it was only a short step for them to seek ways to enjoy lifelong partnerships with each other—and without men.[58] Southern students' close relationships with each other, like their admiration for their favorite teachers, thus offered young women a glimpse of an alternative to their seemingly predestined future as wives and mothers.

Romantic friendships—intense, often exclusive relationships between women—were an important aspect of school life in the Old South. While male students in the antebellum South devoted significant attention to the opposite sex—in the form of either sedate courtships of elite women or sordid liaisons with slaves and prostitutes (and, occasionally, both)—female students, who had limited contact with men, focused their emotional energies on relationships with other women. Reminiscing about schoolgirl friendships during her time at North Carolina's St. Mary's School in the 1850s, Lucy Catharine Moore Capehard wrote: "I know not if it is the custom now [1906] for school girls to have sweethearts among their own sex, but it was in those days; such devotion you cannot imagine. . . . My sweetheart was Ellen Brent Pearson; to get a smile or glance from her . . . made me supremely happy."[59]

The female community of the female academy was the primary reference point for southern schoolgirls. A former student of Harrodsburg, Kentucky's Daughters' College known only as Daisy L. summed up the importance of belonging to the female community in a letter to her friend and schoolmate Belle Price in a Christmas 1857 letter. "The Old Year is dying fast," she reflected. "Pause, with your foot on the threshold and look back into the past. One year ago, to you I was a perfect stranger; I came here knowing no one; no kind hands were held out to welcome me; no eyes looked love into mine; no heart rose to welcome a sister-spirit. . . . Now, I stand among you (shall I say it?) a *beloved sister*. Oh! God knows how I love you *all*, and thank you for it too!"[60]

Within this community of "sister-spirits," young women searched for intimate friends. Southern schoolgirls filled their diaries and letters with lists and descriptions of their fellow students. In some cases, girls had little choice in determining their companions for meals, walks, and study hours. At some academies, in addition to roommates, school authorities assigned "companions" for meals in the dining hall and walks on the grounds. But schoolgirls eagerly sought out the company of kindred spirits with whom they could share their innermost feelings. As Maryland student Susan Mc-Dowall mused in her diary in 1856: "'Tis sweet to have a loving friend in whom one can confide." [61]

Young women were quite particular in their selection of their closest friends, distinguishing between mere classmates and "*intimate friends.*" Lucy Warren explained to her mother, "I know all the girls by name, but only know a few of them." Emma Kimberly complained to her father, "I have two or three friends in school, but none of them are as confidants." "A single true friend," as Susan McDowall expressed it, was worth more than scores of mere acquaintances. [62]

Indeed, the search for "a single true friend" could take up most of school-girls' limited free time. During a five-month period in 1856, Susan Mc-Dowall devoted her diary to her quest to find "some fond friend to whom I can confide my sorrows and troubles." McDowall's "sorrows and troubles" stemmed from her conviction that she was unpopular with the other girls at her school; "I wish I could for one moment take a peep into the hearts of many, and see how I am liked," she wrote in one entry. Despite her insecurity, McDowall continued to seek out her fellow students and to record with pleasure their attentions to her: notes, candy, flowers, and evening visits. "My heart pants for affection and love," she confessed. Indeed, Mc-Dowall's difficulties may have been related to the indiscriminate pleasure she took in female company. Over the course of five months, she mentioned ten girls—Amelia, Annie, Eliza, Mollie, Jennie, Marie, Lissie, Sallie, Grace, and Amanda—with varying degrees of affection, as well as her assorted roommates, her closest friend from home, Belle, and her rival for Marie's affections, Maria Jones. McDowall's eagerness to form friendships with so many girls—"I . . . pine for the love of others," she explained—ran counter to schoolgirl culture, which dictated that young women should form exclusive attachments. "The girls here seem to think, that if you love more than one girl, you are fickle, or you do not love anyone," she explained. [63]

McDowall was atypical in her desire for universal popularity, but she shared with other southern girls her need to be loved and her conviction that she would find that love in the company of other women. Like Mc-Dowall, southern schoolgirls looked to each other for their most important emotional connections. This was not simply a practical response to circumstances—students at female academies, after all, had limited contact with men—but also a result of widely held views that women, as creatures of the "heart," found comfort and consolation with each other more easily than with members of the opposite sex. Virginian Laura Wirt, who was privately educated together with her cousin Louisa Carrington, summed up this attachment in an 1828 letter. "To you, Louisa, I have always spoken my whole heart," she wrote, adding with emphasis, "*you know me.*"[64]

Female friendships were often highly romantic, if not downright erotic. Georgia student Loula Kendall recorded a series of intense schoolgirl crushes during the mid-1850s. At her first school, Kendall was besotted with "my own Bammie" (probably a nickname for Alabama). Kendall's relationship with Bammie colored all her fond recollections of her school, called Culloden. "There was where I first saw my Bammie," she recalled afterward. "How I loved her!" After two years of constant companionship ("Bammie and I were *always* together," Kendall wrote), Kendall and Bammie were separated when the former's parents concluded to send her to another school, Montpelier. They parted in true romantic fashion; Kendall sang a sentimental song ("No more") for her beloved friend, and both girls sobbed as they professed undying friendship.[65]

By the following year, however, Bammie had a rival for Kendall's affections: "My *sweet* Susie." Kendall wrote even more ecstatically about her feelings for Susie than she had about her attachment to Bammie, calling her "the partner of my joys and *sorrows.*" Exclaiming, "I love her so passionately," Kendall indicated that the girls' friendship included physical displays of affection as well as an intense emotional connection. When parted from "my *own darling, my precious, my adored Susie,*" she longed once again to "feel [her] breath on my cheek," to hold "her hand, (*my* hand) clasped in *mine,*" and to feel "her sweet ruby lips pressed to *mine.*" The girls considered their relationship both passionate and permanent; they exchanged rings (Kendall wished to have "our names engraved" on them, but the engraver was not in town), and after Susie left school, they promised each other "to think of each other *every* evening at *twilight.*" Perhaps aware of her companion's fickle nature, Susie also sent her absent lover a picture of herself, which Kendall gazed at for hours on end, daydreaming of the pair's time together and longing for a "nectar kiss" from "her rosy *pouting* lips." Kendall vowed to be faithful to her absent darling. "I *never* will love another girl as I have loved *her,*" she proclaimed. "Did *one* girl *ever* love another as much, and as passionately as *I* do my Susie?" she demanded, answering: "I cannot believe it: *Her* destiny is connected with *mine,* and *without* her love life's path to *me* were a dark and dreary waste."[66]

While southern girls frequently mentioned such affectionate behavior as holding hands and exchanging kisses, they seem to have shared their culture's belief that such actions were innocent—that is, nonsexual. It was not until the late nineteenth century that European "sexologists" defined homosexuality as a disease, and it was not until the early twentieth century that most Americans became conversant with psychological theories of sexual development that stigmatized lesbianism as perverted and unnatural. Prior to the Civil War, then, southern girls were free to engage in intense, romantic relationships with other women without fear of social stigma. Indeed, Tennessee student Eliza Anna Goodwin's friend Lizzie linked same-sex friendship with female chastity, writing: "May our friendship, like the Sacred Lamp of Vesta's Temple, be ever pure, bright and undying."[67]

Limited in their contact with men, living in close proximity to other women, and lacking cultural taboos against same-sex intimacy, southern schoolgirls forged intense attachments—what Anna Louisa Norman's friend Addie described as "ardent love"—to each other.[68] Female friends often were inseparable. In 1829, Mary Louisa Read, a Virginia student, wrote to her cousin, Mary Carrington, about her friendship with "one of the finest girls you ever saw," Maryanna Mugee. "We are great cronies and are never satisfied unless we are together," she commented. When seated separately in the classroom, Read and Mugee communicated with each other by sign language. Even during holidays, schoolgirls maintained their special friendships; they begged their parents to allow their closest friends to accompany them home for vacations, and they wrote each other lengthy letters when they were unsuccessful in their pleas.[69]

Southern schoolgirls recognized romantic friendships as special relationships marked by unique customs. Students at female academies often exchanged gifts of candy and flowers to express their admiration for each other. Millie Birckhead's cousin Sallie, a student at Piedmont Female Academy, explained, "I went in the woods after wild flowers[;] we got a great many then we fixed up bouquet's and sent them to our *loves*." Sallie was delighted to have received four bouquets, including one from "Ida Fancouer . . . the sweetest little thing I ever knew." Particular friends also made each other gifts of books of poetry, golden rings, locks of hair, or daguerreotypes as tokens of their lasting affection.[70]

Choosing deskmates was a ritual repeated at the beginning of each term that announced a special relationship. Writing to Olin Davis during the summer vacation in 1858, Nannie Nottingham could barely contain her anxiety to be reunited with her friend at Wesleyan Female College in Virginia. "Linnie I am almost crazy to see you dearest," she wrote. "I suppose you will not fail to choose our desk and remember we are partners for everything next session." [71]

Close friends also roomed together. Schoolgirls fondly reminisced about
their college roommates. One LaGrange Female College student bewailed her ill fortune in being denied the ability to room with her closest friend, "Cousin Mollie." "Jennie you cannot imagine how much I love Cousin Mollie for she is the sweetest [girl] that ever lived I believe or she appears so in my eyes for you know love covers all defects and failings," she wrote in 1857. [72]

Even more than sharing a desk or a room, sharing a bed was a mark of a particularly close friendship. At many schools, roommates routinely slept together, either in a double bed or in two mattresses placed on a single bed-frame. This was the case at Judson Female Institute, where Mary Elizabeth Whitfield casually referred to her "bedfellow," a young woman she barely knew. Often, however, sharing a bed was a public statement of an important—and usually exclusive—relationship. Wesleyan Female College student Louisiana Burge and her roommate of three years, "Mitt," were most "unwilling to separate" when illness forced Burge to change rooms. "Mitt and I cried like two children," Burge recounted; "she vowed that she had slept with me for three years and would have not other [sic] room-mate." [73]

While it is difficult (if not impossible) to know if girlish displays of affection such as hand-holding, hugging, and kissing extended to sexual intimacy, it is clear that students prized the night hours as a time to share confidences and that they took comfort in each other's company. Susan Mc-Dowall frequently remarked on sleeping arrangements at Patapsco Institute, where girls routinely left their assigned rooms (and McDowall herself) to sleep with their closest friends. Sallie Collinson revealed the connection between romantic love and sharing a bed when she wrote to her schoolmate Anna Louisa Norman: "Dear Lou I never loved any one . . . as much as I do you. . . . I wish you could sleep with me To-night." And Greensboro Female College student Jennie Johnson's cousin recognized the significance of one's choice of bedfellow when she demanded: "Who do you sleep with? . . . Have you a new darling, or do you still cling to *Puss*." [74]

Romantic relationships could create emotional turmoil when one student's affection was not reciprocated. Sallie Collinson, a student at Baltimore Female College in the late 1850s, displayed unrequited love in a series of letters and romantic poetry to her schoolmate Anna Louise Norman, called Lou or Lulu. "Lou you do not know how dearly I love you," Sallie exclaimed. "It seems as if you treat me so coldly but I cannot beleive [sic] you intend it. . . . I have had many crys [sic] about you my darling, last night I sat by my window and the tears trickled down my cheeks, and I do not think my heart ever ached worse and it was all for you Lou." Despite the intervention of a third schoolgirl, who urged Lou to reciprocate Sallie's love, Lou

remained aloof.[75]

Whether they enjoyed the intimacy of Olin Davis and Nannie Nottingham, who were "partners for everything," or suffered the unrequited love of Sallie Collinson, who knew from experience that "O it is the worst of pain, / To love and not be loved again," southern schoolgirls generally believed, as Susan McDowall wrote in her diary, that "to be loved, 'tis surely the greatest happiness below." Moreover, it was to their fellow schoolmates—roommates, deskmates, bedfellows, and romantic friends—that southern girls looked for intimate relationships and emotional satisfaction.[76]

The "romantic attachment" that existed between schoolgirls granted them a temporary reprieve from the demands of conventional southern womanhood. Unlike heterosexual marriage, which required women to subordinate their desires and serve their husbands, homosocial relationships in pre-Freudian America involved few trade-offs; students at the South's female academies found that it was possible, indeed desirable, both to seek self-fulfillment (in the form of academic achievement) and to develop a self-in-relation (in the form of romantic friendship). The joy that many young women took in these rewarding relationships is summed up in Jessie Ferguson's 1859 inscription in her friend Ida Ann Southworth's autograph album: "For with thee true and trusted friend than more dear friend to me / the sweetest moments of my life are those I've passed with thee!" In later life, young women would look to their "true and trusted" female friends for support and encouragement in resisting a future that required them to prioritize patriarchal heterosexual marriage over egalitarian same-sex friendship.[77]

"SCHOOL DAYS ARE THE HAPPIEST": COMMENCEMENT

In their late teens, young women began to anticipate the end of their schooling. As they approached the commencement ceremonies that would mark the end of their "school days" and the beginning of their adult lives, they reflected on the significance of their time at the female academy and on what the future held in store. Many schoolgirls reported reluctance on leaving school. Agreeing with Virginian Elizabeth Nelson's assessment that "our school days [are] the happiest," they regarded commencement as both a marker of adult status and a moment of wrenching separation from their classmates.[78]

Susan McDowall captured schoolgirls' mixed emotions as she prepared for her own commencement from Maryland's Patapsco Institute. In an 1856 diary entry, McDowall anticipated the end of her schooling, her return home, and her separation from her friends and classmates. "Soon school days will be over and we will take our places in the drama of life," she reflected. "Though school has many trials, still it will be sad to sever the ties that have bound us as schoolmates, and fellow labourers, after knowledge. When I look at the future and think upon our different lots, I feel sad to think many of us may never meet more after seperated [sic] here."[79]

During their time at school, young women experimented with a new identity as schoolgirls and forged a new community centered on other women. Commencement threatened the community and the identity that young women built within the confines of the female academy. As Mary Virginia Early wrote to her mother shortly before her own commencement in spring 1842, "Ah! me the ties that are to be sundered next month!!!" Schoolgirls on the brink of graduation frequently reiterated that commencement meant parting from their friends forever. A Wesleyan student wrote to her classmate Olin Davis: "I often think of the many happy hours we have spent together oh! Linnie it is painful to think they have past, past for ever."[80]

Graduating students looked to autograph albums as a way of preserving the friendships that they had formed during their time at the female academy. Autograph albums may be viewed as the nineteenth-century equivalent of modern yearbooks, although antebellum versions were considerably more expressive than their contemporary counterparts. While many "albums of affection," as one particularly elaborate autograph book was titled, were bound in leather, embossed and edged with gold, and lavishly illustrated with romantic or historical scenes, others were simple copybooks. Regardless of their appearance, autograph albums constituted a material culture of female friendship, providing both evidence of girls' attachment to each other and a venue for them to express their emotions.[81]

Schoolgirls filled their autograph albums with mournful tributes to female friendship. More than collections of signatures, autograph albums were repositories for sentimental verse, fond reminiscences, and well-wishing. Young women adorned the pages of their albums with valentines, pictures, and locks of hair, as well as with excerpts from well-known British and American sentimental poetry. Original poems with titles such as "School-Days Remembered" and "My Last Day at School" also proliferated in schoolgirls' autograph albums, suggesting the importance that young women attached to the end of their school years.[82]

Because young women often wrote in autograph books on the eve of parting, albums are a rich source of reflections on the importance of female friendship just as those friendships were threatened by separation. As Emma

Many southern girls formed close friendships while at school. Even after commencement, they hoped to keep in touch with each other, as this autograph album from Lenoir, North Carolina's Davenport Female Academy illustrates. (In the antebellum South, street addresses were not required to send mail; correspondents could simply direct letters to the proper town and state.) (Southern Historical Collection, Wilson Library, University of North Carolina at Chapel Hill)

Graves noted, "Our friends always appear doubly dear to us when we are about to be separated from them. Then all the latent affection that had been slumbering in our hearts is brought forth into action."[83]

Female students' albums were full of odes to female friendship. Entries in Nashville, Tennessee, St. Cecilia's Academy student Eliza Anna Goodwin's album typified this emphasis. Goodwin's friend Mary Bailey praised friendship in verse:

> There is a sweet, and lovely flower,
> That blossoms still the same,
> Amid the sunshine and the shade,
> And "Friendship" is its name.

Likewise, a girl named Mary averred:

> The earth can boast no purer tie,
> No brighter richer gem;
> No jewel of a lovelier die,
> Than friendship's diadem.

Not surprisingly, then, still another friend, Mag (probably short for Maggie), offered this wish for her friend:

A wish for thee—the boon is rare
The choicest heaven bestows:—
A *friend* to share thy every care,
To soften all thy woes.[84]

Young women prized autograph albums as mementoes of youthful friendships. As one signatory, who signed herself "Your True friend S.," wrote in Mary Virginia Early's autograph book in 1840: "The Album is one of Friendship's dearest minions. It is the declared enemy of Oblivion. Its owner may well regard it as of inestimable value. In future years, when the scenes of youth shall have been reckoned among those that 'were, but are not,' this book perchance will be considered a most valuable memento of other days."[85]

In their albums, graduating students bade farewell to their friends at the same time that they reaffirmed the importance and endurance of female friendship. Writing in fellow Greensboro Female Academy (North Carolina) student Martha Ann Kirkpatrick's album, S. A. Brown proclaimed:

Blest be the dear uniting love
That will not let us part
Our bodies may far off remove
Yet still I hope we're joined in *heart*.[86]

School attendance might be temporary, such verses indicated, but female friendships endured.

Commencement prompted southern girls to ponder the importance of friendship. It also inspired them to reflect on the significance of their time at school. Students' comments on the end of schooling suggest that they saw graduation as an important rite of passage, a major milestone on the path from girlhood to womanhood. Anticipating the graduation ceremonies at Wesleyan Female College in 1860, one student wrote to her classmate, Olin Davis:

Well dear Sis Olin Commencement is most here, in a few more weeks
you and I will bid adieu to school days, the pleasant associations of our
childhood, the friends of our youth, to all these we must bid farewell.
Can you my precious realize that in so short a time your school days
will have ended? It seems incredible to me, and I feel glad that I cannot
believe it, since I am afraid my school days are the happiest. Tho' I

shall be so glad to again enjoy the society of my dear friends, I am sorry to part from so many that I love, never again expecting to see them.[87]

Like this young woman, many southern girls drew a sharp contrast between "school days" and adult life. During their time at school, young southern women devoted themselves to intellectual pursuits and female friendship. As they prepared to bid farewell to their schoolmates, they registered reluctance at leaving school and fear of the future. Their comments suggested that although brief, their time away from home at school had a lasting impact on their lives. By offering them even a temporary respite from the demands of southern ladyhood, the academy experience increased both southern girls' reluctance to assume their adult roles and their awareness of alternatives to those roles.

Many schoolgirls reported reluctance on leaving school. They recognized that, just as leaving home for school had meant assuming the identity of a schoolgirl, leaving school for home would require another shift in their sense of themselves. Daughters' College (Kentucky) student Daisy L. wrote to her friend Belle Price on the brink of graduation:

You are now,
"Standing, with reluctant feet,
Where the brook and river meet;
Womanhood and childhood fleet."[88]

Georgia native Loula Kendall likewise recognized commencement as an end as well as a beginning: the end of what she called "*my college life*" and the beginning of a new stage of life as "a young *lady*." Admitting her reservations about the change—"I dread so much to part from my friends and to be a young *lady*," she wrote at the start of her last year at school—she also accepted the shift as inevitable, adding: "It must be so!" On her last day of school, she recorded an extended reflection on the meaning of graduation in which she linked leaving school with losing the relative freedom of girlhood:

Today is my last school day! Time is ever rolling onward, waiting for no one nor regarding our entreaties to travel slower, and the day is here when I am to bid *farewell* to school days! I, who as early as I can remember used to love to study and go to school so much, and never wanted to be a *young lady*, I must now leave such scenes, and mingle with the world's votaries! . . . A few years ago, I was a child my heart as guileless as an angel's, . . . and *now* I am considered as *being grown*, the childish heart must be exchanged for a garb of dignity, the hallowed books must be thrown lightly away, and I am to be ushered a mass of whalebone & starch into the fashionable world—"From our path have fled the flowers, woman['s] lot is on us now"[!] [89]

On her graduation day, Kendall anticipated, she would exchange "the hallowed books" of a schoolgirl first for "the fashionable world" of the belle and then for the duties of a southern matron—what she warily referred to as "woman's lot." Thus, Kendall, like other southern schoolgirls, regarded the end of her time at the female academy as a significant coming-of-age ritual.

Young women marked this transition from girlhood to womanhood with a formal commencement ceremony. While academies sponsored such ceremonies, in part to demonstrate to parents and guardians their success in educating their young charges, girls themselves eagerly took part in commencement, urging their parents, siblings, and friends to attend the ceremony that would make "home girls" and "young ladies" out of erstwhile "school girls." [90]

The ceremony itself was an incongruous amalgam of remembrance and anticipation, combining celebrations of traditional femininity and displays of female intellect. The graduates wore "lovely white dresses" made especially for the occasion, signifying their innocence, youth, and purity, yet they also received "honours," medals, and certificates testifying to their "proficience" in academic subjects. Commencement addresses, delivered by the school principal or by the senior with the highest average, praised young women for bringing joy to the home circle at the same time that they mourned the loss of female friendship. According to Susan Nye Hutchinson, such addresses were "pathetic and elegant" and "deeply affected" those assembled. [91]

In her postbellum commencement address, Wesleyan graduate Josephine Southall hinted at the mixed messages of graduation and recalled the jostling emotions of commencement in her description of the academy's first graduating class's farewell ceremonies:

At the end of the same term thirteen of the maidens were to receive the honors of graduation and return to the homes which they were now considered fitted to adorn. This was in the good times when young ladies completed the College course to become the caressed and honored pets of the home circle, their especial mission being to keep ever shining the sunlight of love in their father's house till they chose to brighten with the same sunlight another's. But the visions of joys the sweetest in reserve did not make them forget that they were leaving the spot the second only to home and each face grew sad at the thought of going away never to return.[92]

Whether they anticipated being "ushered a mass of whalebone & starch into the fashionable world" or becoming "the caressed and honored pets of the home circle," young women departing from school agreed that life after graduation would never be the same. As they laid aside their schoolbooks and bade farewell to their schoolmates, young women in the Old South prepared to take on adult roles and responsibilities in "the drama of life."[93] This transition, however, proved to be a difficult one.

Southern schoolgirls had relished the opportunity to devote themselves to intellectual improvement and female friendship. Keenly aware that marriage and motherhood would curtail their ability to study and socialize, female graduates resisted their preordained future by prolonging each successive life stage and postponing the next. As they did so, they called upon the friends they had made in school for emotional support and practical advice. With their unwavering conviction that "school days are the happiest," they relied on their "sister-spirits" to resist accepting as inevitable "woman's lot" in a patriarchal society. As they left the female academy behind, young women in the Old South took with them the building blocks of a female youth culture of resistance.

"IT WILL NEVER DO FOR ME TO BE
MARRIED": LAURA HENRIETTA WIRT

In 1826, twenty-two-year-old Laura Henrietta Wirt
wrote a letter to her cousin and confidante, Louisa Cabell Carrington, in which she defended her stubborn refusal to marry any of her numerous and persistent suitors. Laura, who had realized her father's fond dream
that she would become "a classical scholar" by excel-
ling in her studies first at home in Virginia and then at a
female academy in Washington, D.C., was reluctant to
exchange the intellectual stimulation of her girlhood
for the domestic responsibilities of adulthood. "Variety for me, forever!" she declared. "It is the essence
of my life and happiness." Laura predicted that marriage would mean a limited life of child care and housekeeping—activities that she disparaged as "disagreeable occupations." "Monotony kills me as dead as a
door nail," she pronounced, concluding, "it will never
do for me to be married."[1] Despite her protests, Laura
did eventually marry, but like many of her counterparts, she first spent several years as a single woman
living at home with her parents. Her correspondence
between the end of her schooling and the beginning
of her married life—from 1820 until 1827—reveals the
difficulties that beset young southern women as they
completed their educations and confronted their adult
destiny as wives and mothers. Laura's reluctance to
commit herself to marriage also illustrates one avenue
of resistance explored by young women in the Old
South.

Born in Richmond, Virginia, in 1803, Laura learned
early in life that the key to attaining love and accep-

tance was to apply herself to her studies. True to his promise to "spare no pains" in raising her, Laura's father, Virginia lawyer and U.S. Attorney General William Wirt, subjected her to a rigorous academic program that included Latin, French, Italian, Spanish, and English grammar, as well as dancing, painting, and piano. An 1810 letter displayed seven-year-old Laura's eagerness to win her father's approval and her readiness to undertake whatever studies he might suggest. "I will try to learn very fast to please my dear Father," she promised.[2]

As Laura entered her teens, however, pleasing her dear father became more complicated. From the beginning, William's vision of female perfection — "an happy union of female gentleness and delicacy, with masculine learning & genius" — required his daughter to walk a fine line between intellectual excellence and feminine modesty. Once Laura entered her teens, the balance shifted. As Laura approached her seventeenth birthday, William abruptly terminated her formal education, adjuring her to dedicate herself to learning the art of pleasing others, which he called "the sweetest charm" of "your sex." An intelligent woman "may be admired," admitted William, "but she will never be beloved."[3]

Meanwhile, Laura's mother, Elizabeth, set about training her daughter in "the *minutia* of housekeeping." Laura was not eager to substitute training in housekeeping for her classical studies. In 1818, Laura admitted to her grandmother that despite "Mama's insisting upon it yesterday that I must learn to ply my needle with more industry," she undertook the task "very reluctantly" and found many excuses to interrupt her progress. The following year, she complained in a letter to her cousin Louisa, "I kept house today and am to do so for this week, besides mending and making my clothes! — darning stockings, and all the other disagreeable occupations that you can imagine." But despite Laura's objections, her mother held firm; Laura, she pronounced, should "take more pleasure & interest in the necessary, tho unintellectual duties of domestic life."[4]

While her parents both pushed her toward and prepared her for marriage, Laura formed other plans. Shortly before the conclusion of her studies, Laura spent a summer at the country home of relatives, where she attended to her lessons in the company of her cousin, Louisa Elizabeth Cabell. Laura and Louisa were already well acquainted thanks to the Wirts' habit of spending many summers at the Cabell plantation. The cousins' friendship intensified during the months they spent together completing their formal schooling, and soon after they parted, Laura and Louisa made a solemn promise to each other to remain single. The two friends planned to found an "Old Maid's Hall," where, together with other like-minded women, they would "live and die in single blessedness." Laura painted an idyllic picture of life in this "Charming happy society," where the denizens would devote themselves to music-making, to the "refined delights" of continued intellectual improvement, and to "promot[ing] the happiness" of others.[5]

For the next seven years, Laura struggled to realize her vision of "single blessedness." At home in Washington, D.C., she continued her studies on her own. "My bed is at this minute covered with charts, historical, geographical and biographical, with books of all sizes and descriptions," she boasted in 1820. But with no definite goal in mind for her studies, Laura feared her commitment might not last: "You cannot imagine how studious I am all o' the sudden, but I fear the fit will go off before long, as you know I am not remarkable for constancy in any respect," she added ruefully.[6]

Laura found a justification for her studiousness when, in the mid-1820s, she set herself up as a governess for her younger siblings. But despite Laura's "enthusiasm" and "perseverance" in undertaking the education of her younger sisters, her parents were reluctant to allow their daughter to "rusticate at home." William insisted on an "excursion" to the fashionable Virginia Springs, where Laura would have an opportunity to meet potential husbands, and Elizabeth enrolled the younger children in a local school so that their education would no longer be an obstacle to Laura's "seeing and being seen."[7]

As she searched with growing despair for a route to the useful independence she had dreamed of, Laura sank into a deep depression. Her father pinpointed the source of Laura's "apathy, lethargy and pining atrophy" even as he conspired to frustrate her hopes of finding purpose and fulfillment as a single woman. "At present," he observed in late 1824, "your mind is without an object in prospect, and no mind can stand that situation. It must have something to achieve. . . . We must have something to do that calls for an exertion of our faculties, or we are miserable," William concluded.[8]

Laura's prolonged and ultimately unsuccessful quest for a meaningful existence as a single woman was poignant but not unique. Indeed, most young women in the Old South spent several years living as single women in their family homes. Although many of these girls agreed with Laura Wirt that "it will never do for me to be married," they saw few alternatives. Ultimately, most concluded that "single blessedness" was only an illusion and dedicated themselves, instead, to the quest for romantic love. Although temporary, the time that young women in the Old South spent as single women was neither brief nor insignificant. Far from eagerly embracing their assigned adult roles, southern girls actively resisted them, vigorously and over an extended time span. Their inability to translate their resistance to the status quo into realistic alternatives says more about the restrictive nature of elite southern society than it does about young women's desire or determination. Young women's attempts to find fulfillment and independence beyond the bounds of matrimony represented a serious and sustained (if ultimately unsuccessful) effort to exert control over their own lives and to free themselves from the strictures of southern patriarchy. By seeking to transform the life stage of a single daughter-at-home into a lifestyle of "single blessedness," young women in the Old South resisted their preordained future as southern ladies.

"THE NARROW CIRCLE OF HOME": SOUTHERN DAUGHTERS' SPHERE

Most young women in the Old South spent their late teens and early twenties living with their parents and filling the role of a "daughter-at-home." This life stage was typical of Anglo-American girls. For many girls, on both sides of the Atlantic Ocean and both north and south of the Mason-Dixon line, the end of formal schooling marked the beginning of this period. At the conclusion of a girl's education, whether at home or at school, parents and daughters alike expected that young women would "enjoy the sweets of home society," as one of Margaret Beall's correspondents expressed it in 1857. But what South Carolinian Grace Elmore called "the narrow circle of home" proved dissatisfying for many southern girls. Rather than finding contentment and pleasure in the family circle, southern-schoolgirls-turned-stay-at-home-daughters frequently complained of loneliness and boredom. The "almost unvaried repetition of daily and wearisome occurrences" caused young single women "restlessness and anxiousness," and they eagerly—and, sadly, usually unsuccessfully—searched for purpose and direction. Virginian Mary Hawes spoke for many of her contemporaries when she wrote: "Daily I ask myself, for what purpose was I made? and hourly feel my insufficiency, to be what I should be."[9]

Although other daughters-at-home also found this life stage challenging, southern girls' quest for companionship and meaning was made especially difficult by the geographic and cultural landscape of their region. The Old South was a predominantly rural society. For many young women, life on isolated plantations was lonely, particularly after spending months or even years in the company of other young women at school. Former classmates conducted extensive correspondence with each other, expressing their desire to see one another again, exchanging daguerreotypes and flowers, and planning periodic reunions. But such contacts were a poor substitute for the constant company of one's closest friends. Elizabeth Nelson revealed both the depth of young women's friendships and the extent of young women's isolation in her numerous letters to her former schoolmate, Mary Carring-

ton. "I have very frequently wished My dearest Mary that we could see more of each other," she wrote in a typical letter. "I have ever retained a very affectionate remembrance of you ever since we were in School together, and though all [personal] intercourse has ceased between us this affection [has] not diminished—I have frequently thought that our school days [were] the happiest of our life and often feel sad to think that of all the girls with whom I went to school some of whom I loved and still love very dearly—with not one of them have I now any communication."[10]

As Elizabeth Nelson's wistful letter suggests, southern girls' desire to maintain female friendships was often frustrated by both physical distance and social conventions. Even local travel was difficult, expensive, and time-consuming in the nineteenth-century South, with its rough roads and reliance on horse-drawn conveyances. Compounding this difficulty was the requirement that a young single woman be accompanied by a male "protector"—usually her father or brother—on even short journeys.[11]

As a result of these constraints, young women's plans to see their friends were often postponed indefinitely. In late 1851, Georgia resident Gertrude Clanton complained that she had been forced to renege on her promise to visit a friend because her father told her that she was "too unwell." Though Clanton disagreed, she had no choice but to defer to her father's judgment: "I however don't happen to agree with him—[but] I suppose I must 'yield to the powers that be' though unwillingly[.]" Fellow Georgian Maria Bryan similarly chafed at the constraints posed by social convention and uncooperative male relatives. "I have been quite anxious lately to go to Scottsborough," she wrote in 1826, "but I have but little idea of doing so, as I have no way of going, nor no one to go with me. Brother prefers waiting on any other person to me, and will leave all his business to go to any place where his whim may incline him, but he always pleads pressing business when I ask him to accompany me. I really feel hurt sometimes when I think of it." Male authority combined with rural geography to severely limit southern daughters' opportunities for mobility and sociability.[12]

In letters to their friends, southern daughters described themselves as virtual prisoners in their own homes. In 1796, Virginian Eleanor Parke Custis wrote to her old school friend Elizabeth Bordley, "[I] stay constantly at home. . . . I have been out but twice since I came here (which is three weeks.)" This situation remained virtually unchanged throughout the antebellum era. More than fifty years later, Mary Berkely of Loudon County, Vir-

ginia, echoed Custis's phrasing when she told her friend and former classmate Ella Noland in 1851, "I stay almost constantly at home."[13]

Restricted in their movements and isolated on rural plantations, many
girls complained that they were "almost dead for want of Society," as
Frances Higginbotham put it in a letter to her sister in 1834.[14] The diary
kept by Louisiana resident Ellen Louise Power in early 1862 typified young
women's loneliness and boredom—compounded, in Power's case, by illness. On January 1, 1862, she wrote: "I have concluded to try and keep a diary
this year, but it is a bad beginning, as I am sick in bed with typhoid fever."
Later entries provided little variation from this theme:

> I have nothing to write, only I am still in bed. I do get so lonesome I
> wish some one would come.

> I have nothing of interest to write today it has been very dull all day.

> I get very lonely sometimes. . . .

> I haven't anything interesting to write.

Small wonder that in February, she exclaimed: "Oh! me! I dread for the time
for me to write in my diary for I haven't any thing to write."[15]

Virginian Elizabeth Ruffin also suffered from boredom, although it did
not prevent her from writing lengthy entries in her diary. Ruffin filled her
journal with complaints about what she called "this every day sameness and
idleness." Although Ruffin recorded a number of activities in her diary, including reading novels, writing letters, playing piano, sewing, entertaining
gentlemen callers, painting, working Chinese puzzles, sleeping, and eating,
all of them soon lost their charm. "I really am most seriously tired of doing
nothing," she wrote in 1827. "Books have nearly failed to entertain. . . . I
have slept till my senses are stupified [sic] beyond recovery, scarcely an idea
now remaining. . . . I have eat till ashamed. . . . All sources of amusement
[are] complete[ly] worn thread bare."[16]

Isolated on rural plantations, unable to maintain contact with their
friends and classmates, and weary of solitary amusements, southern daughters suffered from loneliness, boredom, and melancholy. To escape the restlessness and ennui of life as a daughter-at-home, southern girls cast about
them for something to give their lives meaning and purpose. The search
for "single blessedness," as many referred to this ideal, represented one of
southern girls' most creative—although ultimately unsuccessful—forms of
resistance.

A logical—and indeed, often seemingly unavoidable—choice for these women was marriage. Mary Page suggested as much in a letter she wrote to her close friend and former classmate Lucy McGuire. "I tell you what," she commented wryly, "our forlorn condition often makes me think that *good husbands* would be the best things for us." Young women in the Old South fully embraced the romantic ideal that flourished in nineteenth-century America, hoping in a relationship of mutual love, respect, and trust to achieve the ultimate in personal happiness. But southern girls harbored so many doubts about the supply of "good husbands" that they were in no hurry to marry. As Amanda Jane Cooley put it, "I see so many unhappy matches it almost discourages me."[17]

Southern girls were keen observers. They knew that in marrying, a woman entrusted her economic welfare and her emotional well-being—"all her earthly hopes, her world entire," as one girl expressed it—to her husband. And they also knew that many men did not deserve this sacred trust. In their autograph albums, young women frequently offered each other warnings against "men unqualified and base." According to one selection, men were prone to "a fretful temper," envy, and unkindness; moreover, they were deceitful: "Man when smoothest he appears / Is most to be suspected," one young woman quoted British poet William Cowper. While most southern girls did not classify all men as unrepentant deceivers, they did believe that the faults of men, both as a class and as individuals, posed obstacles to marital bliss. As one of Eliza Cornelia Grantham's correspondents put it, young women had "so little confidence in the *sexe* [*sic*]" that they hesitated to attach themselves to men who might prove thoughtless or even cruel husbands.[18]

Lizzie Davis, a student at Frederick Female Seminary in Maryland, filled her composition book with fictional essays about matrimony that suggested that husbands would either become "miserable drunkard[s]" or die and leave their widows penniless. The critical point, as Davis recognized, was that on their wedding day, women tied their futures to those of their husbands: "She has taken the irrevocable step by which her future destiny is decided. Her happiness is in anothers hand." While few girls cataloged men's faults as completely as Lizzie Davis, many young women expressed doubts about men's ability—or desire—to ensure their wives' happiness.[19]

Southern girls' ambivalence about marriage was widely shared; in nineteenth-century America, many young women experienced what one historian has described as a "marriage trauma" when they contemplated exchanging single life for the married state. Yet for southern girls, contemplating the future may have been especially traumatic, both because marriage was more unavoidable for southern women and because southern women had more to fear from marriage. Northern girls married later than their southern peers; one comparison of southern and northern elites suggests that while the greatest proportion of all women married between ages twenty-one and twenty-five, a significant percentage of southern women married at younger ages, while for northerners, a greater proportion of women married in their late twenties and thirties. For northern women, then, delaying marriage was more likely—and perhaps more acceptable as well—than for southern women. Remaining single for life was also a more realistic option for northern women than for their southern sisters. Comparative statistics for women's marriage patterns in Charleston and Boston indicate that southern women were less likely to remain single than northern women, even when both lived in cities. In 1845, over a third of Boston's women over age twenty were single. The contrast with Charleston was minimal, but suggestive; not quite a third of Charleston's adult white women were single in 1848. But although women over twenty were single at approximately the same rate in both cities, Charleston women were half again as likely as their Boston counterparts to be married by age twenty-five. Once they reached their twentieth birthday, then, southern women seem to have encountered strong cultural, social, and economic forces that pushed them to relinquish their single status more quickly, and more often, than northern women. In addition to experiencing less pressure to marry than their southern counterparts, northern women, once married, enjoyed both legal and cultural protections from male dominance, ranging from the adoption of married women's property acts, enacted in New York in 1848, to the exercise of a form of indirect power, sometimes described as "domestic feminism," which granted some northern wives influence over their husbands and control over their own fertility. By contrast, young women in the Old South confronted more pressure to marry while single and anticipated fewer protections once married.[20]

Southern women's reservations about men also may have been particularly pronounced. The bad behaviors that southern girls attributed to men were commonly identified (and, by northern reformers, often vociferously decried) as male vices. However, southern men, relatively unencumbered by the powerful constraints of female influence that accompanied the feminization of religion in the antebellum North and strongly attracted by the male culture of honor that enjoyed strong support in Old South, may have been particularly likely to engage in activities that threatened the sanctity of marriage and the security of the home: gambling, drinking, and womanizing.[21]

Young women in the Old South indicated that southern men had many
faults that could make for an unhappy match. As Lizzie Davis recognized, alcoholism was the source of numerous marital difficulties, ranging from chronic indebtedness to domestic violence. In the Old South, where the culture of honor sanctioned hard drinking among elite men, alcohol abuse (and sometimes wife abuse as well) may have been a particularly common problem. Virginian Amanda Virginia Edmonds frequently remarked in her diary that her gentleman callers took "too much 'dutch courage [i.e., drank to excess].'" Young women were well aware that such habits contributed to marital difficulties. Ann Eliza Wright wrote to her friend Mary Carrington to comment on an unhappy marriage in 1837: "I have just returned from Powell's, where I rode to meet my old friend Lucy Wharton nee Dabney. She was on her return home. . . . She certainly seems very well satisfied with the state of matrimony. In fine spirits & good health for her. Mrs Stuart her sister was with her. She seems cheerful, but I dont [see] how she can poor woman! with a husband a perfect sot." Although Wright did not elaborate on Mrs. Stuart's difficulties, clearly, she believed that "a perfect sot" could only make an imperfect husband.[22]

Infidelity also held the potential to destroy women's happiness in marriage. While cheating spouses no doubt exist in all times and places, women in the antebellum South had special reasons to be concerned about their husbands' fidelity. In the antebellum North, a vigorous debate over men's sexuality—ranging from seduction literature that depicted men as "inherently immoral," heartless "rakes" to anti-masturbation tracts that advocated a "male chastity ideal"—reflected both men's immoral behavior and reformers' attempts to curb male vice. In the Old South, however, a sexual double standard that stigmatized women for extramarital relationships while it excused elite men's dalliances with poor white or enslaved black women, together with a legal system that permitted divorce only in instances of extreme physical cruelty, the wife's infidelity, or the husband's inability to produce an heir, combined to allow men to indulge their "passion" and to prevent women from objecting to their husbands' wandering ways. At the same time, the physical presence of presumably available female slaves and the proslavery argument that the presence of this group of supposedly debauched women protected elite women from men's voracious sexual appetites both paved the way for slaveholding men to engage in illicit interracial sex. Young women's much-vaunted sexual innocence did not prevent them from knowing about men's infidelities. Nineteen-year-old Texan

Lizzie Scott confided to her diary that her father's indulgence in "illicit love" had destroyed her mother's peace of mind and expressed disbelief that "any man in the world, unless 'tis a *really pious minister*," was truly "moral."[23]

Because it was considered unseemly to mention men's sexual peccadilloes (South Carolinian Mary Boykin Chesnut once acidly commented that southern wives had to pretend that their husbands' illegitimate offspring had fallen from the sky rather than acknowledge their husbands' culpability), young women did not openly discuss men's sexual misbehavior.[24] They did, however, warn each other against mercenary men who married in hopes of bettering their own finances. Because a married woman's property came under her husband's control, men sometimes sought wives in order to improve their economic status. Since (with the exception of Mississippi) southern states tended to lag behind northern states in granting wives control over the property they brought to marriage, this may have been a matter of especial concern for southern women. South Carolina planter James Henry Hammond, for instance, established his wealth by marrying a young woman with money and slaves and urged his sons to follow his example. Just as they circulated information about alcoholic husbands, young women also counseled each other to steer clear of mercenary suitors. Elizabeth McPherson's relatives wrote "to put [her] on [her] guard" against gold diggers, noting of a certain Dr. Pontelance that "he has managed in such a way as to become very much enthralled in money matters and if any Lady of fortune were to marry him his creditors would lean down upon him immediately for their debts."[25]

Young women warned each other about gold diggers, drunkards, and Romeos, but even more frequently, southern women expressed concern that husbands might prove unappreciative or unloving. While less specific and seemingly less serious than women's other concerns about men's trustworthiness, women's doubts about men's lasting affections were particularly significant in a culture that idealized romantic love. In addition, southern girls' concerns about their prospective mates' devotion may have been especially acute, since (as discussed in Chapter 4) romantic love was southern wives' most potent form of protection from male dominance. Without love, as Lizzie Scott expressed it, southern women believed that marriage was a perfect "hell."[26]

Even the ideal husband—loving, faithful, and sober—could not fully erase young women's doubt about marriage, however, for even the best of husbands seemed a poor substitute for the female friends that young women cherished so highly. "The *idea* of my friend's *marrying* makes me feel sad," wrote a friend of Lynchburg, Virginia, resident Mary Virginia Early.

"It seems to me that when one marries, they form new connections, other thoughts and feelings occupy their minds, and thus forming so many new associations, the remembrance of other friends glides imperceptibly from them."[27]

While northern women seem to have successfully combined heterosexual marriage with homosocial friendship (sometimes even ejecting their husbands from the bedchamber to accommodate female friends during extended visits), young women in the Old South saw marriage as a barrier to female friendship. South Carolina twins Mary Adelaide and Carolina Dogan regarded their married friends as "lost" to them. Ann Eliza Wight told her friend Mary Carrington that she feared receiving news that her friend had determined to marry: "I am constantly expecting to hear that the *right one* has at last come I dont know why, ex[ce]pt that the *matrimonial fever* seems to be prevailing to such an alarming degree; that I *fear* the *contagion* will reach you. I say fear because I dont want you to leave me yet a while." Much as their ability to visit their friends might be limited by fathers and brothers, young women evidently regarded husbands as a still more daunting barrier to female friendship.[28]

In 1849, Richmonder Mary Virginia Hawes related a troubling dream to her confidante, Virginia Pearl:

> I had a strange and by no means a comfortable dream last night, I was on a visit to you and enjoying myself of course, when William Matthews arrived and claimed you as his property, winding up by saying that the carriage would be at the door by the time you were ready, you held out for a time stoutly, declaring that you would not go until I went home but he was your stronger half, and by the hour appointed your trunk was strapped on the carriage, you and he in it, the whip cracked, and you were off for Buckingham. I cannot describe the feeling of desolation that came over me, I awoke myself saying, "Powhatan is no place for me now, Eppes has gone."

"Don't go, darling," Hawes concluded.[29]

Hawes's dream contained many elements that help to explain young women's reservations about committing themselves to marriage: she recognized that a married woman not only lost title to any property she might own but actually *became* property herself; she alluded to the possibility of domestic violence by referring to the husband as "the stronger half" of a couple; and she explicitly addressed young women's fears that marriage would permanently separate them from the female friends they loved. Had the domineering figure of Hawes's imagination only carried a bottle of whiskey as well as wielding a whip, her nightmarish depiction of married life would have been complete.

With so many doubts about marriage, some young women in the Old South resolved "to live & die a maiden." In dismissing what Elizabeth Ruffin's friends tried to convince her were the "horrors of *old-maidenhood*" and instead emphasizing the "sweets of independence," young southern women were participating in what one historian has labeled "a cultural reassessment of singlehood" in antebellum America. Whereas women of earlier generations regarded spinsterhood as shameful, women in early-nineteenth-century America began to tout the rewards of the single life, such as the ability to devote one's life to self-improvement and to social reform. Presumably this is what one of Emma Nicholson's friends had in mind when she counseled her: "I hope you will live to be a very good, useful old maid, for I've no doubt it is the happiest way to live."[30]

South Carolina resident Laura Margaret Cole Smith wrote a virtual advertisement for "single blessedness" in the 1830s. Smith expressed grave reservations about marriage, explaining, "I will not give away my heart, and am afraid to exchange it, lest I should not get one in return equally valuable." She also found satisfaction in life as a single woman. Preferring needlework, books, and gardening to either the "gay assemblies" of the "belle" or the "duties" of "becoming madam," she asserted, "single ladies can sometimes have a great many employments." Smith related a "bright day-dream" that detailed the many rewards of the single life: "Give me a little nook in my father's dwelling, a few friends, a few books, a small spot for Flora, and leave for a buoyant spirit to roam unfettered, whilst creating its own world, and I should be far happier than if my mind and affections were controlled by anyone." While few southern women so fully cataloged the advantages of a single life, many commented on the same advantages that Smith noted: close friendships, intellectual improvement, pleasant employments, and personal independence.[31]

Southern women who sought "single blessedness" had few options. As one historian has expressed it, "The culture provided no primary role for unmarried daughters." A "comic Valentine" that Amanda Virginia Edmonds received in 1859 suggested that negative stereotypes of single women persisted in the South long after the "cultural reassessment" of single women had transformed possibilities for northern women. "Quite amusing," she remarked dryly, "telling me I'll be an old maid and the end of old maids, will be pitched up on a fork, and some hideous old witch, looks more like the old scratch than any thing else, holding me up. What a delightful end

Saturday night. Jan 9th 1858.

What is the aim of my life? How many times I have asked myself this question to-day! Must I be like the common butterflies of fashion, make no exertion and care for no higher name than the humble one I bear? God has given me a soul to appreciate His works for which I am thankful, but oh: if I only had the energy and intellect enough to do some thing. I am a happy and wayward child now in my country home, my hands are not obliged to toil but rest in the lap of ease, I can go where I please, read and write as much as I please and ought I not to be happy and cheerful? I am happy for my joyous spirit finds a companion in every warbling bird, moving leaf and rippling stream, and sometimes it seems as if I am perfectly willing to spend life thus, but my summer cannot last always! A time must come when this lovely home will be changed, my darling parents can light it no more in hours of darkness, for theirs may be a faithful rest in Heaven, and where, when they are gone will be my anchor? The King of Destinies only knows where mine may be cast.—

A letter came to my trembling hands today whose well known characters on the outside spoke of the writer ere I opened it.— It was short, respectful, and kind, though sad.— The petals of love he said for him were just beginning to expand in all their sweetness, though I had told him they were crushed for me. I told him to think of me as a sister, he hoped that the day might come when I should be proud of my adopted brother, and asked for my sisterly

Single women in the antebellum South struggled to find meaning and purpose for their lives, as this 1858 entry from Georgian Loula Kendall's journal reveals. For this devout Christian, it was difficult to reconcile the sincere conviction that she had a "soul" with conventions of southern femininity that required elite women to be "butterflies of fashion." Like other young women in the Old South, Loula initially dreamed of a life of "single blessedness" but ultimately searched for fulfillment in marriage. (Special Collections and Archives, Robert W. Woodruff Library, Emory University) to a blossoming lass to be thus shifted to old maidenhood." Most antebellum southerners, sighed Caroline Brooks, viewed the unmarried woman as "a real odity [sic]" whose life was one of "chagrin & disappointment."[32]

In addition to confronting social stigmas, single women in the Old South faced economic difficulties. While women in southern cities, as in northern cities, managed to find useful and rewarding work on behalf of their churches and charities, opportunities for respectable paid employment were extremely limited in the Old South. Most elite women who remained unmarried in the Old South lived within the households of their relatives as unpaid—and often unappreciated—housekeepers, governesses, and nurses. Young women in the Old South thus struggled to define themselves as single women: happy, useful, and independent.[33]

"THE ARDUOUS DUTIES OF HOUSEKEEPING": DOMESTIC RESPONSIBILITIES

For many young southern women, assuming domestic responsibilities was both a route to usefulness and an obstacle to independence. Adopting what North Carolinian Mary Pettigrew called "the new character of housekeeper" allowed women to employ themselves usefully and to fulfill their parents' expectations of them. But at the same time, "keeping house at home" reinforced southern daughters' dependence on their families. As a result, being what one woman disparaged as "a[n] old maid taking care of other peoples interest" failed to provide southern spinsters with the "sweets of independence" that they craved.[34]

Many young women documented their first attempts at housewifery in their teens. Fourteen-year-old Sarah Wadley wrote in 1859: "I have been very busy indoors for the last few days making me a dress; it is my first attempt at dress making and it is quite hard work for me." "How very domestic I am!" eighteen-year-old Gertrude Clanton exclaimed in some surprise in 1852. "Quite a transformation really!" Wadley and Clanton's experiences neatly bracketed the years during which young women, released from school duties, instead devoted themselves to domestic tasks.[35]

A mother's illness or absence often prompted young women to turn "deputy Housekeeper." Under such circumstances, it usually fell to the oldest daughter living at home to serve "in the capacity of Housekeeper." "I have intended writing you ever since you left," M. L. Berkely assured her friend Ella Noland, "but since Mama has been so great an invalid, I[']ve been too busy *housekeeping*, to think of any thing else." Another of Noland's acquaintances wrote with a similar apology, explaining, "Ma has been sick for the last four months and consequently I have been *sole* housekeeper and you know it keeps one busy all the time to keep things in order." Some young women found that their responsibilities were more permanent when their mothers died. In 1857, South Carolinian Susan McDowall reflected in her diary on the impact her own mother's death would have on her own life. "A responsible, burdensome change has fallen to my duty," she soberly wrote. Although not all young women carried the burden of housekeeping as fully as McDowall, what one girl referred to simply as "Work"—sewing, gardening, and assisting with housekeeping and child care—occupied a great deal of southern daughters' time.[36]

For women in slaveholding households, housekeeping largely meant supervising domestic workers at their tasks. Despite their reliance on slave labor, young southern women found that managing a household was a time-consuming occupation. Well-to-do southerners engaged in a remarkable range of productive activities, including dipping candles, stuffing sausages, sewing mattresses, making soap, churning butter, and growing, harvesting, and canning fruit and vegetables, as well as cooking and cleaning. Even if a southern matron—or her deputized daughter—performed none of these tasks herself, merely supervising all these tasks made for a busy schedule, as Virginian Ann Eliza Wright explained in a letter to her friend Mary Carrington. "I . . . have found such full employ for my time, both head & hands, since my return [home] that I have not felt that I could write," she remarked. "Do you ask how it is I am thus closely occupied? Grace has not yet returned; the housekeeping of course devolves upon me. This is to us a new place, much to be done & not many to do it. I have been preserving, too, & the whole care of the Dairy I have. . . . I have the entire management & the [slave] woman we have (in this department at least) is such a novice that I have to watch & direct her as much as I would a child." Finally, she added, "*white washing &c &c*" added to "the *multiplicity of my avocations*" at her family's Ingleside home.[37]

Moreover, most southern women performed at least some household tasks themselves. Women living in households with few or no slaves reported significant involvement in household production. Sisters Amanda Jane and Elizabeth Cooley, the daughters of a small farmer in rural Virginia, filled their diaries with reports on weaving and spinning cloth, sewing clothing for the family, gathering and preserving fruit, sewing and stuffing mattresses, and working in the garden. Even the most privileged women participated directly in some aspects of housekeeping. Gertrude Clanton, the daughter of one of Georgia's wealthiest planters, gathered produce from the garden, straightened the parlor, and pickled and canned fruits and vegetables.[38]

In housekeeping, some southern single women found an occupation that fulfilled their need to feel useful and won them parental approval. St. Mary's School graduate Emily Bland (Blannie) Southall indicated the importance of feeling useful when she assisted her aunt in housekeeping and in educating her children in the early 1860s. "This is the second time I have kept house for her," she wrote to her sister Julia, continuing, "I help her in sewing, too, so that I feel I am of some *use*[.]" Richmonder Mary Hawes, reporting on her *"duties as a housekeeper"* in 1846, glowed with success: "You must positively come down and see what a housekeeper I make, why my dinner elicited a compliment from father himself to-day," she exclaimed. Clearly, some young women found satisfaction in domestic duties.[39]

But there were drawbacks to housekeeping, as well. Many young women found that keeping house, while it fulfilled their need to feel useful, made it even more difficult for them to escape the isolation of their homes to visit with their female friends. Indeed, the unceasing demands of housekeeping often prevented young women even from corresponding with their friends; southern daughters repeatedly excused their tardy or short letters with reference to their domestic responsibilities. "The arduous duties of a housekeeper" left little time to cultivate friendships.[40]

Young women also found that their domestic responsibilities interfered with their attempts at intellectual improvement. Susan Cornwall, a resident of Burke County, Georgia, wrote an amusing poem "while making peach preserves," demonstrating the incompatibility of housekeeping with writing or serious reflection:

Preserves and poetry! Who would suppose
That a woman could rhyme except in repose?
Yet I, tho' I'm watching the sweet as it fuses
Can summon the boldness to challenge the muses.

The kind of preserves I am making is peaches.
This lesson to all pattern housewives it teaches,
That when the thick scum rises up to the top
Whate'er else they're doing, for that they must stop.

For should it be left to boil in the syrup,
The first thing one knows, they will be in a stir up
For peaches and all will begin to ferment,
And that might induce me, to wrath to give vent.

And anger you know, don't agree with this season
So warm as to tempt us to banish all reason;

Beset as we are by ants and by flies
Temptations themselves for the passions to rise.

This pot of preserves might teach us a lesson
Which would we but con, might be to us a blessing;
We'd oftener remember life's gay froth to shun
And seek for the pleasure that lasts till life's done.

Oh, I'm full of grave thought, but hardly have time
A brace of these thought[s] to string into rhyme,
When down goes the pen, and up comes the spoon
For the scum 'gins to rise, I must take it off soon.

Away goes the paper—Away goes the ink—
I haven't the time, to write, or to think—
I thought I would draw from my labor a lesson
But the scum won't allow me a moment to reason.[41]

"I WISH TO GO TO STUDYING AGAIN": INTELLECTUAL IMPROVEMENT

The incompatibility of housewifery and study was a serious problem, for young southern women fairly ached for intellectual improvement. Although fifteen-year-old Sarah Wadley studied Latin, practiced piano, and took watercolor lessons at her home in Louisiana, she yearned for more systematic study. "I wish to go to studying again," she wrote in 1860, "for I feel more than ever my great ignorance in all that pertains to the knowledge of a student. I know nothing of the sciences and no language except my own and a little of the latin, then there are accomplishments, music, which is almost necessary and drawing and painting, which I dearly love. Ah! I have much, *very much* to learn."[42]

Southern girls, especially those who had attended boarding school, also associated continued study with close friendships. Complaining of boredom and loneliness at her country home after an all-too-brief visit with friends in the city, Virginian Ella Noland's cousin threatened to abandon "this 'stand-still' world of ours" and return to the female academy. "I am strongly tempted to go to school again," she declared.[43]

Although few southern women returned to school, many single women spent at least a part of their time at home attempting to further their educations. After her return home from a Washington, D.C., boarding school to her home town of Raleigh, North Carolina, in 1844, Mary Pettigrew made plans to continue her studies. "I am reading Prescott's Conquest of Mexico and find it very interesting," she remarked. "I hope next winter, while at home, to do a great deal of reading and practicing." While living with her adoptive parents, George and Martha Washington, at Mount Vernon, Eleanor Parke Custis rose before five in the morning in order "to get a long Italian lesson" before beginning her day's activities. One young woman who had attended school with Ella Noland told her former schoolmate, "I am reading a great deal this summer, I read about twenty pages of French a day, besides my history." South Carolinian Susan McDowall drew up a plan for "How to employ my time" that called for her to "always strive to blend improvement with amusement" and marked out time for Spanish, French, Italian, and reading "some *solid improving* work" each day.[44] By scheduling regular time for study, young single women attempted to recreate the academic routine they had experienced while attending school.

Eager for the company of other women, as well as for intellectual challenges, southern daughters also seized opportunities to reconstitute the community of learning that many first encountered at boarding school. Many young women formed informal study groups after their return home. A resident of a Virginia plantation known as Wills Forest gave a detailed account of a day she spent reading improving works in the company of her female relatives. "We read & work all day," she described their activities, "& the time passes very pleasantly. . . . We are reading a very interesting book now—'Prescott's Conquest of Mexico'—I read it aloud in the evening & it is as interesting as a novel. . . . Well then, I read an hour or two in 'Alison's French Revolution' aloud every morning—& I am reading 'Ranke's History of the Popes' to myself—thirty pages aday [sic] . . . so you see I'm right busy[.]" This anonymous reader's account reveals both young women's determination to pursue a rigorous course of study and the pleasure they took in sharing the experience with their peers.[45]

Young women in cities probably had the greatest opportunities to meet with other girls to pursue their studies. Baltimore sisters Lizzie, Catharine, Ellen, and Rosa Wirt studied chemistry, botany, and philosophy not only together but also in the company of a neighbor, Henrietta Wilson. In addition, living in the city gave the girls the opportunity to attend public lectures on topics ranging from "the Jewish antiquities" to introductory chemistry.[46]

Even rural residents, however, did their best to replicate the studious companionship of boarding school life. Some young women formed virtual correspondence courses with one another, comparing their activities and progress in their studies. North Carolinian Mary Brown wrote to her former schoolmate Margaret Steele to ask her about her progress in the fine arts. "How goes on your Music drawing &c," she inquired. "My imagination frequently paints you sitting at your Piano; I expect you let no days pass without practising [sic] your many beautiful tunes—I strum on mine sometimes, and daub a little in the painting line—if it was not for my paint box, time would pass heavily, for when alone it is my *favorite amusement*[.]"[47]

Despite their best efforts, southern daughters often found that their studies lacked discipline and direction. In part, this was because southern girls' other activities—including their work as assistant housekeepers—interfered with their studies. But it was equally true that, without a definite aim in mind, southern girls' determination wavered. Home schooling lacked the reports, the compositions, and the examinations that spurred schoolgirls to serious study; away from the competitive culture of the female academy, many girls, like Laura Wirt, floundered in their self-directed studies. South Carolinian Caroline Elliott mourned her inability to stick to a study schedule in 1859. "I am reading French history now . . . but I am not as studious as I should be," she admitted.[48]

Southern daughters might read the same books and study the same subjects as schoolgirls, but they were not able to re-create the atmosphere of companionable study and academic competition that young women found in female academies. As a result, young women found it difficult to continue their studies on their own. Richmonder Sallie Manson was on target when she pointedly observed, "I don't think the studying done at home by young ladies . . . amounts to much[.]"[49]

"THE NOBLEST OF WORKS": CHARITY AND TEACHING

Disappointed in their efforts to continue their educations at home, some southern daughters looked beyond the home for an outlet for their talents. By engaging in activities that appeared to be logical extensions of domesticity and by justifying their actions in terms of religious commitment, single women in the antebellum South expanded their sphere in ways very similar to those adopted by women in the antebellum North. While teaching school and engaging in social reform increased southern women's options, however, both activities were limited in scope; only young women in urban areas had the opportunity to join church-based organizations, and southern schoolteachers suffered from both social isolation and financial insecurity. Therefore, while these activities offered single girls at home an additional outlet for their energies and talents, they did not represent a viable alternative to marriage in the Old South. Nonetheless, southern girls' participation in these activities represented an attempt to redefine their role in society and thus constituted a form of resistance against prevailing definitions of southern womanhood.

Southern cities offered young women ample opportunities to transform religious zeal into social activism. Church-affiliated charitable and reform organizations abounded in antebellum urban centers. Temperance organizations, Dorcas societies, orphan asylums, Sunday schools, and other organizations all relied heavily on women volunteers; while married women dominated the leadership and the membership of such groups, young, single women played a significant role in women's voluntary organizations.[50]

Norfolk, Virginia, resident Mary McPhail had "so many duties to attend to" that she found little time to complain of boredom. "On Monday morning I attend the Education society," she explained in 1832, "and after sewing all the morning find exercise in the evening very necessary, Tuesday I devote to my bible lesson and Catechism and attend the class in the afternoon, every other Wednesday I attend the Dorcas society and friday is spent partly in learning tunes to sing with the choir at night, saturday I am occupied in *setting my house in order* and preparing exercises for my Sabbath School Class." McPhail's account of her activities indicates that urban women had many opportunities to join women's groups and thus maintain relationships with other women of their own age and interests even while living at home.[51]

Most southern women's groups, like Mary McPhail's, were closely linked to churches and limited their activities to evangelism and charity. Some, however, ventured beyond evangelizing and ministering to the poor to urban reform and even antislavery activity. In many southern cities, women participated in church-based charities aimed at assisting poor women and children. In Baltimore, Maryland, for instance, the Wirt girls joined the Dorcas Society and participated in a fund-raiser to benefit an orphanage. Commenting on the aid she had rendered to "a poor but honest woman," Catharine Wirt commented: "My heart ascended in gratitude to God that we were permitted to be the instruments of assisting one of his children in her poverty."[52]

Some pious young women even concluded that African Americans, as God's children, deserved their attention. In the 1830s, Catharine Wirt's younger sister, Ellen, began catechizing the family's bondspeople, holding religious services for the house slaves, and teaching the slave children to read. Such activities could lead to involvement in the relatively mild antislavery reform of raising money to transport free blacks to Liberia. In 1828, one young Virginian reported that "the ladies in Richmond" had formed a

Single women often kept records of their daily activities. Catharine Wirt, who postponed marriage until the advanced age of thirty-one, dedicated her life to serving others. Here, as a twenty-year-old daughter living at home, she expresses her horror of "sloth & inaction" and prays for strength to "do all things to [God's] glory." Other southern spinsters likewise searched for ways to be useful members of society. (The Maryland Historical Society)

Colonization Society. "We have form'd a sewing society in school for the same purpose," she explained, "which I think we shall like very much[.]" [53]

Religious zeal and church-based organizations in the urban South, as in northern cities, offered women the ability to channel their energies and talents into service to others. This sort of female organization was consistent with southern definitions of Christian and self-sacrificing womanhood, and thus socially acceptable, at least as long as it did not directly challenge hierarchies of class, race, and gender. Women who did challenge the slaveholding South's social structure—like South Carolina abolitionist-feminist sisters Sarah and Angelina Grimké—faced social ostracism and even physical danger (the pair was burned in effigy, and they fled to Philadelphia to avoid personal, as opposed to symbolic, violence). Thus, there were limits to the types of moral reforms that southern women could engage in (there was, for instance, no southern counterpart to the North's moral reform societies, which challenged male privilege and protested women's exploitation by rescuing prostitutes from brothels and exposing their clients to public humiliation). Even more circumscribing, however, was the fact that most southern women did not live in cities. Isolated on rural plantations, they lacked both the female network and the institutional backing necessary to create effective women's organizations. [54]

While single women in cities joined forces with other women to engage in charitable work and social reform, rural spinsters more often turned to teaching. As a profession, teaching was "feminized"—that is, it shifted from an occupation dominated by men to one dominated by women—in antebellum America. Although this process occurred more slowly in the South than in the North, southern spinsters, like their northern counterparts, were able to justify their foray into this form of paid work by emphasizing its associations with domesticity (teaching as motherhood) and piety (teaching as missionary work). Teaching offered southern women a degree of financial independence—Caroline Brooks Lilly called teaching "a genteel way of making a living"—as well as the opportunity to use their minds and talents. However, all too often, southern schoolmarms found that their lives were a constant struggle for financial and personal security. [55]

Many schoolteachers were dedicated to their students and to what they regarded as a calling to teach. Mississippi resident Julia Southall, who began her thirty-three-year career as a teacher in 1861, filled her diaries with her reflections on teaching—"the noblest of works"—and wrote letters to her sister Blannie Southall detailing the classroom exercises she invented to make learning a "pleasant" process for the youngsters under her care. For this southern woman, teaching was not merely a way to earn money but a call-ing. Southall saw it as her duty "to set an example of self denying love, and christian forbearance" to her students. "My life must be free of blame," she reflected, "that I may influence some of these dear young girls committed to my care, for usefulness . . . and happiness in Eternity[.]"[56]

Like Southall, many schoolteachers were intensely religious women who regarded teaching as a form of ministry. These teachers were deeply im-pressed with the significance of their work for the welfare of the "little immortals" in their charge. Mary Whitfield's teacher at Alabama's Judson Institute, Lucy Atkinson, felt a tremendous sense of responsibility to her students. "If I have been unfaithful to the high trust committed to me of moulding in some measure, your intellectual & moral character while under my influence, I look for forgiveness to Him who alone is able & willing to pardon the sins of erring mortals," she wrote to Whitfield in 1845.[57]

Teachers also derived a sense of accomplishment from sharing knowl-edge with others, particularly with other women. Veteran schoolteacher Susan Webb took pleasure in her students' ability to learn. In 1864, she re-flected: "I have been teaching 15 years and never had a more delightful and harmonious session; had twenty pupils, all of whom could learn, & did learn very well." Concord, North Carolina teacher Caroline Brooks Lilly felt a call-ing to "the arduous but pleasant and interesting avocation of instructing a number of pupils" and took an especial interest in "the interesting and im-portant cause of female education."[58]

But often, teaching was a frustrating and unrewarding experience. Schoolteachers in the mid-nineteenth-century South complained—as teachers everywhere do—of hard work and low pay. Some teachers, like Mississippian Julia Southall, had to relocate frequently in search of steady employment; others, like North Carolina schoolteacher Susan Webb, lived at home and combined teaching with domestic responsibilities. Because of low wages and uncertain employment, all schoolteachers had to practice what Julia Southall called "rigid economy."[59]

Virginia sisters Amanda Jane and Elizabeth Cooley filled their diaries with their desire for financial independence and educational opportunities. Teaching school, the sisters found, fulfilled neither of these desires. Amanda Jane Cooley's diary in spring 1842 was particularly despondent:

My school is to commence tomorrow week & I fear I shall not like it. . . .

I have now kept school one week and find it very tiresome. . . .

I have kept school another week & find it worse and worse I wish I had never begun. . . .[60]

Both women alternated teaching school with living at home, their desires for independence eluding them. "I would sacrifice most anything to gain my own liv[e]lihood by my own work and to know that I lived altogether on my own exertions," wrote Elizabeth Cooley in 1842. "It would be a satisfaction beyond description." "I sigh for independence but I cannot have it," mourned Amanda Jane Cooley in 1844.[61]

Charitable work and teaching school could give single women a meaningful occupation, but these activities could not provide southern women with the financial independence that they needed to enjoy "single blessedness." Although these activities served as important outlets for some southern women, then, they did not offer a secure route to the "useful independence" that southern spinsters desired.

"I HAVE DONE LITTLE OR NOTHING": MEANINGLESSNESS AND MELANCHOLY

Despite all their efforts to find meaning and purpose as single women, many young women in the Old South described their lives as "idle." Louisiana resident Sarah Wadley lamented that she had lived "a desultory life" since losing her last governess. Georgian Gertrude Clanton marveled at how little news she had to record in her journal: "I can scarcely tell how today has been passed," she wrote in 1848. "I have done little or nothing."[62]

Doing "little or nothing" weighed heavily on girls' consciences. Particularly for graduates of female academies, who had so thoroughly learned the importance of making good use of time, idleness was not only hopelessly dull but also a nearly unforgivable sin. A school essay written by Agnes Miller (who evidently had missed the finer points of noun-pronoun agreement) demonstrated the importance that southern girls attached to usefulness. "All girls should have a purpose in life," she pronounced. "They should deside [sic] what power she possesses, what duties are resting upon her and find pleasure in a true life of usefulness."[63]

But for single southern women, "a true life of usefulness" was difficult to achieve. In the slaveholding South, wealthy planter families had little need for their daughters' labor, and social and political leaders had little interest in women's reform activities, particularly if they seemed to threaten the South's "peculiar institution" of slavery. Thus, while northern girls also struggled with boredom and depression, elite women in the Old South found it particularly difficult to give their lives meaning and purpose. Georgian Loula Kendall expressed typical concerns in an 1858 diary entry that began, "What is the *aim* of my life?" As "a happy and wayward child" in her parents' home, she reflected, "my hands are not obliged to toil but *rest* in the lap of ease; I can go where I please, read and write as much as I please." Despite— perhaps because of—all her advantages, Kendall longed for "the energy and intellect enough to do something!" But the "something" remained elusive.[64]

Even girls who had significantly more to occupy their time than Kendall complained of feeling at loose ends. Elizabeth Cooley, who alternated teaching school with household production, complained in 1842: "My time is not spent to my satisfaction along of late. I am busy as can be but it is still work in the house, such as sewing or something of the kind, I would prefer a more busy life."[65] The situation Cooley identified—being "busy as can be" while wishing for "a more busy life"—suggests that at least some southern women found "work in the house" just as dull as being genuinely idle. Housework filled southern daughters' time, but it did not fulfill the desires for intellectual stimulation, congenial companionship, and social recognition that so many southern girls exhibited during their time away from home at school.

Service to family members, while significant (and expected), often did not seem sufficient to young women who had been taught that women had a worldly mission. Teachers and ministers inadvertently fueled young women's discontent when, seeking to reconcile women to a distinct "sphere" of influence, they delivered sermons and assigned essays on "Woman's Destiny." Mary Virginia Early's 1842 commencement address on this topic at Virginia's Female Collegiate Institute, while drawing clear distinctions between men's strength and women's kindness, nonetheless described women's role in the grandest terms: "*Woman* has never, since the *Fall*, been allowed to fulfil the destiny for which she was created," Early deplored the restrictions placed on women. Yet, she predicted, "Christianity has done much for her, & will ultimately restore her to her first stage." Although conceding women's inferior physical strength, Early averred, "*Woman is possessed of mind*" as well as superior "feelings of the heart." Thus, while being careful to point out that "woman . . . not usurp the province of the '*Lords of Creation*,'" she also insisted that women were not meant to be "subordinate" to "the tyrannical exxactions [sic] of the other sex," and she ridiculed men's "dreams of imagined superiority." "'Tis not [woman's] destiny to be adorned as a doll, treated as a Toy, or to be the companion of a facetious coxcomb," Early pronounced. Instead, the college graduate explained, women had "a noble *destiny*, than which *none* could be nobler." While rooted in the "separate and distinct sphere" of the home rather than in the world beyond where men "perform[ed] the sterner duties of life," women's influence had far-reaching significance:

> Woman's Destiny is to promote peace, love, and happiness in the social circle, to exert a happy influence on all around; to cause every eye to beam with delight at her presence, every ear to listen with profound attention, to the gentle words of wisdom which fall from her lips, & every heart to swell with gratitude for the enjoyment of her influence. 'Tis for her to seek out and to succor the unfortunate and distressed, to step with noiseless tread around the couch of Affliction, & point the dying sinner to a merciful Saviour—to comfort the mourning and afflicted, & pour into their wounded hearts the healing balm of consolation—She is to regulate the corruptions of the age in which she lives, to form characters which are to bear the impress of her hand throughout Eternity. *She* is to *evangelize* the world[!]

Thus, while women were deprived of "the honours of Genious and the Fame of Conquests," their proper role was not less important than—indeed, was arguably more important than—men's achievements. "Is not *Woman's* a *high*, a *noble* Destiny?" demanded Early.[66]

Not surprisingly, then, many young single women regarded their daily lives as falling short. Virginian Mary Hawes, who helped her ailing mother to keep house, nonetheless worried that she was not contributing enough to society. On her twenty-first birthday, she exclaimed, "Heigho! What an old woman I am getting to be! And how little I have done to benefit myself or others. . . . Do you know that I think very much of the duties which my Creator meant that I should perform, the destiny he intended me to achieve, and a horrible fear comes over me often—the fear lest I should die and leave my work undone?" Despite her sense that she had a "destiny" laid upon her, Hawes was unable to envision her future clearly. "Daily I ask myself, for what purpose was I made?" she remarked, "and hourly feel my insufficiency, to be what I should be."[67]

A few particularly perceptive southern women realized that it was not simply their own "insufficiency" but their culture's rules that barred their path to usefulness. What Mary Virginia Early called "Woman's Destiny" (to do good in the world) was simply incompatible with what Loula Kendall called "woman's lot" (to be submissive and obedient).[68] When Virginian Elizabeth Ruffin made invidious contrasts between her own pastimes and the accomplishments of men, she recognized the constraints of her society at the same time that she ridiculed what she regarded as her own worthlessness. "Spent the whole day lolling and reading," she noted in 1827. "No work done, all things neglected and give place to the strange infatuation of novel-reading so popular with us *silly, weak* women whose mental capacities neither desire nor aspire to a higher grade, satisfied with momentary amusement without substantial emolument, and a piece of *weakness rarely indulged* . . . by the more *noble, exalted* and *exemplary* part of society the men of course who seek alone after *fame, honor, solid benefit* and *perpetual profit.*" [69] By emphasizing certain words, Ruffin indicated southerners' widely held (but, she suggested, equally erroneous) beliefs that women's intellectual abilities and aspirations were both limited and inferior to men's quest for fame and fortune.

Mary Hawes also linked her dissatisfaction with herself to the constraining gender roles of the antebellum South. "A man," she reflected, "goes into the broad open world to battle, stimulated by the presence and influence of his fellows, his every action has a witness and is censured or approved— while woman finds her warfare *within*—Oh the battles agonizing and terrible that are fought within that pentralia! the victories, unheralded save by the angels who have seen and sympathized—and the defeats after which she dies, still uncomplaining, perhaps smiling to the last. And the world wonders, 'what could ail her?'" [70] In the "broad open world," men were "stimulated" by their peers and "witnessed" by society; by contrast, after leaving school, women were confined to their homes, imprisoned within their own psyches, "unheralded" by the living, and consigned (perhaps resigned) to silent suffering and death.

The Civil War–era diary of Grace Elmore, a resident of Columbia, South Carolina, helps to illuminate young women's unhappiness in the Old South. Elmore complained frequently of "a dissatisfaction with everything and a grumbling at my lot." Twenty-four years old, Elmore was single and living at home with her mother and several of her siblings. "What a hum drum life mine has been," she exclaimed on her birthday. Although not yet twenty-five, Elmore concluded that "the brightness of life [is] gone." [71] Writing in the midst of the Civil War, Elmore, like Hawes a decade earlier, found her battles within; her reflections are strikingly similar to those of other young women in the antebellum South.

Elmore's introspective diary reveals the basis of her discontent. Although well educated, she found herself unable to take an active interest in her mother's household. With her mother, her sister-in-law, and her sister at hand to take charge of household affairs, she remarked, "If I were to live a hundred years in this house, I would never have a settled object, a life giving interest, because there is no need of me here, I have no work to do, my place had just as well be vacant." As a result of her lack of "a life giving interest,"

Elmore found herself wrestling with "sourness," "touchiness," and "morbid fancies." Her "vexations" and "anxieties," she perceptively noted, were the result of the lack of "that activity which springs from a deffinite [sic] object and gives sufficient employment to the mind & heart." In "the narrow circle of home," Elmore found no pursuits "to prevent the weariness the disgust I may almost say of one who has been educated, to stay at home and be nothing." [72] Thus, like her antebellum counterparts, Elmore complained of idleness, boredom, and dissatisfaction with herself, which resulted not only from a lack of necessary labor but also from insufficient challenge "to the mind & heart" of an educated woman.

Also like some of the women before her, Elmore contrasted her role—"to stay at home and be nothing"—with men's: "A man can seek the outer world, and in the duties belonging to that world restrain that irritability and restless longing that fills the spirit, when without a vocation. Oh how often have I longed to battle with life as men do, and expend in action those energies that work but to excite fretfulness because denied of the true outlet." Like Mary Virginia Early, Elmore believed that women needed a higher destiny—what Elmore called "a vocation." Like Mary Virginia Hawes, she envied men their "battle with life." Like Elizabeth Ruffin, she recognized that female "fretfulness" was the result of societal limitations, not an inborn feminine weakness. Yet for all her perceptiveness, Elmore could not perceive a solution to the dilemma she shared with other young women in the slaveholding South. As a southern woman, and particularly as a daughter in her mother's household, Elmore could find no "outlet" for her pent-up ambitions. "When will calm be mine," she demanded of herself. "When shall I cease to drift on the sea of feeling[?] . . . This ceaseless vexation of spirit is dreadful, & there is no relief." [73]

The musings of this young woman—and those of her antebellum counterparts—convey southern women's inability to alter the situations that caused them so much unhappiness as well as their ability to identify the source of their dissatisfaction. No matter how clearly young women saw the restrictions that hindered their quest for a meaningful existence, they were unable to circumvent them. They might resist their foreordained destiny for a time, but they did not (perhaps, could not) rebel against it. Instead, they sank into depression as they accepted the reality that the only way to escape the status of a dependent daughter was to marry and to become a dutiful wife. This was the conclusion that North Carolinian Penelope Skinner, who spent her single years caring for her ill-tempered father on an isolated plantation, came to in 1840. "I am heartily sick & tired of the life I lead it is too dull & melancholy," she complained, adding, "therefore I have come to the conclusion to be married & that speedily[.]"[74]

Like Skinner, most young women in the Old South eventually relinquished the search for "single blessedness" and devoted themselves, instead, to the quest for marital bliss. As they shifted their energies from single life to seeking a mate, however, they continued to search for ways to shape their own futures. Southern women's quest for self-determination during the process of courtship represented an ongoing form of resistance even as it manifested itself as the cultural ideal of the southern belle.

"A MOST DELIGHTFUL WINTER":
ELLA NOLAND

During the winter of 1850–51, Ella Noland, the
daughter of Virginia planter Lloyd Noland, made an
extended visit to relatives in the North. Fresh from six
years of boarding school—first at Mrs. Edwards's establishment in Leesburg, Virginia, and then at Mrs.
Cary's academy in Baltimore, Maryland—Ella was not
only intelligent and accomplished but also, according
to her mother, Elizabeth, "quite a *beauty.*" Now, under
the chaperonage of "Aunt Sally," Mrs. William Gibson
of Philadelphia, and in the company of her cousins,
Grace and Marion, Ella was prepared to take "the gay
and noisy City" by storm as a "*great Virginia bell[e].*"[1]

Ella—or "Miss Noland," as she was no doubt known
during this period—probably made her first official appearance in society at "Mrs Willing's Ball," which she
described in detail in a letter home in early 1851. "I
would have liked for you to have seen me dressed for
Mrs Willing's Ball," she told her "dear Ma": "My dress
was exceedingly handsome. I wore my light silk suit, a
skirt of white silk [sultan] embroidered all over in bouquets of flowers & a beautiful bustle to suit; Grace's
coral necklace on my hair [and] coral earrings & brace-
let." After her initial appearance, the young Miss Noland was soon inundated with invitations to genteel
social gatherings. Ella was full of praise for "the Club
Ball," a lavish event where the young woman's "cherry
lips, and rosy cheeks" made her a favorite with the gentlemen. "There was a great crowd, between seven &
eight hundred persons—everything was conducted in
the best manner—the supper was *very* handsome—the

table was ornamented by pyramids of most splendid bouquets, which were distributed among the guests during the latter part of the evening," she detailed the scene, adding, "Marion & I danced nearly all the time, & rec[eive]d as much attention as we could have expected. . . . We all enjoyed it exceedingly." Making preparations for "a large party at Mrs. Coleman's" and for an event she called simply "The Assembly," Ella and her cohorts also kept themselves busy "visiting and rec[eivin]g. visitors." "We are all enjoying ourselves very much," Ella pronounced.[2]

Purchasing the finery for such occasions was a time- (and money-) consuming occupation. Included in Ella's sprightly account of her social engagements was her "account" for her clothing (including her dress for Mrs. Willing's ball, which cost $28, a bill at Levy's, $41.75, and $25 for assorted "small articles") and her request for permission to make yet another purchase: a "Spring silk." "Aunt S. thinks I had better get mine So I may have it made & wear it out in the evening," she justified this additional expense. "It can be charged and my bill paid at any time before I leave here," she assured her mother.[3]

With a seemingly unlimited expense account, a host of invitations to choose from, a fun-loving set of female friends, and the attentions of young men from Philadelphia's leading families, Ella's debut seems to have lived up to the expectations expressed in an effusive letter that she received from a former schoolmate, Carrie ("Cad") Sage, in late 1850. "You will no doubt spend a most delightful winter in Philadelphia," she enthused. "How you must be enjoying life now—what can compare with a first winter in Society—no after season in a person's life can ever come so laden with pure unalloyed happiness," she gushed. Yet Ella's friend's excitement on her behalf was tempered with caution. "At the same time," she added soberly, "let me warn you to take extra care of that little heart and do not yield it too readily."[4]

The letters that Ella received from other female correspondents reinforced this message: enjoy your debut, but do not hasten to make a match. While they filled their letters with news of male attentions, innocent flirtations, and rumored engagements, Ella's friends shied away from commitment, and they urged her to follow her example. One friend gave her suitors ridiculous nicknames: "Mr Saussage" [*sic*] and "Mr Pudding." Another, complaining of the dull routine of life in the country after her "gay city life," wrote disparagingly of "*home duties*" and of local women's conversation, which revolved around "*the having of babies*, & the treatment thereof." No doubt aware that these subjects gained new significance for married women, she distanced herself—and her friend—from this future possibility, adding, "both of which topics are I suppose as devoid of interest for you as myself." Carrie Sage warned Ella of the complications likely to arise from agreeing to correspond with male admirers. Her cousin Marion, who went on to Baltimore and Alexandria to continue her career as a belle, commented wryly on the "marrying mania" among some of her peers and expressed her preference for the "glorious liberty" she enjoyed as a single woman. And even Ella's mother, Elizabeth, offered the advice that the young Miss Noland was "quite too young to encumber [herself] with family cares." "Good and clever husbands are rare articles nowadays," she pronounced, and "young ladies should not be in a hurry" to make a match.[5]

Ella Noland seems to have taken this advice to heart. Although she had at least two serious suitors—a Mr. Armstrong in 1850 and a "Mr. G" in 1851— she avoided a commitment to either, apparently preferring to plan reunions with her female friends, who besieged her with invitations like Carrie Sage's: "Oh! how much pleasure will it not be a treat to have a regular coze over old times and the *scrapes* and fun we have had together?" The winter following her successful debut, however, found her instead living at the family plantation, Glen Ora, and tending to "home concerns" and supervising the family's domestic slaves under her mother's supervision. "Tell Joanna to cover the yarn . . . in alum water, wash the yarn that was left in dye, and have all ready to send to the weavers as soon as I return," the older woman directed from Philadelphia. "Have the kitchen whitewashed, and . . . have the dining and chamber curtains put up."[6]

Perhaps Ella found such activities tame after the excitement of her winter in Philadelphia. Possibly she had been waiting for the day when her mother pronounced her old enough to marry a suitor from her school days in Maryland. Her correspondence offers few details on the man who would become her husband or on the couple's courtship. In any event, by the following spring, she was engaged to a Baltimore physician, John MacKenzie, whom she married in 1852. Though this was by no means a whirlwind courtship— Ella had been out in society for nearly two years—the former Miss Noland was well ahead of her peers in settling down to married life. After her own marriage, the newly christened Mrs. MacKenzie continued to receive letters from her female friends, including her girlhood chum, Marion, who had entered society alongside Ella and had been so enthusiastic in her praise of the "glorious liberty" of belledom. In 1854, still single after four years in society, Marion added news of marriages and births to her catalog of social events and suitors, but she remained wary of marriage. "I do think it such a pity for girls to marry so," she wrote acerbically.[7]

Ella Noland and her friends offered one of the most complete accounts of what nineteenth-century southerners called "coming out"—a girl's official debut into society—from the standpoint of a young southern woman. Like Ella Noland, many elite southern girls relished what North Carolinian Mary Walker called "the prestige of being a belle." They dressed up, went to parties, surrounded themselves with admirers, and generally devoted themselves to the pursuit of pleasure. Clearly, many young women in the Old South enjoyed the time they spent in high society—or what many, using their schoolgirl French, styled "the Beau Monde." At the same time, however, they proved remarkably resistant to the intended purpose of this stage of life: finding a husband.[8]

Much like Ella Noland's circle of friends, many young women in the Old South were reluctant to relinquish the "glorious liberty" of a celebrated belle for the "family cares" of a southern matron. Many young single women, like Noland and her friends, reveled in the unprecedented opportunity to seek pleasure, rather than pleasing others. Combining their longstanding reliance on female companionship with a new opportunity to enjoy male company, they threw themselves wholeheartedly into the social whirlwind accepted, even expected, of a southern belle. Yet this stage of life did not lead quickly or directly to the outcome—an advantageous marriage—that southern elders intended, because southern belles, like college girls and daughters-at-home, insisted on setting their own agenda—and avoiding marriage. Some prided themselves on collecting (and rejecting) beaux; others, like Ella, returned to the home circle to devote themselves to domestic duties. Whatever the strategy adopted, most young southern women seem to have done their utmost to prolong their single years and to delay the inevitable outcome of "coming out": marriage. Ultimately, however, most southern belles succumbed to social pressure—and to their own longing for love—and used the rituals of courtship to make a match. As they did so, they strove to base their future marriages on mutual love and respect, rather than (as their parents preferred) on family name and fortune. Whether seeking pleasure, delaying marriage, or selecting a mate, young women in the Old South enacted resistance by prioritizing their own—not others'—desires.

"THAT EVENTFUL EPOQUE": THE DEBUT

In 1859, Lemuella Brickell, a fourteen-year-old Mississippi schoolgirl, looked forward to the time when she would exchange books for beaux. "I only can anticipate that eventful epoque in my life, the 'coming out,'" she mused. "I shall laugh and dance and flirt, haha, am I not going to have a nice time. I will have beaux, plenty of them (that is if I can get some) and go to parties and lead a very pleasant life." Virginia student Mary Miller had a different perspective on "Society." Writing in 1846, she speculated on what the future would hold. "Instead of rejoicing as some girls do at the idea of being released from the restraint and imployment [*sic*] of school and be-comming [*sic*] as the fashionable deem it 'a turned out young lady' I feel exceedingly sad to think that my school days, my hours of pleasure, are gone never to return," she mourned.[9] Despite their very different perspectives, both girls regarded entering society—what nineteenth-century southerners called "coming out"—as an important stage in the female life cycle, one that involved undertaking new activities, such as dancing and flirting, and adopting a new identity, the "turned out young lady"—what contemporary Americans commonly refer to as a southern belle.

For these girls, leaving school was closely associated with becoming a southern belle. While some young women returned home after school, exchanging the identity of a studious schoolgirl for that of a dutiful daughter, others planned to enter "Society" and adopt the role of the southern belle. Still others spent a period of a few months or years living quietly at home prior to their "public entree au monde." Age appears to have been the most important factor; younger girls, like thirteen-year-old Mary Bertron of Mississippi, were told that it was "too soon to make [a] debut into society," while older girls, like seventeen-year-old Virginian Laura Wirt, "turned out" almost immediately following their departure from school. Birth order could also affect the timing of a girl's "coming out," since many southern parents preferred to postpone younger daughters' debuts until the eldest daughter was safely paired off. Expecting marriage to quickly follow the debut, southern adults timed coming out rituals to coincide with the age that they regarded as appropriate for considering marriage, usually in the late teens.[10]

While the precise sequence of events varied, well-bred southern girls in their late teens could expect to adopt a new role: that of the southern belle—or, as young women themselves often put it, as a "turned-out young lady." (While for later generations of southerners, the term "belle" would become synonymous with a young, single woman, antebellum southerners used the word with more precision, preferring the phrase "turned-out young lady" to refer to all girls on the marriage market and reserving "belle" to refer to the subset of such girls who were particularly in demand.)[11] As Lemuella Brickell and Mary Miller's comments suggest, southern girls looked forward to this "eventful epoque" with emotions ranging from enthusiasm to anxiety. But whether they regarded "coming out" with excitement or trepidation, young women attached tremendous importance to the customs and ceremonies that marked their new status—and announced their new identity—as southern belles.

Despite the enduring popularity of the image of the southern belle, sur-prisingly little historical research has been conducted on this stage of life. Perhaps reflecting long-standing assumptions that female coming-of-age was a straightforward process of practicing adult behaviors, historians have not devoted extended analysis to the social rituals of "coming out" in ante-bellum America. Most discussions of debutantes focus on the era following the Civil War, when shaken former slaveholders in the South and up-and-coming industrialists in the North turned to the ritual of presenting their daughters to society as a means of shoring up their claims to elite status. Relying principally upon etiquette guides, newspaper reports, and fictional accounts, these studies tend to portray young women as mere pawns in the elaborate status maneuvers orchestrated by their elders. Nowhere is the ne-glect of "coming out" as a coming-of-age ritual more evident than in the case of young women in the Old South. Although southern women's his-torians have commented upon the anomaly of southern belles' exercise of power in a patriarchal society, the life stage of the debut and the identity of the southern belle have not received sustained scholarly attention. The analysis that follows, based upon young women's own writings, regards the debut as an important rite of passage that marked the start of a significant, and often lengthy, stage of life. Moreover, it suggests that southern belles were much more than emblems of elite status; they were young women ac-tively engaged in intentionally fashioning their own destinies.[12]

Although young women in the Old South did everything in their power to shape their own lives, adults controlled the customs that defined them as southern belles. For some young southern women, particularly those who lived in cities, becoming a belle involved an elaborate ritual that announced a young woman's debut into society and her availability for marriage. Typi-cally this ritual involved the young woman's first appearance at a festive pub-lic occasion, often a fancy ball, dressed in an outfit especially chosen for the occasion. Well aware that their daughters' appearance reflected on their own reputation, wealthy southern families spared no expense. Elite parents often spent months preparing for a daughter's debut, purchasing fine cloth-ing and jewelry for the young debutante and investing in costly and fashion-able furnishings and decorations to prepare their homes to entertain suitors. The time, attention, and money that southern families invested suggested the importance of a young woman's successful debut and the necessity of introducing her to men in the best social circles.[13]

In the nation's capital, young women were presented to society each New Year's Day at the "Presidents Levee." In 1827, sixteen-year-old Catha-rine Wirt wrote to her father to describe the debut of her sister Elizabeth

("Lizzy"), a year her senior: "This has been a great day with us in as much as it was Lizzys debut," she announced. "The rooms were crowded . . . [but] there was not in the whole room a dress which could at all vie with either of our group. . . . After being introduced to Mr & Mrs Adam's—she took her station at Mrs A's right hand—where she has the best chance of seeing *tout le monde*—she says I must tell you that she was very well pleased & gratified." [14]

The following year, Catharine made her own debut. She devoted considerable space in her diary to her "public entree au monde," describing her dress, her family's admiration, and the family's reception. Admitting to some nervousness ("My heart beat a little as I entered," she wrote), she resolved "to take it all calmly," and at the end of an evening spent in a "close & compact crowd" and a "brilliant burst of light," she returned home "in great good humour." [15]

Catharine Wirt wrote especially detailed and revealing accounts of debuts in the antebellum South. The convention of being presented to the president and first lady mimicked the practice of being presented to the king and queen in European courts, suggesting that women played a key role in establishing and maintaining class distinctions in an increasingly democratic society. Young Catharine's use of French phrases to describe the events also indicated the European—and aristocratic—origins of this practice. Americans in the new republic made the practice their own, however, by vying with each other for status through fashionable clothing, available to anybody with sufficient funds, including the rags-to-riches Wirt family. The Wirt girls' privileged position at Mrs. Adams's side, while reminiscent of favored courtiers in royal courts, in this case probably was derived from William Wirt's political post as attorney general in President Adams's administration. While it is unclear from this account whether northern girls also participated in this particular form of being presented to society, the timing of the Wirt girls' Washington City presentations—making one's debut in birth order and in one's late teens—is consistent with other southern women's accounts and with statistics on elite southerners' marriage ages. [16]

Although not all young women in the antebellum South had the opportunity to be presented to the president and the first lady, most elite girls marked their change in status with a special occasion, such as a fancy ball—for rural girls, this often necessitated a visit to a metropolitan area—and a new dress, usually white, to signify a young woman's purity and chastity—traits highly valued in southern white women. [17] North Carolina schoolgirl Lizzie Davis described the archetypal belle's debut in an essay titled "Bubbles": "A young girl is standing before her mirror dressed for a ball. . . . Her dress of virgin white exposes the plump neck, & rounded arm, Pearls

are clasped around her wrist and throat. and twined among her sunny ring-
lets. Yes, she is very lovely[.] A few moments more, & she is the center of
a gay circle. Her merry laugh acts like a charm upon those around her. . . .
She floats gracefully through the dance, a soft flush mantling her fair cheek.
She seems to have all that [is] requisite to render life happy."[18]

Real-life southern belles followed this pattern fairly closely. Alabama
native Virginia Tunstall Clay (who titled her memoirs *A Belle of the Fifties*) recalled that her first trip to Mobile, where she appeared in her first ball gown,
"transformed me . . . as truly as Cinderella was changed into a princess."
Georgia resident Gertrude Clanton, who "made [her] debut in society" the
year following her departure from school at the age of seventeen, also recalled the event as a transformative one, changing her from an innocent
schoolgirl into "a gay girl of fashion."[19]

Such comments suggest that southern girls equated making their debut
with taking on a new identity. Indeed, many young women called attention to their new status by adopting a new name; once a young woman was
the oldest unmarried daughter in her family, she used the title "Miss" followed by her surname, rather than being known by her Christian name. By
doing so, young women (and their parents) announced their "young ladyship" and their eligibility for marriage.[20] At the same time, however, young
women seem to have relished their identity as southern belles not for what
it might lead to for their families—an advantageous match, enhanced reputation, increased wealth, and so on—as much as for what it represented to
them: a truly once-in-a-lifetime opportunity to live like a pampered "princess" (rather than a responsible matron) and to be "a gay girl" (not a dutiful
wife). By becoming southern belles, young women in the Old South took on
an identity that permitted—and even encouraged—them to please themselves rather than pleasing others.

"THE PRESTIGE OF BEING A BELLE": THE PURSUIT OF PLEASURE

Even in the absence of a formal debut, it was quite clear to southern
women what constituted "a *grown, young* lady." Rather than spending her
time "studying harder than I ever did in my life" or assisting her mother
in housekeeping, a "young lady" spent her time "amid the gayeties of the
fashionable world" and devoted herself to being "*exquisitely beautiful* and '*very
fashionable.*'"[21]

Southern girls could not have been ignorant of the fact that the ultimate
aim of the debut was marriage, preferably to a wealthy and prominent mem-

Friday – Nov. 4th 1827 –
Father, Ma, Lizzy, & I went to a
small party at Mrs. Decatur's –
wearing the same dresses & ornaments
we had worn the evening before to
Mrs. McLean & Mr. Campbell's –
we found no one there but Mrs.
Cutts & her daughter Dolly – &
anticipated rather a dull evening –
in the course of the evening
Mr. Vaughn, Doyle, Ousely,
Lisbon, Rebello, Stackebourg
& Mr. & Mrs. Rumple, who was
the only other lady, besides those
enumerated came in – We had
a little music on the guitar &
piano from Mr. Ousely – Lizzy
played two or three waltzes, &
Ma played a little which was
the only deviation from ennuyant
uniformity of the evening – Mr.
Vaughn lead the way to the
card table & was followed by the
rest of the company –

"Turned-out young ladies" filled their time—and the pages of their diaries—with
a dizzying round of social events. In this page from Catharine Wirt's diary, the
Baltimore resident describes two family parties where the entertainment consisted
of music and cards. Despite the presence of eligible men at these and similar
gatherings, Catharine, like other reluctant belles, quickly tired of the "uniformity"
of such occasions. (The Maryland Historical Society)

ber of southern society. Laura Wirt's father, William, was clear on this subject when, in 1809 (when Laura was only six years old), he predicted that she would "enter the world" at age seventeen and be married by age twenty. Laura's brother Robert reinforced this message when "Miss Wirt" made her official debut into Washington society during the winter of 1820–21. Now that Laura had "in reality and bona fide *turned out*," he wrote home from school at West Point, "I . . . wish her success with all my heart:—admonishing her at the same time to be ambitious, and not to be contented with any thing less than a member of congress, or—a soldier."[22]

The defining feature of a belle was her marriageability. North Carolinian Penelope Skinner described this aspect of a belle's identity—and her most time-consuming activity—in a series of letters to her brother Tristrim in the late 1830s. Anticipating the return home of a number of female students in spring 1839, she remarked: "So you see we have the Town full of young girls who will soon be Ladies. I pray some of the old *stock* may be off the carpet before that time arrives." A young lady was "on the Carpet," as Skinner described herself earlier that same year; that is, she was ready to be courted by eligible "Beaux."[23]

Once a young woman had made her first public appearance, therefore, she was expected to assume an air of confidence suited to her new role as an eligible belle and to eagerly embrace opportunities to meet potential mates. After Sarah Garland made her debut into society in Richmond, her mother commented: "As the grand affair of the Ball is over and you have maid [sic] your apperence [sic] at a Richmond assembly, I hope all your perturbation will cease, at going into company." Many parents encouraged their daughters to receive visitors and to participate in social activities that might lead to an advantageous match—even when the girls themselves preferred to spend time quietly at home. "You know I intended to keep *myself*, to *myself*," Mary Virginia Early commented in 1840, "but mama has almost forced me to ride very often."[24]

Yet while parents took pains to convey that the desired result of a successful "season" was marriage, young women themselves often laid more emphasis on their enjoyment of society. Southern girls filled their diaries and letters with detailed accounts of the clothing they wore, the people they saw, the conversations they had, and the events they attended. Men were certainly present in these accounts—they were indispensable as escorts and dance partners—but they were not always, or even often, the focus. Rather, young women in the Old South seem to have relished the rare opportunity to devote themselves primarily to the pursuit of pleasure.

Once young women had made their entrance into society, they spent their days and nights "immersed in dissipation," as North Carolinian Margaret Steele put it. During a visit to the coast town of Wilmington, Steele received a constant stream of invitations to balls, parties, horseback rides, and other activities throughout the fashionable winter season. "Nothing but calls & invitations since I came here," she noted in January 1827. The following month, she reported: "There is scarcely a night in the whole week but we are at the Theatre or private parties which generally terminate in dancing."[25]

Other young women similarly recorded days filled with visiting and nights filled with dancing. Mary Brown excused herself for not writing regularly with the explanation, "I always am in a round of company, dressing; [or] visiting." North Carolinian Margaret Beall received letters from a former schoolmate who was transported with excitement as she described social events in her neighborhood. "Oh! *Maggie* I never enjoyed myself better," she exclaimed. Separated by the passage of fifty years—Brown's debut was in 1807 and Beall's friend's was in 1857—these young southern women were united by their shared enjoyment of the social whirl of southern belledom.[26]

Young women who resided in the countryside often spent the winters with friends or relatives in cities in order to participate in the dizzying round of social events that typified southern cities' winter "seasons," which often spanned several months. Washington, D.C., offered its residents and visitors "endless calls, receptions, dinners and balls." Upon her return home from the capital city in 1849, Ella Noland's friend Mary Berkeley caught up with her correspondence. "I am really ashamed to have delayed writing you so long," she apologized, "but the first of the winter I had nothing interesting to communicate & while in Washington I was too busy attending *parties & balls* to think of letter writing." Baltimore was another popular choice. Noland's cousin Marion, who had made her debut with Noland in Philadelphia, found Baltimore even more to her liking. "I have an engagement for every night next week," she boasted in April 1851. "This has been one glorious winter to me[.]"[27]

Smaller southern towns and northern cities also offered ample scope for socializing. Three of Virginian Eliza Spragins's former classmates at North Carolina's Salem College accompanied each other to Lexington, Kentucky, for a series of social outings in 1842. Kentuckian C. Alice Ready "dived pretty deeply into Nashville society," recording a round of parties and calls during the winter of 1860–61. North Carolina resident Margaret Mordecai went to Philadelphia, a popular destination for the southern elite, for her debut. "You don't know what *a gay winter* I am spending," she wrote home. "I have seen a great deal more company than I did at home for people have been calling on me. . . . I have seen some company most every day since I have been here—and night before last I *went to the theatre . . . last night I was at a large party at Mrs James'.*"[28]

Southern girls clearly enjoyed the opportunities for pleasure-seeking that society afforded, but they did not always take advantage of the potential for husband-hunting that these events offered. When Eliza Spragins's friends Sarah Clay, Mary Combs, and Lizzie McKnight went to Lexington, Kentucky, in fall 1842, they enjoyed "meet[ing] all the elegant beaux" and reveled in being "quite *belles.*" Yet the girls' account (written jointly by Clay and Combs) laid equal emphasis on other aspects of the girls' social rounds, such as the clothing they wore ("I have worn all my winter gloves," commented Combs) and the food they ate (Clay enjoyed "a plate of most delightful cake"). In addition, while all three young women enjoyed the company of "several young gentlemen" and Clay pronounced herself "in *love*" with a "remarkable handsome" Mr. Goode, the young women seem to have derived the most pleasure from the time they spent in each other's company. Indeed, their joint letter sounded much like the correspondence of southern schoolgirls in its focus on female friendship and girlish confidences. "Liz Mary and myself all three slept in *one bed,*" Clay related. "Just imagine us all in one bed we kicked laugh[ed] talked nearly all night," especially enjoying reminiscing about "old times" at school with Spragins at Salem College.[29] While the girls obviously greatly enjoyed their time in Lexington, their career as "*belles*" was only one part of their enjoyment. Rather, the theme of their account was, quite simply, the fun they derived from social interaction—both heterosocial and homosocial.

Like this Lexington threesome, many southern belles seem to have measured their success not by the number of admirers they collected (although, as discussed below, some did) but rather by how much fun they had. The calculus of pleasure included men, but more important variables, judging from girls' correspondence, included the number and variety of social events attended, the type of people encountered, the quality of the refreshments, the richness of dress, and the opportunity to share one's enjoyment of all of these with female friends.

For many southern girls, "coming out" marked the beginning of a period of life devoted to the pursuit of pleasure. The care with which young women listed the visitors they received, the parties they attended, and the balls at which they danced indicates that young women's time "in society" offered them a rare opportunity to enjoy such events—a suggestion borne out by other girls' complaints of boredom and loneliness in isolated rural communities. The southern countryside offered no "gay assemblies where we country girls may display our little finery, our smiles, graces etc.," South

Carolinian Laura Margaret Cole Smith wryly noted, "and we have no better way of cheating ennui, than to engage in all manner of housewifery, which employments are, doubtless, no less creditable than disagreeable." "I have been dreadfully lonesome ever since my return from the city," Virginian Mary Berkeley mourned. "You can imagine how intollerably [sic] dull I find the country after my gay city life." "You know we live out in the country and I confess it is very dull," lamented one rural miss.[30]

In drawing invidious comparisons between "sober" country life and "gay" city life, southern girls also contrasted the "glorious liberty" of southern belles with the "domestic cares" of southern daughters. Yet, aware that marriage would mean a still more serious commitment to domestic tasks, many young women postponed marriage in favor of a prolonged "young ladyhood." Whether by withdrawing from society to "rusticate at home" or by priding themselves on their "adamantine" hearts, many young women sought to extend their youth either as dutiful daughters or as fascinating belles.[31] In doing so, they resisted acquiescing to their assigned adult role as responsible matrons at the same time that they represented the ideal southern lady: beautiful and dependent. By separating these qualities and associating them with particular identities—beautiful belles, dependent daughters—young women excused and extended both groups' refusal to relinquish single life and undertake adult responsibilities.

"THE EMPTY FRIVOLITIES OF THE BEAU MONDE": RELUCTANT BELLES

Although most young women enjoyed their entree into society and welcomed their new identity as belles, some soon tired of what one dismissively referred to as "the empty frivolities of the Beau Monde." The all-encompassing gaiety of belledom left little time or energy for other pursuits. Young women who had made their debut into society often found it difficult to maintain the study schedules or engage in the charitable activities that some single women made a priority. As Mary Elizabeth McPhail worried to her friend Mary Carrington: "It takes up so much time to follow town fashions and customs which leaves too small a portion for more important concerns." Similarly, Mary Cooke wrote to her former schoolmistress, Martha Hunter, about her concern that her previous industriousness had been replaced by "extreme laziness." She blamed "gayety . . . parties, and visiting" for her lack of motivation. "It seems to me that a life of usefulness is inconsistent with a town life unless one fixes a certain hour for study and useful employment and resolutely determines not to be interrupted by visitors," she observed before launching into a sermon on womanly duty. "Richmond certainly is very pleasant, but then pleasure is not every thing, and one feels as if their lives were spent in such frivolous pursuits, there is no end, no aim to obtain, by this mode of being, and it does not seem that we as rational beings, ought to fritter away our lives thus." Society, Cooke concluded, was "too great a wear and tear of time, intellect, and every thing else."[32]

For some young women, the attractions of belledom paled in comparison to their studies. Reflecting the dissimilar perspectives of Lemuella Brickell and Mary Miller on the debut, some girls found more "pleasure" in studying than in flirting. Margaret Steele's friend Mary Brown wrote from Wilmington, North Carolina, that she was surrounded by "a round of company"; as a result, she complained, "I can never find time to sit *seriously* down to read or write[.]" Similarly, Washington resident Laura Wirt complained that society in the capital city made her "dull" and "stupid." Responding to her brother Robert's disparaging remarks on her analysis of literature, she indignantly informed him "that women have sometimes some faint glimmerings of intellect, & often a taste more nice & discriminating that that [i.e., than that] of your own lordly sex . . . tho', Lord keep them! They are obliged, of necessity, to confound their wee bit of native sense with such an imbroglio of ribbons, laces, gauze tassels, &c &c &c as w[oul]d. strike Newton himself 'all of a heap.'"[33] Like other former schoolgirls, these women prioritized intellectual improvement and only reluctantly acquiesced to the demands of social interaction.

Other young women expressed concern that the worldly attractions of society distracted them from both the all-important task of preparing for heaven and the more immediate work of improving society. One of Emily Conrad's friends, possibly a former fellow student at North Carolina's Salem College, worried: "I often think I am committing a great sin in not rendering myself useful to others, but just floating along on the surface like a bubble." Ann Steele, who spent the winter season of 1801–2 in Washington, D.C., regretted that her attention had been drawn away from religion by the "trifling and uninteresting occurrences" of society. "When I review that lapse of time," she lamented, "and consider it as I do now [as] so much time thrown away without gaining any knowledge whatever, without being of service to a single individual and rather acquireing [sic] habits of folly and idleness which may hereafter be a disadvantage to me . . . when I take this survey of past events I feel fully convinced with the psalmist that all is vanity and vexation of spirit but that which is directed to the praise and glory of one only and true God."[34] For young women who believed that they had a destiny laid upon them by God, the pleasures of society seemed at best fleeting, and at worst, sinful.

Virginia Campbell, niece of Virginia governor David Campbell, filled her diary with regrets at the time (and money) taken from religious matters by social commitments. Although Campbell's aunt did her best to introduce her pious niece to Virginia society, Campbell feared the "witchery" of "gay company" and did her best to avoid "sinful mirth." Her diary entries bemoaned each concession made to the social life of a belle. "Went visiting and shopping this morning with aunt, who bo[ught] me a white satin to wear to Miss T's wedding," she recorded in April 1835. "I did not wish to buy so expensive a dress and feel much distressed about it. How many Testaments would the price of it send to the poor savage African or Indian?" In June, she commented: "Spent most of the afternoon answering tickets [i.e., invitations] to a party which is to be on Monday evening. What a waste of time!" Campbell also regarded flirtations with the local beaux as a distraction from more important matters. "Three young men spent the evening," she remarked in November, "but no improvement could be derived from any of them." And the following year, in July 1836, she wrote: "Received invitation to E.S.'s wedding. Constantly feeling the 'nothingness of this world' and of the great importance of preparation for eternity." [35]

Washington, D.C., resident Catharine Wirt likewise became "tire[d] of the scene of hurry & confusion" that characterized the capital city's glittering season only a few short weeks after her debut in the fall of 1827. Weary of recording the endless round of calls, parties, and dances, she ceased writing in her diary for nearly two years. When she resumed her writings in 1829, the eighteen-year-old, now living in Baltimore, Maryland, penned an entry that marked a dramatic transition from her earlier comments on her "public entree" into society and her attempts "to look pretty & be admired." "At this moment," she announced, "I feel profoundly the utter folly & emptiness of every pursuit of my life! They are all bounded to the contracted horizon, of this petty world." [36] While many young women enjoyed the pleasurable activity to be derived from society, then, others criticized the passivity of "look[ing] pretty & be[ing] admired." Despite their differences, however, young southern women shared a dissatisfaction with the "contracted horizon[s]" of southern womanhood.

Weary of society, disenchanted young women often withdrew from the "beau monde" to "rusticate at home." Some hoped to resume their studies with the support of female friends. Virginian Maria Roy dreamed of abandoning society for the company of "the Sister of my soul," Richmonder

Delia Hayes. "Stealing from the noise and bustle of company, Maria flies to the bosom of friendship," she wrote in an 1809 letter. "I wish," she added, "I had it in my power to have a little building erected here, where I would place my piano, library, and writing desk . . . here would I devote many hours to improvement and thinking on the virtues of my delia, try to imitate them." Others devoted themselves to religious studies and charitable societies. Catharine Wirt, who asked God to "point out clearly my line of duty" in 1834, spent the next eight years meditating on "the equality & immortality of women" and dedicating herself to "the poor & needy."[37] Whether they focused on the life of the mind or the state of their souls, these young women, like the hopeful southern spinsters of the previous chapter, sought an alternative to courtship and marriage.

Thus, following their debuts, some reluctant southern belles abandoned high society to return to the home circle. There, they resumed (or undertook) the domestic responsibilities and attempts at self-improvement that characterized the lives of other southern stay-at-home daughters. Despite the trials of single life detailed in Chapter 3, some girls saw such an existence as preferable to either the debut or its intended outcome, marriage. Ann Eliza Wright expressed such sentiments in a letter to her friend Mary Carrington. Wright took pleasure in her domestic responsibilities after her return from Richmond to her family's Virginia plantation. "The fact is," she reflected, "I think I am becoming too fond of seclusion. . . . I have seemed to lose my interest in the *World at large* I hardly like to look at it even through the 'Loopholes of retreat'. I have not *actually retired* in disgust, nor have I *any serious notion of taking the veil*. But I only meant I was growing too fond of this quiet."[38]

"I COUNTED UP MY CONQUESTS": BEWITCHING BELLES

Despite her disclaimer that she had no intention of entering a nunnery, Wright's wry comments reflected the reality that many young southern women seemed unready or unwilling to use their debut for its intended purpose, as a launching pad into southern society as a married woman. While Wright, along with other reluctant belles, chose to curtail her time in society, other girls sought to prolong their reign as southern belles. Priding themselves on their "adamantine" hearts, they "counted up [their] conquests" and reveled in their power over men.[39] Despite the obvious dissimilarities between these bewitching belles and their sober sisters, both groups of young women shared a common reluctance to commit themselves to marriage.

Many young women corresponded ceaselessly about their suitors and news of engagements in their neighborhoods. "Tell me all about your beaux" was a constant refrain.[40] Following their debuts, southern girls filled their letters with news of local courtships, engagements, and weddings. They implored each other for updates on each other's beaux and demanded immediate notification in case a suitor was accepted or rejected. Sarah Brown's 1819 letter to Sarah Garland was typical:

> You were mistaken in charging me with the two remaining beaus and as for Dr V—his continual theme whenever I see him is Miss S. A. G— I can claim no share in his heart of that you reign sole empress[.] I hear of nothing new in our city[.] Miss Nancy Payne has been amongst us for several weeks she will I expect make all the beaus [sic] heads quite dizzy. . . . Mr Jordin is still a pretty constant visitor at Mr Franklins[.] I am in hopes by the time you return Mary Ann will be redy [sic] to give us a wedding, Eliza Moor and P. Walker are shortly to surround the hymenial altar the precise time I do not know, I forgot to tell you we have a new beau Mr Reed from Henry County he is a student of my fathers.[41]

But for all their talk of men and marriage, young women were remarkably reluctant to commit themselves, and they carefully distanced themselves from their hopeful beaux by giving them ridiculous nicknames, describing them in highly unflattering terms, and rejecting them outright.

In their letters to one another, southern girls gave their suitors humorous, often disrespectful, nicknames. Laura Margaret Cole nicknamed a friend's beau, apparently a physician, "Doctor Kill-pill." Ellen Finley referred to beaux generically as "*Johnny horses, Billy goats,* and *Tom boy's.*"[42] Such ridiculous nicknames made it impossible to take suitors seriously—and indeed, many belles suggested that they had no interest in doing so.

Although the ostensible goal of entering society was to make a good match, many young women made their debut with a firm resolve to avoid entanglements. Thus, although Margaret Steele was much pleased with the coastal town of Wilmington, North Carolina, where she made her debut in 1807, she reported to her mother: "I declare Mama I am very much pleased with this place though I have not yet button'd up my heart in any color'd coat, the various perfections of so many Beaux secure it from becoming the slave of any."[43]

More frequently, young women commented on the imperfections of their suitors. Young women often complained, as Washingtonian Ann Steele did in 1801, of an "indifferent a set of beaux . . . not one very captivating[.]"

Saturday 19 July 1856   Washington City

The double throated — Bittern

[reckon you'll]

[find them good]

Southern women frequently poked fun at their suitors. In this entry from Anna Rosalie Quitman's journal, the Mississippi teen caricatures "The double-throated Bittern," a local young man who insisted on presenting the Quitman girls with fruit and flowers despite their distinct lack of enthusiasm for what Quitman elsewhere called his "munificent gifts." Assigning ridiculous nicknames to male admirers was one of several ways that "turned-out young ladies" avoided committing themselves to marriage. (Southern Historical Collection, Wilson Library, University of North Carolina at Chapel Hill)

Mary Page wrote from Clarke that "the beaux here are generally very commonplace—only to be desired as *conveniences* at parties[.]" Arkansas resident Elvira Boswell complained, "I have a great deal of company part of the most pestiferous kind viz—gentlemen." Richmond resident Mary Cooke complained that the men in her neighborhood were "loafers" and "great bores" and that "to crown all there is no such thing as offending them they are wrapped in an impenetrable coat of self conceat [sic] and never dream that they are unwelcome." A Portsmouth, Virginia, woman poked fun at her latest suitor, "the *fat* proffessor [sic]." Fannie Hatcher told her old Salem Academy schoolmate Mary Eugenia Bennett that her beaux consisted of "*a charming little feller*" and "*an old widower.*" Richmonder Mary Virginia Hawes was no more impressed with the list of "conquests" she had made during a trip to the countryside in 1848. She related a conversation with two family friends: " 'I suppose we may expect to see some of them this winter, how is it Miss Almenia?' says Mr Denison 'Well, Jinnie, and have you found the right one?' asks his better half, Truth will out, and as I ran over the list in my mind, I could not help saying, 'I hope not madam.' "[44]

Young women especially poked fun at elderly bachelors and widowers. South Carolinian Susan McDowall ridiculed one of her suitors of advanced years, ironically named Mr. Young: "He is decidedly the most stupid, silly, old man that ever lived," she exclaimed. "The idea of an old bachelor of 36 coming to see a girl of sixteen? Preposterous!!!" Texan Mary Starnes wrote scornfully about the "old widower 60 years old" who had presumed to address her.[45]

Although southern society approved of marriages between older men and much younger women, southern girls themselves expressed much skepticism about such matches. North Carolinian Mary Brown gleefully reported to Margaret Steele in 1810 that "an old Bachelor" in her neighborhood was unsuccessful in his pursuit of the local young ladies, despite his possession of "that *never failing* charm, of being very rich." "He has addressed *one of our Young Ladies,*" Brown noted pointedly, "but she cannot get her *own consent* to become an *Old Mans darling.*" Virginian Elizabeth Ruffin Cocke gave a more detailed and even more damning description of a "frisky widower" named Mr. Thompson, who came to call on her friend Rebecca Dupuy in 1848. After Cocke and several female friends had "concluded there would be no visitors," she wrote humorously, "who should be 'issued in' but the frisky widower Mr Thompson of course leaving at home the 5 children; when he proposes an evening walk, Beck just finds out she is not fond of walking, if riding the same excuse is offered tho' in the interim between his visits both walking and riding are indulged in." Cocke noted that Thompson seemed especially attracted to very young women, remarking with disapproval, "He goes to see Adelaide Payne not yet eighteen." Cocke contrasted the opinions of the local elders with those of young women. "He stands very high in the community as a most estimable, excellent man with plenty of money," she noted, but "none of the girls like him."[46]

Despite adults' acceptance, even encouragement, of matches between older men and younger women, young women clearly regarded older men—particularly those with children from a previous marriage—as undesirable suitors. Norfolk resident Mary McPhail was appalled at the idea that an older gentleman might have proposed to her friend Mary Carrington. "I was much surprised to hear of Mr S. Venable having addressed you," she remarked, "not that I wondered at his loving you, but do not know how a widower with three or four children can have the heart to wish to cast such a charge upon a young girl who may have *whom she chooses*[.]" A few years later, another of Carrington's friends slyly suggested that "a certain Dr." might soon address Carrington, but wondered if Carrington could "get over the *three* objections (*children*)."[47]

Even young men came in for their share of ridicule, however. One Richmond woman described one of her suitors, a Dr. Hamsun (possibly a nickname playing on the word *handsome*), as "gnawing most industriously on his cravat all the time during his visit[s]" to her. "I suppose he has exhausted his supply of handkerchiefs," she jested, "and as times are too hard to purchase more he has commenced on his cravats, think the next time he comes I will give him a large piece of crust of bread to gnaw on. so as to spare his clothes, wouldn't it be a good plan[?]" Georgia resident Maria Bryan regaled her sister with scathing reports of her admirers. Describing one of her suitors, she remarked with amusement: "Seriously, you have no ideas of the airs of consequence that the little fellow put on." Despite Bryan's dislike for the young man, he persisted in staying near her and in boring her with his clumsy attempts at conversation. "He seemed determined to stick it out," despaired Bryan, "and I never was more heartily tired of a person. . . . I really would have showed my contempt very openly had I not remembered that the command to 'Do unto others as we would they should do to us' extended to coxcombs as well as to other people."[48]

While some girls complained of the obligation to entertain "coxcombs," others reveled in the attention of their suitors. Their writings suggest that some southern belles enjoyed the temporary power they wielded over the men who ordinarily held the upper hand in southern society. One of Eliza Spragins's friends wrote to demand "a full account of y[ou]r Conquests." At the front of her journal, Eliza Lavalette Barksdale recorded a list of her admirers, with the notation: "All of these are my boys by right & if any body *dare dispute* the fact let them come forward and do it to my face that I may give them what they deserve." Young women teased each other mercilessly about their hold over men. "I think Delia you are very selfish, to wish to monopolize all the Physicians," Mary Roy wrote to Delia Hayes in 1813. "I have long since heard that, you had made an attack on Doctr. Clarke. . . . Oh! Delia you are a sly girl, you wish to insnare [sic] the other Brother . . . what have you done to poor John he can neither, *eat, sleep, or talk*, You are a *cruel creature.*" The more admirers a young woman had, the better. "It is well I counted up my conquests before I left the country," Mary Virginia Hawes wrote to a friend in 1848, "for I have frequently been asked the number, I always answer carelessly, 'Oh somewhere about a dozen, their ages varying from nineteen to ninety['] It is generally decided from such a reply that I must have had quite a successful summer."[49]

By collecting (and boasting about) male admirers, successful belles discovered a new way of achieving recognition in southern society. While southern schoolgirls sought status through public displays of their intellect, southern belles acquired notoriety by calling attention to their desirability. North Carolinian Penelope Skinner delighted in attracting, and then rejecting, numerous suitors. In 1837, she confided to her brother, Tristrim: "Do not tell if I tell you something I refused three or four [suitors] week before last. So you see your little sister is not forgotten in the crowd[.] a Lady told me the other day she expected I had had more offer's than any other Lady in the state[.] I said nothing but thought it very probable." Informing her brother of a Mr. Mitchell's attentions, she queried: "What do you think of the match," adding hastily, "but do not fear I have given him his *walking ticket.*" The following year, Skinner had once again freed herself from an insistent suitor's attentions. "Well I have discarded Mr French & am again on the Carpet," she reported with good cheer. By 1840—after three years in society—Skinner had rejected thirty offers of marriage. Far from fearing permanent singlehood, Skinner regarded her series of abortive courtships as evidence of her high social standing; multiple (and apparently generally known) offers of marriage ensured that she would not be lost "in the crowd" but rather regarded as one of the preeminent young ladies in North Carolina.[50]

Because a young woman's popularity reflected favorably upon her family's reputation, rejecting numerous suitors was expected and accepted. As a teenager, Washington resident Violet Blair embarked on a quest to collect a dozen proposals before her twenty-first birthday, and she delighted in counting her "victims." She wrote in her diary: "I love no man & yet I wish them all to love me, it flatters my vanity to have it so." Some women apparently led men on simply to obtain a proposal. Kate Rose told her friend

Ella Noland, with great relish, that she had recently rejected a Mr. N. Smith. "Nell it would have amused you to have seen how astonished he was when I said No! . . . How completely I fooled him pretending that I was desperately in love until came to the *pint* [sic] when I summoned all the dignity I could command and laid great emphasis on the word No!" By tolerating women's flirtation and even outright deception, adults unwittingly sanctioned girls' strategies for postponing marriage.[51]

While some belles evidently delighted in collecting male admirers, they resisted any commitment to marriage. In their letters to one another, young women insisted, as Laura Wirt did in 1824 after rejecting three marriage proposals, "I do not fall in love." "I don't believe I shall ever *fall in love*," declared Mary Francis Page. "My heart seems made of granite as far as men are concerned." Violet Blair proclaimed: "It is impossible that I should love any man—I *will not* do so—My heart is *unconquered* & *unconquerable*."[52] With words like these, young southern women helped to create and sustain the idealized image of the southern belle at the same time that they resisted taking on the onerous duties of a plantation mistress. Southern belles thus created an image of themselves as the objects of male desire even as they defined themselves as the makers of their own destiny.

"WHAT DO YOU THINK OF GETTING MARRIED?": MISGIVINGS ABOUT MATRIMONY

Clearly, some girls enjoyed both the opportunities for pleasure-seeking and the chance to wield power over men that belledom afforded. At the same time, they almost universally agreed that accepting a proposal would result in an end of pleasure. Commenting on an acquaintance of hers, an acclaimed belle, Wilmington, North Carolina, resident Mary Brown added: "It is said she is engaged, and if so gaeity will be fled soon—Alas! Alas!" By collecting—and then rejecting—suitors, southern belles were able to prolong the pursuit of pleasure. This motivation was clear in a letter that Matilda Abernathy received from one of her former schoolmates at "old Montrose Academy." "You mustn't *get married* til I get done going to school," she directed, "so we can *fly around* together, awhile first, & have a heap of fun, I dont beleive [sic] in getting married so soon either, I beleive [sic] in enjoying yourself a while first."[53]

But young women's flirtatious—even heartless—behavior was not motivated simply by the desire to "have a heap of fun." Rather, southern girls' fear of commitment reflected their knowledge of the potential drawbacks of marriage. Although young women often spoke teasingly of their courtships — discussing catching a beau and "taking the veil" in the same breath — they recognized that marriage was serious business. Ella Noland's mother commented on the importance of selecting a mate in an 1851 letter to her sister, Sally Gibson, who was playing hostess to Ella and her cousins. "I am glad to hear, *neither of 'the two great Virginia bell[e]s'* have had an *offer*," commented Mrs. Noland. "They are quite too young to encumber themselves with family cares. Good and clever husbands are rare articles nowadays — young ladies should not be in a hurry, it is an important step, and should be weighed well, before taken[.]" Young women echoed this message in their correspondence with each other. Throughout their time "on the carpet," young women circulated information among themselves about the consequences of commitment. The collective knowledge that they shared reinforced their fears of marriage and increased their determination to avoid "the *matrimonial fever.*" [54]

"Oh Lyd," wrote Virginia Taylor to her friend Lydia Russell. "What do you think of getting married[?]" In posing this question, Virginia Taylor spoke for many young women in the Old South. Southern girls eagerly collected information about marriage from their friends. Virginian Fannie Hatcher's letters to her North Carolina schoolmate, Mary Eugenia Bennett, typified such correspondence. While she began by lightheartedly recounting matches made by the young women of their acquaintance, she concluded by speculating on whether following their example was advisable: "Charlotte got acquainted with one of Ben Waddle's cousins not long since, told her all about Ben's getting married. I believe his name is Powell. Beck Catly is married & got a young one. Also Fannie Penn. . . . Oh! I should like to see her & her *old man* so much. *Ask her how she likes married life.* Tell her she must tell so as we may know whether to *follow her example or not.*" Similarly, Washington, D.C., resident Laura Wirt, the daughter of Attorney General William Wirt, wrote to her Virginia cousin, Louisa Cabell Carrington, who had recently married, to demand "the real opinions of my friends, *pro and con*, as the lawyers say." [55]

The "real opinions" of southern girls were largely negative. Many young women saw marriage as a renunciation of their independence. Invoking revolutionary rhetoric about liberty and reflecting personal knowledge of slavery, southern girls pronounced that in marriage, a woman relinquished her "glorious liberty" and "provided herself with a *Lord & Master.*" Such phrasing exaggerated both single women's freedom and married women's bondage. As southern daughters' complaints testified, single women in the Old South confronted significant limitations on their actions. And while marriage did subordinate wives to husbands, it was not tantamount to slavery. White southern women voluntarily "surrendered" themselves to their husbands—South Carolinian Mary Boykin Chesnut once commented that white women, unlike black women, had the dubious privilege of *choosing* their masters—and while wives were second-class citizens, they were not chattel property.[56]

Nonetheless, southern girls knew that the bonds of matrimony, while not the same as the chains of slavery, were no less real. Wives, like slaves, suffered a kind of "civil death"; they were permanently bound to men who possessed the legal right to determine their daily activities, choose their place of residence, and control their sexuality and reproduction. Young women often used metaphors of bondage for marriage, describing engaged and married women as being "caught" in the bonds of matrimony. Mary Francis Page referred to engagement as having "tied hands." Other young women commented on the "matrimonial noose." For young women in the slaveholding South, bondage was a powerful metaphor for the strictures of married life.[57]

Young southern women's rhetoric likened marriage to slavery. It also suggested that marriage ended much more than girls' ability to engage in the pursuit of pleasure; it might end their lives. In 1850, Mary Virginia Hawes wrote to a friend: "So Sally is all but on the scaffold, I hope sincerely she may not find this being noosed, decidedly inconvenient, to say nothing more."[58] The comparison of the bonds of matrimony to an executioner's rope suggested that marriage, in addition to imposing "civil death" on women, could result in literal death as well. In an age before reliable contraception, married women could expect to bear numerous children in rapid succession. Repeated childbearing posed a significant danger to women's health—and to their lives—especially in the Old South, where maternal death rates were double those in the antebellum North. Southern girls knew that, as one historian has remarked, "a possible death sentence came with every pregnancy."[59]

Young women frequently exchanged horror stories about their friends' and acquaintances' repeated pregnancies, nagging health problems, and early deaths. Laura Wirt was horrified at the fate of her friend Ann Van Ness Middleton, who was struck by a terminal illness during her first pregnancy, less than a year after her marriage. After giving birth to a sickly child who lived only a few days, the young bride suffered continually until her own death in late 1822. Laura Wirt's visceral reaction to her friend's agonies may well have reinforced her own desire to delay marriage; her detailed description of the corpse probably also caused her cousin and confidante, Louisa Cabell Carrington, who was recently married and a new mother, considerable anxiety. "Oh, Louisa, how fearfully was she changed by disease and death!" she exclaimed.

> I should never have believed that Ann could look like this inanimate figure. I could not recognize her at all. Her very features seemed changed. She looked like an old woman of sixty. . . . That mouth around which such agreeable smiles used to play was grimly closed in death. Those eyes, once so expressive of the amiable cheerfulness and serenity of her temper were shut forever! . . . Her once tender and snowy skin was now stretched like yellow parchment tightly over the bones, and her cheek, once brilliant with health, sunken, hollow and livid. . . . I could not bring myself to look on the object before me with any other emotion than one of unmixed horror and astonishment. All my affectionate thoughts belonged to Ann as I remembered her . . . shortly after her marriage. . . . Poor, poor Ann![60]

As this lengthy and expressive passage indicates, young southern women understood the connection between early marriage, repeated childbearing, and premature aging and even death. Thus, when girls exchanged updates on the status of their mutual acquaintances—often consisting of lists of marriages and deaths—they were well aware of the connection between wedding bells and funeral dirges. Southern girls knew that marriage was indeed, as North Carolinian Julia Southall described it in 1865, a "fatal step" that posed a serious danger to women's lives.[61]

Well aware of the drawbacks and dangers of marriage and motherhood, young women in the Old South urged each other to resist the "fashion" for getting married, at least for several years. While not all young women advocated "old maidenhood" as the best avenue to "the sweets of independence," many, perhaps most, agreed that young women should not rush into marriage. In contrast to their culture's approval of child brides, young women expressed dismay. Writing to Mary Eugenia Bennett in 1856, Fannie Hatcher commented of a former schoolmate: "I heard not long since that Amanda Fowler was married. Don't you think her quite young?" Young women—occasionally joined by older (always female) relatives—warned each other against loving too soon. Writing to Sarah and Mary Garland in 1819, Jane Garland cautioned her daughters against falling in love too quickly in elegant language (if inexpert spelling). "You are now my Daughters at a time of life that the Hart [sic] is susceptebel [sic] of the tender passhun [sic]," she wrote. "Let me beg of you to gard [sic] it well."[62]

A common theme in young women's letters was the desirability of postponing marriage. One woman, confronted with the rumor that she was engaged, replied with scorn. "The *idea*, my dear Emma of my getting married is too ridiculous," she exclaimed. "Have not the slightest whim of changing my name have never seen what specimen of the 'genus homo' that I would link my fate with and *hope*, I will not (as it is *generally termed*) fall in love for another year. May I make the same wish for you? Please do not think of marrying yet a while I want to see you as Emma P Nicholson once more." Writing to a former classmate from the Edgeworth Female Seminary in Greensboro, North Carolina, Lizzie Cochran reported, "There is to be any quantity of weddings down here this week." Reflecting on her own situation, she added, "Your time and mine will come along after awhile, I hope not for four or five years yet."[63]

Over and over again, young women cautioned each other to guard their feelings—and their reputations—and to postpone marriage. Writing to her friend Julia Conrad, one young woman inquired about the pace of her courtship. "I shall not allow you to make any engagements without first consulting my ladyship," she admonished. "Do you understand?" Similarly, Jane Constance Miller's cousin urged her to "have a delightful winter" but to "remember you are not to be *irrevocably* engaged till I see the *gentleman*—for if he is not some thing more than common he shan't have my little Jennie[.]"[64]

Ultimately, of course, with no compelling alternative, young women resigned themselves to the inevitability of marriage. After a period of as much as several years, they assumed that the "time" would "come along" when marriage was unavoidable. When it did so, they used the rituals of courtship in an effort to assure themselves that the men in whose hands they placed their futures would be "some thing more than common"—persons for whom they felt respect, esteem, and "tender passhun." Moreover, they hoped that by basing their marriages on mutual love and respect, they could provide themselves with safeguards against male dominance. Rather than simply postponing marriage, they sought to exert control over it through the process of courtship. Young women in the Old South attempted to use the rituals of courtship to resist a subordinate role in marriage.

"THE MACHIAVELISM OF THE DRAWING ROOM": THE RITUALS OF COURTSHIP

In nineteenth-century America, personal preference was coming to be considered the most important factor in choosing à mate, and older courtship customs such as marriage in birth order, adult chaperonage, and the requirement of parental consent gradually relaxed to allow men and women greater opportunities to converse freely, assess their compatibility, and form (or break) engagements on their own. However, the customs of courtship remained quite restrictive in the antebellum South. Moreover, the dynamics of courtship, which often took on the appearance of an elaborate—if dangerous—game of cat-and-mouse, interfered with courting couples' efforts to assess each other's true characters. The rituals of courtship in the Old South—what one male southerner referred to "the Machiavelism [sic] of the drawing room"—hindered confidence rather than advancing intimacy.[65]

Courtships often began with a chance meeting at a social occasion, such as a wedding, a graduation ceremony, or one of the innumerable balls, parties, and formal teas that filled the days and nights of young women "on the carpet." After an initial meeting, young women allowed favored suitors to escort them to church; on social outings such as parties, concerts, lectures, and picnics; or on "moonlight walks" and horseback rides—usually as part of a group that included several other young women and men.[66]

Virginian Eliza Lavalette Barksdale kept an unusually detailed diary recording her social contact with several men in her neighborhood. Barksdale's diary recorded the details of courtship practices in the antebellum South. Before venturing away from home with the favored gentleman whom she had agreed to allow to accompany her, she dressed "with all possible care," and she noted in her diary exactly what she wore and how she looked. After arriving at the scene, she no longer was obliged to remain with her escort but rather chatted, played games, danced, or "promenaded" with various gentlemen—sometimes alone in the garden—before returning home with yet another male companion. As she concluded at the end of one especially successful evening, "Upon the whole [I] spent my time very pleasantly."[67]

Courtship settings offered a combination of freedom and constraint. Events like those Barksdale described allowed young people to mix without formal chaperonage, while still ensuring that young women would only meet eligible men of their own social class. While few southern parents in the nineteenth century arranged marriages, they did maintain more subtle forms of control over their daughters' choice of companions. Belle Price's father was relieved that she had refused to entertain a man he described as "a very rough uncouth Fellow" with "very bad habits." Reminding his "dear Daughter" that women "are always judged by the company they keep," he impressed upon her "the importance of being careful in Selecting our association with discretion and good judgement, So as to occupy the proper position our Selves." Young women were encouraged to confide in their parents—particularly their mothers—about their courtships and thus avoid unsuitable attachments. Occasionally, when parents disapproved of particular suitors, daughters were sent to live with relatives away from the man in question to allow the couple's ardor to cool. More frequently, southern parents insisted that their daughters be accompanied by "suitable Company" — a parent or sibling, a trusted family friend, or a "Lady of destintion [sic]" — when they left the house. Laura Wirt's parents, for instance, refused to allow her even to go horseback riding unattended. For the most part, however, the settings in which courtship took place sufficiently limited the pool of potential mates — and offered enough scope for monitoring behavior — that parents and guardians felt comfortable allowing their daughters to interact with their suitors without strict supervision.[68]

Internalized notions of proper ladylike behavior also played an important role in dictating the rituals of courtship. While most well-to-do antebellum Americans upheld the ideal of female purity — virginity before marriage and fidelity within it — female sexual innocence was especially important for wealthy slaveholders, who sometimes defended the institution of slavery by arguing that the sexual availability of enslaved black women ensured the sexual purity of elite white women. Indeed, sexual inexperience was one of the most important distinctions between black "wenches" and white "ladies"; while black teenagers were regularly subjected to sexual abuse and coercion, white teenagers' contacts with the opposite sex were carefully monitored and controlled. Elite southerners thus emphasized the importance of a young woman's reputation, which reflected on her family's status and on her father's honor. "I wish you to be discreet in your conduct," Cary Whitaker reminded his daughter, Anna. "Never act so, as to give the least room for censure." Concerned about appearances, as well as actual practice, status-conscious southerners also called attention to the fragility of female respectability. "One false, imprudent step will blast the reputation of a female forever," exclaimed Alabama resident Elizabeth Ruffin Cocke. In general, then, white southerners agreed with Elizabeth Noland's assessment of the situation and her recommendation to her daughter in an 1846 letter: "My dear little Ella, you cannot be too circumspect in your deportment."[69]

Young women in the Old South were well aware of the rigid constraints on women's behavior and of the high costs of breaking with convention. Interwoven among more lighthearted commentary on persistent suitors and innocent flirtations were sobering reflections on the fate that awaited young women who defied parental and social constraints. In 1840, Raleigh, North Carolina, resident Isabella Miller wrote to her friend Jane Constance Miller about "a very unhappy affair" in her neighborhood involving a young woman named Meredith who had eloped with "one of the apprentices." Worse still, "before that [she] is said to have disgraced herself so as to make it necessary that she should marry the lad." Miller was quick to take warning from the incident. "When I heard of it I was quite sick and it caused me to feel very bad," she commented, adding that it was imperative for young women to remain "pure from all sin and disgrace" and never to "act imprudently."[70]

Both because of the limited privacy available to them and as a result of their own awareness of the need to behave circumspectly, courting couples seem to have limited their conversations to innocent, and often rather impersonal, topics. Alabama belle Virginia Tunstall Clay's memoirs offer some clues about male-female interactions at social occasions. Recalling her first ball and her first crush (who turned out to be married), she wrote: "During the evening he paid me some pretty compliments, remarking upon my hazel eyes and the gleam of gold in my hair, and he touched my curls admiringly, as if they were revered by him. . . . We danced together frequently throughout the evening, and my hero rendered me every attention a kind man may offer." Elizabeth Ruffin, who entertained suitors at her Virginia plantation, described similar conversations. Ruffin and her suitors "discoursed largely on many subjects" but invariably came back to "a wide expatiation on that *theme of themes, Love.*" Ruffin suggested that the subject was of little interest to her and was, rather, a stale topic in courtship settings. The topic of love, she commented with evident impatience, was an "*exhaustless fund* including its numberless ramifications tho' after all to no purpose in as much as no mutual edification was imparted; but why expect any from an everyday topic rendered almost insipid from a universal resort when all others fail to entertain?" Indeed, Ruffin concluded, most male visitors were incapable of conversing on anything other than "many stale topics." In sum, conversation during courtship generally appears to have been a matter of gentlemen paying compliments and young women enjoying—or, in some cases, being bored by—the flattery.[71]

The rituals of courtship in the Old South often functioned to forestall, rather than to promote, intimacy. Many southerners recognized this and deplored the fact that courtship seemed to be more about concealing than revealing one's true self. Women's deception seemed particularly problematic given that many nineteenth-century Americans believed that female emotions were especially transparent and that women were inherently sincere. Yet at the same time, the emphasis that southern adults laid upon female reputation made it difficult, even dangerous, for young women to avoid hypocrisy. One of Emily Conrad's friends indicated the degree to which women's participation in the competitive sport of courtship challenged accepted notions of femininity when she speculated, "I'll tell you what this courting must be dreadful, I would as soon (if I were a man) try to manage an intricate law-suite as the love suits of every day occurrence, think there is more maneuvering required in the latter and so much deceit must be practised."[72] According to this southern woman, courtship was a "dreadful" business characterized by "maneuvering" and "deceit" and carrying serious legal consequences—not unlike a lawsuit. Yet in order to uphold southern standards of propriety, there was no alternative; deception "must be practiced" in courtship. Thus, while the goal of courtship in the South—as elsewhere in the nation—was to achieve a relationship of mutual love and respect, the conventions of the region often made this ideal difficult to achieve.[73]

"A MOST AGREEABLE TETE A TETE": THE SEARCH FOR INTIMACY

In September 1838, Caroline Brooks began to receive visits from her future husband, James Lilly, at her home. Such visits customarily would take place in a young woman's parents' presence, but Brooks, a schoolteacher, lived alone. Therefore, "Mr Lilly" came accompanied by a "Miss D. Mask," who acted as chaperone. By the end of November, charmed by Lilly's frequent (and no longer chaperoned) visits, Brooks was giving serious thought to accepting his marriage proposal. "I have again enjoyed the pleasure of a visit from J. M. L.," she wrote, adding, "The golden hours flew on eagles wings. . . . I have partly promised to give him a decisive answer. . . . Never before did I think so seriously on the subject nor find it so difficult to exclude it from my thoughts." Even though Brooks admitted her attraction to her suitor at the outset—"Felt that my heart was in danger, but prayed for aid to guard it carefully," she confessed in late September—it was only after she had determined to marry James Lilly that she began to call him "James" rather than "Mr Lilly" in her diary. For Brooks, engagement represented liberation from the confining rules of courtship. In mid-December, she recorded "a most agreeable tete a tete" with her intended husband. "I felt under less restraint than usual," she explained, "and we conversed freely on the subject of our intended Union with mutual and unbounded confidence in each others fidelity and attachment."[74]

The course of Caroline Brooks's courtship represented an ideal pattern. As casual acquaintance shaded into serious courtship, those involved gradually abandoned superficial flirtation to undertake serious investigation. During this phase, the goal was to ascertain each others' character and mutual compatibility. In short, as courting couples deepened their relationship, they strove to use courtship to find intimacy with another person. However, the restrictive rituals of courtship continued to frustrate young women's quest for emotional connection. Some women, like Brooks, found that committing themselves to marriage removed the last traces of reserve and allowed them to enjoy "mutual and unbounded confidence" in their intended husbands; for others, the conventions of courtship proved difficult to abandon, and the requirements of feminine propriety posed insurmountable obstacles to intimacy.

While flirtations usually began with chance meetings at social occasions, once such acquaintances moved into realm of courtship, young women, with the cooperation of their families and friends, met with their suitors in less crowded—although rarely private—settings. Some young women entertained their serious suitors "en famille"; that is, they received "gentleman callers" in their own homes and entertained them there by engaging in genteel conversation on literary topics or by displaying their own skills on the guitar, the harp, or the piano. Some couples evidently used such opportunities to discuss important matters, such as their ideas about religion. In such conversations, they ventured closer to intimacy than in drawing rooms and ballrooms. Even in the comparatively intimate setting of family parlors, however, they maintained a sense of reserve—reinforced, in many cases, by the presence of other family members. Writing to his fiancée, Sarah Bennett, in 1835, Erastus Hopkins congratulated himself as well as his intended bride by reflecting on their proper behavior, even when they managed to evade the conventions of chaperonage: "Do you remember those days in November last, when we used so slily [*sic*] to steal into the dining room & talk so *soberly* about these things—when *you* felt so (I hardly know how) & I felt so tender?" he reminisced. "I love to think of those days, for all was conducted with such propriety &, as I trust, on Christian principles. I believe there was not a word or deed which for dignity's sake or conscience's sake we would have recalled."[75]

Hushed conversations on parlor settees, strolls in the garden by moonlight, and stolen private moments at crowded social outings offered courting couples their best opportunities to engage in personal conversations that allowed young women and men to share their inmost thoughts. Because such moments were rarely recorded—and even then, only retrospectively—it is difficult to reconstruct the progress of courtship from them alone. Fortunately for both courting couples and historians, however, there was another way to conduct the search for intimacy: exchanging letters. Courtship correspondence illuminates both southern women's (and men's) desire for romantic love and the difficulties posed by gender conventions.[76]

Men initiated the correspondence with a stiff, formal letter requesting the favor of a reply. John La Bruce's first letter to Charlestonian Jane Allston was typical. "I hope I am not taking a liberty in writing you," he began his letter to "Miss Janie," "but hope that you will gratify me with an epistle occasionally?" The recipients of such letters then determined whether or not to grant the favor of a return letter containing permission for a continued exchange. While southern belles might flirt shamelessly at social functions, young women did not enter into correspondence lightly, for the exchange of the "first love letter" — even one that contained no personal information whatsoever — signified a potentially serious relationship. In 1850, Ella Noland's friend Carrie Sage commended her for returning a letter received from a Mr. Armstrong. "If you really do not care for him," she reflected, "it is much better to discourage the first attempt at a correspondence — which might lead to something more serious[.]" [77]

If and when a young woman agreed to a correspondence with a gentleman, stiff notes on elaborate stationery might be gradually replaced by longer, more candid letters in which the couple carefully investigated the possibility of a serious attachment. Richard Johnson suggested to his fiancée, Isabella ("Bella") Mackay, that they correspond about books that they read as a way to get to know each other: "I think that you and I might improve ourselves by writing to each other about the different literary works," he explained, "and we might in that way discover each others tastes on such matters[.]" In courtship letters — which writers insisted must be kept strictly private — southern women and men ideally "laid aside all formality" and shared their innermost "secrets" with each other.[78]

In these letters, content — not form — was paramount. Young women routinely apologized for their poor paper and scratchy pens but sent their letters anyway, recognizing that their suitors wanted candid self-revelation more than carefully written epistles. "I am sorry to inform you that I am unable to give that all important answer as yet," wrote Mary Miller to Charles Davis in 1848. She explained: "I can never consent to marry you or anyone else unless I am *certain very certain* that I prefer you to all others. . . . Please excuse me for writing on foolscap paper, I have nicer but it blots so that you would not be able to read it, You desired me to speak plainly, I have done so and if there is any thing amiss in what I have said please look over it[.]" [79] "Speak[ing] plainly" — rather than writing elegantly — was the purpose of courtship correspondence.

However, the candid self-disclosure that couples sought in romantic relationships was often hindered by the conventions of courtship, which required women to be circumspect and wary of revealing too much of their

own feelings. Women's need to protect their reputation—and men's recognition of this requirement—resulted in long, convoluted letters whose careful wording obscured more than it revealed. After informing Joseph Skinner
that she was not ready to give him an answer, Maria Lowther received a letter from him asking her to clarify her attitude toward his suit. "I am persuaded a young Lady of modesty, and sensibility almost in the extreme would shrink at the idea of abruptly rejecting an address to her affections, and this inclines me oftentimes to think you have declined mine with more delicacy and politeness than my manner merited," he wrote—in other words, Skinner suggested that Lowther did not reject him out of hand for reasons of "delicacy and politeness" rather than because she had feelings for him. Despite his urgent desire for a more definite answer, Skinner felt he could only ask "so much candor as to assure me whether you have determined *not to favor* my addresses?" "If you have not thus determined," he continued, "would it be presuming too much to enquire if there is more than a mere possibility they will be favored?" Desperate to ascertain his beloved's feelings, Skinner buried his own meaning in an avalanche of double negatives and roundabout phrases. Still, in his next letter he felt compelled to apologize "for having suffered my impatience and disquietude of mind to hurry me so precipitately into an enquiry not strictly consistent with propriety"—that is, for being overly direct! Skinner continued to read and re-read his inamorata's letters, commenting, "Since the receipt of your first letter I have been in doubt as to the construction it should receive." Despite his own "impatience and disquietude of mind," which was exacerbated by his correspondent's carefully constructed (and intentionally uninformative) letter, Skinner praised Lowther's "strict correctness and propriety" in shielding her real feelings from him.[80]

The difficulty of achieving candor in the usual course of courtship may explain why southern women so often married cousins, with whom they could enjoy a relationship freed from the traditional constraints of courtship. As Margaret Lea explained in a letter to her fiancé, "Cousin Charlie": "We met, not as strangers, but, through the intimacy of our families, as already friends." As "friends," cousins could visit, walk, and ride together without chaperones and—equally important—without the internalized restraints that so often characterized courtship. Virginian Sarah Satterlee found that familial ties eased her romantic relationship with her cousin George Satterlee. "He wishes me to call him 'Cousin George,'" she explained to her friend Mary Hudson Ellett, "which I am not at all unwilling to do, for the more I see of him the better I like him. . . . I expect to see a good deal of him, he will have his horse and wagon, and I hope it will not be considered very improper for him to drive out his 'Cousin' occasionally, the relationship being so very *near*." By contrast, Satterlee found it difficult to enjoy the attentions of another suitor, a "Mr. H," because his visits were clearly intended as courtship. "I will tell you, Molly, what I have not told anyone else," confided Satterlee; "if I could see Mr. H. at anyone's house . . . or any where that we visit, if I could see *more* of him perhaps I should love him, see him as *any visitor*, you know what I mean, that perhaps I should change but you know that my constant feeling when knowing him here was only to *repulse* his attentions, listen as little as possible to his *conversation*, and *get away from him*, as I saw that if I appeared pleased in the least with his society that it would encourage him so that there was but one way. This however cannot be accomplished." Relationships with male cousins, then, could develop more naturally than those with unrelated men, who had to be either "repulsed" or "encouraged" at an early stage. Not surprisingly, then, it was often with a favorite cousin that a southern girl felt—or allowed herself to feel—"this first feeling of real affinity."[81]

It was only rarely that a "feeling of real affinity" translated into physical intimacy. Here again, cousins seem to have experienced greater freedom from both internal and external constraints. Even before they were engaged, Emma Sue Gordon and her cousin, Robert Perkins, shared kisses and caresses. "Cousin Robert . . . staid Journal till twelve o'clock [at night]," she wrote in spring 1863, "but it did not seem but a few minutes to me, for Journal with my head resting on his bosom & his arms around me he told me that he loved me, loved me more than anybody else, & now I am happy." Apparently Gordon's parents found nothing amiss either in "Cousin Robert's" late-night visits or in granting the courting couple considerable privacy. Nonetheless, Gordon herself placed limits on the couple's intimacy prior to an official engagement. "He *almost* asked me to be his wife this afternoon," she wrote in mid-May. "*That must* come soon I feel—He begs me so hard to put my arm around his neck & to sit on his lap, but I resist all his entreaties, I will kiss him & that is all."[82]

Although Gordon hesitated to do more than kiss Robert Perkins prior to his proposal, once they were engaged, she was less concerned about appearances. In June 1863, she wrote in her diary: "It seems that Someone, I don't know who was down at the creek the other evening watching Cousin Robert & me well, I hope they were satisfied, I don't care if all the world knows it, I *did* go there to meet him, I *did* kiss him several times . . . & we *did* sit together on the roots of a tree, very close to each other & his arm was around me all the time, but I am engaged to him & what do I care who knows about my meeting him."[83] For Gordon, first her familial relationship to Robert and then her official engagement to him justified both their solitary meetings and their shared intimacies.

Engagement could give other young women the same kind of freedom that Gordon enjoyed with her cousin-fiancé. For some fortunate couples, engagement allowed women to abandon many of the strictures on a proper lady's behavior, including the convention of chaperonage. In many cases, however, young women maintained a steely reserve with their suitors even after they had agreed to marry them. Ironically, the relaxed rules of courtship—which, by midcentury, called for southern women to ask their parents' blessing only after they had already accepted a proposal—led to new strictures. Agreements made in private could also be broken in private—and they often were. Because of the uncertainty involved, many young women kept their engagements secret until shortly before the wedding day. Secrecy was imperative to protect a young woman's reputation. As Cornelia McIver remarked to her friend and relative Lucy McIver, "these long engagements are very uncertain," and a woman whose heart was known to have been claimed—and even more, whose "maiden modesty" was believed to have been compromised—found her chances at marriage appreciably diminished. In a society in which young women's reputations could so easily be destroyed, it was imperative to maintain a flawlessly upright appearance until after marriage. (Indeed, it was not until two days *after* her wedding that Elizabeth Cooley McClure recorded in her diary "the first time I sat in Mr. McClure's lap or he in mine.") As a result, most engaged couples behaved quite circumspectly, limiting their ardor to coy descriptions of erotic dreams. Alluding to his eagerness for physical intimacy, William Henry Wills urged Anna Whitaker to marry him quickly, explaining, "the Cold Etiquette of the world imposes upon us Certain observances which nothing but our Union will Remove." [84]

Even more important than these limitations on physical contact was evidence that some engaged couples found it difficult to discard the conventions of courtship and communicate openly. What Elizabeth Lucas's fiancé called "the cold conventionalisms of this world" interfered with not only physical but also emotional intimacy. Over and over again, couples wrote letters that indicated that they had difficulty discarding their accustomed reserve. "Cousin Lottie," wrote Wyatt Patterson to his fiancée, Lois Dye, in 1863, "I think both of us are rather distant or too much reserved . . . but I hope this will wear off soon." Mary Francis Page remarked that her letters to her fiancé were "of the most commonplace kind. I do'nt generally say even '*my dear*,'" she admitted. Waddy Butler complained that Lucy Wood refused even to write him love letters. "Yes, Lucy, though loving me you find it impossible to talk to me in the language of love," he reflected in 1861, only months before the couple's wedding. Instead, Wood wrote "plain matter-of-fact letters" that did not satisfy Butler's craving for reassurance of her affection. "All this may, and doubtless does, proceed from modesty," Butler acknowledged, but he wished that "frankness and affection," rather than "false modesty" and "cold terms of courtesy and polite remarks," would characterize his beloved's correspondence. "It would be inexpressible happiness for me to pour out my heart and love to you, if you too would act as kindly."[85]

Other engaged couples expressed great joy, not simply in their strong feelings for one another, but in their newfound ability to express them openly. "When I write to you I dip my pen in my own heart," Elizabeth Lucas's fiancé wrote ecstatically; slightly more prosaically, he reflected, "It is pleasurable to feel so much at ease with you, that I can say to you whatever comes up, in the first words that present themselves." Women also found tremendous pleasure and a degree of freedom in candid correspondence. Once she had accepted Thomas Norwood's proposal, Anna Hendree claimed "the right, yes the right to weary you as much as I like." "You see I am confiding much more freely than of old," she remarked; "it is indeed a happiness to feel that there is one who can fully enter into our feelings."[86]

Likewise, Sarah Bennett cast off rules regarding both form and content in the letters she wrote to her fiancé, Erastus Hopkins, in 1835: "There is no need for excuses for writing now, bad as it is, I know you only see it so I care not," she explained. Just as importantly, Bennett felt at liberty to express her feelings for (and to) her fiancé. "O I can hardly believe it is to you I am writing thus freely," she interrupted a long soliloquy on her longing for her absent lover. "You who was but a little while ago a stranger entire to me, and now the one on whom all my earthly happiness depends. This entire confidence is so delightful that we can but regard it as a rich treasure," she thrilled.[87]

For some young women in the Old South, as for Sarah Bennett, a courtship conducted with absolute "propriety," when based "on Christian principles" of mutual respect and self-revelation, could produce the desired result: a union based on "entire confidence." For others, the combative atmosphere and "cold etiquette" of courtship produced strained relationships characterized by stifled passions and "false modesty." In either event, courtship rarely succeeded in reducing young women's fears of commitment or weakening their determination to postpone matrimony. Young women in the Old South did not proceed immediately from courtship to marriage, however; rather, they experienced—and in many cases, insisted upon—a lengthy period of engagement. More than courtship, engagement allowed young women to strive for intimacy with their intended husbands and to

come to terms with their persistent misgivings about marriage. It also enabled them to continue their efforts to use the ideal of romantic love to redefine their role within marriage. Young women in the Old South used the
period of engagement to resist patriarchal control even as they acquiesced
to the inevitability of marriage.

"LOVE WILL UNITE US!": LIZZIE SCOTT

In March 1852, Elizabeth ("Lizzie") Scott, the daughter of a Texas lawyer and politician, commenced a diary. "I intend this book as a faithful repository of my inmost thoughts, my hopes, my sorrows, my joys," she explained.[1] Over the coming months, the nineteen-year-old had many thoughts, hopes, sorrows, and joys to record in her journal—a gift from her intended husband, Will Neblett. In her diary, Lizzie recorded her ideas about romantic love, confessed her fears of marriage, and prepared for her wedding day. In the process, she revealed both the importance that young women in the Old South attached to romantic love and the deep reservations they held about marriage. At the same time, she illustrated how young women sought to prepare themselves for the adult responsibilities of married life at the same time that they held those responsibilities at arm's length during an extended life-stage limbo: engagement.

Like many southern girls, Lizzie believed that romantic love was the surest route to personal happiness. As a teenager, she described herself as being formed for love. "Nature seems to have assigned my heart for loving ardently truly," she reflected, "& has implanted the longing[,] I may say holy desire[,] to be loved." Lizzie found love close to home when, at age thirteen, she first met twenty-year-old Will Neblett, the son of a neighboring physician. Despite the seven-year age difference, Lizzie and Will attended a local school together; after both had finished their formal educations, he studied law with her father. The couple's relationship developed naturally, if not smoothly, over the next six years. Lizzie had at least one other serious suitor, Ben Smith, and she continued to correspond with him during her lengthy engagement to Will Neblett—which she broke off twice in a three-year time period, perhaps in a fit of pique inspired by Will's "indifferent and careless" behavior, which she took as a sign that "he begins to feel certain of the prize." By April 1852, however, Lizzie felt confident that the engagement would terminate in marriage. "I hesitate not, nor falter," she wrote. "I am determined, and know the consequences, 'tis not a step taken rashly and *unadvisedly*." [2]

But, as Lizzie quoted from one of her favorite authors, Shakespeare, "The course of true love never yet run smooth." Although her father gave his "rather reluctant consent" to the match, both of Lizzie's parents warned against it, threatening to disinherit her if she married Will Neblett, who, at age twenty-six, did not yet have a steady income. But "poverty were better with him," Lizzie concluded, "than riches with another. . . . Riches and worldly honors are nothing to me, nor am I any too good to suffer poverty with one I love." Love, Lizzie believed, was the most important ingredient for happiness. "I have no cause to murmur," she wrote in early May, three weeks before her wedding day. "I love, and am beloved! . . . We will have to toil I expect all our lives for the support of Nature, but love will unite us!" [3]

Despite Lizzie's certainty that her feelings for Will (and his for her) were "love, in its warmest purest state," and her professed eagerness "to be his, beyond all doubts," as her wedding day approached, she admitted, "I have a thousand fears, and missgivings [sic] whether I should marry or not." Much as she loved Will, whose faithfulness had won her "whole heart," and as thoroughly convinced as she was of his commitment to her—she was, she wrote, "the love of his boyhood, and love [of] his manhood, the one love of his life"—she worried about "how we will get along." In particular, she expressed concern that the couple's love would not endure. "As long as love lasts I shall feel no fears," she reflected, "but alas! when love *dies*, 'There's the rub,'" she quoted Shakespeare again, "to prevent love dying." Like other southern women (and men), Lizzie believed that it was the wife's responsibility "to prevent love dying," and she worried that her personality—especially her "monster pride" and her "unfortunate temper"—would prevent her from being the kind of self-sacrificing, supportive wife who would earn and retain her husband's love. Small wonder, then, that as her wedding date drew nearer, Lizzie was anxious and despondent. "Our affections tho' they afford us much pleasure," she mused, "often fill our hearts with fear, doubting and grief." [4]

Lizzie also reflected on women's legal and economic powerlessness in marriage. Despite her youth, Lizzie was keenly aware of the legal ramifications of marriage. Three weeks before her marriage, she reflected: "A few more weeks will pass away and I will become a wife—a great responsibility. My identity, my legal existence will be swallowed up in my husband." Indeed, as Lizzie knew, married women had no "legal existence"; they were unable to sign contracts, to own property, or even to appear in court without their husbands' permission. On a woman's wedding day, any property she brought with her to the marriage became her husband's. Marriage simply obliterated a woman's existence in the eyes of the law.[5]

Married women's legal disabilities made them dependent on their husbands for daily necessities, encouraging them to accede to their husbands' preferences in determining where to live. In the weeks leading up to the wedding, Will continually changed his plans about where to begin his fledgling law practice, first proposing settling in Waco ("a perfect grave yard"), then in Marlin ("that remote corner of the earth"), and finally living with his parents. Renouncing her ambitions for "worldly honor" and her desire for a comfortable "home of our own," Lizzie vowed to be "ambitious for *him*" and settle wherever "he can do best" without "murmuring." "I am willing to go any where, put up with any thing do anything for Will, and with him," she explained. Women's legal and economic powerlessness—what Lizzie called "the stern realities of life"—dictated that wives "submit to any privations" to ensure their husbands' success.[6]

"Sometimes I think really that I cannot marry so soon," Lizzie wrote in early May, two weeks before her wedding day. "I am not ready." Although in this instance, Lizzie was referring to the "good deal of sewing" she needed to complete, she also recognized that engagement offered her a final opportunity to prepare herself for marriage. This preparation included accepting the wifely responsibility "to prevent love dying" and expressing selfless willingness to "submit to any privations" for the sake of her husband. Ultimately, as Lizzie recognized, it meant that she needed to "teach [her] heart to be content with [her] lot"—that is, to accept her subordinate position within marriage. For Lizzie, this meant being "hopeful, resigned, and full of trust, and love." In return for the "inestimable gift" of "a loving noble, truthful heart," Lizzie promised to renounce her "monster pride" and her desire for "greatness & fame" and become "meek lowly and deserving" of Will's love. "I *will reform*," she vowed, resolving to "join the Methodist church on probation" to "see if that will aid me any in my reformation."[7]

"What aid will quarreling with existence bring me?" Lizzie demanded. "The boon of life has been bestowed, and now it needs only that I 'work out my own salvation with fear and trembling.'" Although Lizzie had long cherished dreams of achieving fame and fortune and had resisted placing her fate in Will's hands for several years, by spring 1852 she had determined that "view[ing] things in their true and natural light" meant accepting both her limited "existence" as a woman and her responsibility to find "salvation" within the institution of marriage, sweetened by "the boon of life": romantic love. As her wedding day approached, Lizzie's diary entries displayed a combination of excitement and trepidation. "My life will be entirely changed," she reflected soberly. "All my cherished recreations of mind & body must in part be abolished. I will have much to do, and I hope much happiness, if not, miserable will be my exchange."[8]

Like Lizzie Scott, many young women in the Old South used—and prolonged—the period of engagement to contemplate the "exchange" of single life for what they hoped would be marital bliss. This important—and often extended—stage of life gave women a final opportunity to consider their future and to take what steps they could to shape their destiny. Most elite women in the antebellum South ultimately concluded that the aim of their existence was marriage even as they recognized the many ways in which marriage subordinated wives to their husbands. Yet at the same time that young women in the Old South submitted to the bonds of matrimony, they hoped that romantic love would temper their husbands' dominance. Southern women refused to marry simply to gain social approval and economic security; they held out for romantic love. Once committed to marriage, they insisted on a lengthy period of engagement, during which they used love as a tool to negotiate for a favorable position within marriage. As they rehearsed their relationship with their husbands-to-be, southern brides-to-be resisted a subordinate role even as they accepted the inevitability of marriage. The period of engagement, then, proved to be both an important stage in southern women's coming-of-age and a staging ground for their continued resistance. The form this resistance took, however, was not collective, but individual; it was not public, but private. "Blushing brides" in the antebellum South rested their hopes for the future not on their civil rights as women but on their particular circumstances as wives. Ultimately, this proved to be an ineffective strategy. Both assisted and undermined by the cult of romantic love, young women in the Old South found that the life stage of engagement served as a tipping point between resistance and resignation.

"A PURPOSE IN LIFE": THE IMPORTANCE OF MARRIAGE

Despite their many doubts about matrimony (detailed in the previous chapters), southern women generally shared their culture's sentiment that marriage was a woman's destiny. When she agreed to marry her cousin, Henry Williams, Nannie Hoskins wrote in her diary: "Now I have a purpose in life something to live for." Hoskins, like many other southern women, regarded marriage as a sacred calling. As a wife, she wrote, she would be "something that God has made woman to be, a comforter—Henry when he was lonely came to me to comfort him and with Gods help I will be to him a good & faithful companion."[9]

The importance of marriage is indicated by the frequency with which young women engaged in fortune-telling games to forecast their marital prospects. Unlike the rituals of "coming out" discussed in Chapter 4, these guessing games were initiated by young women without adult guidance. Virginian Amanda Edmonds and her friends wrote men's names on pieces of bread and slept with them next to their hearts; those they dreamed of might be their future husbands. Vicksburg, Mississippi, resident Mary Shannon wrote to her sisters about an article she had read that offered another tip for prognostication. "It says among the customs, girls name their two hands after the two admirers best liked, and then plunge them in clear water, and the hand which dries first will indicate the future husband." Shannon was eager for her sisters, then away at school, to try this method for themselves. "Ann, do plunge one in for John & another for Jim, and let me know the result. I wont have the impudence to suggest which two Emma shall select from her numerous admirers," she teased.[10]

The popularity of such fortune-telling games suggests that—notwithstanding some women's professions of aspiring to "single blessedness"— many young women in the Old South found it impossible to visualize a future as single women. When Virginian Elizabeth Cooley and her sisters gave free reign to their imaginations about the future, marriage was integral to the picture they painted, even though they had no particular men in mind. "Last night after we went to bed," Elizabeth Cooley recorded in her diary in 1845, "we indulged our wild and unruly imaginations flying off through the impenetrable future. . . . We said perhaps I would be in a little house a 'sweet companion in arms.' . . . What! Oh what will we be a doing."[11]

Cooley's fantasy of "a little house" and a "sweet companion" suggests both that southern women fully participated in antebellum American's "cult of domesticity," which regarded home and family as the sine qua non of comfort and fulfillment, and that they could not conceive of the possibility of achieving domesticity outside the institution of marriage. Virginian Elizabeth Ruffin was unusual in her desire to have a "home" but not "a house full of husband and children." "No indeed," she declared; "I congratulate myself on the exclusion of all such agreeables and (as is commonly deem'd) indispens-

ables." But most southern girls did indeed regard husbands as "indispensable," if not "agreeable," at least in part because they saw marriage as the only route to a happy home life.[12]

This was not simply a failure to envision alternatives but a realistic assessment of southern women's prospects. As discussed in Chapter 3, it was exceedingly difficult for single women to earn enough income to support an independent establishment. North Carolinian John Steele inferred as much in a letter to his daughter Ann in 1801, in which he commented that he hoped her single friend, "Miss Nessfield," would keep her company "until you, or she shall be married and have a home of your own." The implication, of course, was that single women could not aspire to their own residence; financial necessity forced most unmarried women to make their homes with their parents or other family members. Half a century later and half a continent away, nineteen-year-old Texan Lizzie Scott confronted the same dilemma. Scott married at least in part because she wanted to escape an unhappy home life. After a stormy exchange with her parents in May 1852, she wrote furiously in her diary: "I am done being cursed and threatened to be *cow hided*. . . . Well now, even if I did not love Will, I should be tempted to marry him, if I had the chance to get away from here." Clearly, southern women who sought to make home "a haven in a heartless world" depended on men to make that home a possibility, if not a reality.[13]

But it was not only economic considerations that limited southern women's options. Cultural values played just as important a role in determining the boundaries of possibility. Socialized to regard themselves as members of families and coming of age in an era that celebrated romantic love, these young women found it was virtually impossible to imagine an unattached life, for they believed that life without love was empty. Sarah Satterlee expressed these sentiments when she explained that her desire for love was the only stumbling block to "single blessedness." "So frightful is this many head[ed] monster called Love," she exclaimed in 1855. "Not at all to me a dear little baby Cupid, smiling and full of playful mischief, but a positively disagreeable creature, which makes a terrible row, just as I settle down into comfortable old-maidish apathy . . . then a certain amount of crying, loss of appetite, and paleness has to be gone through, . . . etc. etc." Much as Satterlee might regret Cupid's claims, she regarded them as inexorable. " 'Sich is life!' " she concluded whimsically.[14]

Perhaps more than their northern counterparts, then, most young women in the Old South ultimately concluded that "single blessedness" was a sham; only marriage could grant these women either economic security or personal happiness. Certainly many young southern women, for all their concerns about unhappy matches, believed that it was only within marriage that women could find happiness. "I am glad to hear that Magg is married," wrote one woman to her friend Matilda Abernathy. "You will not think it strange or foolish in person to marry, if you once get married, they [women] are so much happier if they are so fortunate as to get the right kind of a man."[15]

"LOVE MUST BE ALL ABSORBING":
THE CULT OF ROMANTIC LOVE

For most southern women, "the right kind of man" was one for whom they felt true love and who loved them in return. Lizzie Scott was not alone in her belief that marriage without love would constitute "a hell on earth." Southern women repeatedly affirmed that romantic love was not only the ultimate aim of married life but also the only acceptable reason for getting married. "I can never give my hand to one who does not possess my undivided heart," explained Mary Miller, "for by doing so I would embitter my happiness for Life and mar his peace forever[.]" Eliza Harwood echoed Miller's sentiments in an 1846 letter to the man she would eventually marry: "Unless I can love someone so much that I feel my existence dependent upon him, I do not think I can marry. With me love must be all absorbing." In their near-unanimous emphasis on the importance of "all absorbing" love and "undivided" hearts, young women in the Old South participated in an idealization of romance that constituted a deeply held belief system: the cult of romantic love.[16]

Emma Sue Gordon's diary entries on her feelings for her future husband typified young southern women's search for true love. "I do believe I have never really loved before," she reflected. "This feeling for him which fills my heart, that makes my pulse quicken at the sight of him, & my cheek glow at the pressure of his hand, or the glance of his blue eye, I do believe *this is love*." After her suitor declared his love for her, she wrote: "I love him Journal as I never thought to love anyone, as I have never loved before. . . . I love him from my heart of hearts & wish I could be with him henceforward & forever."[17]

The language that Gordon used in her diary suggests that young women in the Old South learned about romantic love from the sentimental novels that abounded in nineteenth-century America. Some southern girls do, indeed, seem to have taken their cues from literature. Caroline Kean Hill recorded her response to a book in her diary in 1846: "I have read such an entertaining book lately. Say & Seal," she referred to Susan Warner's novel.

"I do not think I shall ever fall in love unless I meet with a 'Linden'"—the romantic lead—she added. "I wonder if I ever shall!" [18]

The theme of romantic love was not limited to romance novels, however. Rather, such novels represented the confluence of the "companionate ideal" of the early national period with the fascination with the "self" that prevailed in Victorian America. By midcentury, most well-to-do, white Americans believed that it was in a companionate marriage based on romantic love that individuals would discover their true selves and find true happiness. The ideal of romantic love crossed lines of gender and region (if not race and class); affluent white men and women, North and South, subscribed to its tenets. But the ideal served particular purposes for young women in the Old South. Romantic love was a powerful—and, for southern women, often the only—form of leverage for nineteenth-century women. While northern wives increasingly found opportunities to exercise influence within "woman's sphere"—the urban, middle-class home—southern wives generally remained subordinate to the planter-patriarchs who held the ultimate power "within the plantation household." Thus, while romantic love was an important ideal throughout antebellum America, it was an essential tool for resistance in the Old South. For southern brides-to-be, the cult of romantic love offered at least the possibility of finding a mate who would love, honor, and cherish his wife—thus reducing, if not directly challenging, male dominance. [19]

Adherence to the cult of romantic love allowed southern women to steer a middle course between their fears of marriage and their desires for marital bliss. Like Caroline Hill, many southern women insisted on holding out for an ideal mate, one they loved unreservedly and who gave them unstinting affection in return. Because of the risks inherent in marriage, young women resolved to marry only if they were sure of a good match. A North Carolina resident summed up young women's ideas about marriage in a letter to her friend Emily Conrad in 1855: "My advice to all is—If you can marry well do so; if not remain as you are." [20]

For young women in the Old South, marrying "well" meant marrying for love. Parents, guardians, and other relatives considered wealth, social standing, and family name to be important attributes of a prospective husband. Mississippian Bazil Kiger expressed deep concern about his sister's engagement to a "milk & cider youth" with poor health and poorer prospects. According to Kiger, although the young man was "good natured, kind in his disposition, [and] moral in his habits," there was "nothing on God's Earth to recommend him as a Husband." By disparaging the suitor's good disposition and asserting that "more than this is necessary in a Husband,"

Kiger indicated that practical factors such as status and money were more important than personal factors such as compatibility and affection.[21]

Southern girls, however, had their own ideas about mate selection. Although most young women hoped to find husbands of whom their parents would approve, they did not believe in marrying simply to please their parents. Southern girls especially shuddered at the thought of marrying for money. A friend of Eliza Cornelia Grantham was horrified at the mere thought. "Adversity can not drive me to the extremity of marrying for mammon," she assured Grantham. "O no I should die at the idea of taking so false a vow."[22]

Only true love, young women were convinced, would bring them happiness in marriage. Young southern women shrank from the idea of marrying for mercenary gain—what Alice Ready called "that curse of humanity." Mary Shannon, who regularly included sprightly accounts of neighborhood romances in her letters, commented with disapproval on a match based on money in an 1858 letter to her sisters: "Miss Georgiana is soon to be united to Mr. Brown or rather his money bags, I say." When a wealthy man proposed to her in 1838, Caroline Brooks was horrified: "To my utter astonishment Mr L Simmons came here on last evening and actually proposed marriage[.] Nothing could be further from my thoughts than the idea of acceeding [sic] to the proposition even if he were possessed of the wealth of the Indias[.] He takes a great deal of pains to have it known that he is rich and goes so far as to say he is independent. Be it so He is welcome to enjoy it.—I want it not. I would rather work for [blank—love?] in a cottage than to possess princely honours with him."[23]

For young women in the Old South, romantic love was more important than "princely honours." Charlestonian Sally Elmore was typical in her resolve not to marry until she met a man who would be "a husband and lover still, who brings you flowers" even in old age. "I shall marry," she told her friend Rosine della Torre, "when I find one whom I know will do this."[24]

Holding out for romantic love was not just about getting flowers, however. Southern women recognized that, in a society in which wives had few legal rights or economic assets, romantic love was the most important source of influence that women possessed in marriage. Thus, by refusing to marry unless and until they found the ideal mate, young women resisted accepting a subordinate role in marriage. As Mary Brown explained to her friend Margaret Steele, she had not yet married because she had not found the right man: "I had never seen the one yet that I cou'd resign my hand and heart to," she explained. "The one," of course, was one for whom a young woman felt she gained sufficient exchange for "resigning" her liberty. Mar-

Successful courtships resulted in emotional (and, less frequently, physical) intimacy. Georgian Loula Kendall indicated the desirability of this ideal in her sketch of cooing "lovebirds" in her journal in 1858. Even women who achieved this desideratum, however, usually insisted on lengthy engagements to consider—and postpone—the new responsibilities that awaited them in marriage. (Special Collections and Archives, Robert W. Woodruff Library, Emory University)

riage might be an uneven exchange in many respects—men gained power, and women lost it—but in at least one way, it could be an even one: one heart for another. Brown promised her friends that she would "take *special care of*" her heart "untill [sic] I am sure and certain of havei[ng a] *good* one in return."[25]

Many young women in the Old South resolved to marry only if they found men who truly loved them—and could thus be trusted to treat them well. Elizabeth Cooley demonstrated this logic in her diary when she reflected: "I would get married if I could obtain . . . the love and confidence of such a one as I could place my confidence on for a partner for life."[26]

Southern girls' fervent conviction that romantic love was an indispensable prerequisite to marriage allowed them to be selective in their choice of partners and to postpone committing to a mate. By insisting on love and devotion before committing themselves to marriage, young women in the Old South demanded a form of emotional insurance within marriage—what Elizabeth Cooley called "confidence." The cult of romantic love thus offered young women a socially acceptable way to resist male dominance. But holding out for the ideal mate was not the only way that southern women exercised control over their relationships. Young women in the Old South had limited options, but they made full use of them in their efforts to bargain for the best possible situation. Therefore, once they had committed themselves to marriage, young women used the lengthy period of engagement to contemplate their decision, negotiate for a favorable position in marriage, and prepare for their new responsibilities.

"STILL SOMEWHAT OF AN OLD MAID IN MY HABITS": LOVE IN LIMBO

As detailed in Chapter 4, young women attempted to determine their potential husband's character and commitment in the process of courtship. In many cases, however, the complicated rituals and constrained interactions of courtship prevented this desired outcome. For this reason, engagement was an indispensable phase in young women's transition from singlehood to married life. Lengthy engagements were commonplace in antebellum America. This transitional period permitted courting couples increased freedom to explore their feelings for one another—and, on occasion, to call off the wedding if the results of this exploration were unsatisfactory. For southern brides-to-be, engagement was a final testing ground that determined their future in important ways. The wedding day might be, as one southern woman put it, "the day to fix my fate," but most young women in the Old South preceded that day with months and even years of forethought, preparation, and negotiation.[27]

Hesitant at the prospect of married life yet convinced that only in marriage could they find true fulfillment, many southern women steered a middle course by insisting upon lengthy engagements. Although confident that "no two people ever were so happy before," Sarah Satterlee refused her fiancé's desire for a quick marriage. "You ask when we shall be married," she wrote to a friend in February 1858, "probably not until the autumn, for it seems to be the general opinion that that is a better time than the spring, and it is decidedly my wish, for you know being still somewhat of an old maid in my habits, I don't much like being hurried about anything, altho' George [her fiancé] rebels a little."[28] Like Satterlee, many young women in the Old South claimed a long engagement as their prerogative, one that took precedence over men's preferences. Thus, lengthy periods of engagement, like the cult of romantic love, served as a form of female resistance that enabled women to prioritize their own desires over those of their future husbands.

While southern men, like Satterlee's rebellious George, tended to be "desperately impatient" to consummate their marriages, southern women were almost universally reluctant to set a definite date. "I am becoming very impatient for our marriage," wrote Waddy Butler to Lucy Wood in 1860, "for I am wearied, tired at times almost to madness, of my present mode of life; I long for a home of my own and some one, to whom I can give my whole confidence and my whole heart, to preside over it." Yet Wood, pleading health concerns, postponed the wedding until the following year. Georgian Loula Kendall, who confided her reservations about both her fiancé (shorter and younger than her ideal mate) and marriage to her diary, used her mother as a scapegoat, claiming in letters to her anxious bridegroom that it was her mother, not Loula herself, who wished to postpone the wedding day. Even the happiest brides insisted on lengthy engagements. Bettie Bernard, although eager to gain her mother's consent to her marriage, did not plan to marry quickly. "I *do not wish* to marry yet," she assured her mother, "have no idea of it for *one* or *two years.*"[29]

Like Bernard, many southern women drew a clear distinction between a promise to marry and the actual wedding day. In the Old South, marriage was not only a rite of passage from one life stage to another; it was also a gateway between a female youth culture of resistance and a southern women's culture of resignation. Small wonder, then, that so many brides-to-be in the antebellum South hesitated on the brink. By postponing their marriages, they prolonged their resistance.

Engagements were more than power plays or delaying tactics, however. Southern women used long engagements as final testing grounds that gave them time to come to terms with their fears of marriage—or, if that failed, to end the relationship. It was not uncommon for engagements to be broken in the antebellum South. Kate Rose's correspondence with her friend Ella Noland revealed that she had been engaged, then "broken off" the engagement, then "partly renewed" the agreement. Planning on a lengthy engagement, Rose correctly pointed out that "strange things may develope [sic] in the course of four years and I am sorry to say that I cant disclose to you now those things for the good but simple reason that I have three years to contemplate those matters & may probably change my mind by the expiration of that time."[30] Southern women insisted on lengthy engagements so that they could have time to "reflect" on their choice before making the "final resolve" and entering the unbreakable bonds of matrimony. They also used this important interval to test their intended husbands' love and devotion, to negotiate for a favorable position in marriage, and to rehearse their roles in marriage. First, however, they had to come to terms with their persistent fears about marriage.

For young women in the Old South, engagement was an important stage of life fraught with meaning—and anxiety as well. Shortly after accepting James McClure's proposal in 1845, Virginian Elizabeth Cooley expressed satisfaction with her choice of a life partner and optimism about their shared future in her diary. "I have long sought for one on whose confidence to rely," she reflected, "to whom I can without restraint, pour out my inmost secrets 'from out their thousand secret cells,' one who can love and confide and bear with me through all the various vicissitudes of life; for such a one I long have sought and now I (think) have found. May such be the case." [31] But other southern women instead spent their engagement in "a most doubtful unsettled frame of mind," as Lucy Randolph Page wrote regarding her sister, Mary Francis Page.[32] Indeed, for many—perhaps most—southern women, engagement prompted a severe crisis during which they questioned their affection for their intended husbands, their fiancés' degree of commitment, and their own ability to adapt to the demands of marriage.

Although courtships were often conducted through correspondence, engagements usually were contracted in person. As a result, written accounts of proposals are limited. Elizabeth Cooley, however, took the time to record the details of her marriage proposal in her diary in 1845. Her account tallies with the hints offered in other women's writings and offers insight into this important encounter. Cooley wrote: "Last Sunday J. W. McClure came here and it was cold and misty, but nevertheless *we* went into the garden and stayed about two hours . . . and during that time made a bargain between us that is to last forever . . . a bargain that is to seal our happiness or ruin for life. Our fates hereafter will inevitably be linked as one, and I hope, and pray, that nothing but harmony and love will accompany us as way farers through this life." [33]

Like other young women in the Old South, Cooley took advantage of the relative privacy offered to courting couples to speak privately with her lover about their future. Although hopeful that "nothing but harmony and love" would characterize the pair's relationship, Cooley also recognized the tremendous significance of the step she had taken—ensuring "happiness or ruin for life." The results would be most important for the bride-to-be, for while husband and wife were "one," that one, by law, was the husband. Finally, Cooley's use of the word "inevitably" suggests her awareness of the limited options available to southern women; as a former schoolteacher and

POPPING THE QUESTION.

Although women had the power to accept or reject offers of marriage, "popping the question" was a male prerogative. This 1846 lithograph of a marriage proposal in progress represents the man as a supplicant and the woman as fully in control of the encounter—a situation that would reverse itself the moment she said "yes." (Library of Congress)

daughter-at-home, Cooley knew only too well that marriage was the best "bargain" a woman could hope to make in the antebellum South.

Engagements often took place without parental knowledge (as Cooley's emphasis on her own and her beloved's agency suggests), but most southern couples sought parental approval once they came to an agreement. Indeed, many couples sought not only parental approval but also the best wishes of all their friends and relatives. As Tristrim Skinner wrote to his fiancée, Eliza Harwood, in 1848, "I truly desire that our union may not only afford us true & lasting happiness, but that it may be looked upon with pleasure by all who have any possible interest in it." It was only in rare instances, however, that parents or guardians refused their approval. Having exercised considerable control over the process of courtship, parents and guardians usually gave their stamp of approval to women's choice.[34]

The difficulty was not external opposition but internal conflict. For many southern women, engagement triggered a "marriage trauma," forcing them to ponder the meaning of marriage and often causing them tremendous anxiety. In many cases, becoming engaged seemed a matter for mourning rather than celebration. Brides-to-be complained of a "spirit of gloom" hovering over them, described themselves as "frightfully oppressed by the blues," and expressed a sense of "fear and trembling" as the wedding day drew near. Some southern women even manifested symptoms of psychosomatic illness during their engagements.[35]

Single women friends and acquaintances regarded such feelings as natural and understandable, demonstrating remarkable empathy for their engaged peers in the letters they circulated among themselves. Hearing that her friend Virginia Pearl was engaged and "terribly low-spirited about it," Mary Virginia Hawes repeated the sage comment of a mutual acquaintance that the bride-to-be "has not got her own consent yet, I reckon."[36]

Southern women had good reason to suffer from anxiety, depression, and "neuralgia" during their engagements, for they correctly viewed their impending marriages as life-changing—even identity-changing—events. "The important change which is so soon to take place, Occupies a large share of my thoughts," Caroline Brooks wrote in 1838, "and will not suffer my mind to dwell long on any other subject." The change was indeed a momentous one. Apologizing to a friend for a poorly written letter, Mary Polk explained that she was to be married the following week. "*My nerves are very much agitated,*" she wrote with emphasis. "*How can you expect a young Lady just on the eve of matrimony to be quite herself?*" Indeed, "a young Lady just on the eve of matrimony" was no longer "quite herself," for when women married, they assumed a new identity. Anticipating her wedding day, Nannie Hoskins reflected, "One year from now, *I will no longer be myself as I am* but *the good wife of a good man.*"[37]

Becoming "the good wife of a good man" (or a bad one, for that matter) had profound repercussions in the nineteenth-century South. When a woman married, she surrendered her legal identity, her fortune, indeed, her very existence, to her husband. Under the legal convention of coverture, husband and wife became one—and that one was the husband. As a *femme covert*, or "covered woman," a married woman could not own property, represent herself in a court of law, or testify against her husband. Moreover, the doctrine of marital unity that coverture represented meant that the marriage contract, while decidedly unequal, was generally permanent. While in the antebellum North, state legislatures adopted increasingly liberal divorce laws, enabling wives to escape unhappy marriages with greater ease, southern courts and congressmen maintained a conservative commitment to marital unity, refusing to grant divorces except in cases of extreme physical cruelty, the wife's adultery, or the husband's inability to provide for his family or to produce heirs. By denying married women a legal identity and curtailing their economic rights, marriage law and southern lawmakers ensured that southern wives had few avenues of resistance.[38]

The practice of assuming the husband's name was symbolic of a young woman's new—and permanent—identity as "a wife." Southern girls were keenly aware of this symbolism. After James Lilly proposed to her, Caroline Brooks practiced writing her new name, "Mrs Caroline M Lilly," in her diary. "Tomorrow fortnight," wrote Penelope Skinner in 1840, "I am to become Mrs Dr Warren." The night before her own wedding, Emma Sue Gordon, who had previously called herself "Emma Sue Gordon Spinster," noted in her diary: "Well Journal this is I suppose the last I will write as Miss Gordon."[39] The stress that young women placed on their impending name change suggests their awareness of the legal ramifications of marriage and their anxieties about entering the bonds of matrimony. Marriage, they understood, marked both the adoption of a new female identity as a married woman and a diminished ability to engage in a culture of resistance.

In addition to their more general concerns about marriage, women feared the changes that marriage would bring to their lives, even in the best of marriages. Young women well knew that marriage would bring new and demanding duties. Southern girls may not have received extensive practical instruction in the details of housewifery, but they knew from observing— and occasionally assisting—their mothers how arduous keeping house in the antebellum South was. Moreover, they understood the connection between fulfilling household responsibilities and retaining their husbands' affections. Anna Hendree suggested prospective brides' awareness of their future duties—and their reluctance to assume them prematurely—when she wrote to her intended husband that "marriage involves so much of responsibility, so much of care that I cannot enter lightly on it."[40]

Virginian Bettie Bernard explained her desire for a long engagement in terms of the responsibilities of marriage, which she realized differed from the romance of courtship. "I know," she told her family, "that now I have no cares, my wishes are all gratified, whilst were I married, there would be many things, that I would have to do, because it was my duty." Like the southern belles discussed in Chapter 4, Bernard was in no hurry to exchange self-gratification for self-sacrifice.[41]

Should a young woman be disposed to overlook the new duties that would become hers after the wedding day, friends and family members stood by to offer pointed reminders, as well as practical advice. When Anna Higginbotham announced her engagement, her sister congratulated her, but she also reminded her of the duties shortly to become hers. "You have no doubt dear Anna considered how responsible then will be your situation: for the wife has her husbands happiness in a great measure in her hands—and besides that we are answerable in a *manner* for the example we set those under our influence," she wrote. Young women in the Old South learned early in life that they were "responsible" for and to others, but after an extended period of self-improvement and selfish pleasures, many were reluctant to enter a permanent "situation" in which they would be "answerable" to another for the rest of their lives.[42]

Southern brides regarded the prospect of wifely responsibilities with some trepidation. After agreeing to marry Mr. Cooke, Mary Page wrote: "I dont know whether to feel happy or horrified at the step I've taken." Nannie Hoskins repeatedly begged God for "*strength, patience & forbearance*" to fulfill her new responsibilities. Mary Virginia Hawes explained her conflicted feelings in an 1856 letter:

> Never—I say it gladly, thankfully—never for one instant since my betrothal, have I doubted the wisdom of my choice, or contemplated this life-long union except with happy hope. Every hour of intercourse, every letter has seemed to draw our hearts more closely together,—yet there are times when the sense of the importance of such a trust as the happiness of another, and that one the best-beloved, makes me tremble. There are many and solemn thoughts that come to me in hours of solitary reflection. I never before knew and felt my own deficiencies as I do now. I shudder at the thought of impairing his usefulness or clouding his life with disappointment.[43]

Dreaming of happiness but dreading disappointment, southern brides-to-be utilized the interlude between accepting a proposal and saying their vows to test their intended husbands' love, bargain for loving consideration, and practice for their new roles as wives.

"THE FINAL RESOLVE": THE TEST OF LOVE

Southern women shared the nineteenth century's idealization of marriage as a relationship of mutual love and respect. Yet at the same time that southerners participated in the shift "from patriarchy to companionship," couples in the South confronted major obstacles to true companionship. In addition to their superior legal and economic power, southern husbands often held the advantages of age, experience, and education over their wives.

Only a husband's devotion to his wife, therefore, countered the power that men held over women even in the most intimate of relationships. Because romantic love was often the only form of control that southern women had in what one historian has described as "the political economy of marriage," it was important to test and strengthen it. As Mary Page expressed it in a letter to her friend Lucy McGuire, "It must take a world of love to make married life happy."[44]

Not surprisingly, then, young women resisted committing themselves until they were sure of their intended husbands' devotion. Mary Cooke did not engage herself to be married until she found the "one whom I love most sincerely and whose affection for me has been too plainly shewn by every word and act for me to doubt any longer his devotion." But even after engagement, southern women worried about the staying power of their bridegrooms' affection. Emma Sue Gordon, although deliriously happy at the prospect of marrying her cousin, Robert Perkins, was terrified that his love might fade with the passage of time. "Oh if he should cease to love me when I am his (& I fear he will) or if his love should diminish & his loving caressing ways wear off, after I am his wife how deep will be my disappointment," she wrote.[45]

The connection that Gordon drew between her fiancé's love for her and his "loving caressing ways" was an important one; like Gordon, many southern brides relied on romantic love to temper their husbands' dominance and guarantee them marital happiness. The cult of romantic love thus not only offered young women a winnowing tool during courtship but also a form of power within marriage. Before relinquishing their freedom, then, southern women often insisted on proofs of their future husband's love—and, relatedly, their willingness to concede certain privileges. Looking back from the vantage point of her first anniversary, Bettie Maney Kimberly told her sister that during the Kimberlys' "grand Champagne supper," "Baby set up a yell." Although John Kimberly at first "insisted upon my going to see what was the matter with 'his darling little pet baby,'" his wife refused. As she explained to her sister: "I told him I did not promise to do it that time a year ago and I did not intend to do anything I did not promise to do then."[46]

More frequently, young women suggested that they hoped their husbands would yield to their wishes at least insofar is it pertained to remaining near their homes, families, and friends—an important consideration in the antebellum South, where men on the make often evinced a "disposition to migrate" from the worn-out tobacco fields of the Chesapeake to the fertile cotton fields of the Old Southwest. Some brides insisted on being able to visit their friends. Ann Eliza Wright whimsically proposed making it a condition of marriage that her husband would take her to visit her friend Mary Carrington. In a light-hearted, teasing letter, Anna Hendree informed her husband-to-be that she had no intention of yielding to his every whim. "Per-

haps one of these days you may find some *simple hearted, wild, romantic girl*," she wrote, "who would even resign a visit to an old schoolfriend where *beaux*, and pleasure were in abundance promised, simply to gratify you. I am sure I would not be so *silly!*" In letters like these, southern women indicated that while they had resigned themselves to marriage, they refused to give up the female friendships that fostered their resistance.[47]

Because so much hinged upon a husband's love for his wife, brides-to-be often subjected their fiancés to tests of devotion. Responding to a despondent letter from Waddy Butler, in which he worried that he would never earn enough money to support her in style, Lucy Wood responded that she was willing to "endure a life of poverty" with him but questioned whether his misgivings indicated that he was "ready and willing to renounce all claims to [her] heart and hand." "If your love is too weak to stand the test then tell me so," she commanded, "for if this is the case it is not worth having." Similarly, Anna Hendree offered her fiancé the chance to terminate their agreement if he felt the responsibility of supporting her was too great. "Remember the responsibility is a great one, for I *require*, not wealth or style but *perfect independence*," she admonished him. "And years must pass ere this can be obtained. . . . Now answer me candidly . . . would you not feel freer, happier *if for the time you were released*[?] . . . Remember if at any time you find your task more than you can perform you have but to say so, and you are free."[48]

Although these women phrased their tests in terms of their fiancés' ability to support their wives, their questions also were designed to elicit professions of deep devotion from their husbands-to-be; their letters suggested that if the men hesitated at all in declaring their love, the women would call the weddings off. Interestingly, the almost-menacing letters in which southern women threatened to end their engagements were significantly more direct than their courtship letters, which were discreet to the point of obscurity. In engagement, the stakes were still higher than during courtship; at this stage of life, however, the most important consideration was not protecting a woman's sexual reputation but ensuring her future happiness.

Some women subjected their lovers to a series of tests. Like the heroines of the "double proposal plot" romance novels to which many southern girls were addicted, young women might initially reject a suitor—or call off a wedding—only to resume the relationship once they had received assurances of undying love and devotion, which might result in a more egalitarian match. Anna Hendree illustrates this pattern well. In addition to questioning his ability to support her, Hendree also tested her husband-to-be's devotion by insisting on being able to choose her own company in her new home, demanding a lengthy engagement, and reminding him that she had other suitors waiting in the wings. "I know I have tested you," she wrote in 1852. "I believe now I know you *perfectly*—*bravely* have you endured all, and I thank you a thousand times for your kind, your generous, your true, appreciation of my character."[49]

As in fiction, real-life lovers usually passed the test and convinced their fiancées to go forward with the wedding. After a long period of single life, courtship, and engagement, the majority of southern women eventually entered the bonds of matrimony, hoping that romantic love would soften the outlines of patriarchy and that within marriage, they would find true happiness. "I sometimes resolve to write and release you," Anna Hendree wrote to Thomas Norwood in 1851, "but then my own heart rises in rebellion and I fear to do so lest I should blight forever, my happiness and our future peace. And I determine to reflect even more than ever, ere the final resolve is mad[e]."[50]

"STRANGE CONTRADICTIONS": LOVE AND POWER

Southern women tried to protect themselves from an abuse of male power by holding out for the perfect mate—one who showed them love and respect. Of course, the corollary was that young women had to return their fiancés' devotion. Although less frequently than they expressed concern about their intended husbands' feelings, some brides-to-be worried about their ability to reciprocate their fiancés' love. Mary Francis Page hesitated on the brink of engagement for two years. Although certain that her suitor "*loves me with his whole soul*," she worried that her own feelings did not match his. "Unless I love him devotedly I have no strength to commit my destinies to his keeping," she reflected. "T'would be a sin against God & him to give a hand when the heart is not with it." When young women yielded their hearts, they relinquished much of their ability to negotiate for a favorable position in marriage—and to resist their subordinate position in southern society.[51]

Many young women in the Old South viewed marriage as an inherently hierarchical relationship. Mary Francis Page hoped for "a protector to love & guide me." When she finally "surrendered" to her husband-to-be, she wrote: "'Tis a comfort now to think that I have [him] to shield and guide me through life's trials." Speaking of herself and her future husband in the third person, Anna Hendree wrote: "*They* had promised to brave the world *together. Together* were they to begin the voyage of life, *the one as guide and pro-*

tector, the other as *friend* and comforter." (Both Hendree and her bridegroom clearly understood which individual was "guide and protector" and which was "friend and comforter"; the assumption that the male would guide and the female would comfort was so ingrained that it did not need to be stated explicitly.) Vicksburg, Mississippi, bride Emma Shannon Crutcher likewise expected her new husband to take "the reins" in their relationship. He would be, she wrote, "the *head* and governor, the *monarch* of my little kingdom." Georgian Gertrude Thomas summed up the expected relationship between husband and wife when she wrote: "True to my sex, I delight in *looking up* and love to feel my woman's weakness protected by man's superior strength." [52]

During engagement, brides and grooms prepared to assume their respective positions in the southern patriarchy, with wives under the firm, albeit loving, control of their husbands. Preparation for marriage thus represented an inversion of the power relations of the "beau monde," in which young women (as discussed in Chapter 4) delighted in their unaccustomed power over men. Georgia bride Elizabeth Lucas received a letter from her South Carolina suitor, "Cuthbert," in which he commented with "exceeding great wonder" on the hold she had on him during their courtship. "I will bow to no man;—no one shall ever get the mastery of me," he proudly proclaimed his independence. But, he added with some bewilderment: "And yet a weak girl can rule me by the turning of her finger: I am the veriest slave to her that crawls; & strange to say, I wear her chains not only patiently but am content to do so, yes & find a pride & pleasure in so doing." "Cuthbert" revealed the contradictions between southern patriarchy—which assumed men's dominance over women—and southern courtship—which sanctioned women's "rule" over men. Small wonder that he concluded his reverie: "What a mystery is the heart of man!" [53]

But once southern men secured women's promise to marry, they reasserted their dominance. Erastus Hopkins, a gentle soul who offered frequent professions of his affection, nonetheless set out his preferred terms in an 1835 letter to his fiancée, Sarah Bennett. Disapproving of a "Mr C." whose "feelings" for a young lady had overcome his "good sense & reason," he explained that although in courtship, "the power of the ladies over men is very great," in day-to-day life, it was inappropriate for women to wield power over men. "A gentleman appears to great disadvantage when he allows himself to be so complete at the disposal of woman, when nature has ordained that things sh[oul]d be the other way," he pronounced. [54]

Isabella Mackay's letters from her fiancé, Richard Love Johnson, demonstrated considerably more forcefulness. Johnson alluded to women's power in courtship, referring to southern belles collectively as "that fickle, deceitful, bewitching race of creatures who wear petticoats and lead poor men astray." He then made it clear that he would not tolerate "any such rebellious and disrespectful conduct" from his future wife. Referring to a mutual acquaintance, a male friend he referred to as "Mr. S.," he devised what he called "a plan to keep you all in order," including asking Mr. S. to "make you a good docile little wife for me." If that plan failed, he added, he would take more drastic action: "The fact is I am getting so incensed at your insubordination that I will return some time, like Othello, and smother my little Desdemona—yes I'll smother you—with kisses." Johnson's final sexual innuendo did not erase—and may even have highlighted—his evident intention to claim the upper hand in his relationship with his bride-to-be. Perhaps Bella's distrust of her fiancé—who had been on his "Ps and Qs" during the couple's courtship but who now warned his intended bride, "the more you know me the less you will like me"—contributed to her reluctance to set a date for the wedding (the "insubordination" to which Johnson referred). Johnson's somewhat ominous admonition, "I will expect you to do better after we are married," may also have caused Bella some concern; certainly it indicated that he intended to put a stop to Bella's "rebellious" tendencies after the wedding and mold his "fickle" and "disrespectful" fiancée into a "good docile little wife." [55]

Future husbands often assumed the role of adviser in the letters they wrote their brides-to-be. Although he promised not to give his fiancé a "moral lecture," Tristrim Skinner could not resist urging her to study seriously in her last winter before the pair's planned marriage. "You should prepare yourself for the very important change in life which you have determined upon," he advised, "in order that in your new character, your future course may be characterized as much by its happiness, its nobleness, and its usefulness, as the past has been by its brilliancy[.]" [56] Skinner's phrasing reflected his understanding that marriage represented a female rite of passage—it was an "important change in life," he wrote—that marked the assumption of a new identity—a "new character"—in which women undertook a new role, or "future course," defined by "usefulness" to others rather than by self-aggrandizing "brilliancy." The scope of this change made it especially important that young women in the Old South use the period of engagement to "prepare" themselves to enter adulthood.

While brides-to-be were expected to accept, and even welcome, advice from their husbands-to-be (Loula Kendall requested of her fiancé, "Let me know all you admire most in woman, so I can aspire to be what is excellent in your sight."), giving advice was a male prerogative. In her diary, Gertrude Clanton revealed the potential for force that underlay men's paternalistic counsel. She and her fiancé, Jeff Thomas, argued over his career; she hoped that he would become a physician, while he planned to become a planter. "A little misunderstanding occurred. All my fault though," she framed the exchange. "I made use of some remark jesting, and he looked up with such a look of sterness [sic]! It startled me! and for a moment my old feeling of pride o'ercame me and I felt the blood gush to my cheek. I had almost said too much. Thank Heaven! I did refrain and now I love him more, oh how much more than ever. Oh Love thou art formed of such strange contradictions!" Indeed, entering marriage in the Old South was a matter of "strange contradictions." While women sought love in marriage, they also prepared to yield to their husbands' wishes and to learn that any problems were "all my fault." Rather than rebelling against this situation, most brides, like Clanton, accepted it, thus taking an important step away from resistance—and toward resignation. "That one look accomplished so much," she reflected. "I respected him more then than I ever had before." [57]

Young women in the Old South tried to use the romantic ideal to their advantage during their engagements, hoping that love would soften the harsh outlines of patriarchy and blunt husbands' power over their wives. But as the wedding day approached, the power of love lent itself instead toward a reassertion of patriarchy, encouraging southern women to accede to the demands of a male-dominated society and to respect their husbands' authority. The cult of romantic love proved to be a shaky basis on which to build egalitarian marriages in the Old South.[58]

"TO BEGIN THE VOYAGE OF LIFE": REHEARSING ROLES

Although southern women attempted to use the period of engagement to negotiate a favorable position in marriage—or, if that failed, to call off the engagement—once women accepted marriage proposals and acquiesced to patriarchal relationships, they found another purpose in engagement: practicing for marriage. In their correspondence and their interactions with their future husbands, brides-to-be rehearsed their roles in marriage, discussing with their future husbands the purpose of matrimony and their respective positions within it. During this phase of engagement, southern women shifted their focus from resisting matrimony itself to resisting male power within marriage. Although young women in the Old South gained certain concessions as moral advisers and domestic authorities, they were unable to translate feminine influence into female resistance. Instead, the cult of romantic love that women had hoped to use to enhance their status within the institution of marriage and increase their control over their own lives proved to be an effective force in reconciling women to their subordinate status and introducing them to a culture of resignation.

Engaged couples in the antebellum South, in keeping with the companionate ideal, agreed that the purpose of marriage was mutual happiness. "Through the remainder of our lives we are to journey hand in hand," wrote Tristrim Skinner to his fiancée, Eliza Harwood, in 1849, "it being the chief business, as it will be the chief pleasure, of each, to render the other perfectly happy." Similarly, William Henry Wills reveled in the prospect of marriage in an 1835 letter to Anna Whitaker: "How sweet it will be for us to think alike, to act alike; and influenced by the [only?] pure motive, striving each to advance the others interest here." Women recorded similar thoughts on marriage. Nannie Hoskins expected her wedding day to be "the happiest day of my life," the day that "Henry will be mine & I His, we will love, comfort & honor each other." [59]

Although the ultimate goal of marriage—mutual happiness—was the same for husbands and wives, their roles were different. Even before marriage, young women prepared to take on new responsibilities as domestic managers. Writing to his fiancée, Tristrim Skinner informed her that his own father was eager to welcome her as "a wife & a daughter in the same person," as well as "mistress of [his son's] household." Men, on the other hand, were expected to take on the responsibility of making a name for themselves in the world and, if not a fortune, a respectable living for their family. "To you & your happiness you know my future life is deddicated [sic]," Julian Moore wrote to his fiancée, Blannie Southall, in 1863. "I shall ever strive to be worthy of the trust you have put in my hands, to this end my life & energies will ever be at work." Waddy Butler assured his bride-to-be, Lucy Wood, that he planned to change his "idle listless life" and enter "man's estate" as a lawyer. Only then would he be qualified to "come for [his] betrothed." [60] Women's and men's different roles in marriage were prefigured by their actions and their correspondence during engagement.

As they anticipated their wedding day, many southern women took a new interest in housekeeping duties. Once she had agreed to marry Thomas Randall, Laura Wirt, who had previously disparaged housekeeping activities as "disagreeable occupations," took a new interest in caring for her clothing and in becoming "an excellent manager" of her slave maid. As Gertrude Clanton prepared for her marriage in 1852, she recorded her household activities, including gathering produce from the garden, making pickles, and straightening up the house. "How very domestic I am!" she exclaimed in some surprise, adding that it was "quite a transformation really!" These daughters-at-home-turned-domestic-divas might have little control over their husbands' career choices, but they could—like their northern peers—stake out a power base by establishing authority over domestic affairs.[61]

In addition to preparing for their role as housekeeper, young wives-to-be also rehearsed for the other duties of a wife: encouraging a husband to be diligent at his business and to be moral in his behavior. Despite southern men's penchant for dispensing paternal wisdom, antebellum southerners shared the Victorian belief that naturally pious women were appropriate spiritual advisers. This gave future wives an important, although limited, avenue of influence. Young women often urged their future husbands to read the Bible on a daily basis. Many brides-to-be, like Nannie Hoskins, prayed for strength to "exert a good influence" over her husband-to-be; "if I do my duty in this," she wrote, "I shall feel that I have not lived in vain."[62]

Women's "good influence" could extend to worldly, as well as spiritual, matters. Although wives were not permitted to advise their husbands on the choice of a career, nineteenth-century southerners expected wives to support their husbands in whatever careers the men chose, taking an active "interest" in their husbands' work and, on occasion, even spurring them on to undertake that work. Lucy Wood urged her fiancé, Waddy Butler, to overcome his feelings of depression, devote his energies to his career, and become "a wiser and a better man." Butler quickly took the hint, apologizing for his "unmanly weakness and pitiful despair" and assuring his bride-to-be that her encouragement would enable him to succeed. "Your love, dear Lucy, will, I trust, prove the means of my regeneration," he wrote.[63]

So long as their wifely influence reinforced conventional gender roles and did not challenge male prerogatives, married women in the Old South, like their northern counterparts, could tentatively begin to explore the possibilities of female influence. However, this influence had clear limits, and the boundaries of female influence were more constricted in the South than in the North. A southern wife might urge her husband to read the Bible, but she could not enforce his moral behavior, as northern women did by forming moral reform and prohibition societies. She was permitted—indeed, expected—to support him in his career, but she was not allowed any say in his choice of occupation. Moreover, as the wives of southern professionals increasingly imitated their northern counterparts by providing a comfortable home life to balance the competitiveness of the male workplace, they discovered new forms of marital oppression that were not relieved by increased access to the public sphere.[64]

While they encouraged their fiancés to devote themselves to their work, brides also learned to suppress their own desires for their lovers' company and to prioritize (men's) professional success over (women's) personal satisfaction. Anna Hendree practiced the self-denial of a wife supporting her husband in his career in her engagement letters to her schoolteacher-fiancé Thomas Norwood in the 1850s. "You say every impulse of your nature bears you north [to her], and that you are tempted to dismiss your School forever," she responded to an 1851 missive. "*Dismiss* such thoughts. Performing *every duty, then* will come the reward." In the meantime, she promised, "I shall write often to cheer you." Similarly, Mary Miller urged her fiancé, Charles Davis, not to leave his work in Richmond to visit her at her family's Virginia plantation. "As to your comming [sic] up it is what I can not expect of you — and therefore I will not bid you come," she wrote, adding, "You have repeately [sic] told me that your business was of such a nature that it required your undivided attention and I can not ask you to neglect that for me[.]" In letters like these, women offered — or agreed to — a model of marriage in which husband and wife had distinct roles; the man would devote himself to his work with might and main; the woman would support him without question or complaint.[65]

Although both husband and wife had obligations in this model of marriage, women's obligation to encourage their husbands in their careers gave men the upper hand in marriage in concrete ways. Lucy Wood told her fiancé that the decision of where to make the newlyweds' home was his to make since his intended career as a lawyer would be the most important criterion. "I think it would be much better for you to . . . choose your home wherever you may think best," she wrote, "and to commence business, . . . of course you know much more of such matters than I do." Because the choice of a home would affect the couple's income, Wood left the decision up to her husband-to-be, even though this might well mean moving from her native state of Virginia to Florida. "I will willingly accede to your wishes," she vowed. Likewise, Virginian Bettie Bernard pledged to "cheerfully" move to Florida with her husband-to-be, even though he offered to remove to her home state to allow her to remain near her family. "Of course I would be happier near my friends, yet I would not urge him to move as I know that it is best for him to be here," she explained to her mother.[66]

The writings of Gertrude Clanton, Lucy Wood, Bettie Bernard, and other southern brides-to-be suggest that during the period of engagement, the balance of power within the relationship tipped in the groom's favor; while women sought marriages based on love at least in part because they hoped such matches would protect them from abuses of patriarchal power, as the wedding day neared, they found that love also held the potential to bolster husbands' control over their wives. This stage of life thus helps to reveal the complexities of elite women's place in the Old South as both privileged and oppressed members of the southern patriarchy. In order to gain the privileges of elite southern womanhood, young women had to accept the strictures of white male dominance. To come of age, a southern girl had to relinquish resistance and adopt resignation.

"SO CRUEL A PROOF OF MY AFFECTION": MIGRATION AND MARRIAGE

Ironically, southern women's cult of romantic love helped to destroy their female youth culture of resistance. The case of migration vividly illustrates this pattern. Bettie Bernard's decision to relinquish her ties to her family in order to advance her husband's career was not uncommon in the Old South. As men responded to the lure of the frontier, marriage increasingly meant migration from the established Upper South to the crude Lower South. Migration on this scale meant enduring not only "the privations and inconveniences of a new country" but also prolonged—or even permanent—separation from friends and family members. For southern women, who were accustomed to operating within a network of friends, neighbors, and kin, this represented a major sacrifice in the name of romantic love.[67]

Many women regarded the prospect of migration with profound dread. Inviting her friend and cousin Emma Nicholson to her wedding, Mary Massenburg remarked: "I fear we wont have much of an opportunity to be with each other after this, as it is my destiny to make my home in a distant clime and among strangers. You cant imagine how much I dread the idea of parting with my loved ones." Remarking on the marriage and migration of a mutual acquaintance in a letter to Matilda Abernathy, Mary Moor reflected, "I should think it a great undertaking to quit all of my friends for the sake of one and go so far from any of my kindred."[68]

Laura Wirt's response to her fiancé's plan to move from her comfortable home in the nation's capital to a crude cabin in the newly established Florida territory typified young women's anxieties about migration. "I cannot endure the thought! The very prospect breaks my heart!" she exclaimed. As her departure date drew closer, her fears increased. "My heart falters," she wrote shortly before her marriage (and migration). "It dies within me when I think how soon I must bid (perhaps) a last farewell to those who have so tenderly cherished me from my infancy and who have been so closely entwined with my dearest affections. I kill myself by dwelling on this, and I must not do it. It is unjust to one who would without a sigh resign everything for me."[69] The question of migration throws into sharp relief the connections between love and power in southern brides' lives. Despite Laura Wirt's conviction that her husband-to-be would "resign everything" for her, in reality, it was usually the brides who resigned themselves to their fiancés' wishes.

Some southern women capitalized on romantic love to persuade their husbands to resist the "disposition to emigrate." Speculating on a match between Caroline Moore and a Mr. Caban, who would move with his young bride far away from her family, Mary Moor commented hopefully, "I havent the least idea but what he will use her well perhaps she made him promise if she was dissatisfied that he would move back[.]" Mary Virginia Hawes wrote admiringly about Margaretta Mitchell, who flatly refused to remain in Kentucky with her "pigmy" husband "eight years her junior," despite the fact that his career was thriving there. "Her powers of ruling *tickle* me most wonderfully," Hawes jested, "am half in the notion of engaging myself to the handsomest little boy of my acquaintance—it's a convenient plan. . . . No cross words, or slamming doors as the 'lords of creation,' stalks off *dignifiedly* angry leaving you shedding tears by the tubful. . . . Only fancy the exquisite delight of sovereign [sic] power over one's husband." Of course, at the same time that Hawes's comments suggested the hold that beloved wives could hold over considerate husbands, they also revealed that her vision of having "power over one's husband" was not the usual pattern for southern brides.[70]

Indeed, in most cases, southern brides concluded that true love required them to accede to their husbands' preferences. Laura Wirt shrank from the prospect of moving from the Upper South to the southern frontier. "I should be glad," she confided to her friend Louisa Cabell Carrington, "that he would not make so cruel a proof of my affection." But ultimately, she decided that love demanded the sacrifice. "It would go very hard with me to be transplanted to this new country," she reflected, "and there is but one man under the moon for whose sake I would consent to it."[71]

Like Laura Wirt, many southern women felt that true love meant that they should be willing to make any sacrifice to marry the right man. Nannie Hoskins explained: "Long since have I determined not to marry any man that I would not be willing to go to the furthermost parts of the earth with him if necessary. And so it is I love Henry and will live with him any where." Bettie Bernard, a Virginian who traveled to Florida in hopes of improving her health, met and fell in love with a Floridian. Although sorrowful at the prospect of a lengthy separation from her parents and siblings, she assured them: "I've weighed the matter well. . . . Not only will I have to leave the home of my childhood, & the many loved & long tried friends in that house; but also many comforts & conveniences. . . . I have thought *calmly & seriously;*

yes I have *counted the cost*. Although the sacrifice will be *very great, I can make it cheerfully.*"[72]

Like Bettie Bernard, many southern brides-to-be believed that it was necessary to give up everything familiar—family and friends, comfort and convenience—to attain romantic love. Moreover, because of the tremendous importance they attached to romantic love, they concluded that they should not merely make the "sacrifice," but make it "cheerfully." Romantic love thus facilitated the transition from resistance to resignation.

"IF MY LOT IS NOT HAPPY, . . . IT MUST BE MY FAULT": THE POLITICAL ECONOMY OF MARRIAGE

Young women in the Old South insisted on marriages based on romantic love, hoping that a relationship of mutual affection would also prove to be a relationship of mutual interests in which a husband would consider his wife's welfare first and foremost. Yet once they committed themselves to marriage, brides-to-be acquiesced to a model of marriage characterized by rigid gender roles and by the expectation that men's success—not women's welfare—took priority. Thus, the emotional leverage that southern brides-to-be sought all too often ended up being wielded in favor of their husbands-to-be rather than in their own interests. As they made final preparations for their wedding day, young women recognized this reality and readjusted their expectations of marriage to accord with it.

Young women's reflections on the eve of their weddings frequently suggested that wives would bear a greater responsibility for ensuring the success of the marriage than would their husbands. While some women, consistent with the companionate ideal, expected men to bear an equal share of the burden, men generally viewed marital happiness as the wife's responsibility. As Ella Noland prepared for her marriage in 1852, she received two letters, one from a female friend and one from her brother, reflecting these different views. Cornelia Taylor wrote to congratulate her friend on her good fortune, saying, "I trust he will make you very happy." But Richard Noland wrote: "I doubt not you will be happy for happiness in married life depends in a great degree upon the wife & any woman of good sense & good temper will make a good wife." While both correspondents agreed that happiness was the goal of marriage, they differed in their assumptions regarding who was responsible for creating and maintaining that happiness.[73]

Most women understood, however, that the responsibility lay with them. After months and even years of engagement, most southern brides-to-be accepted the task of maintaining a relationship as the cost of romantic love. While they continued to hope for marital bliss, they placed the onus of responsibility on themselves, rather than on their husbands-to-be. As Mary Page put it in a letter to her friend Lucy McGuire, "If my lot is not happy it seems to me it must be my fault."[74]

By accepting a subordinate role in marriage, young women took an important step toward accepting the inferior status assigned to elite women in the Old South. For many southern women, the wedding day would prove to be a threshold between a culture of resistance and one of resignation, as well as a transition from the relative freedom of girlhood to the adult responsibilities of womanhood. Small wonder, then, that so many "blushing brides" hesitated for so long before taking the "fatal step" of matrimony.

FROM SANCTIFIED LOVE TO LARD AND SAUSAGES: LOULA KENDALL ROGERS

Louisa Winifred Kendall—"Loula"—was an incurable romantic. For years before she met her future husband, James Henry Rogers, she filled her journal with daydreams of the perfect mate, a noble figure who would closely resemble the romantic heroes of the sentimental novels to which the young Georgian was addicted. Although Loula, who pronounced herself averse to two things above all others—sewing and marriage—repeatedly expressed her wish to remain single for life, that desire ran counter to her conviction that love was the ultimate aim of existence. As she wrote in 1860, "What are all the joys of earth, the fleeting pleasures, pomp and glory without love? *Nothing!*" Loula's certainty that to be a wife was "woman's highest mission" on earth was reinforced by her strong religious beliefs, which taught her that marriage was "Heaven's holiest institution." "I know marriage is right," she reflected in her journal, "and intended by the Almighty to change our selfish being for the *better*." Loula's lifelong "craving for love" intensified after her father's death in 1860, when she reached the uncomfortable conclusion that she had "*no one on earth* to depend on for protection" from the "cold & uncharitable" world.[1]

When Loula met "Private Henry" later that year, she declared that she had found her "*real destiny*": to share in "holy affection" with a mate selected for her by God. Certain that "*He* hath made us to love one another," she dreamed of "a life of labor and love" in which she and Henry would enjoy a "union of *heart, soul,* and *mind*— all *one,* to work together, to study together, to do good together, and to pray together!" In her dreams of the future, Loula focused on the higher purposes of marriage. "We are made to mould each other, to teach all we know of what is bright and holy, and to live for the good and happiness of a *whole world*, not for ourselves alone, and may the great Creator . . . help us to do it," she mused.[2]

Loula hoped for a sacred union with a true soulmate. "All that is beautiful and elevating we both would love together," she daydreamed, "nature, music, painting, poetry and flowers!" At the same time that she eagerly anticipated a holy union with her husband, Loula dreaded the "innumerable cares," "bewildering trials," and "hum drum sameness" of married life. Once married, she anticipated "*button holes to work, patches to make*, servants to manage, and a thousand other disagreeable things too numerous to think of. . . . Ugh! how it makes my head ache!" she exclaimed. Aware of both her shortcomings as a household manager and the challenges posed by her "wild wayward" disposition, she prayed, "God . . . help to make me a good and gentle wife, submissive to my husband, and the delight of his eye." As she prepared to take "the solemn vow . . . which separate[d her] from girlhood forever & forever," she concentrated on the "holy mission" of earthly marriage, writing in her private journal about the "divine origin" of the "sacred affection" that she felt for her intended husband.[3]

Loula's "Bridal Morn" dawned dark and dreary. Clad in "robes of snowy whiteness," wearing a bonnet adorned with orange blossoms, and keenly aware that January 6, 1863, was "the day that most affects my future happiness or misery on earth," Loula prayed for "grace & strength to bear with christian fortitude all & everything." Despite the ominous circumstances of her wedding day and her sad realization that her "girlhood" was "Gone! Gone! Gone! . . . never to be reclaimed upon earth or in eternity," Loula found much to be thankful for in her "new life" as a married woman. The newlyweds knelt together twice a day to "commune with the Author of our being"; to these joint prayers, Loula added her own: "May God watch over our love forever, preserve it pure and holy, and consecrate it to his own glory."[4]

Soon after her wedding day, however, Loula's focus on the twin themes of romance and religion shifted. Now, she concentrated on caring for her "darling Henry" and on the "hard realities" of housework. "I have just found out what I was made for," she exclaimed three months after marrying Henry: "to render him always happy." When Henry was home, Loula knew that it was her duty "to support his drooping head in affliction's dark hour"; when he was absent, she felt that the world was "a *blank*"; "it seems the ruling power of life has departed," she wrote the first time that Henry left her at home

Loula Kendall Rogers, who married at the beginning of the Civil War, bewailed the transition from sacred vows to sausage-making. The shift from romantic love to domestic responsibilities was an important aspect of coming-of-age as a southern woman and exchanging a female youth culture of resistance for a southern women's culture of resignation. (Special Collections and Archives, Robert W. Woodruff Library, Emory University)

alone. Loula filled the empty hours with domestic tasks. Perhaps because it was difficult to reconcile these chores with "the spirit of poesy" that she loved so well, her journal became sporadic, although she continued to carefully record her anniversaries for the first two years. She recorded her third anniversary after the fact: "On the third anniversary of our marriage," she explained, "I was busy *doing up lard*, and *making up sausage meat* all day, so it was not even thought of!" Wryly drawing a comparison between her present activities and her youthful daydreams, she concluded: "Farewell sentiment, poetry, beauty and flowers!" [5]

The trajectory that Loula Kendall Rogers recorded — from sanctified love to lard and sausages — while occurring during the upheaval of the Civil War, typified the experience of many young wives in the antebellum South. After an extended period of delaying, contemplating, and preparing for marriage, most young women in the Old South ultimately resigned themselves to their destiny and entered the bonds of matrimony. When they said their wedding vows, southern women bade a permanent farewell to the relative independence of girlhood and accepted a subordinate role in marriage in exchange for the promise of love and protection. This role involved devoting themselves to domestic duties, living where and how their husbands wished, and depending on their husbands for emotional satisfaction. Southern women's experiences of marriage varied depending on a variety of circumstances, including their own and their husbands' personalities; while some women found marriage deeply fulfilling, others discovered that married life was full of hardship. Regardless of their own happiness or sadness, southern wives accepted married life as their destiny and worked unceasingly to fulfill their assigned role.

For young women in the Old South, marriage was a major step toward exchanging a female youth culture of resistance for a southern women's culture of resignation. As with other life stages, however, young women's adjustment to married life was neither immediate nor uncomplicated; it involved a number of phases, each demarcated by distinct rituals, that strengthened southern women's acceptance of their role in slaveholding society—and weakened their resistance.

"THE MOST EVENTFUL DAY OF MY LIFE": THE WEDDING AND ITS MEANING

In June 1857, nineteen-year-old bride Anne Eliza Pleasants Gordon reflected in her diary:

> It is needless to dwell on the many varied and conflicting emotions of my wedding day, the 20th May, since no time can obliterate their freshness,—the mixture of joy and sorrow, the pain of adieus and separation from my home and kindred, the happiness of loving and being loved, the natural and inevitable regret over a spent girl-hood, the grave responsibility of the future, the fear of unworthiness, the overflowing gratitude to God for the wisdom and happiness of my choice. These and a thousand other feelings make that day one ever to be remembered.[6]

The key themes that Pleasants identified—the mixture of joy at being united with a loving partner and sorrow at separation from friends and family and the sense that the carefree pleasures of girlhood would soon be supplanted by matronly responsibilities—were common in the writings of young women in the Old South. Southern women attached tremendous significance to the exchange of vows, expressing near-universal agreement that the wedding day was "that most important one in woman's life."[7]

Mary Fries Patterson spoke for countless other young women when she described her wedding day as "the most eventful day of my life." The wedding day marked a young woman's assumption of a new identity: that of a wife. Newlyweds filled their journals with reflections on the importance of the wedding day. Elizabeth Cooley McClure commemorated her 1846 wedding day with the solemn announcement: "The wedding is over, I am MARRIED." More poetically, North Carolina bride Ellie Hunter recorded: "The orange blossoms have trembled upon my brow; I've taken the sacred vows upon me, and been crowned with the name of wife." Over and over again, young women indicated that they saw the wedding day as a life- and identity-changing event. As Mary Polk Badger expressed it, on her wedding day, a young woman "assumed the most sacred and dignified station *a wife.*"[8]

Such a "great event" required careful preparations. In the weeks leading up to a wedding, the bride, her female relatives, and her girlfriends sewed the wedding dress, decorated the house or garden, and baked elaborate cakes. Once the preparations were complete, the bride awaited her bridegroom's arrival. Occasionally, difficulties in communication or traveling caused delays. In other instances, the extended absence of a bride's father required a couple to postpone the wedding date.[9]

Such flexibility was possible because marriage ceremonies were not elaborate in the Old South. Weddings were usually family affairs, their size varying depending on the number of relatives and family friends in attendance. The "best and dearest friends" of the bride and groom gathered at the bride's home for a brief ceremony conducted by a local minister. Dinner and dancing sometimes followed the exchange of vows. In her postwar reminiscences, Gay Robertson Blackford described her mother's 1856 wedding at "The Meadows" in Washington County, Virginia, as "typical and significant of the lavish generosity of the time—there was so much food on the table that it broke down." But such descriptions said more about defeated Confederates' tendency to wax nostalgic about the Old South than they did about actual weddings in the antebellum era. Most couples contented themselves with "a small party" on the day of the wedding and, perhaps, a series of social gatherings in the neighborhood in the following weeks, including ritual visits for the bride and "punch drinking" for the groom.[10]

For young women in the Old South, wedding days revolved not around elaborate ceremonies but around the meaning of marriage itself. Just as young women commemorated the end of their school years in friendships albums, they marked the end of single life in verse and prose. In 1835, while Rosina Ursula Young of Virginia was making preparations for her marriage, her female friends wrote a series of poems marking the rite of passage.[11] Their entries do much to illuminate young southern women's thoughts on the significance of the wedding day.

> "The bride comes forth! her tears no more
>   are falling
> To leave the chamber of her infant years;
> Playing voices from a distant home are calling;
> She comes like day-spring, she hath done with
> tears:
> Now must her dark eye shine on other flowers;
> Her soft smile gladdens other hearts than ours!"
>
>   M. T. S.

> "A man that hath friends must show
> himself friendly; and there is a friend
> that sticketh closer than a brother."
>
>   C. Storrs.

Young women in the Old South viewed marriage as a wrenching departure from friends and family. In autograph albums, they copied sentimental poems that called attention to this dramatic transformation at the same time that they testified to the enduring power of female friendship. Here, a selection from the perennially popular British poet Felicia Hemans reminds the reader that after marriage, the bride's "soft smile" must "gladden other hearts than ours." (Virginia Historical Society, Richmond, Virginia)

Marriage, the entries in this album suggested, spelled separation from both female friends and family members. Much like entries in schoolgirls' autograph books, those in wedding albums mourned the loss of female friendship. As a selection from British poet Felicia Hemans (a popular choice) put it: "Now must her dark eye shine on other flowers, / Her soft smile gladden other hearts than ours!" Whereas graduation spelled the exchange of female friendship for the family circle, however, marriage meant bidding farewell to home and family, as well as to female friends. On her wedding day, as another Hemans poem recorded in Young's album pointed out, a woman left "the chamber of her infant years" for a "distant home." Marriage, then, meant loss, first and foremost; on her wedding day, a bride bade farewell to familiar circumstances, family ties, and female friends.[12]

Weddings also provoked reflections on "connubial cares." Pauline's inscription, "To Rosina on her Bridal-day," typified the contrast that young women drew between the carefree joys of youth and the conjugal cares of adulthood.

> From the home of childhood's glee,
> From the days of laughter free,
> From the love of many years,
> Thou art gone to cares and fears,
> To another path and guide,
> To a bosom yet untried!
> Bright one! oh! there well may be
> Trembling midst our joy for thee![13]

Other poems—and other albums—offered more specific examples of the "cares and fears" of married life. A common theme was women's dependence and submissiveness in marriage. While some verses presented an optimistic view of marriage as a "paradise of love," nearly all entries acknowledged that "Hymen's gentle pow'rs" would be reinforced by men's firm control. Writing in Sophia Coutts's album, Rebecca chose a poem titled "Woman's Love," in which she explained: "'Man's love is of his life a thing apart;—'Tis woman's whole existence.'" Because of the different importance of love to marriage partners, men had the ability to dominate women within the marriage relationship. "Woman's Love" continued:

> If once she loves you, she her place will know,
> And high as she has risen, will stoop as low;
> And your's will be the undisturbed control,
> The homage of her whole devoted soul.

Another poem in the same album, titled simply "Woman," offered similar sentiments, referring to "fair woman's . . . soft submission" to "man . . . her protector, the high mark of all her earthly hopes, her world entire, Centre and continent of all she owns."[14]

Inscriptions in autograph albums emphasized not only a good wife's submissive posture but also her greater responsibility for maintaining conjugal harmony. In 1835, Mahaly Pleasants wrote in Rosina Young's album:

Be it her care to keep her owne,
The heart her vergin sweetness won.
Kind to his friends and those he love
Be shure to like whome he approv[e]s.[15]

Antebellum wedding albums focused on the high cost of marriage to southern brides. In marrying, a young woman gave up her own home, her family support, and her female friends. In exchange, she might gain her husband's love, but she also became responsible for domestic tasks, wifely submission, and marital success. In their musings on the wedding day, then, young southern women suggested that growing up meant giving up. On her wedding day, a bride said farewell to both girlhood and resistance.

This message was complicated and contested, however, by plaudits to the enduring power of women's relationships with each other. At the same time that wedding ceremonies publicly affirmed the paramount importance of the husband-wife relationship, the messages that women inscribed in wedding albums privately asserted the continued importance of female friendship. Marriage might separate female friends, but it would not destroy their emotional connection. As one friend wrote in Rosina Ursula Young's album: "Thy love, thy fate, dear girl, to share / Must never be my happy lot." Nonetheless, the friendship would endure: "But thou may'st grant this humble prayer, / Forget me not, Forget me not."[16] Marriage, wedding albums suggested, meant leaving female friends and family ties behind for a new life of domestic cares and male dominance. But while female friends might be separated, their continued support remained vital. Thus, while female resistance was muted, female friendship—one of the essential building blocks of a female youth culture of resistance—remained central to young women's lives.

Wedding ceremonies offered similar messages about the meaning of marriage. Although antebellum weddings generally had few guests outside of immediate family, most brides insisted on one last visit with those who were "near and dear" to them: their female friends. Young women frequently demanded that their closest female friends attend and serve as bridesmaids. These attendants helped the bride prepare for the ceremony, provided emotional support, and sometimes even accompanied the newlyweds on their wedding trip. Serving as a bridesmaid was additionally important because it was the last time that a young woman could be surrounded by her friends before she committed herself to her husband's custody. Lucy Taylor revealed the importance of this ritual when she lamented to her friend Elizabeth

Kane: "Dear Bessie I must tell you how *very* sorry I am that you cannot be my Bridesmaid and how dreadfully disappointed I am that you are not to be at my Wedding. Nothing can make up for your absence now, but a *long* visit to me at some other time."[17]

In addition to remarking upon the challenges to and confirming the importance of female friendship, wedding ceremonies attached tremendous symbolic meaning to a new bride's transition from her old home to her new one. On her wedding day, a young woman exchanged the "hand of friendship" for the "indissoluble tie" of marriage. "There and then our fates were linked, bound, and sealed together while life should last," Elizabeth Cooley McClure reflected on her wedding ceremony. In marrying, women transferred their allegiances from their friends and families to their husbands and in-laws. As Tristrim Skinner expressed it to his fiancée, Eliza Harwood, a bride prepared "to leave the home & associates of [her] childhood" in order to make a "new home" with her husband. At the same time, young women acquired a whole new set of kin. This shift was dramatized at Mary Virginia Early Brown's wedding when her new in-laws attended the wedding, which was held at "papa's house." "Mr B's dear *good mother* was there," she recalled afterward, "& came as soon as the ceremony was performed, & kissing me called me *her daughter*[.]" Other southern wives likewise adopted—or were adopted by—their husbands' relatives, referring to their in-laws as "Papa" and "Mama." If, as one historian has suggested, female identity in the Old South was primarily a matter of family membership, it underwent a major shift at marriage, when a young bride exchanged one family for another.[18]

Marrying introduced young women not only to a new family but also to a "new life" as a married woman. "From this time the scenes and whole tenor of my life, would change," reflected Samuella Hart Curd. Young brides regarded their wedding day as the beginning of a life filled with responsibilities. Many young wives prayed for what Caroline Brooks Lilly called "Divine aid to perform religiously the marriage vows." After recording the details of her wedding in her diary, Mary Fries Patterson concluded: "My earnest prayer is that I will be blessed with wisdom & strength sufficient to meet all the new cares & responsibilities & be enabled to discharge my duty faithfully." Marriage meant adopting a new identity as a wife and new duties as a married woman.[19]

Ultimately, young women understood, a married woman's role was one of dependence, and a wife's responsibilities came down to submitting to her husband's will. Emma Sue Gordon's wedding attendants brought this message home by reading "The Taming of the Shrew" aloud after completing

Marriage solidified male dominance in Victorian America. In accordance with the companionate ideal, this 1848 marriage certificate reminds both men and women that a loving marriage was the ideal, but it also asserts—with scriptural backing— women's special duty to serve and submit to their husbands. (Library of Congress)

wedding preparations. "I was taught by Kate my duty as a wife," the bride recorded in her diary. A woman's "duty as a wife," according to both Shakespeare's play and southern society, was to submit to male dominance.[20]

Bidding farewell to family and friends, moving to a new home, entering a permanent union, assuming household responsibilities, accepting a subordinate role in marriage—for young women in the Old South, all of these changes, marked by the wedding ceremony, added up to a major transformation—the shift from girlhood to womanhood. As Loula Kendall Rogers expressed it, on a woman's wedding day, she "bid farewell to . . . girlhood forever" and exchanged "all the pleasures of young lady's life" for "*womanhood's* cares and trials." Small wonder, then, that young women in the Old South regarded the wedding day as "a sad & solemn time indeed."[21] The changes prefigured by wedding albums and wedding ceremonies would play out in the weeks and months to come. However, the major evidence for these changes—women's correspondence—also testified to the continuing importance of female friendship.

By midcentury, some young women followed their wedding ceremonies with a wedding trip, ranging from a visit of a few weeks to a nearby city to a sojourn in Europe lasting several months. Bettie Maney and her new husband, John Kimberly, spent over a year in Europe after their wedding. More typical was the experience of Samuella Hart Curd, who went with her new husband and the rest of the wedding party (the bride and groom's attendants) to Washington, D.C., for two weeks of sightseeing and shopping.[22]

The convention of a "honeymoon" offered some brides an easy transition from girlhood to womanhood. For some newlyweds, the honeymoon was a prolonged period that carried no responsibilities and offered the opportunity to revel in romance. Anne Eliza Pleasants, who spent five months making "the tour of Europe" with her new husband, described the wedding trip as "the happiest period of my life." For newlyweds like Curd, who spent a portion of her wedding trip hat-shopping with her girlfriends, the honeymoon served another purpose by allowing young women to ease the shift from homosocial relationships to heterosexual marriage. For some fortunate young women, then, a honeymoon allowed new brides to prolong the period of engagement and to postpone the assumption of the responsibilities of marriage, and thus to delay the shift from girlhood to womanhood.[23]

For most young women in the Old South, however, the transition to married life was both more abrupt and more practical. In general, married couples in the antebellum era proceeded immediately to their new homes following the wedding ceremony and accompanying festivities. The day after her wedding, Caroline Brooks Lilly recorded in her diary: "Escorted by my James and attended by a few individuals I went to my *new Home*."[24] The move to a new home symbolized young women's assumption of their new duties as married women; young women's dramatic accounts of their homecomings suggest the profound meaning that they attached to the move.

For some southern women, marriage meant making a new home far from their families and friends. Those southern brides for whom migration followed marriage lavished attention on the event, offering detailed descriptions of the farewell scene and heartrending accounts of their own sadness. Samuella Hart Curd, a Richmond native, set out for Missouri with her husband after a two-week honeymoon in Washington, D.C. "It was an evening to me of peculiar sadness," she reflected. "From this time the scenes and whole tenor of my life, would change, I would soon turn my face Westward, away from the scenes of home and childhood. . . . As the last sound of good night fell on my ears, I could not but ask Will we? Can we ever meet thus again? And a voice within whispered, never!"[25]

Virginian Elizabeth Cooley McClure, who saw in westward migration a hope of achieving the financial independence she had always desired, was torn between her desire to move west and her love for her family. "I do not know yet what to do," she wrote in her diary. "I want to go to Texas but yet it seems like it will break my heart to leave all my friends behind." McClure changed her mind hourly about what course to take. "During all this time my feelings have been changeable, sometimes fine spirits, then the next moment almost insupportable, sometimes almost perfectly happy, others miserable," she wrote in late March 1846, as she and her new husband prepared to move west. In this extremity, McClure looked for divine guidance and support:

> I have earthly love almost to perfection and I am fixing to go to Texas, a country to which I had rather go than anywhere else, and to leave my *dear* old native land for a new and untried place of residence, quit my *old*, *true* and long tried friends for new and untried love and friendship: at times my spirits are as dark and gloomy as the grave. . . . Oh! Lord I humbly beseech thee hear my prayers and have tender mercy on me, . . . and spare Oh! Lord, my feeling from the dreaded and harrowing feelings of ever repenting my choice in a companion for life and a spot on earth on which we have or may select to live.[26]

These women's accounts of the day of departure emphasized the event as a dramatic demonstration of the requirement that they choose between familiar surroundings, supportive family members, and female friends and an uncertain future, an isolated setting, and a husband's preferences. In writing these descriptions, migrant wives attempted to reconnect with the loved ones they left behind and, no doubt, sought to alleviate their loneliness by writing lengthy letters. Yet women who moved comparatively short distances wrote similarly detailed descriptions. Whether they moved across the country, or merely across town, newlyweds regarded going to "my new home" as a significant event.[27]

Eliza Harwood Skinner's account of her move was typical of southern brides. The new Mrs. Skinner moved from her family home in Virginia to her father-in-law's North Carolina plantation the day after her marriage to Tristrim Skinner in 1849. "Now I'll tell you something of my movements since I bid farewell to my native land," she wrote to the relatives she left behind. "My eyes were fixed on the Grove till it faded in the distance when I could no longer see it—I gave myself up to sad thoughts of home and you—praying that your life might not be a lonely one and that I should always have you near me. . . . When I parted with cousin Dickie I could no longer restrain my feelings; but rushed to my room in a paroxysm of tears. . . . I cannot describe to you my feelings—as my foot touched Carolina soil. . . . I scarcely spoke during the ride. My feelings were too deep for utterance."[28]

Skinner's description of her move dramatized the shift in her sense of place and identity from her own family to that of her husband. Upon her arrival in her new home, her new relatives did their best to make her feel at home; in the process, they also reminded her of her new relationship to them. "Dr Warren [Tristrim Skinner's brother-in-law] was in advance of us —and heralded our arrival," she continued. "He met us and helped me out of the carriage and presented me to the 'old man.' Who welcomed me very cordially as his *daughter* and *mistress of the establishment*—with a kiss." As Old Man Skinner's welcome made clear, in marrying, the younger generation was taking on the responsibilities of the older. "The evening of my arrival 'Pa' gave up the management of all domestic affairs," Skinner explained. "He said he was tired of housekeeping and farming and he assigned both to Trim and me." In the Old South, assuming responsibility for "domestic affairs" meant exercising authority over slaves; after being greeted by the family patriarch, Skinner was welcomed by the household slaves in her new role as plantation mistress. She related: "Annie and Harriet—the two principal members of the household met me at the door—with a 'howdye do mistress['] — 'Welcome home' — 'we have been looking for you a long time.'" Finally, Skinner described her first appearance as "mistress of the establishment," which symbolized her new role as domestic manager:

> I have not seen the keys yet, but I have presided at table, with annie's assistance. Yesterday morning I was led to the head of the table—and got through the performance tolerably well. . . . My dress for dinner was my blue silk with the high body—I expected company to dinner, but the weather was so bad that no one came but Mrs Joshua Skinner and little Maria Warren. I am delighted with my "Aunt Betsy" and Maria is a sweet little thing. . . . I wished to resign my seat at dinner yesterday but no one would take it. I had to get Mr Burgwin's assistance in carving.

Despite her diffidence, the new Mrs. Skinner had the comfort of knowing that her ten-course meal was well received. After the last course was cleared, "a toast was drunk to the mistress."[29]

Margaret Mordecai Devereux's description of her welcome at her new home was similar. She began by evoking the sense of loneliness and displacement she felt as she traveled from her home in Raleigh, North Carolina, to her husband's plantation, Runiroi, "in the *mashes*" (that is, marshes) of rural Bertie County. "I felt sad enough when I left my dear sweet home, and my own dear mother and sister and so many that I love," she confessed, "but I knew it would do no good to give up to my feelings so I would not suffer myself to think of you all, and though my throat did feel mighty tight and *hurty* yet I finally conquered and though I did not feel very happy yet I was not very miserable." Devereux also expressed her anxiety about her arrival in her new home and took pleasure in the warm reception she found there. "I dreaded the getting here very much," she wrote to her mother. "My breath almost stopped when the carriage drew up before the door, but Mr Devereux [Sr.] was out to welcome us and seemed so glad to see us and *Nerve* [and] *Clarissa* [the household slaves] . . . looked so clean and smiling, that I soon felt quite easy. . . . Every thing had been fixed mighty nicely for us. Manerva or *Nerve* had even dressed flower pots, both in my room and the dining room." Immediately after her arrival, Devereux symbolically assumed her position as mistress by doing "the *honour's* at the head of the table with great decorum." Like Skinner, she carefully described each course of the meal, noting that "even though there were only three people," they had a "bountiful" feast consisting of eleven different dishes.[30]

Skinner's and Devereux's accounts of their move to their new home contained all the elements typical of such letters: the sad farewell, the joyful welcome (complete with devoted servants welcoming the new "missus"), and the new wife's first duty: presiding at the head of the dinner table.[31] These descriptions symbolized young wives' adoption into a new family and their assumption of a new set of domestic responsibilities. When a new bride moved into her new home, she also adopted a new role: that of a housekeeper.

"TO PERFORM THE DUTIES OF A HOUSEKEEPER": GOING TO HOUSEKEEPING

An event that many young women regarded as quite as significant as the wedding itself was setting up housekeeping. "Going to housekeeping," in the parlance of the times, marked a young woman's assumption of her new role as mistress of a household. This was a position of great responsibility. In the nineteenth-century South, households were units of production rather than consumption. Southerners relied on domestic production, not on the marketplace, to provide themselves with such basic necessities as

Marriage marked women's assumption of domestic responsibilities. Most well-to-do southern brides proceeded immediately from the wedding ceremony to their new home, where they undertook the duties of keeping house and experienced the privileges of slave ownership. The rapid pace with which young lovers became "young housekeepers" is indicated by this 1848 Currier & Ives lithograph depicting "the day after marriage." (Library of Congress)

clothing, bedding, linens, candles, and soap. Southern gardens and stables, not grocery stores, were the source of such staples as fruits, vegetables, butter, cheese, ham, and sausage. Although elite white women could rely on the labor of enslaved African Americans to produce and process many of these goods, they were ultimately responsible for ensuring that all of the necessary tasks were accomplished. Whether as supervisors or as fellow workers, then, southern mistresses felt the weight of their responsibilities keenly. As Eliza Steele MacNamara wrote home to her parents in 1815, "a housekeeper has more thoughts to occupy their minds than those which have not that trouble to attend to." [32]

Some young women regarded the "trouble" of housekeeping with trepidation. Writing to Ella Noland MacKenzie, who already had borne her first child, Carrie Sage inquired: "How do you like the idea of taking the responsibility and care of a house upon yourself[?]" No doubt the new Mrs. MacKenzie would have agreed with Caroline Brooks Lilly, who mused: "To perform the duties of housekeeper will require much skill and fortitude." [33]

However, many young women looked forward to going to housekeeping as a sign of their new status—and privileges—as adult women. "I am quite anxious to enter upon the 'cares' of housekeeping, as they are called," Sarah Satterlee confided to her friend Mary Ellett. "But I have my own ideas about that matter. I believe there is a great deal of *fun* too." Like Satterlee, some young women suggested that a measure of authority came with assuming the role of housekeeper. Indeed, the attention that young matrons devoted to their new position suggested that they found domestic authority to be one of the most concrete benefits of marriage. "By this time you have probably returned to Baltimore and are settled down once more in your own home," Ella Noland MacKenzie's friend Carrie Sage speculated in 1854. "Is it not pleasant to feel that you are Mistress, and to have the direction of Everything[?]" In marrying, young women relinquished a degree of personal freedom, but at the same time, they also gained a new status as "Mistress" with "the direction of Everything" in the household. [34]

Mary Miller Davis's correspondence likewise suggested that young women took a certain degree of satisfaction in having a household under their direction. Davis and her husband, Charles, began their married life in a boardinghouse; although she initially remarked, "it is immaterial with me whether I board or keep house," she quickly added, "I might feel more at liberty in my own house." Once the Davises were settled in their own home, one of Mary Davis's friends wrote to inquire: "Marie what do you feel like house keeping; just sitting up in the house *thinking you are the boss* while Charlie is gone[?]" [35]

Such comments suggest that southern wives enjoyed a significant level of autonomy (what Miller called "liberty") and a degree of authority as the mistress (or "boss") of the household. Although nobody questioned the husband's ultimate preeminence as "the Lord and master of the mansion," on a daily basis, wives enjoyed considerable authority in household matters, particularly when their husbands' duties took them away from home for extended periods of time. Moreover, while southern wives were subject to their husbands' guidance, they wielded authority over their own subjects: household slaves and domestic servants. While some southern mistresses struggled to maintain control over surly servants and malingering slaves, others found that their control over their social inferiors bolstered their own status. On occasion, wives' authority might even eclipse that of their husbands'; Margaret Mordecai Devereux's husband, John, complained that he was no more than a "cipher" in household discussions; with the assistance of an experienced slave, the new Mrs. Devereux capably managed the household without the "master's" guidance.[36]

Young wives did not achieve this degree of competence overnight, however. Rather, newly married women underwent a lengthy apprenticeship in the mysteries of housekeeping, relying on both the advice of older women relatives and on the labor of enslaved African Americans to attain the "*matronly air*" of "*a housekeeper.*" It was only once this transformation had been completed that young women felt comfortable in their new homes. Caroline Brooks Lilly's diary illuminated this change. Although initially she felt "as if I was on a *visit only* and not at home," once she had spent a few weeks outfitting the kitchen and decorating the hall, she wrote: "Find my attachment to my home hour encreasing [sic] and realize far more pleasure in my new situation than I anticipated."[37]

Many brides began their married life in the homes of relatives or in boardinghouses. Richmond resident Harriet Payne Turner, for instance, began her married life in 1838 "very comfortably located with Mrs Anderson a widow lady with 6 children," but later lived at the home of her brother-in-law while the newlyweds' house was being built. This practice allowed young women to settle into their new role as married women (and sometimes as mothers) before taking on the additional duties of keeping house.[38]

Although intended to lighten young wives' burdens, such arrangements could bring their own difficulties. South Carolinian Sally Taylor Elmore, who "had a perfect genius at not being a favorite with my mother-in-law," chafed at the requirement that she attend weekly gatherings of the extended family. "At Edge Hill, among the mysterious charms of this patriarchal community to which I had to accord my practice, was the 'spending the day,'" she recalled, a "clan gathering" that prevented her from playing on her new piano or singing "the wicked opera drama I then reveled in." Nevertheless, with her mother-in-law present to attend to household matters, it was not until two years after her marriage that Taylor was required to take on one of the fundamental duties of a plantation mistress: sewing clothing for the slaves. Unfortunately for Taylor's relationship with her mother-in-law, she did not relish this task:

> I could not imagine myself cutting out a little brown calico frock which came to me from my Mother-in-law two years after I was married. The gown was ticketed as were sundry other "models", and with them in the basket, a letter, resigning to her son's wife, the "duty" which had been her's as Directress for the Negro Woman's comfort in certain circumstances [i.e., impending childbirth]. A layette of any sort had not ever come under my immediate supervision, and these provisions for plantation events were further from my sense of duty than Mrs. Jellaby's making up flannels for the Hottentots.

Even as a married woman, Elmore remained subject to an older woman's supervision. She released her pent-up frustration at this situation via racism, comparing African American slaves to African "Hottentots." For this young matron, as for southern daughters-at-home, household responsibility did not bring domestic authority. Not surprisingly, then, many young wives looked forward to the day when they could write, as Martha Harrison did in 1843, "I am delighted with my own home."[39]

Whether they began their careers as housekeepers in rented rooms or in a grand mansion, newlyweds devoted lengthy letters and diary entries to descriptions of their arrival in their new homes and to the challenges they confronted in setting up a household for the first time. "My rooms are very nice and comfortable," wrote Bettie Maney Kimberly from her Chapel Hill, North Carolina, boardinghouse in 1861.

> But I wish you could have seen them when we got here last Wednesday at one o'clock, all bare and desolate with unpacked furniture piled up to the very ceiling. But I forthwith sent off for a negro woman, broom, floor cloth and hot water all of which soon made their appearance and while Mr Kimberly and two negro men moved and opened boxes I superintended the sweeping, scrubbing and dusting, and before night we had a carpet down, some chairs out, Babys cradle up and our mattress on the floor and with a great blazing fire we looked and felt quite comfortable.

Despite initial difficulties, Kimberly took pride in her ability to create order from chaos at the same time that she revealed her reliance on the labor of others. "[I] had the satisfaction of seeing every thing straight and in its place," she concluded.[40]

Once settled in, young matrons welcomed visitors to their new homes. This ritual allowed a new wife to display her housekeeping skills as well as satisfying the neighbors' curiosity. As Bettie Kimberly put it, "I had any number of visitors for you must know that all Chapel Hill is nearly consumed with curiosity to know what manner of 'hanimal' Mrs Kimberly is. . . . I have made a most tremendous sensation my Sissie darling, the whole village is doing nothing but talking and thinking about me." Visits to a newly married woman's home also allowed a young woman to announce her new identity as the mistress of a household. Mary Polk Badger looked forward to welcoming her relatives to her new home. "I should be happy, most happy to welcome you at *my own house*," she emphasized.[41]

Young brides and their acquaintances measured their success as adults by how well they filled their new role. Margaret Steele, who accompanied her sister Eliza Steele MacNamara to her new home in Columbia, South Carolina, informed their mother: "We have been housekeeping some time & Sister is a much better manager with the assistance of her Husband than I had any idea of—she graces the head of the table quite well." Laura Wirt Randall's mother, Elizabeth, reported her uncle's favorable comments on Randall's apparently successful adjustment to her now role: "Your Uncle Cabell . . . is lauding you to the skies," she told her daughter, "for being so 'domesticated, sober, home-loving, a country wife' & so 'perfectly reconciled & happy'" to her new situation as a plantation mistress.[42]

Many young wives found a source of pride in their domestic abilities and took pains to update their family and friends on their successes in meeting the responsibilities of keeping house. "I have become quite a housewife in every sence [sic] of the word," Eliza Steele MacNamara boasted to her mother in 1815. "I have cut Harry and London two Breaches [sic] and Jackets and stattira and rosetta a habet [sic] each they set as well as if a tailor h[ad cu]t them . . . dont you think now I was pretty expert[?]"[43] MacNamara's letter indicated the additional work that slaves required, as well as the essential labor that they supplied, as she detailed her own work in sewing clothing for her enslaved labor force. But for MacNamara, the most important point was that she had displayed her own abilities as "a housewife" in a slaveholding household and thus was justified in claiming her new status as an adult southern woman.

Southern wives emphasized particular tasks as symbolic of their new position. In addition to sewing for servants and presiding over the table, a mistress carried the keys to the household, maintaining control over stores of candles, flour, and meat. Thus, when a servant interrupted her unpacking "to go with her to get some flour," Margaret Devereux commented, "Though it was some trouble, it gave me such a womanish feeling that I felt really flattered[.]" Becoming a woman—or more precisely, the elite mistress of a southern household—was "some trouble," but it also brought with it the rewards of domestic authority and the labor of household slaves. Devereux's husband, John, called attention to the importance of a mistress's tasks and status when he described his wife's "womanish" role and manner: "Peggy is beginning to keep house in earnest," he remarked, "and *totes* the keys in style."[44]

These achievements were important for a variety of reasons, ranging from the practical to the symbolic. No plantation household could operate without a storeroom full of supplies, and no elite family could showcase its status without a well-laid table waited upon by well-trained servants. But for young white women, the real importance of these accomplishments was that they marked their assumption of adult status. As Nathalie Baylies remarked to her friend Mary Hudson Ellett soon after the latter's marriage, "I really should like to see you looking dignified & old-ladyfied!"[45]

"THE CARES OF A SOUTHERN HOUSEHOLD": POWER AND PRIVILEGE

Young southern women achieved a measure of authority when they assumed their adult roles as housekeepers. However, they did not achieve independence. Rather, successfully fulfilling the duties of housekeeping highlighted young southern women's dependent status as they relied on the advice of other women, the work of slaves, and the goodwill of their husbands.

Newly married women relied on other women for advice and assistance as they undertook the responsibilities of keeping house. Some fortunate women had the assistance of unmarried sisters or cousins as they set up housekeeping. Eliza Lucinda Garnett was accompanied to her new home by a relative, Florentina Morena Garnett, to whom she surrendered the keys to the establishment. Sisters Gay and Lizzie Blackford "made such a scene" when it was time for Lizzie to leave home with her new husband, Arthur Lloyd, "that Pa said Gay could go along with them," where the newlyweds shared two rooms in a boardinghouse with the bride's sister. More commonly, young matrons engaged in copious correspondence with women friends and female kin to exchange everything from household hints to clothing patterns.[46]

Many young wives relied heavily on their mothers for both household basics and domestic advice. In doing so, they assumed the role of apprentice and prepared to follow in their mothers' footsteps. Writing from her new home in Columbia, South Carolina, Eliza Steele MacNamara asked her mother for assistance: "I hope my dear Mother you will not forget to send me the coverleds [sic] and other small things which you promised me indeed my good Mother I shall thank you for any thing which you would think would be of benefit to me." Margaret Mordecai Devereux thanked her mother for "all the nice, pretty, and good things that you sent us" to start housekeeping. Judith McGuire gave her daughter Mary Anna McGuire Claiborne advice on matters ranging from organizing storerooms to managing servants and, when the younger woman desired a new cook, kept her informed of possibilities. From the nation's capital, Laura Wirt Randall's mother sent her daughter china, crystal, and furniture, as well as foodstuffs, to assist her in setting up her household in Florida. In addition, Elizabeth Wirt assisted her newly married daughter in locating both slave and free servants for her new home.[47]

New housekeepers' inclusion of household assistants in their lists of household essentials calls attention to a peculiarity of southern housekeeping: the role of slave labor. Mary McPhail Smith called attention to southern women's reliance on others' labor when, writing to her friend Mary Carrington from the boardinghouse where she began her married life, she speculated that her workload might be less once she went to housekeeping. "I sometimes [think], that if I were keeping house that I should have less trouble," she explained, "for then [I would have more] than one servant to call upon." While Smith, like other urban southerners, may have relied upon a combination of free and slave labor, she probably was following convention in referring to a slave with domestic duties as a "servant." Moreover, like her rural peers, while she may have employed free white servants for certain specialized tasks, such as sewing and child care, she probably relied on African American bondspeople—especially, although not exclusively, women and children—to perform most household tasks.[48]

Managing household slaves was very important to southern matrons, both to complete necessary tasks and to claim elite status. Caroline Brooks Lilly learned this less than a week after her wedding, when her husband presented her with "a little negro girl named Sophy" on the condition that Lilly "would make her a good house girl." An important part of going to housekeeping was establishing control over domestic slaves, no small task for young women with limited experience. As Judith McGuire explained to her daughter, it was all too easy for slaves to "lose all respect" for a timid new mistress. Bettie Maney Kimberly's letters to her sister Annie Maney were filled with complaints about her sole household assistant, an ailing black woman. "You can possibly imagine what a delightful fix I am in," she wrote sarcastically, with "that Satan of a negro to attend to and our rooms to clean up and not a soul to do a thing except ourselves[.]" Eliza MacNamara Steele wrote that her cook needed "close watching" but that she herself was doing "tollerably well in house keeping." Caroline Brooks Lilly lamented, "I find myself miserably deficient in the management of servants."[49]

Margaret Mordecai Devereux, despite her husband's claim that she reserved a heavy iron key to keep "the small descendants of Ham" in check, successfully managed her household staff by conceding a degree of authority to a slave woman named Manerva. Devereux and "Nerve," as the slave was known, conferred on domestic matters and presented a united front against Mr. Devereux. "I wish you could see her how she tries 'to come the old housekeeper' over me when ever I am a little too much in the way," wrote John Devereux in a postscript to his wife's sister, Ellen Mordecai. "You would be amused to see how wise she looks whenever she can get Nerva on her side in any housekeeping discussion."[50]

While Devereux's tactics may have been atypical, her description of herself "giving out" dinner and directions to her enslaved staff in "a most matronly and knowing manner" typified slaveholding wives' reliance on the slaves in their household for the fulfillment of most domestic tasks. Nonetheless, the mistress was responsible for supervising the work, a task that required a certain degree of expertise, if only to maintain the servants' respect—and to legitimize white women's claims to authority. "On Monday morning bright and early I have got to [boil] fat and make sausage meat," Devereux worried to her sister. "And what, shall I do? wont I feel and look like a monkey when I set about it[?]"[51]

Nevertheless, within two years of her marriage, Devereux had learned how to present at least the appearance of control over all household activities. "You ought to see how like a grown up lady I look every morning giving out meal and meat and pretending as if [I] knew all about it," she wrote to her sister. With the help of her female slaves, Devereux had learned the basics of southern housekeeping. "I have made sausage and souse [i.e., soap], and candles, and I have got Clara back in the kitchen—and I have had that cleaned and scalded and fixed so that it looks like a different thing—and I attend to the cows and the milk and we have just as much butter and milk as we know what to do with," she boasted in 1844, adding, "I wish you could see some pastry that I made yesterday—it is really sublime!" By learning to complete these tasks—either on her own or with her servants' assistance— Devereux had earned the right to call herself "quite a steady matron." "Is not this a real housekeeper's letter," she teased. "I will change the style lest it should smell of lard." [52]

Young matrons' descriptions of their housekeeping trials and successes revealed that southern wives had both privilege and power: the privilege of material possessions and the power to supervise household servants. But the purpose of all this privilege and power was not to enjoy oneself, but to please one's husband. As Elizabeth Wirt cautioned her daughter, Laura Wirt Randall, "*the performance of duties*," not "personal gratification," defined married women's lives. Young women's writings, therefore, shed light on one of the central paradoxes of elite women's lives in the slaveholding South: they were simultaneously privileged and oppressed, powerful and powerless. [53]

Elite women in Victorian America, in accordance with the popular doctrine of "separate spheres" for women and men, believed that it was women's duty to make home a pleasant retreat for their husbands. Southern wives echoed these sentiments, albeit with a southern accent. Caroline Brooks Lilly wrote that she "anticipated no small degree of pleasure in superintending my domestic concerns and in endeavouring to contribute to the happiness of my beloved husband, who, I am persuaded, is altogether worthy of my *esteem & love*." [54]

Southern women thus linked their success as a mistress with their duties as a wife. As Mary Virginia Early Brown expressed it on her fifth anniversary: "I feel an increased desire to be a more faithful wife and fill my place as mother & mistress with more firmness & consistence. A better husband no one ever had, & I must try to make every thing comfortable at home[.]" Only by using their privilege and power to advance their husbands' comfort would southern wives earn their husbands' love, gain social approval, and retain the prerogatives granted to them by southern patriarchs. As Carrie Sage remarked in 1854, it was a woman's duty and pleasure "to anticipate Every wish of the one we love best and make his home so attractive that he has no desire to seek amusement Elsewhere." [55]

When they drew a connection between their husbands' "esteem & love" and their own efforts, young matrons indicated that they understood that their privileged position as "mistress" and the power that it gave them over slaves ultimately depended on their success at pleasing their husbands. One young wife who drew especial attention to this dynamic was Martha Hunter

Hitchcock, who migrated from Virginia to Texas with her husband in the 1840s. Hitchcock lamented the exchange of books for cookbooks. "I am going to seed, very fast," she wrote to her cousin, Martha Hunter. "I read very little, and never write a line, except in the way of letters—but I am growing a notable housewife—make puddings, and darn stockings—sew on buttons, & other intellectual accomplishments," she commented sarcastically. While Hitchcock recognized the link between keeping a neat house and sustaining her husband's attachment, she resented the duties that fell upon her shoulders. She did not even have the time for fancy sewing, she remarked. "Indeed, I find it, quite as much as I can do, to darn my husband's stockings, and to sew on his buttons, when he breaks them off, which is very frequently the case. . . . I have a husband to please, and this is quite enough, to occupy the whole of a woman's time." Hitchcock did not relish the privileges of her station or her power over slaves; instead, she regarded domestic tasks as a burden and recognized her dependence on her husband. Keenly aware that if she were unmarried, she would be destitute, she nonetheless repeatedly lamented, "The cares of a southern household, fill up all my time."[56]

Hitchcock's musings reveal a fundamental truth about elite southern women's lives; the power they possessed was not their own, but their husbands', and women wielded it only with their husbands' assent. Thus, to maintain their own authority within their households, wives had to submit to their husbands' authority within their marriages. In marriage, then, southern women had to come to terms with an institution that upheld male dominance even within a relationship of mutual affection. Whether young wives emphasized the former or the latter aspect of marriage depended upon personal experience and influenced their assessments of married life.

"I AM AS MUCH IN LOVE AS EVER": POSITIVE ASSESSMENTS OF MARRIAGE

Some young wives experienced fulfilling marriages marked by both emotional and physical intimacy. Lucy Taylor Wickham, who married at the tender age of fourteen, assured her friend Elizabeth Kane that she enjoyed her new life. "Of my husband I never could say enough," she wrote in 1847. "So will only tell you that I am as much in love as ever and am perfectly happy." Wickham especially relished the time she spent alone with her husband. "[We] sit in our own pretty room, and read & talk until tea-time," every afternoon, she explained. Wickham found that marriage was unalloyed joy. "All my anticipations have been more than fully realized," she rejoiced, "and I have not been disappointed."[57]

Despite widespread anxiety about marriage, once the wedding day was over, many—perhaps most—southern women pronounced themselves happy with their new life. For all their concerns about what they gave up to marry, many young women found that married life offered an important consolation prize: their husbands' affection. Despite her earlier hesitation at committing herself to matrimony, Penelope Skinner Warren pronounced herself happy with her choice. "I think I can easily guess which life you love the best—married or single," she teased her husband. "I judge of your tastes by my own—I think the former *far preferable* & wonder much that we should have been so long a time making up our minds concerning it." "Five months of my fleeting life Has kind Providence permitted me to spend in the utmost harmony with my beloved husband," reflected Caroline Brooks Lilly in her diary in 1839. "The bonds of affection which first united our hearts are becoming stronger & stronger and I look upon the possession of such a husband as my *James* has been to me, as one of the greatest earthly bless-ing[s] I can enjoy." More succinctly, Emma Sue Gordon Perkins confided to her journal: "My own Robin is all that the most tender & loving husband can be, & I love him with all my heart[.]"[58]

Some young women, indeed, were so delighted with their new lives that they encouraged others to follow in their footsteps. Mary McPhail Smith wrote to her friend Mary Carrington to evangelize on behalf of wedded life. "When I first left home I felt very sad indeed, for it was a severe trial to give up my home," she admitted, "but notwithstan[ding] this Mary, I never was so happy as I am now, and I would advise you, my dear Mary, to follow my ex-ample." Martha Harrison wrote to Eliza Spragins to assure her that "a good husband makes one happ[ier than] all things el[se] and indeed I have one of the [best. The] Dr is all that I imagined him to be, kind, aff[ectionate] and ever ready to gratify my every wish—may you [be as] fortunate." One of Matilda Abernathy's friends wrote to her, a year after her own wedding, to assure her of her happiness and to encourage her to take the same step. "You say you *hope* I'm as happy as I was a year ago," she began. "Yes dear child I am—and if possible a *leetle* more so. Marriage has not proved decep-tive with me in point of happiness—*so far* at least. I hope Mag will find it equally as charming and will find in her future companion, one, as constant, faithful and devoted in their affections as I have found[.]"[59]

Clearly, despite their initial hesitance, many southern women found ful-fillment in their roles as housekeepers and happiness in their relationships with their husbands. For these women, while adult responsibilities offered challenges, they offered rewards as well, and these rewards made the ex-change of girlhood for womanhood worthwhile. Happily married women, then, readily (if belatedly) relinquished their independence, abandoned resistance, and resigned themselves to their designated role in southern society.

"THE DAYS OF ROMANCE & ILLUSIONS ARE OVER": NEGATIVE ASSESSMENTS OF MARRIAGE

Other southern women experienced marriages that were deeply dissatisfying. Laura Wirt Randall, who moved with her husband from Washington, D.C., to the Florida frontier in 1826, pronounced herself "disappointed in everything" with her new life. In addition to "the privations and inconveniences of a new country," one of Laura's greatest disappointments was her relationship with Thomas Randall, to whom she still referred formally as "my husband" or "Colonel Randall," hinting that she had not achieved the intimacy she had hoped for with her husband. Despite his romantic behavior while he courted Laura, she wrote that Randall had since "*lost*" the "charms" that had attracted her. Indeed, "I never was less happy in my life than the two first months of my marriage," Laura confided to her cousin, Louisa Cabell Carrington. Laura concluded that her hopes of wedded bliss had been mere "charming illusions." She would "learn to be happy under the change of circumstances," she told her cousin in 1828, two years after her marriage, by lowering her expectations and devoting herself to her duties as a wife and mother. In the first six years of her married life, Laura gave birth to four children and became an adept household manager of a two-story frame house that frequently served as a gathering spot for the local elites. However, she never learned to enjoy the "regular and unvarying routine" of housework, and her frequent pregnancies contributed to the "feeble health" that made it increasingly difficult for her to fulfill her domestic responsibilities—and her husband's expectations. "I am now," remarked Laura in 1831, "as my husband declares 'the most miserable, poor, good-for-nothing woman he ever saw[.]'" [60]

When Texan Lizzie Scott Neblett penned "a review of the past eight years" in 1860, she also revealed profound discontent with her life as "a married woman." In the intervening years, Will Neblett had moved the family to a small town where he practiced law, farmed, and edited a local newspaper; Lizzie had given birth to three children and was pregnant with a fourth, a circumstance that surely contributed to her despondent reflections and gloomy forebodings. "Eight years of checkered good and ill," she reflected, "and yet thro' all it seems the most of the ill has fallen to my lot, until now my poor weak cowardly heart sighs only for its final resting place, where sorrow grief nor pain can never reach it more." Although Neblett did not initially blame her husband for her unhappiness, calling him "kinder than I perhaps deserved," she went on to describe him as often distant and insensitive—"indifferent"—to her trials. "It seems to me," she addressed her husband, "that you regard all things that approach towards sentiment or sentimentality as beneath your notice, and that the wife of [to]day is a far different creature from the bride of eight years ago, that she has not the same call upon your love and sympathy that she had then."[61]

Martha Hunter Hitchcock wrote many plaintive letters from Georgia, Florida, and North Carolina to her kin in Virginia after her marriage to an army physician whose work took the young couple far away from her close-knit family. Hitchcock had much to complain of: her husband was often away from home; she suspected him of infidelity; she suffered from repeated miscarriages; and she was forced to move with her husband to the frontier, which meant "sacrificing *every* comfort, and leaving behind me, every trace of civilization." "I have been sorely tried of late," she wrote in 1841. "[I] have been obliged to endure many things which I *once thought*, could never have fallen to the share of *one*, whose life had hitherto been but one series, of love and affection." Among those trials was her suspicion that her husband had been unfaithful. "If I had never married how much of pain, and dissatisfaction, should I have escaped," she reflected; "at all events I should never have known what *jealousy* is." Although Hitchcock tried to be philosophical about her lot in life—"every situation has its trials," she reassured herself—she found it impossible to reconcile herself to her fate. "In despite of all my good resolutions," she explained, "I find it impossible *always* to struggle against my nature—the school of indulgence, in which I was educated, was little calculated to teach me, those lessons of *forbearance*, which I have had to practise so frequently, since my marriage[.]" Hitchcock concluded that marital happiness was only an illusion. "Believe me," she wrote in 1841, "matrimony is to a woman, a perfect state of servitude[.]"[62]

The negative assessments of marriage offered by Laura Randall, Lizzie Neblett, and Martha Hitchcock temper the optimistic appraisals of Lucy Wickham, Caroline Lilly, and Mary Smith. While some women enjoyed married life and marital responsibilities, others described themselves as slaves to their husbands' unceasing demands and to their own strictly defined roles. "I despise my calling and rebel at it most furiously," pronounced Lizzie Neblett. Calling herself "an unwilling slave," Neblett tried to be philosophical about her situation. "Woman was made for such things, and when she tries to evade them is only kicking against the thorns," she reasoned. Yet even as she described herself as "designed to be a slave," Neblett continued to "struggle with [her] bonds."[63]

Unreconciled to their lot in life yet unable to change their situations, unhappy wives like Lizzie Neblett kept introspective diaries and carried on voluminous correspondence in which they protested the social, cultural, and economic strictures that subjected them to male dominance and domestic duties. Such women might aspire to resignation—as Neblett demanded, "What aid will quarreling with existence bring me?"—but they did not achieve it. Rather, they continued to "kick against the thorns"—to resist accepting their position in southern society—even as they fulfilled the requirements of their roles as "unwilling slaves."[64]

"MATRIMONY IS . . . A PERFECT STATE OF SERVITUDE": THE POWER OF LOVE

Women's experiences of wedded life depended on a number of circumstances. Women who described married life negatively shared several characteristics: they were isolated from friends and family; they suffered multiple (and often difficult) pregnancies; and they disliked housework. Women who described themselves as happy in marriage, by contrast, tended to remain close to their childhood homes; had only one or two children; and enjoyed considerable domestic authority. For all this variation, however, there was one constant: Young wives depended on their husbands for their own happiness.[65]

Women's emotional dependence on their husbands reinforced men's economic dominance. Theoretically, romantic love offered women a source of leverage in marriage that could counterbalance men's many advantages of age, education, and status. But in practice, most southern wives found that the power of love instead reinforced patriarchal power. Whether they pronounced themselves deeply happy or profoundly dissatisfied with married life, southern wives admitted their emotional dependence on their husbands and found that their happiness depended in large measure on their husbands' physical and emotional closeness—a closeness that men's power in the larger society gave them the right (and sometimes the obligation) to deny their wives. As a result, even the best marriages were marred by frequent separations—and even the happiest wives at least occasionally complained of deep depression. As Margaret Lea Graves explained to her husband, Charles, "I cannot be happy, darling while you, *my all*, are away[.]"[66]

Women's emotional dependence on their husbands was linked to men's economic dominance. As previously discussed, men's duty to support their wives gave them the right to determine where the couple would live. Whether professionals or planters, newly married men often determined that the best chances for success were far from their wives' childhood homes. Thus, for women, marriage often meant bidding farewell to family and friends. Elvira Boswell Fowler, who moved from Kentucky to Arkansas after her marriage in 1834, made this connection apparent when she remarked: "Since my marriage I have been seperated [sic] from all my nearer relatives." Southern brides' mournful anticipations of parting with friends and family, then, proved to be accurate forecasts of married life.[67]

Separation from friends and families increased wives' reliance on their husbands for emotional sustenance. Elizabeth Cooley McClure, who moved from Virginia to Missouri after her marriage, linked her new emotional dependence on her husband, James McClure, with her separation from her family. "It is a dangerous undertaking," she wrote in her diary. "I feel I can't tell how I love James Mc. and it is all I have with me now to love. I have broken the last tie which bound me to home; I have thrown myself away and I fear never more can meet those that are now so unreasonably dear to me." Even when marriage was not followed by migration, many southern women experienced increased isolation from family and friends as they devoted themselves to home and husband. Having exchanged long-standing ties for romantic love, young brides understandably placed tremendous importance on their new relationships with their husbands. Noting that she found it more difficult to form friendships since her marriage, Sarah Satterlee told her old schoolmate Mary Ellett: "My dear George is everything to me."[68]

However, men's careers—whether as planters, professionals, or politicians—often took them away from their wives, leaving them lonely and unhappy. As Elizabeth Gordon remarked in 1816, "A lawyers wife in the country must have many a lonely hour." Charles Graves's work as a naval officer took him away from his young bride shortly after the wedding, when she was pregnant with their first child. "You cannot imagine how very painful has been our separation to me," she confided to him; "I shall not be happy until I am once more folded to your bosom." "My Dear Husband," North Carolinian Anna Whitaker Wills wrote to William Henry Wills, whose work as both a merchant and a minister took him away from home in 1835. "Oh! the time does seem so long since you left me and it is not much more than half out."[69]

While Martha Hunter Hitchcock had more to complain of than most southern wives, she shared with them her sorrow at "the many weary hours, I must pass in solitude." Her husband, a physician, first moved Hitchcock to a series of isolated rural outposts, then left her at home alone while he attended to his practice. "Alas!" she exclaimed in 1841. "It seems my destiny, never to enjoy the intimate companionship of a fond friend—I am so much alone—Charles' profession keeps him from me nearly all of the time—all day, at least—and oftentimes I remain in this large house all alone, three nights out of the seven[.]"[70] Hitchcock's situation sheds light on the ways in which men's economic dominance—their right to determine place of residence and their right to leave the residence they chose—both reinforced and exploited women's emotional dependence.

Men's work responsibilities gave them the right to leave their wives alone, as well as the right to determine where they would live. Southern wives, who often had practiced for this situation during the period of engagement, did not question this prerogative even when loneliness preyed on their minds and dampened their spirits. "Oh my Dearest Love," wrote Penelope Skinner Warren to her physician-husband in 1840. "It is so trying to be seperated [sic] from you were it not that I felt it my duty—I could hardly bear it[.]" Submitting to separations was a wife's duty just as leaving home to attend to business was a husband's. "Consult your own interests entirely," Warren wrote. "I shall be perfectly willing to abide by your choice. . . . I am sure my situation is much better than that of some Ladies who do not see their husbands for years. so I must be content." North Carolina bride Mary Polk Badger also strove to overcome her feelings of loneliness in order to support her husband in his career. "To become accustomed to your absence, now, appears impossible," she reflected in 1827. "However I hope to conquer this dejected feeling as becomes a Lawyer's wife."[71]

As wives, young women placed their husbands' interests before their own happiness. Yet because married women invested so much of themselves in their identities as wives, they felt anxious and uncertain when their husbands were away from home. Many young wives described themselves as "a little lost" without their husbands. "I feel as if I were lost sometimes," wrote Margaret Lea Graves to her absent husband. "Such strange feelings oppress me." "How do you feel about being separated from your husband?" queried one of Ella Noland MacKenzie's friends in 1853. "Pretty much as I do I expect—not exactly *homesick*, but you feel somehow unsettled and glad when the time comes for you to step back into the usual path 'with its cares and pleasures.'" In comments like these, southern women revealed a central paradox of southern womanhood. When they married, young wives in the Old South invested in an identity that was dependent on another person; that is, they successfully achieved the other-directed self that the ideal of the southern lady demanded. Yet in the absence of the other, what happened to the other-directed self?[72]

Women, who found their sense of identity in marriage, suffered from loneliness to a greater degree than men, who possessed an independent identity as public actors. Penelope Skinner Warren pointed this discrepancy out to her husband in an 1840 letter: "I have nothing to do but to think on my sorrows—while you have your business to attend to & young companions to associate with." While men could look to their careers, their colleagues, and their families for emotional sustenance, young wives depended entirely on their husbands for happiness. As Mary Polk Badger admonished her husband, "You have no idea my dearest husband, how much I miss you, to judge by your own feelings is not a proper mode, for your business occupies most of your time, while I have nothing to employ my thoughts."[73]

While women's emotional dependence and men's economic dominance reinforced men's sense of self, then, these defining aspects of southern marriage endangered women's identity. Men's choices increased women's need for their husbands' affection at the same time that men's careers limited husbands' availability to their wives. As a result, the power of love, rather than drawing husbands and wives together, reinforced men's dominance over women—and undermined women's resistance. Penelope Skinner Warren's correspondence illuminates this trend. The previously confident and strong-willed Miss Skinner—she who had rejected thirty suitors as the reigning belle of North Carolina—became quite a different person after her marriage to Thomas Warren, who promptly left her in the couple's townhome in Hillsboro, North Carolina, while he returned to the family's Edenton plantation. "Being absent from you," the new Mrs. Warren wrote to her husband, "has the same effect on me that sickness has—it perfectly subdues me—makes me as meek & gentle as possible & I sincerely trust that when we meet you will find me much improved in disposition."[74]

Even women who declared themselves "rebellious" as they entered marriage—thus evidencing a continuing allegiance to a culture of resistance—soon acquiesced to their husbands' dominance, becoming "meek," "gentle," and "subdued." According to patriarchal notions of femininity, this resulted in dutiful wives who were "much improved in disposition"; at the same time, lonely wives' emotions—which so closely resembled the traits expected of southern ladies—helped to create a southern women's culture of resignation. Emma Shannon Crutcher summed up the necessary transformation in an 1861 letter to her new husband, Will, assuring him that she would be "a much better wife" upon his return home after a three-month absence: "Under any other circumstances I never would have had the time and coolness for the dispassionate course of reflections which has enabled me to arrive at a sense of my true position—being a wife, and the exact nature of the duty which I owed you. When we were married, I had by no means made up my mind that you were from henceforth to be the *head* and governor, the *monarch* of my little kingdom. . . . I never resolved my thoughts down to a theory, but walked into the net, only knowing that I felt very rebellious." However, upon reflection, Crutcher was ready to assume her "proper relative position" in marriage, though she yielded to her husband's dominance only under the condition that his love would never waver. "I can give up the reins to you without any uneasiness," she explained, "for I know you wont *domineer*—you love me too well for that, but—*if you ever neglect me*, you will find a *mule, for stubbornness, rock for immovability, ice for coldness* and *quinine for bitterness.*"[75] Crutcher's letter to her husband neatly summed up the compromise that many southern women made in marriage; while insisting on the companionate ideal's emphasis on romantic love, they accepted the submissive position of more traditional ideals of marriage in the hope that by yielding themselves to their husbands, they would gain their mates' undying affection. In the process, they learned that their "proper position" in marriage was one of loving dependence. Young wives thus experimented with a middle ground between resistance and resignation; while they resigned themselves to a subordinate role in marriage, they insisted upon certain privileges within marriage: their husbands' eternal devotion.

"THE DISCHARGE OF MY DUTIES": LOVE AND DUTY

Notwithstanding southern women's commitment to the companionate ideal, devotion to duty, not romantic love, often defined married women's lives. Once married, many young women felt not only an increased sense of dependence but also a strong conviction of their duties. Mary Virginia Early Brown filled her diary with resolutions "to try harder to be more consistent in the discharge of my duties as, Wife, Mother, & Mistres [sic]." Fulfilling the duties of married life required women to attend to numerous details and to be constantly on the lookout for ways to improve. Brown prayed for "patience under the little trials of life" and for the power to "watch constantly over, my thoughts, words & actions[.]" For Brown, as for other southern wives, the goal of completing these domestic duties was to earn (or maintain) their husbands' love. But when that goal proved illusory, southern wives tried to be content with fulfilling their role within marriage. As Elizabeth Gamble Wirt, who lived apart from her husband, U.S. Attorney General William Wirt, for ten months of the year, put it in an 1827 letter to her absent mate: "We are not & cannot be, so *gay* & *happy*, as while you are with us—But we try to busy ourselves in our duties."[76]

Southern wives assumed primary responsibility for the success of their marriages. As newlywed Samuella Hart Curd wrote in her diary: "On me in great measure must depend the making of a home, happy or miserable." Southern wives expected their husbands to be, as Eliza MacNamara expressed it, "industrious and indulgent," but because a good husband also was "very attentive to his business," it was up to the wife to keep romance alive. In a letter to newlywed Mary Hudson Ellett, Louisa Livingston reminded her friend both of the responsibility that rested upon her and of the necessity of fulfilling that duty. "I hope there is no need of beseeching you to cherish *the one dear friend*, dear above all others, dearer than life itself, in whom indeed life and all its interests are bound up," she charged. "It only depends upon yourself, whether the love and admiration you have awakened shall continue."[77]

Wives' need for their husbands' "love and admiration" encouraged them to invest their domestic duties with tremendous significance. As Mary Stuart McGuire confessed in a letter to her mother, her husband's love was conditional on her complaisance: "I believe my old man is very fond of me," she wrote, "but he wouldnt be long if I didn't wait on him & fuss over him a little." With so much depending on wives' successful fulfillment of their new role, it was small wonder that young matrons devoted so much time and effort to their domestic duties. They did so even when their husbands did not appreciate—or even notice—their efforts. Even after five years of marriage, Mary Virginia Early Brown worried that she did not fulfill her husband's expectations of her. But far from giving up, she devoted herself to her role with renewed zeal. "I feel resolved to be a better wife," she wrote in 1852, "to be more than ever watchful over his interests, & attentive to his wishes."[78]

Many young wives, like Mary Brown, regarded love and duty as natural corollaries; by fulfilling her duties, a wife gained her husband's love. But on a day-to-day basis, married women often found that duty was more important—and perhaps more dependable—than love. Given the responsibility to make a successful marriage but denied the ability to control their husbands' behavior, some wives learned to replace love with duty. As Laura Wirt Randall's mother advised her, it was incumbent upon women to "seek . . . happiness . . . in the respect and affection" of their husbands, "and," she added, almost as an afterthought, "in the conscientious discharge of [domestic] duties." Husbands might fail to deliver "respect and affection," Elizabeth Wirt knew from experience, but "the everyday duties of life" never failed. Thus, all wives, regardless of their personal "situations," could "labour to the same end": "the faithful & conscientious discharge of our duties."[79]

Confronted with the difficulty of reconciling male dominance with mutual affection, many southern wives resigned themselves to a life that revolved around responsibilities rather than romance. The romantic ideal held out the promise of egalitarian relationships and offered women a way to influence their partners' behavior, but once married, most southern women accepted their subordinate role and strove to fulfill their husbands' expectations of them. By replacing "the *fansy* of *youth*" with "life's hard realities," young women took an important step toward adulthood—and away from resistance. They learned by experience "that life is a play day no longer and woman's lot not *all* a scene of flowering beauty & love," but instead that adult womanhood was quite "different from sunny girlhood."[80]

Marriage was an important marker—and maker—of adult status in the antebellum South. It set the stage for well-to-do white women to practice adult responsibilities and enjoy elite status as the wives of powerful men and the mistresses of slaveholding households. It also set new limits on southern women's resistance: their ability to envision (or enact) alternatives to the status quo. Yet in the correspondence that they continued to carry on with female friends and family members, southern women revealed that they did not consider the transformation from girlhood to womanhood complete until they had achieved one additional feminine role: motherhood. While many southern women resigned themselves to the "hard realities" of "woman's lot" after marriage, some continued to resist their fate—to "kick at the thorns" that hemmed them into dissatisfying roles and unhappy marriages. It would take the even more demanding—but often more fulfilling—role of motherhood to reconcile these women to their fate and terminate their resistance.

"SINCE I ARRIVED AT WOMAN'S ESTATE":
MARTHA HUNTER HITCHCOCK

Martha Hunter Hitchcock grew up in Virginia surrounded by a closely knit network of relatives. After
her marriage to an army physician in 1840, she led an
itinerant and isolated life in which her loneliness was
relieved only by the many lengthy letters she wrote to
her female kin. Posted from New York, Florida, North
Carolina, Georgia, and Texas, these letters reflected
Hitchcock's conviction that "the school of indulgence,
in which I was educated, was little calculated to teach
me, those lessons of *forbearance*, which I have had to
practise [*sic*] so frequently, since my marriage."[1]

While Hitchcock had many complaints about married life (as detailed in Chapter 6), she also devoted
significant attention to another theme: motherhood.
During the first six years of her marriage, Hitchcock
filled her letters with detailed accounts of her repeated
pregnancies and her experience of motherhood. Hitchcock's desperation for "the companionship, of those
of her own age, her own sex, and her own condition"
thus led her to record an unusually complete record of
the process by which young women assumed their fully
adult identity as devoted mothers—the last phase of
the long process of female coming-of-age in the Old
South.[2]

Hitchcock was unfortunate. Although she became
pregnant shortly after her wedding, she did not carry
a pregnancy to term until five years later, in 1845. Not
surprisingly, then, many of her letters are extended la-
ments about her repeated "illnesses"—a covert reference to reproductive ailments that called attention to

the danger that pregnancy and childbirth posed to women's health. In September 1840, informing her cousin Martha Hunter of a recent miscarriage, she mourned:

> I verily believe, that, in the whole course of our correspondence, I have never written you a letter, which did not contain some account of my ill health, or the consequences thereof:—and I, as firmly believe that should it continue (as I trust it will) to the end of my existence, you will never receive one, which will not inform you, either of my being, or of my having been very sick—for never, since I arrived at woman's estate, have I enjoyed three months, of uninterrupted health—and repeated illnesses, have so broken down my constitution, that I have little reason to hope, for any permanent exemption, from the sickness, and suffering, to which I have so long been the unwilling heir.

The miscarriage that prompted this letter—brought on, Hitchcock believed, by overexertion while she was in a "delicate situation"—was not the first; although married only a few months, Hitchcock alluded to "the many disappointments, to which my frequent miscarriages had subjected me." Unfortunately for Hitchcock, it was not her last, either.[3]

In 1843, Hitchcock was again pregnant. "So much alone" during her husband's extended absences, Hitchcock again turned to "those whom I best love, for society, and consolation." Convinced that she would die in childbirth, Hitchcock begged her cousin to pay her a visit: "I am filled, with a thousand presentiments of approaching evil," she explained, "and I want your kind companionship, above all things. . . . I know not why, but it seems to me, that if you do not come, I shall never see you again." Hitchcock survived, but once again, her pregnancy terminated in sadness; it was not until 1845 that she at last realized her "expectations of at length becoming a mother" and gave birth to a living child, "our little Lillie."[4]

Although devoted to her daughter, Hitchcock found that motherhood did not bring an end to "sickness, and sadness in [her] family." Instead, she simply shifted the focus of her concern from her own health to that of her young daughter. Lily—sometimes spelled "Lillie" or "Lilly" in Hitchcock's letters—suffered more than her share of the many illnesses that threatened children's health in the nineteenth-century South, making her both her mother's "greatest source of happiness" and her "greatest source of anxiety." Proclaiming, "there is no such *slave* in the world, as the woman, who has but one child," Hitchcock anxiously watched over her delicate daughter, moving into the nursery so that she could be by her side around the clock. "My life is a constant vigil," she confessed in 1846. "There is nothing which wearies mind, and body, so much, as watching a sickly child."[5]

As Hitchcock devoted herself to Lily's care, she transferred her loyalties from her husband to her child. As she wrote in June 1846, "The Dr. is absent, for an indefinite time, and I have nothing but her, to cling to[.]" At the same time, she adopted a new identity, defining herself as a mother, rather than as a wife. Brushing aside her physician-husband's reassurances, she declared with emphasis that only a "*mother*" could accurately assess and sufficiently tend to a child's needs. Indeed, Hitchcock increasingly invested her entire identity in motherhood, looking for fulfillment not in romantic love but in childish affection. "Every day, she becomes more, and more necessary to my happiness—almost to my existence," she wrote of her young daughter, adding, "it really seems, as if she was my life."[6]

Like Hitchcock, many young women in the Old South devoted significant attention to the process of becoming a mother and to the significance of motherhood. Bearing a child marked a new stage of life, one that was characterized both by new responsibilities for child care and by new opportunities for personal fulfillment. Although some women lamented their inability to control their reproduction and the dangers that accompanied pregnancy and childbirth, most agreed that "becoming a mother" was both unavoidable and necessary to achieve what Hitchcock called "woman's estate": full status as an adult woman. With few exceptions, once southern women had attained this status, they also abandoned their earlier efforts to redefine southern womanhood. Instead, they adopted a new identity that revolved around maternity. Motherhood proved to be both the most demanding and the most rewarding adult role available to white women in the antebellum South. For young women in the Old South, then, becoming a mother was both the final stage of coming-of-age and an effective end to female resistance.

"MY LONGING WEARS A CURB": SEX

It is a truism that nineteenth-century Americans were reluctant to discuss sex. Long cited as evidence of Victorians' legendary repression, this reticence has recently been reinterpreted as simply another manifestation of the sharp distinction that nineteenth-century Americans drew between the public and the private. Women and men recognized, valued, and appreciated sexuality—at least within the bounds of marriage—this analysis suggests, but they regarded open discussion of this most private expression of romantic love as inappropriate.[7] Women in the antebellum South discussed

sexual behavior only rarely, and even then, they often cloaked their expressions of sexual desire in innuendo, dreams, and jest. However, it is clear from the clues that these women included in their private writings that many married women enjoyed (and sometimes initiated) sexual activity with their husbands.

Married couples' correspondence occasionally hints at the pleasure both parties took in physical contact. Elizabeth Wirt and her husband, William, apparently enjoyed a mutually satisfying sexual relationship. When business called William away from home soon after the couple's wedding, he ecstatically recalled, "How sweet was the embrace" that they had shared. Elizabeth wrote similarly during separations from her husband, writing of her eagerness to be "in his arms, pressed to his bosom throbbing with affection."[8]

The most explicit discussions of sexuality emerged in half-humorous innuendo. For instance, Civil War bride Ellen Shackelford Gift, referring to a recent furlough, teased her husband about their sex life in a letter in which she used the word "Shanghai" as a code word for sexual intercourse. "I am so very glad that you were drugged or 'Shanghaied' on your last visit, & was it not a sweet little visit after all Darling?" she inquired. "I am sure you think so, because you could not have given me so much happiness without experiencing at least a reflection of it. When you come [again] I shall repeat that dose of Shanghai, may I?"[9]

But pleasure did not come without pain. In an age before reliable contraception, married women could expect to bear numerous children in rapid succession. Although national birthrates declined over the course of the nineteenth century, and some southern women convinced their husbands to cooperate with them in limiting family size (using a combination of primitive contraceptives and periodic abstinence), birthrates remained high in the Old South, and southern women in the antebellum era bore children approximately every two years until menopause.[10]

Young women's correspondence indicated that motherhood followed marriage quickly and inevitably. Calculating her likely delivery date in spring 1830, Richmonder Elizabeth Higginbotham Fischer explained, "I count from the middle of October"—that is, from her wedding day the previous fall. Indicating both the speed with which motherhood followed marriage and the certainty of pregnancy, Elizabeth Noland remarked to Ella Noland: "Mr. M has not brought his bride to town yet—I'll make a bold effort to pay my respects to the bride before she has an *increase*."[11]

Repeated childbearing posed a significant danger to women's health—and even to their lives. As one historian has remarked, "A possible death

THE YOUNG HOUSEKEEPERS.
A YEAR AFTER MARRIAGE.

In the antebellum South, motherhood quickly followed marriage. This 1848 Currier & Ives lithograph indicates the speed with which nineteenth-century couples began their families; titled "The Young Housekeepers—A Year After Marriage," it depicts a recently married couple cherishing their first child. (Library of Congress) sentence came with every pregnancy." Young southern women were well aware of these dangers. Commenting on neighborhood news, one of Ella Noland's friends remarked of a mutual acquaintance: "Poor Orra Orr has had a ha[rd] time since she got married, has been sick ever [since &] is now confined to her bed—I went to see her a short time ago found her looking [very] badly."[12]

The diary kept by newlywed Samuella Hart Curd illuminates southern women's preoccupation with the possibility of pregnancy and their concern about the dangers associated with it. Prior to her own pregnancy, Curd filled her diary with notes on her acquaintances' pregnancies and childbirths, which frequently ended fatally. In the space of only four months in 1860, Curd recorded the death of three infants and one woman in childbirth. Curd's attention to the difficulties of carrying and giving birth to a child only increased the following year, when she discovered her own pregnancy. Curd's diary entries for 1861, although brief, indicated the grave concern with which she witnessed the hazards to women's health posed by frequent pregnancy and childbirth:

Heard that Mrs. Ed Price had a baby. married only 8 months 4 days! Sad.

Cousin A[ngy] has three babies, it is such a charge for so delicate a person. . . .

Betsy & I went out early, first to see Mrs. George, from there to Lizzie Morton's, found the latter quite unwell, has an infant, little girl, about 4 weeks old, this is her 5th child, it seems most impossible. . . .

Mary Dowden had a boy last night. her next to the youngest only 13 months old, she is to be pitied.

Although Curd did not comment on her own situation, her attention to the difficulties of her neighbors undoubtedly reflected her own intense fears, as well as the simple fact of the dangers of pregnancy and childbirth.[13]

Because of the hazards to women's health, some women expressed a desire to control their reproduction, either by limiting or by spacing out their pregnancies. "Have you not fully recovered from the birth of your baby?" inquired Sarah Satterlee of her friend Mary Ellett in 1860. "Don't have anymore now, two is a very good number." Elizabeth Fischer regretted the haste with which she became pregnant after the birth of her second child (her first died in infancy). "Only to think of my being confined *again* next summer just a year from the last," she groaned. Southern women's wishes to exert a measure of control over their own fertility suggested that marriage had neither eliminated their resistance to patriarchal control nor diminished their determination to shape their own destinies.[14]

Women's desire to control their reproduction, however, coexisted with their conviction that birth control was either impossible or unnatural—and perhaps both. Ella Noland MacKenzie's friend Carrie Sage congratulated each of them on having only one child apiece and no "prospect" of a "rival." Yet at the same time, Sage accepted unplanned pregnancies as a normal—and unavoidable—part of a woman's life. "Poor Marion!" she remarked of a friend who was pregnant with a second child shortly after the birth of her first. "I am sorry for her, but these things must be—and the only way is to take such favors patiently[.]" Interfering with reproduction, many southern women believed, was to resist "God's will" and refuse "His gift." Remarking that she thought that even one child was "rather too many," Sarah Satterlee quickly recanted: "But then I suppose I am very wicked and bad to say so."[15]

Such attitudes, combined with the unavailability and unreliability of birth control methods in nineteenth-century America, severely limited women's ability to control their reproduction. By midcentury, women in U.S. urban centers had access to such barrier methods of contraception as condoms, sponges, and diaphragms, although none was entirely reliable. When "preventives" failed, as they often did—Lizzie Scott Neblett became pregnant five times in ten years, despite using contraceptives—the only remaining option was to procure what Neblett called "devilish things": the instruments for inducing an abortion. But although not yet stigmatized by organized religion or criminalized by state courts, abortion remained, as one historian has described it, "woman's last resort" in nineteenth-century America. There is no evidence that any of the women in this study ever induced an abortion, although Neblett was prevented from doing so only by her husband's refusal to obtain the necessary tools. Therefore, for most southern women, pregnancy was not only dangerous; it was unavoidable.[16]

With such serious—and inevitable—consequences, it is small wonder that southern women regarded sexual activity with dread as well as desire. As Lizzie Neblett, whose husband refused either to cooperate with her in abstinence or to assist her in acquiring abortifacients, put it, "Our affections tho' they afford us much pleasure, yet often fill our hearts with fear, doubting and grief." At least for this young wife (and mother of five), her fear of pregnancy interfered with her appreciation of sex. "This constant & never ceasing horror I have of childbearing constantly obtrudes itself between me & my desire & longing to see & clasp you round the neck once more," Neblett wrote to her husband, "& thus my longing wears a curb."[17]

In early 1831, Virginia matron Elizabeth Fischer wrote a letter filled with advice to her sister, Anna Higginbotham Hoskins, who believed that she might be pregnant. Offering a list of possible symptoms, including vertigo, fatigue, and a "sense of fulness in your head," Fischer counseled: "Take a great deal of care of yourself." [18] This letter neatly summed up two of the essential elements of women's experience of pregnancy in the antebellum South: Viewing pregnancy in terms of illness, and relying on other women for advice and assistance.

Expectant mothers monitored the progress of their pregnancies closely. In the early stages of pregnancy, young women were rather reticent. Southern women informed their friends (and sometimes their husbands) of their situation in a variety of roundabout ways that reflected their reluctance to discuss sex openly. (Richard Johnson was frustrated by his wife Isabella's "unsatisfactory hints": "Just tell me when you have good reason to believe you can give me what you know I will think good news," he urged.) Some made coy references to "the little *stranger*" who would soon be coming to visit; others simply announced that they were busy sewing, leaving it to the recipient of the letter to guess the nature of their sewing. Ellen Shackelford Gift asked her husband, who was away from home during her pregnancy, to purchase "any pretty *baby clothes* you see!" Other young women informed their families of their pregnancies by announcing their weight gain. "I have been well *very well* since you left me," Mary Polk Badger wrote to her husband in 1827, "and *strange* to tell, I increase so rapidly in size." Men joined in this sort of teasing. John Devereux commented on his wife's pregnancy in a joint letter that the couple wrote to Margaret Mordecai Devereux's mother in 1842: "She is actually got to be 'fat ragged and saucy,'" he exclaimed, adding, "I weighed her the other day and find that her weight is 102 *gross* what it would be *neat* I cannot say." [19]

By far the most common way for mothers-to-be to describe their pregnancies, however, was by alluding to illness. Many women repeatedly described themselves as "sick" over a period of several months, with only their eventual delivery making it clear that their symptoms were those of pregnancy. In 1839, Caroline Brooks Lilly recorded her first bout with morning sickness in her diary with these words: "Intended rising early but was too unwell. . . . For one hour, or more I was very sick *indeed*." Only Lilly's final comment indicated the nature of her ailment: "I have not the least expectation of enjoying anything like perfect health for several months to come." Nineteenth-century southerners understood such covert references perfectly, however. Responding to a letter from her daughter, Mary Anna McGuire Claiborne, Judith McGuire wrote: "I guessed that your *indisposition* was not very serious. . . . As you marked it at least I hoped I understood it."[20]

Given the many health problems associated with pregnancy and childbirth in the nineteenth-century South, it was sadly appropriate for expectant mothers to describe their situation in terms of illness and disease. The correspondence of the women of the Stuart family of Virginia highlights the link between pregnancy and illness. Sisters Frances Stuart Atkinson and Mary Stuart McGuire exchanged a series of letters with each other and with their mother, Frances Baldwin Stuart, discussing the health problems of young wives and mothers. Frances Atkinson underwent extensive medical treatment for "*a slight displacement*," probably a fallen womb, while her sister Mary McGuire suffered from "a great many aches & disagreeable feelings" during her pregnancy.[21]

Reticent about sex, southern women were positively voluble about the symptoms of pregnancy, which included morning sickness, indigestion, and hemorrhoids (or "piles"). Margaret Lea Graves described herself as "a little sea-sick" during her pregnancy. Caroline Brooks Lilly complained of persistent heartburn that was not relieved by her usual remedy, milk of magnesia. Penelope Skinner Warren complained of a "troublesome" condition that, with the help of a neighbor woman, she identified as "Piles." Whether describing particular symptoms or their "present state of mind, and body," then, southern women almost universally described pregnancy in terms of illness. Writing to inform her mother of a friend who was expecting, Mary Stuart McGuire (who was herself pregnant) utilized the common illness motif: "Poor Mary Johns has caught the disease prevailing in the McG connection & will be confined in the latter part of the winter."[22]

Building on a lifetime of female friendship, southern women relied on other women for support during pregnancy. Female friends, relatives, and neighbors were invaluable sources of information, advice, and comfort. Penelope Skinner Warren relied on her friends and neighbors for practical assistance, confiding her symptoms to them and asking them to help in interpreting and treating them. "Whenever I have any strange pains," she remarked in 1840, "Cousin Annie says I must come to her & she will explain them to me." Warren also relied upon an older woman, Mrs. Jones, for advice and support. "Mrs Jones will come for me whenever I will go out," she assured her anxious husband. Caroline Brooks Lilly looked to other women for emotional support. Suffering from a difficult pregnancy and nervous about childbirth, the expectant mother felt "much better" after a visit with two women friends in August 1839. "Mrs Pemberton & Eliza Christian paid me a kind & social visit," she recorded in her diary, "& said many things to cheer & enliven my drooping spirits." Women also relied on each other for advice on diet and exercise and exchanged recipes for soothing ointments and reviving tonics. Expectant mothers in the Old South found the support of other women indispensable.[23]

Mothers-to-be monitored their health closely. Despite—or perhaps because of—the hazards of pregnancy and childbirth in the Old South, expectant mothers did their best to exert control over their health by paying special attention to their dress, diet, and exercise. "I am very careful & am determined no mishaps shall occur, if the utmost caution will prevent it," explained Margaret Lea Graves. Similarly, Sallie Emory wrote to her friend Ella Noland MacKenzie to ask for advice. "I want to use every precaution in my power," she asserted.[24]

Some women kept extensive records of the "precautions" that they took to increase their chances of a healthy pregnancy and a live birth. These records revealed both their understanding of the threat that pregnancy posed to their personal welfare and their reliance on a community of women for practical and emotional support. Early in her pregnancy, Caroline Brooks Lilly received a letter from a Mrs. Hutcheson advising her "to take daily a spoonful of sweet oil," which the correspondent promised would "have a tendency to relax the system and probably mitigate the sufferings" of childbirth. A few months later, Lilly recorded her regimen in her diary. "Adhered to my simple diet of cornbread & sweet milk which appears to be the food best adapted to check those fits of heartburn & indigestion which so often annoy me," she wrote. "At the suggestion of my freinds [sic] I daily wash my breasts in french brandy to prevent sore nipples[.]"[25]

Penelope Skinner Warren also took special precautions during her pregnancy. In accordance with the medical advice of the day, she went out for "a little walk morning & evening," eliminated molasses from her diet, sewed "*loose dresses*" to accommodate her changing body, and "determined to be cheerful," proclaiming, "I find that cheerful spirits has an excellent effect on me." Warren summed up her efforts to prevent mishaps in a letter to her husband: "I try to take great care of myself."[26]

Despite every precaution, pregnancies were often accompanied by complications ranging from the uncomfortable to the disastrous. Penelope Skinner Warren experienced her share of both. In summer 1840, puzzled by a "troublesome" but "hardly at all painful" condition that she could not identify, she consulted a Mrs. Burgwin for advice: "She told me directly what it was [hemorrhoids] & that it was common to ladies in my situation & told me also what to do for them, I have followed her advice in a measure & find great relief," she explained. Warren again turned to her female acquaintances for assistance and comfort under more serious circumstances. "I had quite an accident yesterday," she related in a letter to her husband in August.

> I went to walk as usual in the entry & dining room & it looked so tempting in the little garden by the side door . . . that I thought I would venture out—as I started I observed a *dog* lying near the door & asked the servants to call him in the house which they did—the dog however got away from them—I had my back to the door—& hearing something coming after me looked behind—& saw the animal in the act of sprin[g]ing on me—I was exceedingly frightened as you may im[agine] . . . & screamed & on attempting to run I fell—I was so much agitated that I do not remember what I did or the dog either. after I got up they brought me in the house & I got on the bed Mrs Johnstone sent a glass of Harshorn for me to take & it composed me a great deal—I experienced no pain at all—but was so fearful of the consequences that I sent for Aunt Nash directly & she came as soon as she received the message. Mrs Burgwin also got here by the time & she hearing of it came down stairs to see me—she remained until Aunt Nash [came] & told me not to be alarmed that she did not think any harm would result from it & that I must keep perfectly quiet—Aunt was very glad that I sent for her—& told me that no danger was to be apprehended at all—as I had not felt it by that time. . . . I cannot tell you my Love how thankful I was that I escaped so well—words cannot express my feelings[.] The whole household seemed stirred up—& expressed great interest for me—they were all affraid [sic] that it might end badly.

After this alarming incident, Warren's "dread of dogs" kept her inside for the remainder of her pregnancy. Nevertheless, despite her own precautions and her female friends' assistance, Warren died shortly after giving birth to her first child, a girl, in January 1841.[27]

"THE GREATEST TRIAL THAT WOMAN IS CALLED UPON TO BEAR": CHILDBIRTH

As Warren's story illustrates, childbirth in the nineteenth-century South was a dangerous business. According to the 1850 federal census, at least one out of twenty-five white women in the South who died that year died in childbirth—twice the maternal mortality rate in the North. Young women's letters and diaries were filled with references to their fears of dying in childbirth. "Have thought much of Death," recorded Caroline Brooks Lilly in August 1839. "Seldom have I felt a stronger or more forcible presentiment of approaching disolution [sic] than on this evening. The grave banished other thoughts from my mind & while leaning on my affectionate husbands breast. the inquiry arose where will they bury me?"[28]

Women also worried lest their children should be born dead or sickly. Elizabeth Fischer, who had lost a child in 1830 or 1831, asked her sister to "remember me daily in your most earnest supplications that I may be safely delivered of a healthy, living infant" when she again found herself pregnant in 1842. Lizzie Scott Neblett, who was exposed to measles in the last weeks of her first pregnancy, suffered from, as she described it, "many many fears, that my poor little Babe will die with them and how sad, sad, and grieved it makes me feel. It seems to me, if I live, and it dies I cannot possibly get over its death."[29]

Perhaps more than anything else, however, southern women dreaded labor itself—what Carrie Sage called "the greatest trial that woman is called upon to bear." Although some women in the Victorian North enjoyed the dubious benefits of "twilight sleep" (drug-induced unconsciousness during labor), women in the Old South regarded pain in childbirth, like pregnancy itself, as inevitable and unavoidable. As Sallie Emory put it in an 1854 letter to her friend Ella Noland MacKenzie, "I have no hopes of not suffering very much in my approaching confinement."[30]

Many women regarded both the discomfort of pregnancy and the pangs of labor as divine judgment resulting from Eve's disobedience in the Garden of Eden. Lizzie Scott Neblett believed that "God fixed [her] to have children in pain & sorrow," while Sally Emory wrote that "if anything goes wrong," it must be "the Will of Providence." Caroline Brooks Lilly, whose pregnancy was accompanied by "distressing pains in various parts of [her] system," accepted her difficulties as part of a divine plan: "Truly Woman is afflicted with many evils in *consequence of her sinful disobedience*," she reflected, adding: "I pray for resignation & submission to the chastisements of my Heavenly Father[.]"[31]

Much as they might pray for "resignation & submission" to God's will, however, young women dreaded "the misery & pain of woman's lot." "Oh! my sister," exclaimed Elizabeth Fischer, "nature dreads the approaching suffering." Carrie Sage referred to childbirth as "the dreaded ordeal." "I will never dread death as much as I dread the suffering of my coming confinement," Lizzie Scott Neblett told her husband, "for death pangs are, methinks, as nothing compared with the pains of labor."[32]

Given the importance that young women attached to motherhood and their fears of labor, it is not surprising that they had mixed emotions about their impending births. Expecting to be "confined" in April 1853 (less than a year after her wedding day), Lizzie Scott Neblett looked forward to mother-hood even as her fear of childbirth made her "low spirited" and gave her the "histericks." "The coming event occupies my mind continually," she confided in her diary in late 1852; "tis the one great thought of my brain the one joy of my heart." Trying to ignore the pain and risk that awaited her, the expectant mother concentrated on the fulfillment she hoped to gain from her new role as a mother. In a few months, she wrote in an optimistic mood, "I will be a Mother—and feel all a mothers love, the holiest passion in the human breast."[33]

Writing to her friend (and new mother) Ella Noland MacKenzie, Carrie Sage also displayed ambivalence. "I expect you will not hear very often from me until after the important Event takes place," she wrote in February 1854. "It is a trying time indeed, and I begin to feel a little nervous and anxious as is natural—but I trust all will go well." Although Sage looked forward to motherhood, her fears of childbirth cast a shadow over her anticipation. "I long for the Spring when, if all goes well, I shall have so much that is pleasant to enjoy and occupy my time," she wrote, adding, "I feel as if I could not anticipate anything with much certainty" until after "the dreaded ordeal."[34]

"Mingled emotions of hopes & fear" were commonplace for women anticipating parturition, but most concluded that all they could do was wait and pray. Sarah Bennett Hopkins, whose husband, Erastus, was away from home during the final months of her pregnancy, mused: "God in mercy grant there may be a happy reunion before very long," but added, "all I can do, is to *wait patiently*." Patience and hope were more than virtues for expectant mothers; they were necessities. "I hope that I shall keep well & be brought safely through it all" was a common refrain.[35]

Caroline Brooks Lilly's musings captured the combination of excitement, terror, and faith that many expectant mothers experienced:

Time in its undeviating course is swiftly bearing me on to an important period in the history of my life. Viz, "partui Infants," [i.e., childbirth] the anticipation of which fills me with mingled emotions of hope & fear—But will not a kind & benevolent Providence who has conducted many millions safely through the scene of terror vouchsafe to strengthen me for the trial which in a few weeks I must pass through. To his care I do most earnestly desire, wholly to commit myself, and to be enabled to say from the sincerity of my heart Thy Will O God be done, and to feel that to me, "To live in Christ & to die is gain[.]"[36]

Southern mothers-to-be, more than southern schoolgirls, celebrated belles, or blushing brides, indicated that they had little control over their own destinies. Regarding pregnancy and pain as unavoidable facts of life or divinely ordained punishment, they resigned themselves to passively awaiting the outcome and placed their fate in God's hands. When it came to giving birth, however, young women reasserted control over their own lives by resisting new medical technology in favor of accustomed female support.

Notwithstanding the weeks and months of anxiety and anticipation, most new mothers spent comparatively little time detailing childbirth (commonly referred to as "confinement"). Most women were attended by family members, female friends, and an experienced midwife, with "efficient medical aid" in reserve in case of emergencies. Husbands were sometimes present—Caroline Brooks Lilly reported, "my affectionate and beloved husband supported me in the trying hour and did all that the utmost fondness could prompt him to do—to cheer & console me"—and male physicians often hovered in the background, but the laboring woman and her female attendants were the most important actors.[37]

Southern women's descriptions of parturition suggest that they only partially accepted the shift from "social childbirth"—an experience defined and controlled by women—to "medical childbirth"—an event defined and controlled by male physicians—described by historians of childbirth. In the nineteenth century, the emerging medical profession seized upon obstetrics as a way to advance the status and the fortunes of its all-male practitioners. Simultaneously criticizing the unscientific methods of midwives and celebrating the alleged advances of medical science, members of the exclusive fraternity of the medical profession urged expectant mothers to shun the advice, support, and assistance of other women and to rely instead on male physicians' expertise, drugs, and surgical tools. Although births continued to take place at home throughout the nineteenth century, the introduction of ether (a drug that induced unconsciousness) and the exclusion of female attendants (as dangerous distractions during the drug's administration) were precursors to the twentieth-century practice of giving birth in hospitals.[38] But, much as they had earlier resisted assuming adult responsibilities, young women in the Old South also resisted a wholehearted embrace of the new approach to childbirth.

Southern women had good reason to resist the medicalization of childbirth. While traditional childbirth practices treated giving birth as a natural (if often painful) process that necessitated mostly emotional support, modern obstetrics defined childbirth as a medical emergency that required a doctor's intervention. Midwives and other female attendants preferred minimal intervention in labor, and then only in difficult deliveries, such as breech (feet-first) births. Male physicians, by contrast, advocated the use of drugs and forceps to hasten even ordinary deliveries, which often led to complications, ranging from vaginal tearing to dismemberment of the infant. Moreover, the adoption of instrument-assisted delivery prior to the discovery of germs meant that unsterilized instruments often introduced dangerous bacteria into tears in the vaginal wall, leading to puerperal (childbed) fever, among other infections. In addition to increasing the chances of injury, illness, and death, medical childbirth reduced women's agency by requiring that the woman in labor recline (sometimes in a state of drug-induced unconsciousness), elevating her legs and lower body to permit the attending physician to apply forceps. In social childbirth, by contrast, midwives encouraged the woman in labor to walk about the room and to give birth in an upright position, physically supported by her female attendants. Such practices strengthened contractions without the use of drugs and allowed gravity to assist the laboring woman in delivery. Although, as discussed above, southern women accepted the medical profession's characterization of pregnancy as a form of illness, they did not allow male expertise to supplant female experience.[39]

The experience of Charlestonian Sarah Bennett Hopkins illuminates the selective way in which southern women responded to the medical profession's attempts to supplant female attendants in the birthing room. Pregnant with her first child in 1836, Hopkins hoped to retain the services of a skilled physician to attend her in her "hour of trial," but after being turned away by the first two she approached, she finally concluded to engage "young Dr Tom Prideau, who has been highly recommended." She did not intend to rely solely on the inexperienced physician, however; rather, she anticipated having the assistance of Dinah, "a colored nurse." After her difficulties in finding a physician, she explained, "There is great comfort . . . in having one by your sick bed like that good woman. May she be a blessing to me." For this southern woman, at least, women's support was more important than men's medicine.[40]

Nearly three decades later, Virginia native Samuella Hart Curd recorded an unusually detailed account of her parturition in her diary. Her description suggests the continued importance of female attendants as well as the new presence of male doctors. Most important to Curd, however, were her own feelings:

I felt badly and had pains during the night & day, they grew worse, after dinner I sent for cousin Mary, who was up stairs & asked her what she thought of the case, she said I was going to be sick so I made my plans for it, sent for Mrs. McKinny & cousin Mary & later for Dr. Abbott, about supper I was taken with a sick stomache [sic], which lasted all night only ceasing while the pains were on me. I was not relieved until half past 5 o'clock in the morning at which hour the baby was born. I had heard all say there was suffering, but the half had not been told.[41]

Curd's diary entry read much like colonial accounts of childbirth; she experienced a painful and lengthy (although apparently uncomplicated) labor with the assistance and support of other women, calling for a doctor only toward the end of her long ordeal. In addition to placing more emphasis on her female attendants than on her male physician, Curd highlighted her own agency, repeatedly using the pronoun "I" to call attention to her central role in the drama. Only when she referred to her newborn infant did she change to the passive voice, virtually giving the baby credit for birthing itself. Curd's account of labor and childbirth, with its shift from herself to her child, typified the trajectory followed by young mothers in the Old South.

Once they had survived the "Ordeal" of childbirth, new mothers shifted their focus from their own trials to their new children. Margaret Lea Graves's account of her delivery, which took place while her husband, Charles, was away at sea, omitted all the details of labor. Instead, Graves described her relief at having passed through childbirth safely and her love for her baby, a boy named for his father. "Oh!" she exclaimed. "Let us bless & magnify the Lord for his merciful kindness in sparing my life through the perils of Childbirth & giving us in His infinite wisdom so beautiful a babe—a little blue-eyed boy—of *perfect* form & feature—& *his Father's image*." In the weeks and months that followed childbirth, young mothers rejoiced in the "novelty" of their new role, focusing their attention on their "sweet babes" and devoting themselves wholeheartedly to what Caroline Brooks Lilly termed "the sweets of maternal felicity."[42] More than the duties of marriage, the demands of motherhood took up all of young women's time and attention.

"A LITTLE BABY TAKES UP A GREAT DEAL OF TIME": CHILD CARE

"The sweets of maternal felicity" were accompanied by tremendous responsibilities. Nineteenth-century Americans regarded children as precious beings and mothers as their best caretakers. Mothers were responsible not only for preserving their children's lives but for molding their characters.

Educators and advice books explained that by fulfilling their duties in raising good children, mothers played a vital role in the production of virtuous citizens and, by extension, in the maintenance of a Christian and democratic nation. Southern women fully embraced these popular ideas about the importance of childhood and the significance of motherhood. As Lizzie Scott Neblett expressed it, it was a mother's charge "to provide, to educate, both brain and heart, and fit them to take their place in the world as useful & good citizens."[43]

New mothers were inundated with reminders of the importance of their new role. Sarah Bennett Hopkins's aunt wrote promptly after the birth of Hopkins's first child to "rejoice" with her on the birth of "a living & perfect child." She also took advantage of the occasion to remind the new mother, "a precious soul is committed to your care," and concluded by praying, "May you be enabled to bring it up in the way in which it should go." Hopkins's mother echoed this advice. She reminded her daughter that "the moment you become a mother; *that* moment the work of education begins" and recommended one of antebellum America's popular child rearing periodicals, "the Mothers Magazine," to the new mother. Expressing "constant praise & gratitude" for "Gods mercies toward you, in a very trying season," she urged her daughter to think seriously about "what we shall render to our Lord for all his benefits towards us." In southern women's writings, motherhood became not merely an earthly responsibility but a sacred charge.[44]

Many young mothers reflected soberly on their new duties. Lucy Wickham, who gave birth to twins in 1850, admitted that although her children were "darling little creatures," she was sometimes overwhelmed at the thought of being in charge of their welfare. "It quite frightens me when I think of how much responsibility rests upon us, in bringing them up," she told her friend Elizabeth Kane. Mary Virginia Early Brown recorded her thoughts in her diary after her first child's baptism: "I feel solemn indeed under the responsibility," she reflected. "You enquire dearest sister how I feel on again becoming a mother," Elizabeth Fischer wrote to Anna Hoskins in 1839. "I feel with you that my responsibilities are doubled; and sometimes am almost in despair about ever being able to do my duty."[45]

Young mothers eased their assumption of their new role by hiring baby nurses (who sometimes doubled as wet nurses) and by delegating responsibility for routine child care to slave caretakers. Women also turned to their mothers, sisters, cousins, and neighbors for assistance and advice. Still, most southern women took primary responsibility for their infants, breastfeeding them, watching over them as they slept, and caring for them in illness.[46]

Loula Kendall Rogers's diary entries after the "Birth Of My First Born" in 1864 indicate southern white women's onerous maternal responsibilities. Alternately enraptured and irritated with her "dear little troublesome boy," she lamented her loss of sleep due to the newborn's incessant demands for food and comfort: "I fear I am not very charitable towards babies," she mused, "as I find myself at such times wishing for 'a lodge in some vast wilderness, where the cry of babies might never reach me more[.]'" She continued with a detailed explanation of the colicky baby's behavior and her own ambivalent feelings toward him: "He wakes up three times every night, & from 4 o'clock till breakfast wont sleep one bit, but keeps us all waiting on him when most we want to sleep—I love the dear little fellow very much in the day when he is quiet & laughing, but have ever so many hard thoughts against him, when he keeps waking me up so often & wont go to sleep[.]" Given these trying (although by no means unusual) circumstances, it is not surprising that the young mother wished for her husband to take a more active role in caring for the baby. "Let us both try to do our duty towards him," she proposed in a letter to her absent husband, making child care "a responsibility . . . that is equally shared by each of us." But when fatherly assistance was not forthcoming, Rogers reconciled herself to being the primary caregiver to her son and prayed for "more patience to bear with all the troubles & trials attendant on his 'babyhood[.]'"[47]

There were both practical and philosophical reasons for southern white mothers to take the lead in infant care, particularly breast-feeding. In the antebellum South, prior to the introduction of refrigeration, it was nearly impossible to keep milk fresh and disease-free; nursing was both the most convenient and the most healthful way to nourish a baby. In addition, the celebration of motherhood that characterized Victorian America attached tremendous importance to the mother-child bond, which elite Americans believed was formed and strengthened by maternal breast-feeding. Thus, despite the widespread belief in contemporary America that black nurse-maids took charge of white children, most women in the Old South nursed their own children.[48]

The importance of maternal breast-feeding is indicated by the correspondence of Sarah Bennett Hopkins and her husband, Erastus. After giving birth to "a fine, lovely babe" in May 1836, Hopkins suffered a spell of severe fever, probably puerperal (childbed) fever, an illness caused by the use of unsterilized medical instruments. Despite her own health problems, Hopkins breast-fed her "dear little Boy," who grew "finely." In June, the new mother complained about the "*drain* . . . upon my system" and determined to augment breast milk with "a little *light food* once or twice a day"; "nursing this dear *great* Boy is enough . . . to keep any one weak for some weeks," she observed. Erastus disapproved of his wife's methods, but in her husband's extended absence, Hopkins resolved to continue the practice "until," she wrote, "I find it *hurts him*, or until I see you when you can *judge for yourself* and advise." But Erastus did not wait to see the child to pass judgment; he was firmly convinced that it would harm the baby to "*stuff* him" with solid food and that only mother's milk would ensure his health. When he filed his wife's letter, he marked it simply: "Merited reproof."[49]

Even for women like Laura Wirt Randall, who had both a white nurse and several slaves to assist her, "the fatigue of nursing" was considerable. Randall did not trust anybody else to diaper her first-born child, and breast-feeding was her constant occupation. "It is an incessant business this nursing," she remarked in 1828. Mary Virginia Early Brown spent many "sleepless nights" tending to her first child. Samuella Hart Curd summed up the situation for many new mothers when she wrote in her diary: "A little baby takes up a great deal of time."[50]

Not all women adjusted easily to their new responsibilities. Although Caroline Brooks Lilly reported herself "quite easy and . . . pleased with the novelty of [her] situation" the day after giving birth to twin girls, Samuella Hart Curd still felt "awkward and ignorant" with her baby a month after delivery. Curd relied heavily on her female friends (mentioning visits from six different women) as she recovered her health and learned how to care for her first child.[51]

The around-the-clock duties of child care took a toll on young mothers. Commenting on the incessant demands of a nursing infant, Laura Wirt Randall came close to despair: "I declare if I tho't I was to be thus occupied for the rest of my life, I w[oul]d—I was going to say—*lie down & die*. It w[oul]d be a slavery beyond that of all the galleys—& for a lifetime too!" Bettie Maney Kimberly pronounced herself "perfectly worn out" in 1861. "I never suffered so much from fatigue in my life," she complained, "and am even yet sadly in need of both rest and sleep." Samuella Hart Curd succinctly summed up the situation of many young mothers in an 1861 diary entry: "I feel very tired both going & coming."[52]

Such comments, taken together with the common practice of placing the baby's crib or cradle at the mother's bedside, suggest that the image of white children's care by black nursemaids owes more to mythology than to fact. Slaves certainly participated in child care, but the care of young infants—particularly breast-feeding—was a mother's responsibility. Unless ill health prevented them from doing so, southern mothers insisted on nursing their children themselves, reserving the labor of their slaves and servants for other tasks. The 1839 diary of Caroline Brooks Lilly, who was a school-teacher as well as the mother of twin girls, illuminates the usual allocation of duties. While "Charlotte," the girls' slave "nurse," watched after the children "very carefully" while Lilly kept school, Lilly alone was responsible for breast-feeding. "The nursing of my sweet babes will unavoidably occupy a large portion of time," she explained.[53]

Even women who customarily delegated routine child care to slaves assumed full responsibility when their children suffered from one of the Old South's ubiquitous illnesses. Measles, malaria, scarlet fever, yellow fever, and whooping cough were only a few of the many diseases that flourished in the nineteenth-century South.[54] Young mothers anxiously watched over their sick children, dosing them with medicine, bathing them with cool damp cloths, and praying for them. Carrie Sage expressed empathy for her friend Ella Noland MacKenzie in the fall of 1854, when MacKenzie's child was ill. "You have, no doubt dear Ella had much anxiety this Summer," she commiserated, "and the hardest of all to bear—to see your little darling suffering and to find yourself utterly powerless to help him—This is indeed the greatest trial next to death—which a Mother is called upon to bear[.]"[55]

"SINCE I HAVE BECOME A MOTHER": MATERNITY AND IDENTITY

Like Carrie Sage, many young women reflected seriously on what it meant to be "a Mother" in the antebellum South. "Becoming a mother" meant more than undertaking responsibility for child care; it meant investing oneself in one's children and adopting a new identity that revolved around them. Many southern women, like Mary Virginia Early Brown, demarcated their lives into the period prior to childbirth and the time "since I have become a mother." Such expressions indicated the paramount importance of maternity to adult female identity. Whether they experienced motherhood as "one of the greatest blessings" of life or as its "greatest source of anxiety," young women in the Old South acknowledged the centrality of motherhood to their identity as adult women.[56]

Most young mothers would probably have agreed with Lizzie Scott Neblett that "a mothers love" was "the holiest passion in the human breast." Although a few women, like Sarah Satterlee, were initially "very rebellious and unhappy" at the prospect of undergoing pregnancy and childbirth and devoting themselves to child care, they accepted motherhood as their mission in life. Indeed, given the realities of life in the nineteenth-century South,

THE HAPPY MOTHER.

Notwithstanding popular images of slave "mammies" nurturing the children of slaveholders, white women in the Old South were primary caretakers for their children. For many young women in the Old South, motherhood was a source of personal identity and profound satisfaction. Southern mothers' lived experiences thus closely resembled popular iconography of "the happy mother" produced in the Victorian North. (Library of Congress) married women had no realistic alternative to a life dominated by pregnancy, childbirth, and child care. Whether "reconciled" or "pleased" at the prospect of motherhood, therefore, once southern women bore children, they devoted themselves wholeheartedly to their welfare—or, as one new mother put it, to "fulfill[ing] a mother's part."[57]

Young mothers invested a tremendous amount of love and concern in their offspring, glorying in their children's accomplishments and in their own position as "Mama." In letters to friends and family members, new mothers reveled in their children's charms and accomplishments. "Well my dear Sis I can write the glorious news at last," crowed Bettie Maney Kimberly in 1861. "*Baby walks*, actually trots all over the room by herself—is it not delightful? Nothing has happened to please me as much in a long time I can tell you." "I want you very much Bessie to see our dearest little Baby," Lucy Wickham wrote to her friend Elizabeth Kane in 1849. "You don't know how sweet he is and what a pet. He is very fair with blue eyes and the sweetest expression, . . . of course in our eyes he is a piece of perfection." Laura Wirt Randall was devoted to her young daughter. "Bless her little Soul!" she exclaimed in 1828. "She has improved very much lately. She *talks* now most sweetly—And has a new trick of holding up her *fists* before her at arms length, & admiring them—Sometimes crossing her arms in that position & seeming to contemplate them with much interest.—What a smart child! Isn't she?"[58]

Many women took great "pleasure and pride" in motherhood. As Carrie Sage expressed it in 1856, "These little ones are a comfort indeed and add a great charm to home." Loula Kendall Rogers doted on her "bright little boy," describing his "winning little ways" and admitting, "He is endearing himself to my heart every moment more strongly." Despite her early difficulties, by the time her infant was two months old, Samuella Hart Curd was extremely attached to him. "The baby is as fat as a butter ball, & is getting so interesting," she wrote, adding, almost with surprise: "How the little creature enlists ones affections."[59]

For some women, what Loula Kendall Rogers called "a mother's holy rapture" became the primary source of happiness. Motherhood offered southern women the opportunity for both pleasant companionship and a meaningful occupation—benefits that were all too often lacking in marriage and housekeeping. Describing her daughter Nan as her "constant little companion," Margaret Mordecai Devereux confessed, "I sometimes think that she will become too necessary for my happiness[.]" Many young mothers devoted their letters and diaries almost exclusively to news of their children, who seemed to have provided them with more happiness than their often-absent husbands. "As usual you give me no news except that dear little Mary

Ann is well," Elizabeth Fischer remarked in a letter to her sister in 1834, adding, "you do not mention your husband."[60]

For southern women, motherhood was both a distinct stage of life and an important source of identity. Young mothers associated motherhood both with increased responsibility and with increased happiness. "My happiness for ten months past *has been doubly increased* by becoming a mother," Judith Nelson confided to her friend Maria Lowther Skinner in 1805, adding that her pleasure in the company of her "sweet smiling little cherub" was accompanied by new "*maternal cares*." For young women in the Old South, the combination of "*maternal cares*" and "the sweets of maternal felicity" added up to a new identity as "a *mother*." In that capacity, they prayed for—and sometimes achieved—the ability to, as Lizzie Neblett put it, "forget myself entirely, and live for my children alone."[61] As they did so, they abandoned their earlier efforts at resistance to fulfill their demanding roles as mothers.

For young women in the Old South, coming-of-age was a lengthy and trying experience. To achieve full stature as adult women, southern girls underwent a series of rites of passage that marked the transitions from one life stage to another and required them to adopt new roles and responsibilities. At each stage, southern women-in-the-making tried on new identities as students, daughters, belles, brides, wives, and mothers. Young women in the Old South resisted these transformations, but they also regarded them as unavoidable and inevitable—as part and parcel of growing up. As they assumed the responsibilities of adulthood, southern women also acquiesced to the subordination of womanhood. The upheaval of civil war, however, changed this situation dramatically. The American Civil War was a rite of passage in and of itself; moreover, it permanently altered the possibilities open to young southern women and thereby fundamentally changed the process and the meaning of growing up female in the American South.

WAR

"IF I WAS ONLY A MAN!": SARAH MORGAN

In early 1862, nineteen-year-old Sarah Morgan, the youngest daughter of prominent Baton Rouge jurist Thomas Gibbes Morgan, commenced a diary in "an old book" given to her by one of her eight siblings. The previous year had "promised much pleasure," she recalled, but had instead been filled with tragedy: the secession of her home state of Louisiana, the establishment of the Confederate States of America, the outbreak of the Civil War, the occupation of both Baton Rouge and New Orleans by Union forces, and—most importantly for Sarah—the deaths of both Sarah's favorite brother and her beloved father (her brother in a duel, her father from a respiratory ailment). Sarah Morgan would forever remember 1861 as the year that the "unclouded happiness" of her early years was replaced by "long days and nights of heart breaking grief."[1]

Initially, the diarist's grief was focused on personal tragedy, not political drama; like Judge Morgan, "father's 'Little daughter,'" as Sarah was known, was a "reluctant Confederate" who preferred a peaceable resolution to the sectional crisis. But over the course of the war, which resulted in the deaths of two more family members (one brother was killed in battle and another died as a prisoner of war) and forced Sarah, her widowed mother, and her sisters to refugee first to the family's rural plantation, Linwood, and then to New Orleans and the home of Sarah's oldest brother, the young Louisianan became a stalwart Confederate. "I confess my self a rebel, body and soul," she announced toward the end of the conflict, adding: "*Confess?* I glory in it!"[2]

Yet for Sarah Morgan, as for other young southern women, the journey from southern lady to she-rebel was a difficult one. For Sarah, as for other young women in the Southern Confederacy, the Civil War exacerbated southern girls' discomfort with the status quo by producing tension between a customary gender identity (as a southern lady) and a new political identity (as a Confederate rebel). Thus, for young women in the Civil War South, the nation's political turmoil mirrored their own inner conflict. At the same time, war brought new responsibilities and new opportunities for ladies-in-the-making. During the Civil War, young women like Sarah struggled to adapt to the demands of the war-torn South and to work the necessary changes in their identities into a new definition of southern womanhood. Sarah and her peers both relished and resisted the newfound independence —and increased responsibility—which the Civil War imposed upon them. Ultimately, however, southern girls discovered that the Civil War offered them unprecedented—and often welcome—opportunities to translate their long-standing resistance to the status quo into overt rebellion against the ideal of the southern lady. Over the course of the war, young women in the Southern Confederacy—female youth who had not entirely assumed their adult gender role or been fully socialized into compliance with the status quo—created a new female identity: the rebel lady.

Throughout the Civil War, Sarah struggled to reconcile the political loyalties she adopted during the conflict with the feminine propriety with which she had been imbued in her childhood. Initially, she recoiled from even a hint of immodesty. In May 1861, after marching with a group of other young women to the State House to wave the Confederate banner in front of the occupying Union troops, Morgan was overcome with a sense of shame at her "conspicuous"—and immodest—appearance. "I—I am disgusted with myself," she wrote. Morgan's "unladylike display of defiance" and her shame at being involved in "such a display," she hoped, would "be a lesson . . . always to remember a lady can gain nothing by such displays." "Never again!" she vowed.[3]

Morgan resolved that wartime "shall not make me less the lady." She decried women's political talk—"I hate to hear women on political subjects," she declared, as "they invariably make fools of themselves"—and refused to take part in the gatherings of women who met to discuss the war. When news reached her of the rude behavior of "the so called *ladies* of New Orleans," who insulted General "Beast" Butler's men, who occupied the town, Morgan criticized them for their "ugly" and "unladylike" behavior. "In my opinion," she reflected, "the Southern women . . . have disgraced themselves by their rude, ill mannered behavior. . . . 'Loud' women, what a contempt I have for you! How I despise your vulgarity!" Yet in her own efforts to show herself a lady—which took the form of conversing politely with a Union officer she encountered on a train—Morgan worried that "in behaving like a lady I have forfeited my self-respect" as a southerner.[4]

Morgan attempted to remain aloof from the war of manners, but she realized that the Civil War caused many of her peers to abandon prewar patterns. She was particularly concerned by women's abandonment of "charity" for "Politics"—and by the bloodthirsty sentiments that many women expressed. "Let historians extol blood shedding," she wrote; "it is woman's place to abhor it." Yet Morgan knew that many women abhorred Yankees even more than they abhorred violence. "This is a dreadful war," she reflected in May 1862, "to make even the hearts of women so bitter! I hardly know myself these last few weeks. I, who have such a horror of bloodshed, consider even killing in self defense murder, who cannot wish them the slightest evil, whose only prayer is to have them sent back in peace to their own country, I talk of killing them!" Although Morgan struggled against such feelings, she observed that many women—including herself—had been changed by the war. "This war has brought out wicked, malignant feelings that I did not believe could dwell in woman's heart," she remarked regretfully. "O woman! into what loathsome violence you have debased your holy mission! God will punish us for our hardheartedness," she soberly added, including herself in the group she excoriated.[5]

Sarah did her best to adapt her old training as a southern lady to her new circumstances as a southern rebel. Forced to refugee repeatedly in the face of Union troops' advances during the summer of 1862, she packed dresses, corsets, combs, toothbrushes, face powder, lace collars, and hairpins in readiness for departure in case of enemy attack and laid out a fresh dress each night so that she could "run respectably." Sarah also struggled to find an appropriately feminine outlet for her patriotic impulses. Early in the conflict, she resolved to "devote all my red, white, and blue silk to the manufacture of Confederate flags" and determined to make a miniature Stars and Bars the finishing touch to her dress. Soon, she found a more practical use for her sewing skills. In September 1862, she proudly recorded that she and her sisters had taken on "a very important task": sewing shirts for soldiers. "We cannot do too much, or even enough for our soldiers," she declared. "I believe that is the universal sentiment of the women of the south."[6]

Yet even as she deplored southern women's—and her own—"unladylike" thoughts and actions and attempted to uphold antebellum ideals of femi-

April 26th 1862.

There is no word in the English language which can express the state in which we are all now, and have been for the last three days. Day before yesterday news came early in the morning of three of the enemy's boats passing the forts, and then the excitement commenced, and increased so rapidly on hearing of the sinking of eight of our gunboats in the engagement, the capture of the forts, and last night of the burning of the wharves and cotton in the city, while the Yankees were taking possession, that to day the excitement has reached almost the crazy point. I believe that I am one of the most self possessed in my small circle of acquaintance, and yet, I feel such a craving for news from Miriam, and mother and Jimmy, who are in the city, such patriotic and enthusiastic sentiments etc, that I believe I am as crazy as the rest, and it is all humbug when they tell me I am cool. Nothing can be heard positively, for every report except that our gunboats were sunk, and theirs coming up to the city, has been contradicted, until we do not really know whether it is in their possession or not. We only know we had best be prepared for anything, so day before yesterday Lilly and I secured what little jewelry we had, that we may yet be of some use to us if we must run. I vow I will not move one step, unless forced away! I remain here, come what will. We went this morning to see the cotton

During the upheaval of the war years, many young women's lives were changed by occupation and refugeeing. In this page from Civil War diarist Sarah Morgan's diary, the stalwart young Confederate reports the latest news from the front and vows to "be prepared for anything." (Rare Book, Manuscript, and Special Collections Library, Duke University, Durham, North Carolina) ninity, Sarah lamented the fact of her womanhood, repeatedly expressing her desire to be a man so that she could fight—and even die—for the Confederacy. Fascinated by weapons and by her brother's gray uniform, Morgan used her diary to express her dissatisfaction with her passive role in the war and her desire to free herself of the restrictions of feminine propriety. As a woman, she explained, she would have to "repent for ever after in sack cloth and ashes" if she harmed anybody, even an invading and "insolent" Union soldier. But if she were a man, she speculated, the situation would be very different. "O if I was only a man!" she cried. "Then I could don the breeches, and slay them with a will!"[7]

Over and over, Morgan expressed her regret at her limitations as a woman. Denied even the option of nursing ailing soldiers, Morgan declared herself "a chained bear." Rather than being the "coward, helpless woman that I am," she wished to be "free"—and the freedom and "independence" that she longed for, Morgan associated with men. "We worthless women," she believed, were "of no value or importance to ourselves or the rest of the world." "What is the use of all these worthless women, in war times?" she demanded. "Why was I not a man?" Sarah knew that her sentiments were widely shared. "If I was only a man!" she repeated her old war cry. "I dont know a woman here who does not groan over her misfortune in being clothed in petticoats," she added.[8]

Ultimately, even as she struggled to uphold feminine propriety, Sarah concluded that the traits traditionally associated with southern femininity were not always desirable. Submissiveness—previously an esteemed characteristic in southern women—became anathema to loyal Confederates who described the Civil War as a war for southern self-determination. Sarah recognized the dissonance between her old identity as a southern lady and her new one as a southern rebel when she proclaimed: "Bondage, woman that I am, I can never stand!" Small wonder, then, that she imagined being able to cast aside the bonds of womanhood. "Pshaw!" she exclaimed in May 1862. "There are no women here! We are all men!"[9]

Sarah never acted on her desire to become a man. Although strongly tempted to try on her brother's Confederate uniform, she turned aside at the last moment for fear that her pet bird, a canary, might witness her in male attire. Yet in less obvious, yet no less significant, ways, Sarah modified her definition of southern womanhood. Like her antebellum counterparts, she experimented with alternatives to the ideal of the southern lady; unlike them, she considered her future in the mist of change and even chaos. Thus, the Civil War offered Sarah and other daughters of the Confederacy a unique opportunity to embrace a changed identity in a changing South. In ways both forced and chosen, the reluctant-Confederate-turned-rebel-lady began to contemplate and prepare for an independent future. In a feminine invocation of martial imagery, she envisioned her new self as "Diana the huntress . . . cold, calm, and independent" and capable of "stand[ing] alone, alone, and fight[ing] the battle of life out single handed."[10] Sarah would not become a man, but she would become an independent woman.

Morgan had never regarded marriage as the sine qua non of a woman's existence. As a teenager, although she reveled in balls and beaux, she had more interest in books than in babies. Like many of the young women described in Chapter 3, Morgan saw much to recommend a single life. She disagreed with a friend, who said that "marriage is awful, but to be an old maid more awful still." "I wont agree," Morgan declared. "I mean to be an old maid myself, and show the world what such a life can be." The war may have reinforced Sarah's commitment to singlehood by inspiring a hatred of tyranny. Referring to President Lincoln, she chafed at being "governed by the despotism of one man, whose word is our law!" Morgan's comment might just as well have referred to a wife's subjection to her husband. Certainly Morgan had no intention of yielding herself to any ordinary man, although she sometimes fantasized about her ideal mate: intelligent, amiable, and brave. "I can fancy no greater hell," she mused, "than to be tied to a man you could not respect and love perfectly." Ridiculing her male admirers as "horrid" "silly," "soft," and "rattle brain[ed]," she seems to have welcomed the opportunity to reject one suitor with the excuse "that these were not 'marrying' times." By late 1863, Sarah and her sister Marion had resolved to set up household together as confirmed spinsters. "What blissful, happy, quiet days we will spend!" Sarah predicted gleefully. "We will grow old insensibly, without regret, live without care, and die in peace when we are called. And the secret of such bliss as this quiet life would be, is to be found in the motto to be inscribed above the door 'No gentlemen or children admitted.'"[11]

Although Sarah did not fear life as a single woman, she did fear poverty. "I look forward to my future life with a shudder," she wrote in July 1862. Faced with the prospect of needing to provide for herself, Sarah concluded that teaching was the most logical choice for self-support, although she regarded the prospect with distaste. "If we are to be pennyless, as well as homeless," she concluded, "I'll work for my living. How I wonder? I will teach!" Although teaching was Morgan's immediate solution to her financial woes, she sometimes felt, "I would rather die than teach. . . . My soul revolts from the drudgery," she explained. "I never see a governess that my heart does not ache for her." As a governess, Morgan predicted, she would have to endure "hard crusts," "bitter words," and "poverty"; the work, she forecast, would "speedily lay [her] in [her] grave." Yet she could see no other alternative, and by the end of the war she was instructing her niece, Charlotte, in order to prepare herself for postwar teaching work.[12]

Sarah also recognized the necessity of learning to perform the menial household tasks that had fallen to the family's slaves before the war. As early as June 1862, she wryly detailed her new accomplishments: "I discovered I could empty a dirty hearth, dust, move heavy weights, [and] make myself generally useful and dirty." Despite Sarah's lack of enthusiasm for her newfound abilities, they did provide her with the opportunity to achieve her cherished dream of "single blessedness." As she told her mother in late 1863: "You see I can take care of myself, so there is no necessity for my getting married." [13]

As the war drew to a close, Sarah's diary, always a document of internal turmoil, as well as external strife, became still more introspective. Much like her antebellum counterparts, Sarah believed that she needed a mission to make life meaningful. "I am aweary of my monotonous, aimless life," she sighed, explaining that her "soul" demanded "more! more! light from above, nobler thoughts, nobler aspirations, a wider, or new field in life! Something nobler, Something beyond!" Carefully (if erroneously) distinguishing herself from "most women," Sarah explained that she found it "irksome" to "walk in the same dull, empty, simpering round that thousands have trod before" and that she longed for a "new part to play" in the drama of life. "In every day life," she mused, "I walk the beaten track apparently content to be numbered with the rest. But I am not! I wish there was a new school for woman," she concluded. "I dont exactly know what I want, except that it is something new." [14]

Although Sarah did not fully realize it, the Civil War had been, in fact, "a new school for woman." In that school, young southern women learned to replace submissiveness with self-reliance, dependence with independence, and frailty with strength. Although it was not yet clear "exactly" how they would do it, the next generation of southern white women would find a "new part to play" in the New South. Their experiences in the Civil War era prepared them to do it.[15]

"THE WAR IS THE ALL ABSORBING TOPIC": THE POLITICIZATION OF SOUTHERN GIRLS

In 1861, Lucy Wood wrote a long letter on "the disunion question" to her fiancé, Waddy Butler. Yet at the conclusion of her letter, the young Virginian demurred: "But I have no political opinion, and have a peculiar dislike to all females who discuss such matters." This blatant falsehood, paired with Wood's sophisticated analysis of secession politics (at least when measured by southern standards) suggest that from the very beginning, the politicization that accompanied the onset of the Civil War would force fundamental changes in young southern women's definition of themselves.[16]

As Wood's self-deprecating comments indicated, for southern women, expressing political opinions was a break from tradition. Although recent scholarship has revealed that southern women took an active interest in politics from the colonial era onward, by the 1850s, women's role in politics was passive; playing anything but a symbolic role threatened the southern patriarchy and left women vulnerable to charges of abolitionism, feminism, and other subversive doctrines. But as political sectionalism increased, southern women found it impossible to ignore the conflict, and young women were no exception. Indeed, it was southern girls and young women—those who were (as demonstrated in the preceding chapters) most committed to resisting the status quo and reworking southern female identity—who were most attracted to the new doctrine of Confederate loyalty, which offered a socially sanctioned avenue to a new definition of southern womanhood. For young women in the Southern Confederacy, politicization and resistance went hand in hand.[17]

Young women eagerly debated politics even before the outbreak of the Civil War. While Kentuckian Lizzie Hardin complained that many girls suffered from "political ignorance," Virginian Kate Cox Logan claimed that she "had been fed on political questions since early childhood." But the Civil War made politics a more pervasive force in southern society. As war drew nearer, more and more southern girls traded political ignorance for southern partisanship. As Tennessean Alice Ready put it in 1861: "The War is the all absorbing topic of conversation and letters."[18]

For many southern girls and young women, the secession crisis and the outbreak of civil war prompted a new interest in political matters, transforming schoolgirls, daughters-at-home, and southern belles alike into "very enthusiastic little 'rebels.'" Georgia resident Anna Maria Green began her diary in January 1861 to keep track of "the great national events that are now transpiring." Although few girls had the opportunity that twenty-year-old Kate Virginia Cox Logan had to accompany her father to the secession convention in Richmond, Virginia, many young women used their journals to record political news, which they gleaned from conversations with family members, newspaper accounts, correspondence from the front, and gossip—what Ellen House termed "madam rumor." Writing from "the quiet of Glen Alpine," her family's upcountry plantation, in 1862, Virginian

Sally Munford described herself and her family as "completely excluded from all this commotion." Nonetheless, the Munford girls kept abreast of developments by reading the newspapers. Although the girls spent their time "with our books and writing," their thoughts were occupied differently. "Our minds are so completely absorbed in the war," Sally Munford explained, "that we think of nothing beyond the arrival of the mail, and the news which the papers may contain." Over and over again, young women indicated that the coming of the Civil War had profoundly changed their thoughts and conversations—even if not (yet) their daily actions. "The war and public matters occupy my thoughts so much," wrote seventeen-year-old Louisianan Sarah Wadley in 1862, "that I scarcely think of noting down the events of our quiet life." [19]

Even schoolgirls were caught up in the excitement. Although some female academies were "turned into hospitals," abandoned in the face of approaching troops, or closed for lack of funds, many young women continued to attend school during the Civil War. Raleigh, North Carolina's St. Mary's School, for instance, was in operation for the duration of the war. Like other female academies, the school was a popular choice for parents who hoped to spare their daughters the hardships of war. Attending boarding school, however, did not exempt young women from the changes wrought by the Civil War. At many schools, as at Athens, Georgia's Lucy Cobb Institute, "the progress of the war was the main topic of conversation." Some teachers, capitalizing on girls' interest in war news, made the secession crisis and the progress of the war topics for student compositions, thus transforming an assignment that upheld conventional definitions of femininity into one that encouraged girls to adopt a new political identity. As in the antebellum era, however, southern students developed interests independently of their instructors. Even when their teachers tried to keep them to their lessons, Civil War–era schoolgirls persisted in their political interests; at schools in New Orleans, students "drew secession flags in their books." While parents may have sent their daughters to school to protect them from the ravages of war, they could not isolate them from the politicization of the era. As a student at Missouri's Danville Female Academy expressed it, "During the War we had some very exciting times for school girls." [20]

Southern schoolgirls followed the secession crisis closely. Fourteen-year-old Louise Wigfall, who felt "like a stranger in a foreign land" at her Boston boarding school, read about the firing on Fort Sumter in the northern papers and wrote home to rejoice with her father, a Confederate senator. One of the most dramatic accounts of schoolgirls' response to secession was Sophia Haskell Cheves's reminiscences of "M[ada]me Togno's Establishment for young ladies—the fashionable Charleston boarding school in 1860–61." Apprised of the Confederate demand that the Union evacuate Fort Sumter, just off the coast of Charleston, or be fired upon, the "half frightened" and "wildly excited" girls stayed awake all night, waiting for the "bombardment." Just as dawn was breaking, Cheves wrote, "one deep awful boom resounded through the air, and we knew that the battle had begun."[21]

Even if they had wished to (and most, apparently, did not), it would have been impossible for many young women to ignore the conflict. Although some women, like Louisiana resident Kate Stone, initially isolated themselves from the conflict by entertaining themselves "with a new novel and a plate of candy," most girls and young women found that their lives were profoundly changed by war. Schoolgirls found that political discussions and military maneuvers disrupted their studies; debutantes found themselves (depending on their location) either overrun with beaux or lacking them entirely; and daughters at home found that wartime shortages, patriotic contributions to the war effort, and the absence of male relatives and slaves placed new demands on their shoulders. Under these circumstances, most southern girls found it imperative to keep abreast of political and military developments.[22]

Virginian Kate Corbin captured young women's new relationship to politics in the Civil War South in an 1861 letter to her school friend, Sally Munford. "I too am taking intense interest in every movement among our statesmen & the states themselves & sometimes feel surprised at myself for it, I have hitherto been so totally indifferent to all such topics," she remarked. "But we are all to be so intimately concerned in the threatened & inevitable war that it is not to be wondered at after all."[23]

Young southern women attained new political acumen during the war years. While such knowledge might seem unremarkable under the changed circumstances of the Civil War era, the results were indeed, as Corbin expressed it, something to be wondered at, because political allegiances could lead young women into unladylike behavior. Southern girls' politicization—particularly in the form of unwavering support for the Confederate cause—sometimes had unexpected results. As North Carolinian Elizabeth Collier worried in 1862: "The great love I bear my country will I fear lead me to extremes." As the war progressed, it would become increasingly apparent that as southern ladies adopted a new identity as "She Rebels," they might rebel against southern codes of femininity, as well as against the "blue devils" of the invading Union army. Girls and young women may have been attracted to southern nationalism in part because they saw a parallel between the

Confederacy's assertions of independence and their own attempts at resistance.[24]

"OUR CAUSE IS JUST": SOUTHERN GIRLS AS SOUTHERN NATIONALISTS

During the war, the South's adult women earned a reputation as stalwart Confederates. As Unionist Frances Dallam Peter put it, "secesh ladies" flaunted their political views both in their dress—with "streamers of red white & red on their dresses or bonnets"—and in their words and actions —by "abusing the [Union] soldiers." Charleston resident Emma Holmes proudly recorded a comment she overheard: "'Secession,' said a gentleman, was born in the hearts of Carolina women." Southern women's support for the Civil War is well documented, recorded in popular songs, Confederate memoirs, and scholarly histories. But what is rarely mentioned in these accounts is that many of the most vociferous supporters of the South were girls and young women. As a member of the Union forces that occupied Vicksburg, Mississippi, wryly acknowledged, "The young ladies were great rebels."[25]

The majority of southern girls supported the Confederacy wholeheartedly. Most echoed the views of South Carolinian Lottie Dye, who, despite her conviction that "civil war is the worst evil that can befall a Country," believed that the South was in the right and could not fail. "The South has to maintain her rights and *stand her ground*, or be subjugated," she explained in June 1861, "and you know that she never will be conquered." "Yankee craft and cunning," these loyal Rebels were certain, would be no match for southern bravery and honor. Louisianan Kate Stone summed up the sentiment of many young women when she wrote in her diary: "Our Cause is just and must prevail."[26]

At St. Mary's School in Raleigh, North Carolina, Confederate nationalism quickly swept the campus. Girls wrote compositions on "Our Opinions of the Present War" and displayed Confederate flags. Although Principal Aldert Smedes attempted to remain aloof from the conflict, he yielded to the students' petition for two and a half days' holiday from class in order to make mattresses and towels for Confederate soldiers. And although the schoolgirls shook their fists behind Sherman's back when Raleigh was occupied in 1865, they welcomed the "delightful serenades" of Confederate soldiers. Students at Madame Togno's select school for young ladies in Charleston, South Carolina, also were well schooled in southern partisanship. In 1861, alumna Sophia Haskell Cheves recalled, all the girls were "in great excitement about Secession" and had long talks "about States Rights . . . and of how wicked it was of the Yankees for thier [sic] own efforts to try to force us to remain in the Union."[27]

Young women's analysis of what was at stake ("States Rights"), of the reason for war (defending the South against "wicked Yankees"), and of the likely outcome (resounding victory) was not particularly insightful. Georgia resident Loula Kendall's interpretation of the conflict was standard Confederate fare: "Our poor persecuted South" had to "fight for its rights, or submit to the base assassins who are wicked enough to rob us of our homes, and not only to convert them into black smoking ruins, but to murder us all, men, women and children in cold blood!" Kendall, like most white southerners, dwelled on images of a helpless population forced to defend themselves against armed invasion and avoided any discussion of the people that they held in bondage; she hinted at the issue of slavery only in her disparaging description of the enemy as the "Black Republican party."[28] This myopic view owed more to (white) southern loyalties than to female ignorance; Kendall, like other young Confederates, simply echoed the language of the South's politicians.

Young women's understanding of the sectional conflict may not have been original, but their ways of showing support for the Confederate cause were unique. Dress, an important badge of southern ladyhood in the antebellum era, became an equally significant marker of Confederate loyalty in the Civil War years. Many young women sported red cockades—or, after the Confederate flag had been designed, a miniature Stars and Bars—on their clothing as a show of their support. Louisiana resident Sarah Morgan indicated the inflammatory potential—and the political significance—of Confederate fashion when she responded to occupying Union commander General Butler's ban on Confederate displays by vowing to wear a small Confederate flag "pinned to [her] bosom" for the duration of the conflict: "The man who says take it off, will have to pull it off for himself," she grimly asserted; "the man who dares attempt it—well! a pistol in my pocket will fill up the gap." Morgan made good on her promise at the next opportunity, wearing a five-inch-long flag on her shoulder and walking downtown when four Union ships arrived in the harbor. Morgan called attention both to her rebelliousness and to her youth when she noted that she and her sister, twenty-two-year-old Marie Antoinette (Nettie), "were the only two who ventured" to thus openly proclaim their loyalties. Indeed, even in Unionist territory, southern girls insisted on using their clothing to announce their politics. Surrounded by Union sympathizers in Maryland and unable to express their views openly, Lizette Woodworth and her cousin wore red and white "Confederate" underwear. For young women in the Civil War South, dress, formerly a means of reinforcing the constraints of southern ladyhood, became instead a way to resist those constraints.[29]

Young women's loyalties sometimes led them to defy not only occupying troops but also members of their own families. While most young women probably adopted the political allegiances of their parents, not all did. Some southern girls defied their parents — including their fathers — by supporting the Confederate cause. Eliza Frances Andrews, whose father was "almost the only man in Georgia who stood out openly for the Union," secretly sewed a Confederate banner to display at the courthouse "while the bells were ringing for secession." During the war, Andrews recorded frequent arguments among her family members about the Civil War. Andrews's refusal either to adopt her father's politics or to remain silent about her own sentiments suggested the ways in which the politicization of southern girls contested the dutifulness of southern daughters. "Poor, dear, old father," she reflected, "how I have disobeyed him and gone against his wishes ever since the war began." Such behavior undermined the southern patriarchy at the same time that it supported the Confederate cause.[30]

Young women in the Confederate South proudly proclaimed their political allegiances in their writings and through their dress. To do so, they sometimes challenged male authority as well as Yankee rule. Translating their ardent support of southern nationalism into concrete action, however, posed a problem for these daughters of the Confederacy: How could they reconcile their new identities as fierce defenders of southern freedom with their accustomed roles as gentle examples of southern womanhood? Confronting this question would cause a crisis for southern girls' identity that was, in its own way, just as profound as the crisis of southern identity that faced the newly established Confederate nation.

"A PART TO PERFORM": SUPPORTING THE WAR EFFORT

Virginian Lucy Wood, who was twenty years old and newly engaged when the Civil War began, spent the war years sewing for soldiers and encouraging her fiancé, Waddy Butler, to fight bravely in the war. In a May 1861 diary entry, she asserted the necessity of women's contributions to the war effort. At the same time, she called attention to the limited nature of those contributions.

We have a part to perform as well as the rest: we must make our men comfortable, we must encourage them by brave words and keeping stout hearts, we must try to turn their hearts to the guider of all destinies, and we must cry mightily unto Him day and night, and must trust in Him to deliver us. Yes, yes, we women have mighty work to perform for which we will be responsible. We have no glory, no fame to gain on earth, but it is ours to calm the fierce feelings of hatred and revenge, to be with and minister to the dying and the wounded; ours to point and lead the way for others—to attain for ourselves a glorious eternity and victory over our worst enemy.[31]

Wood's extended reflection on women's role in the Civil War demonstrated her successful integration of southern womanhood and Confederate loyalty. Women had "a part to perform" in the war effort, yet their "mighty work" took place behind the scenes and in the service of the "dying and the wounded" male soldiers; like the ideal woman depicted in antebellum compositions, women in the Civil War era were expected to devote themselves to making life easier "for others" while they satisfied themselves with the hope of a heavenly reward: "a glorious eternity." Confederate women also remained subject to male authority; God simply took the place of absent fathers and husbands, and helpless women could only "trust in Him to deliver us." Wood's philosophy was consistent with public pronouncements on southern women's wartime role. While Confederate boosters hoped to encourage the South's women to support the war effort, they also attempted to maintain antebellum ideals of femininity. Women and men should both contribute to the war effort, advice-givers proclaimed, but in different ways. "Manhood's energy and woman's faith," as one young woman summarized such views, were both indispensable to southern independence. Newspaper editors and politicians alike worked hard to convince the South's women that "feminine heroism" consisted of self-sacrifice, submissiveness, and support of male soldiers.[32] Many young women, like Wood, accepted this limited mission and worked with a will to fulfill it. In the process, however, they sometimes deviated from their prescribed role as they worked collaboratively, developed new skills, and, increasingly, chafed at the restrictions of southern femininity.

Despite opinion-makers' insistence that supporting the war effort was consistent with womanly self-sacrifice, war work proved to be a venue for female agency. Although challenging accepted notions of southern womanhood and exploiting opportunities for expanded roles were not new in and of themselves—young women had, after all, been doing just that throughout the antebellum era—the Civil War represented a new context for female resistance. As Confederate politicians and pundits encouraged southern women and girls to support the war effort, they also authorized them to expand their role in southern society. When Confederate officers and soldiers turned to girls and women to provide war supplies, they also gave them leeway to define themselves as defenders of the South, rather than as dependents of southern men. And as Confederate girls and women formed soldiers' aid societies, they recreated the environment of congenial companionship and the sense of higher purpose that so many southern schoolgirls had found was an introduction to a female youth culture of resistance in the Old South. In all these ways, women's work for the war also became a way for them to work out their own identities.

The Civil War offered southern girls unprecedented opportunities for organizing. The Confederate army needed supplies, and it called on women to provide them. As soon as the war broke out, Harrodsburg, Kentucky, resident Lizzie Hardin described the scene of "continual hurry and preparation," with women "picking lint [for bandages], making knapsacks, haversacks, and covering canteens." Women also made military supplies; in Charleston, South Carolina, directly after the firing at Fort Sumter, "the ladies immediate[ly] went to work to supply the demand" for cartridge bags. With fewer household responsibilities than their adult counterparts, southern girls rallied to support their troops. (Mississippian Emma Shannon Crutcher believed that the poor health of "married women" accounted for the greater involvement of young, single women.) Young women joined soldiers' aid societies that produced socks, bandages, and flags for Confederate troops and held "tableaux" and bazaars to raise money for the Confederate cause.[33] In Confederate aid societies, young women in the Civil War South found their first significant opportunity—outside of the female academy— to work side by side. They also discovered new practical abilities.

Sewing—important even before the war—took on new importance during the Civil War. The cause of southern independence imbued even the smallest domestic tasks with tremendous political significance. As thirteen-year-old Floridian Susan Bradford expressed it, "Even if the stitches were few, when the fingers were unskilled, those few stitches represented the deepest love for our country and her brave defenders."[34]

Many young women drew a connection between sewing and southern loyalty. Emily Voss devoted herself to producing socks for soldiers in November 1861. "[I] shall continue my 'labor of love' during the entire Winter," she resolved, "& hope to make some comfortable—which little as it is, is a comfort to *me* in such a cause—& unfortunately all I *can* do—I feel anxious to devote my whole time to our poor soldiers, & hate to do anything else[.]" Lizzie Hardin called sewing "a woman's part in peace or war." The image of the southern woman stitching for her country appeared in songs, as well as in diaries and correspondence. Lizzie Cary Daniel's "Confederate Scrap-Book" featured an extended homage to sewing, "The Southern Woman's Song" ("Stitch, stitch, stitch, / Little needle, swiftly fly . . ."). As Charlottesville, Virginia, resident Lucy Wood put it in 1861: "Our needles are now our weapons."[35]

"Darning socks for soldiers" became a constant occupation for young southern women, many of whom displayed more enthusiasm for this task than they did for simple housework. While Tennessean Ellen Renshaw House, who was seventeen years old when the war broke out, often mourned her lack of progress on her own sewing, she took on the task of sewing for soldiers with determination, frequently recording her own and her sister's participation in a local sewing circle. In 1863, she remarked on their success in sewing "drawers" for Confederate soldiers. "Sister cut them out and we got them all made," she wrote, "that is we sent them around to the girls near us. I never knew a dozen pair could be made in so short a time." As the war continued, House and her sister continued to be active participants in Knoxville's sewing society, as well as in local efforts to raise funds to purchase blankets and shoes for soldiers.[36]

Like House, many other young women regarded sewing for the cause—and as part of a group—as more rewarding than sewing alone for themselves and their families. Liberty Hill, South Carolina, resident Lottie Dye was typical in her enthusiasm for her new responsibilities. "I attended our Society last Wednesday," she wrote in December 1861. "We are still working for the 'guards'. It gives me great pleasure to think I have it in my power to be any way of service to our Soldiers, and I feel that my time could not be more happily employed than in working for their comfort, who are now undergoing so many hardships." While Dye emphasized the "great pleasure" she took in helping "our Soldiers," she no doubt also enjoyed the company of her fellow society members. As Louisianan Sarah Wadley described the new situation for many soldiers' aid volunteers, "We all worked together."[37]

Working in all-female groups, young women learned new skills. The main aim of soldiers' relief societies was to provide the troops with uniforms. To do this, young women laid aside fancy work and learned to produce mundane items, such as flannel shirts and men's underclothing. In August 1861, Emma Holmes recorded in her diary that she had "spent the morning learning to work the machine & made nearly a whole flannel shirt." "Both being my particular dislike," she continued, "it needed all my patriotism to bring me to 'the sticking point.'" As the South began to suffer from a shortage of northern- and foreign-manufactured goods, including cloth, many young women also took up knitting socks for soldiers. According to Lizzie Hardin, "knitting was the favorite employment of the young ladies." Charleston resident Emma Holmes wrote that knitting "has become so fashionable that the girls carry their knitting when they go to take tea." Not all women enjoyed this new handiwork, however. Sarah Wadley complained, "My hand is now quite lame from constant knitting"; and Virginian Lucy Breckinridge moaned in 1862: "I have been knitting so much that I hardly know how to write." Nonetheless, young women gained a new sense of importance from—and sometimes garnered public recognition for—their war work. Commenting on a newspaper story on a "Mrs Clark & her daughters," who had "knit ninety-five pair," Williamsburg, Virginia, resident Patty Vest asked Sally Munford: "Are you as busy knitting socks as every one else I see? In James City Co., you never see a lady without her knitting." Perhaps inspired by the example of her neighbors and the story in the paper, Vest concluded: "I intend beginning a sock next week, though I must confess I know nothing in the world about knitting."[38]

Such activities changed the daily lives of southern daughters. Rose P. Ravenel, who was only eleven years old at the war's outbreak, remembered that she was "made to knit one or 2 p[ai]r of socks for the Soldiers every month," and that even her lessons did not interfere with her work: "Read french aloud every day to Mamma," she later recalled, "made to knit while I read." Kate Stone, who could barely knit at the start of the war, was an expert by its end. "I have knitted so many gloves," she reflected in 1865; "I wish I had kept account of the numbers of pairs." Emma Holmes captured the transformation in her description of one of her acquaintances. Before the war, she observed, "she lived wholly among books, & her ideas always seemed confused when she came in contact with the practical every day world. Now she has devoted herself most enthusiastically to working & knitting for the soldiers & her Italian & French has given way to drawers, shirts, & socks." Like many stay-at-home daughters in the antebellum era, this unnamed southern girl apparently had led a desultory life consisting of sporadic study and light reading. But unlike her antebellum counterparts, this young woman found that the Civil War provided her with the sense of purpose that so many single southern women craved. Holmes concluded: "The war really has wrought wonders."[39]

As the war went on, a few young women managed to overcome their customary modesty far enough to nurse wounded soldiers. According to one Virginian, "Up to that time the younger girls had been regarded as superfluities in hospital service," but when the number of wounded Confederates swelled, southern girls were "proud" to be "installed as responsible nurses" in makeshift hospitals. Young women were especially eager to work as nurses. As Louise Wigfall's mother wrote in May 1861, "The young ladies are exceedingly anxious to imitate Florence Nightingale, and distinguish themselves in the Army." But both the availability of slaves to serve as nurses and the need to maintain feminine propriety often barred elite young women from doing so—many adult southerners maintained that hospital wards were "no place" for young single women—and nursing never became as important an occupation for southern women as it did for northern women in the Civil War era.[40]

The "ministering angels" who tended to wounded soldiers and the aid society members who knitted socks for them may have been working in the interests of their country and their men, but they also gained something for themselves from the experience of war work. For Emma Shannon Crutcher, war work—in her case, distributing food to poor families—opened her eyes to the ways in which rigid gender roles condemned well-to-do women to both physical frailty and a "perfect night of ignorance and stupidity." "They go on," she pronounced, "from silly, vapid youth, to soured, venomous old age, and dying, leave the world, *worse* than if they had never lived." Crutcher's solution to this situation was for women to work toward "a *full* employment of all the powers of soul, mind, heart and body"; then, and only then, she believed, would southern women attain "perfect happiness—the ultimate object of all."[41]

Young southern women saw the Civil War not only as an opportunity to serve their new country but also as an opportunity to find "a *full* employment of all the powers of soul, mind, heart and body." In the company of other women, they learned new skills and put them to work in the service of what they regarded as a great cause. Had this been the only outcome of the Civil War, it would have been significant—although not subversive. But it was not the only outcome, because many young women found that "darning socks for soldiers" did not satisfy them.[42] The young southern women who were unable to reconcile their dual identities as rebels and as ladies challenged the prevailing ideal of southern womanhood. In doing so, even as they supported the Southern Confederacy, they shook the ideal of southern ladyhood to its foundations.

"SHE-REBELS": GENDER WARS IN THE CONFEDERATE SOUTH

Tennessean Ellen Renshaw House typified many young women's growing outrage against the "blue devils" who occupied her hometown, Knoxville, in 1863, shortly after House's twentieth birthday. Despite repeated resolves to "behave as a lady," House, who described herself as a "very violent rebel," quickly found that her identity as a "She Rebel" could not be reconciled with the behavior of a southern lady. House's growing hatred for the invading troops — and her desire to see them come to harm — were incompatible with guidelines for feminine propriety, which counseled gentle submission and a nurturing outlook. "I feel perfectly fiendish," wrote House in her diary in February 1864. "I believe I would kill a Yankee and not a muscle quiver. Oh! the intensity with which I hate them." House predicted that she would soon be forced to do "something devilish," adding, "that is just the word, though not a lady like one."[43]

House quickly earned a reputation as "an outrageous rebel," a term that applied not only to her political loyalties but also to her improper behavior. In January 1864, she and several other young women — a group House described as "Rebel girls" — waved gloves and handkerchiefs at the Confederate prisoners who were on their way to the railroad station. The degree to which this behavior flew in the face of feminine modesty was recognized — if exaggerated — by the Unionist newspaper editor, who reported that the young "she-rebels" had been guilty of "bold, impudent flirting demonstrations." House's behavior toward Yankees was also uncharacteristically "bold." "It seems to me sometimes that I feel perfectly reckless of what I say or do," she remarked in March 1864. Surrounded by Union soldiers, House refused to treat them with politeness, as strictures of ladylike behavior demanded, even in trying circumstances. "I cant contain myself," she explained. "I say all sorts of things about all their officers & men, abuse Carter or any of them, and say every thing impudent that comes into my head."[44]

So threatening did the Union soldiers find this young woman that in April 1864, they ordered her to leave the state and go south. House's experiences demonstrated that a term she coined in November 1863 — "rebel Ladies" — was considered an oxymoron in the war-torn South. Young women in the Civil War era often were forced to choose between their identity as rebels and their identity as ladies, and some, like House, chose the former.[45]

Ellen House's story dramatically illustrates a growing trend in the Confederate South: young women's willingness to surrender their status as proper young ladies in order to defend their beloved Confederate Nation. The Civil War forced a major crisis in southern culture, pitting the ideals of southern ladyhood and southern independence against one another. Prior to the conflict, southern femininity and regional loyalty not only were consistent with each other but were also mutually reinforcing. Proslavery theorists defended the supposedly "natural" hierarchy of white over black by comparison with another so-called natural hierarchy: the subordination of women to men. Moreover, they argued that the presence of slavery elevated the position of white women, placing "the southern lady" on a pedestal that rested on the bent backs of enslaved African Americans. The presence of southern ladies, then, demonstrated the alleged superiority of southern society and its "peculiar institution," slavery. By accepting their own position in southern society, elite white women quite literally embodied the southern defense of slavery.[46] The Civil War changed this situation, however. In their display of Confederate—as opposed to simply southern—loyalty, southern white women often acted in ways that contradicted their assigned role as passive supporters of the system. This was particularly true for the South's young women. As southern girls demonstrated their commitment to maintaining the Confederacy, including slavery, they abandoned their pedestals and rebelled, not only against the Union, but also against prescriptions of southern femininity.

Confederate men—prominent politicians, newspaper editors, and religious leaders—attempted to reconcile old definitions of southern womanhood with the new demands of Civil War by recommending a role for women that revolved around suffering and sacrifice. While adult women may have (at least temporarily) accepted their role as Spartan mothers, popularized in Augusta Jane Evans's blockbuster wartime novel, *Macaria; or, Altars of Sacrifice,* many young women realized that a term coined by one Virginian —"feminine heroism"—was an oxymoron. Where southern mothers counseled patience, forbearance, and submission, Confederate daughters displayed impatience, dissatisfaction, and rebellion.[47]

When Louisianan Kate Stone's two brothers left for the front, she felt nearly as sorry for herself as she did for them. "They go to bear all hardships, to brave all dangers, and to face death in every form," she reflected, "while we whom they go to protect are lapped safe in luxurious ease." Nonetheless, Stone envied her brothers. "Oh! the weary days of watching and waiting that stretch before us!" she sighed. "We who stay behind," she predicted soberly, "may find it harder than they who go. They will have new scenes and constant excitement to buoy them up and the consciousness of duty done."[48]

This girl's reluctance to resign herself to "watching and waiting"—the very essence of "feminine heroism"—was shared by other daughters of the Confederacy. Many young women echoed seventeen-year-old Sarah Wadley's complaint: "My spirit often makes me chafe at the regulations . . . a woman should submit to." "Poor woman!" cried Elizabeth Collier. "How can she bear it?" Emma Holmes described herself as "a caged bird, vainly beating its wings against its prison bars and pining for freedom." Like other young women in the Confederate South, Holmes found her prescribed role too limited. "I read & knit all day," she wrote, "but it does not satisfy me." Maggie Munford, sequestered at her family's Virginia plantation during the war, felt "perfectly useless and good for nothing." "I hate weary days of inaction," mourned Kate Stone. "Yet what can women do but wait and suffer?"[49]

The passive—and private—role recommended to Confederate ladies seemed inadequate to many young women, who craved an active—and acknowledged—part in the war effort. Virginia Wilson Hankins, who despite her attempts to convince herself that "a woman cares not for fame—but will work for the love her spirit craves," described her life as "a blank," summed up the restlessness of many young Confederate women in a poem she inscribed in her diary in 1863:

My Father! thou hast knowledge, only thou,
How weary 'tis for women to sit still
On winter nights by solitary fires,
And hear the nations praising them far off
Too far! ay, praising our quick sense of love.[50]

This aspiring poetess, like a growing number of "rebel girls," criticized the limitations imposed by gender during the war years. While single women in the antebellum South sometimes registered similar "weary" impatience with their "solitary" lives and the "far off" (or nonexistent) recognition of their successes and failures, young women in the Southern Confederacy were particularly prone to draw invidious comparisons between male soldiers' public role and their own private one. In their eagerness to support the Southern Confederacy, these young women became increasingly reluctant to accept their role as southern ladies.

Some southern girls not only expressed resentment at their limited role but found it difficult to fulfill. For many young women, the "quick sense of love" that was supposed to come naturally to women was missing. While southern adults do not seem to have altered their antebellum expectations for feminine emotions and deportment—meek and mild—young women found that they were unable, or perhaps unwilling, to adhere to these codes of femininity. Girls who prided themselves with the depth of their commitment to the Confederacy shocked themselves with the unchristian—and unfeminine—strength of their hatred for the enemy. Seventeen-year-old Mississippian Victoria Batchelor earned a reputation as a "thorough enumerator of hate." Hatred quickly translated into violence, or at least the desire to do violence: Georgian Eliza Andrews, who witnessed the destruction of General Sherman's (in)famous "March to the Sea" firsthand, was not the only young woman to exclaim: "I almost felt as if I should like to hang a Yankee myself."[51]

Many young Confederate women expressed a desire to take up arms against the invading Yankees—a wish that revealed not only an unfeminine bloodlust but also a desire to possess that quintessential emblem of male power, the gun. When Union soldiers entered Lucy Buck's Virginia home to request something to eat in 1862, Buck was so enraged by their "impudence" that she "would have liked to have shot them." "I wish the women could fight," exclaimed fellow Virginian Lucy Breckinridge in 1863. "I would gladly shoulder my pistol and shoot some Yankees if it were allowable." Tennessean Alice Ready, expecting the invasion of Union soldiers at any moment, wrote in 1862: "I felt last night, and believe that if they were to attempt to harm me or enter my room I could shoot them, and one after another fast as they came, I could do as David Crockett, pile their dead bodies at the door as they attempted to enter." Ready's comments indicated both the fierceness of her emotions and the limitations of her gender. "It is no boast," she wrote. "I believe I could do it—If I only had a pistol."[52]

Young women did not (as a rule) have pistols, but they did have diaries. During the Civil War, they filled their diaries with expressions of unladylike rage and unfeminine bloodlust. For many girls, diaries seem to have been the only safe outlet for unacceptable anger. Tennessean Nannie Haskins, responding to the Battle of Fredericksburg in late 1862, was bursting with rage: "I feel as if I could fight myself," she wrote. "[I] never see [a Yankee] but what I roll my eyes, grit my teeth, and almost shake my fist at him, and then bite my lip involuntarily and turn away in disgust—God save us!" Furious when Union soldiers invaded her beloved plantation, Bel Air, in May 1862, Lucy Buck pronounced herself "so weary and exhausted with rage that I could scarcely drag myself up to my room tonight." Buck drew a sharp contrast between her own unladylike "rage" and her mother's emotional self-control. While the older woman counseled restraint, Buck was unable to suppress her anger at the idea of having "a houseful of Yankees." "Ma tells me it is so wicked to allow my passions to get such an ascendancy over my better feelings," she worried, "but I cannot help it—it seems as if I am *possessed* of an evil spirit as well as *surrounded* by them." Indeed, later that summer she remarked that she would not "object much" if one of the occupying Yankee soldiers were to break his neck. Similarly, when seventeen-year-old Emma LeConte heard a report that "a great many Yankees" had been wounded by exploding shells and an ensuing fire, she confided to her diary: "How I rejoice to think of any of them being killed. . . . If only the whole army could have been roasted alive!"[53]

Such bloodthirsty pronouncements were in sharp contrast to the morality and modesty expected of southern girls before the Civil War, as Tennessean Alice Ready recognized. Since the war broke out, she remarked, she used "many harsh expressions." Not only Ready's expressions, but also her sentiments, were indeed harsh. "There are a great many sick," she wrote of Union prisoners in 1862. "I rejoice to hear of their dying, because then our men will have fewer to kill." While Ready realized that her sentiments were "hard hearted, unwomanlike . . . even unChristian," she did not repent, instead writing: "O! how I wish I was a man." "I never before wished I was a man," she reflected, "[but] now I feel so keenly my weakness. and dependence. I cannot do or say anything—for 'it would be unbecoming in a young lady'—How I should love to fight and even die for my Country—our glorious beautiful South—what a privilege I should esteem it, but am denied it because I am a woman." [54]

Ready was not alone in expressing a desire to cast aside the limitations of gender. During the Civil War, a striking number of young women, weary of the strictures of ladyhood, expressed a desire to become men. "It is woman's lot to wait and pray," Sarah Wadley attempted to soothe her troubled spirits, but she could not help speculating on how her contributions would be different "if [she] were a man." Even the usually gentle Lucy Wood longed to be a man in spring 1862, when "the Yankee tyrant" occupied Nashville. "But I, being merely a woman, must sit still, with my weak sisters, for fear of doing aught unwomanly," she reminded herself. [55]

More dramatically than anything else in their young lives, the Civil War demonstrated to future southern ladies the restrictions that came with the title of "young lady." Young women's response to this situation was both conservative and revolutionary. As conservatives, they continued to honor traditional definitions of southern ladyhood—if as often in the breach as in the observance. As revolutionaries, they dared to consider casting aside their gender identity and its limitations—at least for the duration of the war.

Southern girls could not, of course, become men, any more than Sarah Morgan could don her brother's breeches. But they could—and did—incorporate one quintessentially masculine characteristic into their definition of themselves as "rebel ladies": independence. During the Civil War, "submission," previously a desirable feminine trait, became a "disgraceful word"; only "perfect independence" would do. Like Alice Ready, many young women in the Confederacy concluded that life was worthless without "liberty and independence." Because they adopted the cause of southern nationalism so thoroughly, and because they so unquestioningly accepted the aim of the Civil War as "perfect independence," the South's "rebel girls" adopted the ideal of "liberty and independence" for themselves, as well as for their beloved country.[56]

Indeed, young women in the Confederate South seem to have embraced the cause of southern independence more thoroughly than their adult counterparts. Many southern women experienced a "crisis of southern nationalism" as the war, which was initially expected to last only a short time, stretched from one year to two, from two to three, and finally from three to four. Because Confederate leaders, ministers, and women frequently identified the Confederacy's cause as God's cause, the South's repeated defeats prompted a crisis of faith, as well as a crisis of confidence. One historian has even suggested that southern women's despair, by leading them to criticize the Confederacy's leadership and encourage desertion from its army, contributed to the Confederacy's downfall.[57]

Yet young women do not seem to have shared older women's discouragement. Judging from their writings, daughters of the Confederacy did not experience either a crisis of confidence in the cause of southern nationalism or a crisis of faith in a God who sanctioned slavery. More than two years into the war, in September 1863, newlywed Loula Kendall Rogers felt sure that "Kind Providence" would protect her soldier-husband. She urged him to "let them *see* that you are a *christian*, let your light so shine that they may see your good works and glorify your Father which is in Heaven." By the end of the following year, Rogers, now both a refugee and a mother, had more in common with the "mothers of invention" that populate studies of adult women in the Civil War; lamenting both the demands of motherhood and "the suffering abroad now in our land," she abandoned hope, writing, "It gets worse instead of better."[58]

Loula Rogers's resignation—to both her own trials as an adult woman and her nation's difficulties in wartime—was not typical of young, single women, however. Identifying themselves with the defeated Confederacy, southern girls refused to admit their country's—or their own—subjugation. As late as May 1865, teenager Sarah Broyles refused to acknowledge defeat. "I will not give up that our Sunny South is subjugated," she asserted, "until I am thoroughly convinced that she is *going—going—gone*." Youth and resistance were closely linked for Confederate women. According to Freedman's Bureau agents in Florida, "silly girls" were the most determined and outspoken opponents of Union occupation. Yet young southern women's obstinacy was far from "silly." In refusing to accept the Confederacy's defeat, southern girls also refused to accept what North Carolina refugee Elizabeth Collier termed "subjugation, with all its horrors."[59]

Southern loyalty thus prompted (and permitted) young women to reject old standards of femininity, in which submission—that dreaded "subjugation"—had been an indispensable requirement. According to one antebellum authority on ideal femininity, proslavery writer George Fitzhugh, women gained men's love, affection, and protection by being "weak, helpless and dependent"; any woman who became "masculine or rebellious" forfeited her claim to protection. Yet in wartime, many southern girls rebelled not only against the Union but also against this definition of ideal womanhood. To borrow Fitzhugh's terminology, as southern girls became "rebellious," they also became "masculine"—or at least markedly less ladylike.[60]

The Civil War was a formative experience for young southern women. While very few adult women openly rejected their assigned role, many daughters of the Confederacy criticized, questioned, and challenged received wisdom about southern womanhood. As Sarah Morgan suggested, the war had shown the South's young women that the traits traditionally associated with femininity were not always desirable. "Bondage," she wrote, "woman that I am, I can never stand!" Like Morgan, many southern girls in the Civil War era began to weaken the link between womanhood and bondage. Thus, even as they upheld many aspects of the ideal of southern ladyhood, they changed it in one very significant way by replacing feminine dependence with masculine independence. The practical applications of this philosophical shift would become increasingly apparent as young women adapted to the exigencies of war and prepared for their future in the postwar South.[61]

"HARD WAR TIMES": ADAPTING TO CHANGE

The Civil War altered young women's daily activities as well as their identities. For southerners, there was little difference between the home front and the front lines. As Virginian Lucy Buck, whose Bel Air plantation was overrun by Yankees and Rebels, by turns, put it: "Oh, dear! Such vicissitude! One day in the very heart of our army the next abandoned in the hands of the Yankees." During the war, the constantly shifting battle lines meant that many young women either endured occupation, like the rebellious Tennessean Ellen House, or moved repeatedly in an effort to avoid the conflict, like Georgian Eliza Frances Andrews, who spent nine months traveling throughout her war-ravaged state. Either way, young women were forced to adapt to new circumstances. Imogene Hoyle, who barely escaped the burning city of Atlanta in the summer of 1864 to take shelter at "Refuge Lodge" in rural Georgia, expressed the necessity of adaptability when she proclaimed, "We can become accustomed to most any thing 'these war times.'" Hoyle's use of quotation marks indicated that during the Civil War, the requirements of what Eliza Frances Andrews called "hard war times"—and women's ability to meet those requirements—had become a cliché. During the four years of armed conflict, young women proved themselves able to change with the times.[62]

"The exigencies of the times" forced some young women to sever family ties in the interest of personal safety. Some families refugeed together. Kate Stone, her widowed mother, her young brothers and sisters, and her aunt and cousin all shared a two-year exile in Texas—"the dark corner" of the Confederacy—after fleeing the Stones' Louisiana plantation, Brokenburn, in 1863. But many other families split up for the duration of the war. The Munfords of Richmond, Virginia, for example, sent three of their six daughters—Sallie, Maggie, and Lizzie—inland to "Glen Alpine" and a fourth—Jennie—to "Buena Vista" during the summer of 1862; Fannie and Lucy, who were still in school, remained in Richmond with their mother until the following summer, when they went to "Clover Pasture" to spend the remainder of the war at their aunt's home. These were "troublous times," remarked Mrs. Munford, imploring her daughters to write regularly to her and to each other during their long separation.[63]

Female refugees sacrificed feminine propriety as well as family togetherness. Often, older women remained in their homes in the South's urban centers (and military targets) to protect them from looting and plunder, while "children and young girls" were sent to live with relatives in the countryside. As Sallie Munford explained, "It is not thought right for young ladies to be in town" during the war. In the absence of their fathers, brothers, and uncles, young women in the war years frequently traveled long distances without a "male protector," which had been considered "indispensable" before the war.[64]

Whether they traveled long distances or remained at home, young women in the Confederate South resided in households that were markedly different from antebellum ones. Eliza Fain described her Tennessee home as inhabited by "a family of women and children" after her husband and grown sons departed for the Confederate army. As men and boys left for the front lines, the home front became "a world of femininity" and southern women recreated domestic life in an exclusively female setting. Emma Holmes's Charleston, South Carolina, "menage on a war footing" was typical; she called her all-female household, composed of herself, her mother, and her sisters, "Old Maid Hall." While Holmes's household consisted of the female members of her immediate family, other women joined households during the war. To keep their daughter company during the war years, for instance,

Young women in the Civil War South frequently resided in all-female households and worked in women's aid societies. Such settings replicated the female academy, which many southern schoolgirls before the war regarded as "a perfect paradise." Here, an unidentified group of six North Carolina women joins ranks. (The Museum of the Confederacy, Richmond, Virginia)

South Carolinian Pauline DeCaradeuc's parents invited her friend, Carrie Griswold, and Griswold's mother and aunt to share their residence for the duration of the war. Refugee women, in particular, pooled their resources and created shared homes. Despite the circumstances, some young women enjoyed the opportunity to live in large groups of their peers. South Carolinian Lou Wilkinson, for example, pronounced herself "*delighted*" at the opportunity to reunite with her "boarding school friends" under her "refugee roof" in 1864.[65] Refugee households in the countryside, like soldiers' aid societies in the city, brought young women together in a setting that strikingly resembled antebellum boarding schools. Just as they did at school and in aid societies, southern girls learned new skills in these all-female settings.

Housework—cleaning, cooking, baking, sewing, and knitting—gained new importance in wartime households. While teenaged girls and single women in the Old South assumed some domestic duties, most young women in the antebellum era did not undertake full responsibility for housekeeping until after marriage. Moreover, the duty of keeping house was accompanied by authority over the slaves and servants who performed the bulk of the labor. In the Civil War South, however, girls and young women of all ages and stages of life took on the burden of household labor, and they did so in a setting in which domestic help was no longer guaranteed—or in which formerly elite females might find themselves domestic servants. Virginian Kate Corbin called attention to these changes as early as 1861. Surprised to learn that the Munford girls were learning to bake bread, Corbin wrote to her friends during the first year of the conflict to inquire about their new skill. "If the Yankees whip us," she wryly predicted, "I may go out as their *help* and must needs know how to do every thing about the house." By the following year, Corbin had joined her friends in their new work. She was, she wrote with a mixture of pride and chagrin, "in full command at the *Cowpen*" in the capacity of "milk-maid" for her family.[66]

Two major factors contributed to young women's increased workload during the Civil War. First, wartime shortages required southern households to produce, rather than purchase, basic necessities: clothing and bedding. Of course, southern households had produced many of their own needs even before the war, but the embargo on trade with England and the boycott of goods from the Union meant that even supplies, such as thread and cloth, had to be either made or recycled. While many young women enthusiastically took on the task of making up linens for soldiers, they found the work of remaking old clothing less to their liking. "As patching, mending, and turning old clothes is much more troublesome than making up new ones," complained Sally Munford in late 1863, "I find my Fall work unusually boring."[67]

Second, as the war progressed, the threat of emancipation—and, in some areas, the self-emancipation of slaves who escaped to Union lines and freedom—shifted the burden of household work from domestic servants to family members. As more and more slaves departed in search of freedom, southern girls found it necessary to learn household tasks that they had previously taken for granted. As Kate Corbin explained to her friend Sally Munford in late 1862, "The loss of all our servants . . . has thrown the chief burden of all our household duties on our own shoulders." Although most elite families managed to retain a few house servants (Corbin admitted that her family retained two slaves, but she described them as "very inefficient ones"), the "constant ebb & flow of servants" meant that white women had to learn the rudiments of housekeeping themselves.[68]

Many young women recorded learning "household duties" from their remaining slaves "preparatory to the coming emancipation." As early as

1862, Kate Stone found it necessary to learn the "unaccustomed work" of weaving cloth. In 1863, Charleston resident Emma Holmes and her sister Carrie spent their time "becoming accomplished chambermaids, laundresses, & housekeepers." Seventeen-year-old Mississippi resident Victoria Batchelor, working alongside her northern-born governess, learned to iron. Even young girls, like eleven-year-old Katie Wallace, learned basic housekeeping tasks. "I came down stairs early this morning and swept & dusted the sitting room," she wrote in her diary in 1864. "Helped Sister make the beds." While southern girls in the antebellum era learned household tasks in preparation for marriage, young women in the Confederate South found it necessary to perform housework simply to meet their daily needs.[69]

Even before emancipation, then, young southern women learned, more thoroughly than their peacetime predecessors, the intricacies of household work. Moreover, they learned not simply how to manage a household, as young matrons in the Old South did, but how to maintain it themselves. Although two house servants remained, Eliza Andrews and her sister Metta did "most of the housework," she wrote in 1865. "It is very different from having a servant always at hand to attend to your smallest need," she reflected, "but I can't say that I altogether regret the change; in fact, I had a very merry time over my work."[70]

Some young women, like Andrews, enjoyed the sense of independence they derived from performing household tasks. Kate Corbin reported that she "thrived on the hard work" of milking cows and churning butter. "It has given me a large experience which will be at all times useful, and I do not consider it dearly bought," she reflected in November 1862, adding: "I wish I could send you down today's churning. I do it all with my own hands." In June 1862, Lucy Buck of Virginia not only "made up [her] first biscuit" but also helped wash dishes and set the table. Although she felt "tired enough" by even these small tasks, Buck also was proud of her achievements: "I feel a great deal better satisfied with myself to know that I am competent to discharge these duties than I would to know that I was a mere idler useless to myself and all around me," she concluded.[71] Such comments indicate that some southern women gained a welcome feeling of self-reliance when they learned to perform essential tasks; they boasted of their new usefulness and self-consciously contrasted it to the idleness that had often characterized young women's daily lives in the Old South.

Not all girls expressed so much satisfaction with their new housekeeping duties, however. Nell Grey, a Virginian, remembered her first experience in washing clothing vividly. "We found some tubs and drew our water, and made up some fire under a pot, as we had seen the negroes do," she wrote, but despite her best efforts, the clothes refused to become fully clean. Wearily, Grey concluded: "I have never in all my life worked so hard as I worked that day trying to wash my clothes out." Lucy Buck, who had pronounced herself so satisfied with her skill in baking biscuits and washing up cups and saucers in 1862, was less pleased with her work in 1863, when she was forced to milk cows, bake bread, and care for the younger children. "Oh such a weary time as we had of it," she sighed. "The children were sleepy and fretful, the stove wouldn't get hot, the bread would not bake and the cows would run."[72] Reflections like these serve as a reminder that young women's new "experience" was, despite Kate Corbin's pronouncements to the contrary, "dearly bought"; it came at the cost of both hard labor and class privilege.

Part of the reason for girls' complaints was that the work they described was physically demanding. Housework in nineteenth-century households — which encompassed such tasks as harvesting and preserving garden produce, slaughtering animals and smoking the meat, manufacturing candles and soap, milking cows and churning butter, as well as cooking over open fires and cleaning with primitive utensils — was no easy task, and it contrasted dramatically with the leisurely activities that filled the lives of "daughters at home" before the Civil War. Young women's descriptions of their fatigue and exasperation reflect both the rigor of the work that had previously been performed by slaves and southern daughters' comparative inexperience with routine household tasks. "You may imagine," wrote Kate Corbin, "how weary we are when night comes, and the day's labours are accomplished."[73] Physical exhaustion, therefore, played a significant role in young women's difficulties in adjusting to the new demands of wartime labor.

But more to the point, performing domestic labor marked a change in southern women's role as they adopted work previously performed only by the most degraded members of society. Even the optimistic Andrews, who took pride in her new accomplishments, felt that household chores were beneath her. "It does seem to me a waste of time for people who are capable of doing something better to spend their time sweeping and dusting," she complained, "while scores of lazy negroes that are fit for nothing else are lying around idle." Andrews might receive some satisfaction from seeing the fruit of her own labors ("we do it so much better than the negroes," she claimed), but that was poor compensation for seeing former slaves receive freedom while former ladies were turned into chambermaids (wearing an apron and with her hair tied in a kerchief, the fashion-conscious Andrews described herself as a proper "Bridget"). Such scenes convinced young women that, as Emma Holmes put it in June 1865, "the very foundations of society are uprooted." Perhaps more troubling than the physical demands of housework, then, were the cultural connotations, which to many southern daughters appeared as the most immediate and meaningful result of the end of slavery on American soil.[74]

Young women's class- and race-conscious comments on their new household tasks suggest that, just as the years of war did not dampen their enthusiasm for the Confederate cause, neither did their initial experiences with emancipation alter their deep-seated convictions about white supremacy. Indeed, southern girls' dislike for the most arduous tasks—those most closely associated with African American "negroes" and Irish American "Bridgets"—may actually have reinforced their racism. Confederate daughters might reject time-honored gender conventions, but they clung all the more tightly to slave society's racist beliefs.

Emancipation notwithstanding, most southern women, despite the difficulties of the war and postwar years, managed to delegate the most difficult and dirty jobs to black women. As Mississippi resident Emilie Riley McKinley described her situation, "We do all our own work now, except the cooking and washing"; these tasks were assigned to the family's one remaining slave, a woman named Henrietta. Writing to her cousin Mary Maxcy Leverett in 1866, Georgia resident Sarah Bull Barnwell remarked that in her neighborhood, "young girls were washing their clothes. . . . I hope y[ou]r daughters are not obliged to do that yet for themselves."[75] Such comments reveal that certain tasks—washing in particular—were both especially demanding and particularly demeaning. White women did their best to avoid such activities, no matter how dire the situation.

Even in reduced circumstances, most families attempted to protect white women—particularly girls—from certain forms of heavy labor. Virginian Susan Dabney Smedes recalled that her father did the laundry himself, defiantly proclaiming: "General Sherman has not brought my daughters to the wash-tub. I could not stand that." Similarly, Kate Corbin's father hauled water from the well, cut firewood, and built the kitchen fire to spare his daughter from this labor. "It touched me deeply to see him so submissive under his reverses," she wrote.[76] In some families, then, white male heads of household assumed the tasks formerly performed by slaves, thereby protecting their daughters from both the physical and the psychic challenges of such work.

In most cases, however, white women's comparative leisure came as a result of the work of black women. Even at the very end of the war, the women in Nell Grey's boardinghouse pooled resources to have "an old negress" cook for them. And nearly all white women, no matter how dire the circumstances, managed to hire black women to take care of their laundry. In a striking example of how important it was to avoid this particular task, Emma and Sue Holmes devoted June 1865 to "taking in sewing to assist in paying for our washing, etc." Even after the war had ended, many young women found ways to avoid the tasks they least cared for—that is, those that were most difficult and most demeaning. Kate Stone's family "managed to keep a cook as that is new and disagreeable work to us all."[77] Young women in the Civil War South thus resisted becoming inferior drudges even as they embraced a new identity as independent women.

Whether they regarded their new work with equanimity or with distaste, by the end of the Civil War, young women had found the answer to Williamsburg, Virginia, resident Patty Vest's plaintive comment in 1861: "I dont know how the rising generation will be educated." For young women in the Confederate South, the Civil War proved to be an education in self-reliance. Living in all-female households without either male protection or slave labor, southern girls learned "the useful art" of housekeeping.[78] How they would use their newfound skills—whether in the service of victorious Yankee masters or defeated Confederate husbands—remained to be seen.

"THE MATRIMONIAL QUESTION": SINGLE BLESSEDNESS IN THE CONFEDERATE SOUTH

The Civil War had a profound impact on young women's prospects for marriage. According to both popular opinion and scholarly treatments, one of the fatalities of the Civil War was young women's hopes of marriage. The absence of men during the war (and the shortage of—and damage to—men after Confederate defeat), common sense would seem to dictate, reduced young women's opportunities to find and wed suitable mates. Ardella Brown's poignant (if poorly spelled and creatively capitalized) letter to a friend late in the war summed up this logic: "if I Can get any Body to have me you Shall get to a weding But there is nobody a Bout here only Some old widiwers for all the young men has gone to the army." Yet this analysis, while plausible, is inaccurate. Young women's prospects for marriage were not substantially reduced; rather, young women's opportunities to live independently of men were dramatically increased. During and after the Civil War, more southern women than ever before were able to realize the dreams of "single blessedness" that many had cherished long before the outbreak of hostilities between North and South.[79]

Some young women, like Ardella Brown, did complain of what Georgian Eliza Andrews called "the dearth of men available for social functions" during the Civil War. In the absence of Confederate troops, Alice Ready wrote, "beaux are a *very* scarce article." Mary Lucas told her sister, Emma, who was preparing to return home from school, that the social landscape had undergone a profound transformation. "I am affraid [sic] you will be very lonesome when you return," she wrote in 1864. "You will see nothing but one legged & one arm soldiers . . . old men & little boys[;] a young man in citizens dress, is a strange sight." Kate Corbin described Richmond in 1861 as "very doleful . . . , now all the 'phellers' are away." In 1863, Nancy Royall whimsically wrote to her friend Cynthia Blair: "I think boys would bring a good price every where this fall for they are scarce about hear [sic] I can tell you."[80] Such complaints would suggest that young women's social lives were profoundly—and adversely—affected by the Civil War.

Yet for other young women, particularly (although not exclusively) in urban areas, the war ushered in a whirl of sociability—what the sober-minded Charlestonian Emma Holmes disparagingly called "the universal fashion of gaiety." As Richmonder Louise Wigfall commented, "It is curious to note how youth will extract gayety and pleasure out of adverse surroundings." Wigfall noted a proliferation of "sundry delightful parties," picnics, and serenades in the Confederate capital. South Carolinian Lou Wilkinson told her friend Jane Allston in 1864: "We have been quite gay up here, going to pic-nics, and dances in the evenings." Tennessean Nannie Haskins recorded concerts, parties, picnics, and even a May Festival in her wartime diary. According to Eliza Andrews, the final years of the war, in particular, were characterized by "thoughtless gayety," at least among "the young people." "It was a case of 'eat drink, and be merry, for to-morrow we die,'" she explained.[81]

In some ways, the Civil War actually created new opportunities for socializing with the opposite sex. According to spinster schoolteacher Julia Southall, the small town of Columbus, Mississippi, had "changed a great deal" since the start of the war. The previously sedate community, "once renowned for its modest young ladies, can now boast of a dozen as fast ladies as any town in the Confederate states," she commented with evident distaste, adding, "this is all together owing to the effect of having soldiers near in the town[.]" Emma Cassandra Rieley, a resident of rural Virginia who was only thirteen years old at the onset of hostilities, recalled that the presence of soldiers during the war forced her to become "a full fledged young lady" at an early age; with so many men in uniform about, she explained, "every girl was compelled to be a belle." All "the girls had a lovely time" flirting with the soldiers, "for brass buttons and gold lace were very attractive," she reminisced, adding proudly, "I wasn't a wall flower by any means, and had as many beaux as I could well handle at one time."[82] Such comments suggest that, far from reducing young women's contacts with marriageable men, the Civil War actually improved their opportunities to meet potential mates.

The arrival—or imminent departure—of Confederate soldiers inspired many southern communities to organize parties, picnics, and other amusements. When "several pleasant officers of the Louisiana Army" were stationed near her home, Baton Rouge resident Sarah Morgan remarked that they "made quite an agreeable addition to" a series of "small parties" in the neighborhood. Georgian Eliza Andrews explained, "Albany is so full of charming refugees and Confederate officers and their families that there is always plenty of good company." Minnie Bacot, writing from Society Hill, South Carolina, told her friend Jane Allston: "Mamma and I are going down to Mars Bluff in the morning & I expect to enjoy myself amongst so many gents." In Macon, Georgia, where "young officers" often "pass[ed] to and fro on sick leave, or during periods of cessation of hostilities," one "charming matron" held "informal gatherings upon every available occasion."[83]

Virginian Amanda Edmonds found that the many soldiers who passed through her community offered a fine distraction from her books. "All scenes and late changes suit my wild restless spirit," she remarked. "It is thus I should like to pass my life—no dull monotony, but all change and variety, full of novelty and romance." Edmonds, a shameless coquette, recorded many "a delightful day spent at home with the Rebels eating grapes, peaches, flirting &c." For Edmonds, the excitement of the war years was a pleasure. "I have become perfectly devoted to the Society of Rebels," she reflected in 1863. "I can look back when the war is over and recall some of the happiest moments of my life—yes, even in this terrible war with all its grief and strife. I have spent many happy days full of change, variety and romance. Excitement is the thing that just suits my fancy."[84] The experiences of Edmonds and other women in communities that hosted soldiers suggest that the "Society of Rebels" provided hopeful southern belles with a happy hunting ground rather than the barren wasteland suggested by Ardella Brown and popular thought.

The Civil War may have increased young women's offers of marriage, as well as their opportunities for socializing with soldiers. There was, recalled Sophia Haskell Cheves, "abundance of lovemaking and marriage" during the exciting war years. Men on their way to the front were eager to marry. As Texas refugee Kate Stone explained, "One must not distress a soldier by saying No when he is on furlough." Sallie Bowcock, writing to her friend Millie

Birckhead about weddings in her neighborhood in the summer of 1861, remarked: "I reckon it is a right good chance for the *old maids* to get married now[.]"[85]

As the emphasis Bowcock laid on the phrase "old maids" indicates, the prolonged absence of men led many young women to reflect on their prospects for marriage. Kentuckian Lizzie Hardin recorded a discussion she and her friends held about the possibility of singlehood early in the war:

> Someone asked dolefully how long we supposed the war would last.
> "Perhaps thirty years," I said, "like the one in Europe."
> This struck the group into a ghastly silence, broken soon by low voices counting how old we would be "when the boys came home."
> "Oh dear," said one, "we'll all be old maids."[86]

As the use of the phrase "old maids" indicated, some young women in the Confederate South dreaded the prospect of remaining single. As previously discussed, the "cultural reassessment of singlehood" was delayed, or at any rate incomplete, in the South. Notwithstanding some southern girls' dreams of "single blessedness," others continued to look to marriage as the best opportunity for economic security and emotional fulfillment. Socialized to think of themselves as "clinging and dependent," it was difficult for southern girls to imagine an independent existence. Although increasing numbers of young women defended spinsters, particularly at midcentury—"I do not feel that the life of a single woman is necessarily aimless or useless or wretched," one Civil War–era woman wrote—not all of them wanted such a future for themselves. Life as a single woman, to many, seemed "without a single aim or ray of joy." For young women who feared permanent singlehood, the staggering fatality rates of the Civil War must have seemed like a death knell to their hopes of marital bliss. In 1866, Georgian Anna Maria Green lamented that "woman . . . [is] created longing for the companionship of man" and admitted, "The true secret of my present restless state of feeling is the dread of remaining single." Indeed, she confessed, "I almost feel that death were preferable to remaining alone in the world, and essentially so as a single woman." Small wonder, then, that some young women in the Southern Confederacy regarded single life as a hardship and defined wartime spinsterhood as a sacrifice for the southern cause. When a rumor circulated in May 1865 that women would have to take the oath of allegiance to the Union before getting married, one young woman demanded: "Talk about dying for your country, but what is that to being an old maid for it?"[87] Clearly, many young women regarded the fate of "being an old maid" as one to be avoided if at all possible.

Desperate to avoid the stigma attached to being an old maid and the loneliness of singlehood, some young women rushed into marriage during the
war years, creating what some contemporary observers called a "marrying
mania." After all, as one young woman expressed it, "if some of us wait
for the war to end we will be old, un-marriageable women before it's over."
Emma Holmes of Charleston commented frequently—and disapprovingly
—on "the strange marriages & matches made by the war." In 1865, she
noted: "All the youths of 21 or 22 are crazy on the matrimonial question." As
a result of both men's eagerness to marry and their imminent departure, she
asserted, "girls [are] willing now to take any offer, without regard to suit-
ability."[88] The unmarried Holmes's observations—although, interestingly,
not her actions—suggested that southern "girls" were in desperate straits
about "the matrimonial question" during the Civil War and, as a result, were
"willing now to take any offer" to avoid spinsterhood.

Not all young women rushed into marriage, however, despite the "exigencies of the times." Lucy Buck of Virginia, for instance, never married;
nor did her three sisters. Similarly, the three daughters of the Leverett family
of South Carolina remained single for life. This was not simply because
of a shortage of men. By August 1862, Jennie Munford had "refused three
offers of hand and *fortune*." Her sister Sallie, despite numerous offers, also
resisted committing herself, much to her friend Kate Corbin's relief. Despite her complaints that the "phellers" had all left for war, Corbin did not
regret the obstacle this posed to marriage. "Dearest Sallie," she wrote, "I
most heartily endorse your views on the subject of '*entanglements*' which you
expressed so freely in your last letter. I am thankful I am in no scrape of the
sort." Clearly, not all young women in the Confederate South allowed the
possibility of permanent spinsterhood to rush them into married life—and
out of what Confederate Sarah Morgan, much like many of her antebellum
counterparts, called "single blessedness."[89]

Rather, the Civil War seems to have provided young women with a ready
excuse to postpone—or avoid—marriage. Many young women who had already accepted offers of marriage postponed their wedding dates during the
war. One reason for this was women's desire to wait to marry until peace—
and, presumably, southern independence—was assured. Writing in January
1861, one of Cynthia Blair's (apparently engaged) friends responded to her
inquiries: "You wanted to know if I was married I am not I thought I would
wait until the war is over." Other women preferred not to marry during a time
of so much uncertainty. As early as 1860, Lucy Wood resisted her fiancé's
urgings to set a wedding date, writing: "I feel so sure that a great calamity
will ere long befall us and our country that I dread the idea of making plans

for the future." Women in the Civil War South also knew that marriage might be quickly followed by widowhood; understandably, they balked at the prospect of marrying their sweethearts only to send them off to battle—and, perhaps, to death.[90] For a variety of reasons, then, the Civil War prompted women to delay their marriages for the duration of the war.

But still other women, like their antebellum counterparts, simply wished to delay marriage altogether. Virginian Kate Corbin, who in 1861 had been "thankful" to be unencumbered by an engagement, agreed to marry her longtime suitor, a Confederate officer, in 1863, but she still regarded herself as "'o'er young to marry yet.'" Colonel Pendleton, however, was anxious to be married, and Corbin, who cried daily at the prospect of being separated from her sister, was "in great straits about getting married." Despite her fiancé's desires for a quick wedding, Corbin hoped for "several months more of freedom." For this woman, it was marriage—not spinsterhood—that was her "sacrifice" for the Confederate cause.[91]

Many young women in the Civil War South proudly proclaimed their independence, asserting that they preferred "the pleasures of single blessedness" to the responsibilities of married life. South Carolinian Grace Elmore, who desired above all her "own establishment independent of every one else," dreamed of a home "without the appendage of a husband." Julia M. Southall, who never married, expressed these sentiments well in both her writings and her actions. Southall, an aspiring author and amateur poet who regarded marrying for money as "repulsive," broke off her engagement in early 1864 after accepting a teaching position in Columbus, Mississippi. "Doing too well to think of marrying for an establishment am I not?" she demanded. "Freedom is *too sweet*," she asserted, "to think of changing my present situation." In her journals, Southall reflected seriously on women's proper role—"Woman should not shut herself up in a band box because she is a woman, but understand what is going on and educate herself to take part in the world's work," she proclaimed—and regarded single women as valuable members of southern society. She elaborated her defense of unmarried women in poetry:

Or even suppose all the women were married;
By whom would superfluous babies be carried?
Where would be the good aunts that knit all the stockings?
Or nurses, to do up the cryings and rockings?
Wise spinsters, to lay down their wonderful rules,
And with theories rare to enlighten the fools
Or to look after orphans and primary schools?[92]

According to Southall and others like her, "wise spinsters" were better off than unhappy wives.

Such views diminished southern women's sorrow at the absence and death of southern men. While young women certainly mourned the deaths of male admirers—as they did the deaths of male relatives—they did not necessarily bemoan their own lives as single women. South Carolinian Pauline DeCaradeuc's marital possibilities were adversely affected by the war, but she displayed little concern about her diminished prospects for marriage. A popular and attractive young woman who "inspire[d] *general* admiration . . . every where," DeCaradeuc recorded numerous flirtations during the war years but displayed little interest in marriage until she met her future husband, Guerard Heyward, in late 1865. At least two of her suitors were killed in the conflict. While DeCaradeuc mourned their deaths, the possibility of remaining single for life caused her no anguish. "Clara . . . thinks we'll all be old maids yet," she recorded a friend's predictions in July 1863, adding, "I don't doubt it, neither do I care very much."[93]

Confederate women's writings on "single blessedness" are nearly indistinguishable from those of their antebellum counterparts. Civil War spinsters preferred the "freedom" of single life to the "entanglements" of "male companionship." While marriage was a risky "lottery" that subjected women to "the despotism of one man," singlehood offered women the opportunity to "take part in the world's work" as teachers, writers, and reformers. What had changed was not women's attitude toward marriage, but their alternatives to it; as Sarah Morgan explained to her mother, there was no "necessity" for the self-sufficient, self-supporting women of the Southern Confederacy to marry.[94]

Most scholarly accounts of southern women's supposed shortage of suitors begin and end in the Civil War era. Reading single women's professions of "single blessedness" within the context of Confederate defeat, many observers logically enough theorize that such comments were simply a form of sour grapes. But given the serious doubts that many girls had entertained about marriage even before the outbreak of the war, it would be naive to assume that their assertions of "single blessedness" during the war years were simply a matter of rejecting what they could not attain. Rather than denying them the ability to marry, the Civil War gave some hopeful southern spinsters the ability to avoid marriage—what Louisianan Kate Stone once called "the great lottery."[95]

The much-commented-upon (if exaggerated) shortage of marriageable men did not force young women to forego marriage; rather, it offered them an acceptable excuse for remaining single. Indeed, during the Civil War, a

new genre of southern novel, featuring a single heroine, gained popularity; many young readers may have read Augusta Jane Evans's wildly popular 1864 novel *Macaria* more for its championship of "single blessedness" (the title
character remains single after her one true love is killed in battle) than for its message of self-sacrifice.[96] The Civil War may well have increased southern women's likelihood of remaining single, but for women who entertained doubts about marriage, this was an opportunity rather than a disappointment.

"A NEW & PECULIAR FEELING OF INDEPENDENCE": THE CRUCIBLE OF WAR

The Civil War had a profound impact on young southern women. As Georgian Eliza Frances Andrews reflected "after the lapse of nearly half a century," the war created a generation gap of vast proportions between those who came of age during the conflict and those who reached adulthood before secession. "A social and intellectual chasm as broad almost as the lapse of a thousand years," she wrote, separated the experiences of antebellum and postbellum southerners. "In the lifetime of a single generation," she averred, "the people of the South have been called upon to pass through changes that the rest of the world has taken centuries to accomplish."[97]

Eliza Andrews spoke for a generation of young southern women. Scholars have rightly called attention to the multitude of ways in which white southerners strove to minimize the changes wrought by Civil War, Confederate defeat, and African American emancipation. Elite women especially attempted to shore up the crumbling foundations of patriarchy in the postwar era. But girls and young women—those who came of age during the Civil War—adopted a different strategy. Like their adult counterparts, southern girls revered the Old South and celebrated the Lost Cause. But unlike older women, they also accepted—and often welcomed—the changed world of the New South. More easily than mature women, young women adapted to the changes wrought by the social and economic upheavals of the Civil War era. Integrating their newly necessary role as workers with their growing appreciation for personal independence, they emerged from the "fiery furnace" of the war years with a new sense of themselves as self-supporting women. As Charlestonian Emma Holmes put it, the war and its aftermath had given young southern women "a new & peculiar feeling of independence."[98]

"I've said farewell to my old home, and to my old life too," wrote Grace Elmore in September 1865. "Now our vocation is work, and we all recognize

The Civil War changed the southern landscape and altered southern girls' futures. In this photograph of the ruins of homes in Baton Rouge, Louisiana, after an 1862 engagement during which the Union army burned portions of the city, an unidentified girl returns the photographer's gaze. (Andrew D. Lytle Collection, Louisiana and Lower Mississippi Valley Collection, LSU Libraries, Louisiana State University)

it to be so, for young and old, men and women are pushed by a necessity, before unknown, the need of bread." Like Elmore, many southern women were less concerned by the Civil War's effects on their marital prospects than on its implications for the South's plantation economy. As Confederate defeat and African American freedom became first possibilities, then probabilities, and finally realities, young women attempted to come to terms with what the new order might bring by envisioning a future in which they would need to contribute to their own support. As Emma LeConte reflected in early 1865, "Perhaps we will all have to work for a living before long."[99]

Even before the war's conclusion, many young women began to engage in paid work. Traditional domestic work was the obvious choice for many women. Emma Holmes and her sister Sue took in sewing, transforming what had once been domestic, and then patriotic, work into a source of income. Mary Bull Leverett and her sisters earned money by selling embroidery, making butter, and collecting eggs. Eleven-year-old Katie Darling Wallace demonstrated the ability of even the youngest southern women to contribute to their families' income through needlework. "I have taken in an apron to make for Eleanor," she wrote in 1864, adding, "anything for a little money these times."[100]

Although domestic work was familiar, it was also poorly paid; Holmes described seamstresses as "a dreadfully ill-paid class." Seeking better pay, greater intellectual challenges, and increased independence, a growing number of southern women turned to teaching—what lifelong schoolmistress Julia Southall called "the noblest of works." Teaching was a relatively uncommon career for women in the antebellum South, although it had already become feminized in the North. The war both spurred women to take jobs as teachers and made positions—formerly reserved for men—available for them. Before the war, for example, only 7.5 percent of North Carolina's public school teachers were women; by 1863, the proportion had risen to 40 percent. Capitalizing on the antebellum South's support for women's schools and banking on the postbellum South's need for female teachers, young women in the Confederate South regarded higher education as the key to financial independence.[101]

Anticipating the need to support themselves after the war was over, many young women prepared themselves for work as teachers while the Civil War raged around them. In 1865, seventeen-year-old Emma LeConte determined to teach her younger sister, Sallie. Young women had engaged in such activities before the war, but LeConte and her family recognized that in the postwar era, teaching might become a vocation rather than an avocation. Although she hoped that she might be able to "get some kind of employment" with the Confederate government, LeConte regarded teaching as a more likely prospect, and she undertook her studies with renewed zeal to prepare herself for this task. "I feel I must study," she wrote in her diary. The Civil War—and the prospect of black emancipation and white poverty that it augured—gave female scholarship new urgency. "An education now is more important to me than ever," LeConte explained, because "the only work I can look forward to is teaching." Studying, however, was not enough; LeConte recognized that she needed to put her plans into practice. "[Father] and Mother agree to let me teach Sallie," she recorded in early February, "both that she may be studying and that I may learn to teach." By the end of the month, LeConte boasted: "I am now fairly launched as a school-ma'am."[102]

Charlestonian Emma Holmes, who disliked sewing and had "always wished . . . to be, a schoolmistress," also was encouraged to do so by the exigencies of the war years. Inspired by the example of a friend who, "very desirous of doing something for herself, especially in these times," had convinced her male relatives to allow her to take charge of a school, Holmes assisted in an established school and worked as a private governess during the war. Like LeConte, Holmes enjoyed her new work even though necessity had driven her to it; teaching, she found, offered an escape from the "aimless, useless existence" that she dreaded. For Holmes, as for other young women who went to work in the war years, the Civil War and its aftermath both inspired and enabled "a new and peculiar feeling of independence."[103] Young women's independence may have been the result of defeat, emancipation, and poverty, but it nevertheless dramatically changed young women's visions of the future and profoundly reshaped southern womanhood.

In May 1865, shortly after the conclusion of the Civil War, Tennessee schoolgirl Sally Broyles's teacher assigned a composition subject that clearly reflected the Confederacy's loss: "'Sweet are the uses of adversity' is our subject," recorded Broyles in her diary.[104] For young southern women, the Civil War proved to be an extended lesson on "the uses of adversity." During the course of the war, young women learned new skills as housekeepers and wage earners. They also adopted new ideas about their role in society, incorporating political opinion, social action, and personal independence into their definition of southern womanhood. The Civil War offered southern girls, who had long sought an alternative to their assigned role as southern ladies, the opportunity to define and enact that alternative. The upheaval of the war years gave young southern women a chance to translate long-standing resistance into outright rebellion. Southern girls and young women—who, unlike older matrons and mothers, had not yet exchanged a female youth culture of resistance for an adult women's culture of resignation—took advantage of the opening. As "rebel ladies," young women in the Southern Confederacy adapted to the demands of the Civil War South and prepared themselves to survive—and thrive—in the New South.

TOMORROW IS ANOTHER DAY:
NEW WOMEN IN THE NEW SOUTH

A generation after the end of the Civil War, a new women's organization, the United Daughters of the Confederacy, arose in the American South. While clearly founded both by and for the New South, the organization capitalized on—and helped to create—the myth of the Old South that would reach its apotheosis in Margaret Mitchell's epic novel, *Gone With the Wind*. Although this was only one of several southern women's organizations dedicated to preserving and praising a particular image of the Old South, it has garnered the most popular and scholarly interest, perhaps because of its founders' media savvy in naming the organization in order to appeal, among other things, to notions of youth, femininity, and regionalism. The United Daughters of the Confederacy thus became one of the key forces in white southerners' postwar attempts to ward off challenges to white supremacy: a force composed of, led by, and named for southern women.[1]

Historians of the New South and southern women have recently drawn attention to the myriad ways in which southern white women participated in—and in some cases led—a regional movement to maintain white supremacy, bolster male superiority, and preserve class privilege in the post–Civil War South. Interpreting the Civil War itself as "a crisis in gender" and the postwar decades as a period of "gendered strife and confusion," they have called attention to the ways in which southern women helped to rebuild the New South in the image of the Old. Although forced by necessity to adopt to new demands at home and work, such analyses suggest that the South's "mothers of invention" expended their creativity on preventing— and, when that failed, containing—change in their home region and in their own roles.[2]

This wave of scholarship challenges Anne Firor Scott's contention, in her landmark book, *The Southern Lady*, that the Civil War was a major watershed in the history of elite southern women, the turning point in white women's journey "from pedestal to politics" in the American South. While the current generation of scholars agrees with Scott that the turbulence of the war years prompted—or, perhaps, forced—southern white women to take on new public roles as workers, authors, and organizers, they regard elite women as

reactionaries, not rebels. Limited by their adherence to white supremacy—which they saw as endangered by female equality—white southern women were incapable of conceptualizing, much less creating, real social change. Southern women's inability to reject the ideal of the southern lady (and its foundation of racial oppression) placed "limits [on] the possible"; as a result, "southern feminism has been shaped by women's sense of their own limitations."[3]

And yet feminism did emerge in the postwar South. Southern women in the latter half of the nineteenth century increased both their personal independence and their public presence as they taught school, wrote for publication, and organized for suffrage. They challenged both male privilege and white supremacy through their involvement in such progressive social reforms as the temperance movement, the social gospel movement, and the labor movement. In the twentieth century, a few advocated interracial cooperation and publicly challenged the most visible tool in the maintenance of white supremacy: lynch law. Historians' discussions of these activities, whether implicitly or explicitly, call attention to the pivotal role of the Civil War in southern women's role and in the emergence of southern feminism, for such developments certainly did not characterize the antebellum South. Indeed, the extent and scope of southern white women's activities in the postwar era seem to support Jane Turner Censer's recent contention that the years between the end of the Civil War and the turn of the century may best be seen as "the reconstruction of white southern womanhood."[4]

How can we reconcile these disparate visions of southern women: conservative or progressive, reactionary or rebellious? And how can we explain the appearance of a conflicted image of southern women in place of the unified motif of the southern lady? I believe the answer to both questions is to be found in the words and experiences of "Scarlett's sisters": young women of the Old South. Unlike their adult counterparts, young women were ready and willing both to adopt new roles in southern society and to adapt their own understanding of southern womanhood.[5] It was Scarlett's sisters, not mature matrons, who redefined their identities and reconstructed their region's possibilities in the Civil War era and beyond.

Although they found their opportunity to change during the Civil War, their desire for change was already there, based in their marginal status as southern ladies and their critical perspective on southern femininity—both of which owed as much to their age as to their gender. As individuals engaged in the process of becoming southern ladies, young women in the Old

South had the opportunity to critically assess their culture's definition of white femininity. As elite southern women-in-the-making, young women in the Civil War South had the ability to unmake—and remake—southern womanhood. While the options were limited by the privileges of class and race that young women took for granted, they were made possible by the constraints of gender and age that young women found so troubling. Southern feminism may have been shaped by adult women's sense of their own limitations, but it was created from young women's sense of their own possibilities. While their vision of a "new woman" for the "New South" continued to be limited by their elitism and racism, their age and gender enabled them to become makers of change—to demonstrate in their lives and actions that, as Scarlett expressed it at the end of *Gone With the Wind*, "Tomorrow is another day!"

NOTES

Auburn   Auburn University, Auburn, Alabama

CAH   Center for American History, University of Texas, Austin, Texas

Duke   Duke University Special Collections, Durham, North Carolina

Emory   Emory University Libraries (Robert W. Woodruff Library), Atlanta, Georgia

MHS   Maryland Historical Society, Baltimore, Maryland

SCHS   South Carolina Historical Society, Charleston, South Carolina

SHC   Southern Historical Collection, University of North Carolina, Chapel Hill, North Carolina

SHC microfilm   Originals at Southern Historical Collection, University of North Carolina, Chapel Hill, North Carolina; also available on microfilm as *Southern Women and Their Families in the 19th Century: Papers and Diaries. Series A, Holdings of the Southern Historical Collection*, ed. Anne Firor Scott (Bethesda, Md.: University Publications of America, 1991).

VHS   Virginia Historical Society, Richmond, Virginia

1   A detailed discussion of the symbolism and significance of *Gone With the Wind* and its female protagonist is beyond the scope of this project. Interested readers may wish to consult Faust et al., "Coming to Terms with Scarlett"; and Fox-Genovese, "Scarlett O'Hara."

2   Anne Firor Scott's classic study, originally published in 1970, has recently been re-issued; see *Southern Lady*. Laura F. Edwards's book incorporates much of the new scholarship on a wide variety of southern women; see *Scarlett Doesn't Live Here Anymore*. Other important studies of white women in the Old South include Clinton, *Plantation Mistress*; Fox-Genovese, *Within the Plantation Household*; and Friedman, *Enclosed Garden*.

For recent work on young men in the Old South, see Pace, *Halls of Honor*; and Friend and Glover, eds., *Southern Manhood*. Books on this subject are also under way by Lorri Glover and by W. Stephen Berry. For recent work on young women in the Victorian Northeast, see Brumberg, *Body Project*; and Hunter, *How Young Ladies Became Girls*. An important exception to the tendency to overlook young southern women is Charlene Boyer Lewis's examination of youth culture (male and female) in *Ladies and Gentlemen on Display*.

See for examples of books on southern "belles," Farnham, *Education of the Southern Belle*; and Roberts, *Confederate Belle*. An insightful—but brief—study of southern girls is Stowe, "Growing Up Female."

The few studies of southern white females to call special attention to the importance of age (or generation) focus on the postbellum period. See Censer, *Reconstruction of White Southern Womanhood*, and Florence Elliott Cook, "Growing Up White, Genteel, and Female." Recent studies of slave children and youth (male and female) are King, *Stolen Childhood*; and Schwartz, *Born in Bondage*.

3   Thus far, the only book-length studies of southern white females to call special attention to the importance of age (or generation) focus on the postbellum period. See Censer, *Reconstruction of White Southern Womanhood*, and Florence Elliott Cook, "Growing Up White, Genteel, and Female." By contrast, the topic of slave childhood has drawn more scholarly interest. Recent studies of slave children and youth (male and female) are King, *Stolen Childhood*; and Schwartz, *Born in Bondage*.

4   Indeed, in the most recent study of American youth, which includes both male and female youth, Rodney Hessinger focuses on the urban northeast (Philadelphia in particular). See *Seduced, Abandoned, and Reborn*. On the history of adolescence, see Hawes, "Strange History of Female Adolescence"; and Kett, *Rites of Passage*, 137. For women's historians' early interpretations, see, for example, Ryan, *Cradle of the Middle Class*, 193–94; for more recent treatments, see Brumberg, *Body Project*; Nelson and Vallone, eds., *Girl's Own*; Maynes, Soland, and Benninghaus, eds., *Secret Gardens, Satanic Mills*; and Rishoi, *From Girl to Woman*. Although Hunter's book, *How Young Ladies Became Girls*, includes some Civil War–era southern examples, the bulk of her evidence and the basis for her conclusions come from the Victorian North. In her study of the Virginia Springs, Charlene Boyer Lewis examines the develop-

ment of a distinct youth culture among southern elites; see *Ladies and Gentlemen on Display*, esp. 142–51.

5 On male youth and adolescence, see Hessinger, *Seduced, Abandoned, and Reborn*, and Kett, *Rites of Passage*; on girls and girlhood, see Hunter, *How Young Ladies Became Girls*, 2; Maynes, Søland, and Benninghaus, eds., *Secret Gardens, Satanic Mills*, introduction; and Nelson and Vallone, eds., *Girl's Own*. Rishoi, *From Girl to Woman*, perceptively notes that for women, "coming-of-age" is a lifelong process, rather than one with a definite end date.

6 This approach is similar to that used in Charlene Boyer Lewis, *Ladies and Gentlemen on Display*, especially pp. 7–9. For Boyer Lewis, the historical context is the Virginia Springs, which both relaxed and reified elite southerners' racial, class, and gendered identities.

I am currently working on a comparative study of childhood in the Civil War South, forthcoming from Ivan R. Dee.

7 Faust, *Mothers of Invention*; Censer, *Reconstruction of Southern Womanhood*. Studies of young men do link the country's internal conflict with (male) coming-of-age. See especially Mitchell, "Soldiering, Manhood, and Coming of Age"; see also Blight, "No Desperate Hero"; and Cullen, " 'I's a Man Now.' "

8 For a more extended discussion of autograph albums, see Jabour, "Albums of Affection." On girls' diaries, see Hunter, "Inscribing the Self"; and Hunter, *How Young Ladies Became Girls*, chap. 2. On family correspondence, see Stowe, "Rhetoric of Authority"; and Stowe, "Singleton's Tooth."

9 On challenges to patriarchy and youthful liberties in the urban North, see, for example, Hessinger, *Seduced, Abandoned, and Reborn*, introduction.

10 On southern women and the Civil War, in addition to Faust, *Mothers of Invention*, and Anne Firor Scott, *Southern Lady*, see Campbell and Rice, eds., *Woman's War*; Clinton, *Tara Revisited*; Clinton and Silber, eds., *Divided Houses*; and Rable, *Civil Wars*.

11 Cashin, ed., *Our Common Affairs*, 2.

12 The dean of the so-called Dunning school was U. B. Phillips, whose *American Negro Slavery* set forth many of the assumptions about the supposedly benevolent system of slavery that would be challenged by revisionist historians, beginning with Kenneth Stampp's *The Peculiar Institution*. My understanding of slave resistance has been shaped by the scholarship of John Blassingame (*Slave Community*), Genovese (*Roll, Jordan, Roll*), Herbert Gutman (*Black Family in Slavery and Freedom*), Albert Raboteau (*Slave Religion*), and the theoretical work of James C. Scott (*Weapons of the Weak* and *Domination and the Arts of Resistance*). On slave resistance in the American South, see especially the work of Douglas Egerton: *Gabriel's Rebellion*, *He Shall Go Out Free*, and *Rebels, Reformers, and Revolutionaries*.

Theorizing based on the actions of (male) European peasants and African American slaves, political scientist James C. Scott explains that members of oppressed groups use the "arts of resistance" to create a "dissident subculture" that creates and maintains a "hidden transcript" that critiques the (im)balance of power. Exhibiting a "prudent awareness of the balance of power," this subculture sanctions a variety of subtle forms of resistance that, taken together, constitute an "undeclared ideological guerrilla war." Scholars of slave resistance validate Scott's assertion that these covert acts of resistance are inseparable from overt rebellion; indeed, the indirect "infrapolitics of the powerless" are the necessary precondition for direct political challenges to the dominant order. See Scott, *Domination and the Arts of Resistance*, 108, 137, 154, 183, 198.

13 Woodward and Muhlenfeld, *Private Mary Chesnut*, 21; DuBois, *Elizabeth Cady Stanton–Susan B. Anthony Reader*, 48. For more on the linkages between abolitionism and feminism (and between proslavery and patriarchy), see Gay, "Tangled Skein"; and Sklar, *Women's Rights*.

14 Anne Firor Scott, *Southern Lady*, 17; Clinton, *Plantation Mistress*, chap. 1, especially pp. 3–4, 6, and 15 (quotation p. 61). See also Leslie, "Myth of the Southern Lady."

15 Fox-Genovese, *Within the Plantation Household*, chap. 1; Faust, *Mothers of Invention*, xiii. A related, and still vigorous, debate questions whether elite white women were secret abolitionists or slavery's staunchest supporters. For an introduction to this debate, see Fox-Genovese, *Within the Plantation Household*, chap. 7; Lebsock, *Free Women of Petersburg*, chap. 5; Anne Firor Scott, "Women's Perspective on the Patriarchy"; and Wiener, *Mistresses and Slaves*.

16 In James Scott's theoretical framework, both the subordinate status of women and the enslavement of blacks represented "an institutionalized arrangement for appropriating labor, goods, and services from a subordinate population." The means of control, as well as the mechanisms of control, also exhibit similarities. Both white women and black slaves in the Old South lacked political and civil rights; both were subject to "assumptions about inferiority and superiority"; and both were kept in place, in part, through the use or threat of coercion. The subordination of white women and the enslavement of black people, then, while not identical, "bear a family resemblance to one another." See Scott, *Domination and the Arts of Resistance*, x–xi.

17 On southern white women's isolation on rural plantations and integration with their male oppressors, see Clinton, *Plantation Mistress*, chap. 9; Fox-Genovese, *Within the Plantation Household*, introduction; and Friedman, *Enclosed Garden*. On the creation of dissident space, see James Scott, *Domination and the Arts of Resistance*, xi.

18 Charlene Boyer Lewis examines the creation of a "youth culture" at the Virginia Springs, while Christine Jacobson Carter reveals the existence of a web of female friendship and women's associations in the South's urban centers. See Charlene Boyer Lewis, *Ladies and Gentlemen on Display*, and Carter, *Southern Single Blessedness*. Both never-married and widowed women found sanction for unconventional behavior in the concept of duty to family. See Broussard, "Female Solitaires," and Wood, *Masterful Women*.

19 James Scott, *Domination and the Arts of Resistance*, 108, 137, 154, 183, 198.

CHAPTER ONE

1 Aunt Mary to Emma and Lizzie Kimberly, September 10, 1856, Kimberly Papers, SHC.

2 Lizzie Kimberly to John Kimberly, November 14, 1857, ibid.

3 Ibid., February 13, 1858.

4 Ibid., May 18, October 2, 1858.

5 Emma Kimberly to John Kimberly, April 12, 1858; Lizzie Kimberly to John Kimberly, May 10, 1858, Kimberly Papers, SHC.

6 Lizzie Kimberly to John Kimberly, March 29, April 7, 1858, ibid.

7 Emma Kimberly to John Kimberly, [April 10, 1858]; Lizzie Kimberly to John Kimberly, November 20, 1858, ibid.

8 Lizzie Kimberly to John Kimberly, April 20, May 15, July 22, 1858; Sarah Smedes to John Kimberly, April 18, [1861], ibid.

9 Lizzie Kimberly to John Kimberly, March 29, [1859], ibid.

10 Very little has been written about female adolescence in the southern United States —or, indeed, in the antebellum United States at all. As Joseph M. Hawes expressed it, "the strange history of female adolescence in the United States" has yet to receive its scholarly due. See Hawes, "Strange History of Female Adolescence." The most recent and comprehensive study available focuses on northern girls and on the latter half of the nineteenth century, although it includes some examples from the Old South. See Hunter, *How Young Ladies Became Girls*. For an unpublished study of southern girls' coming-of-age experiences in a later time period, see Florence Elliott Cook, "Growing Up White, Genteel, and Female." British historians have shown more interest in the topic. See, for example, Dyhouse, *Girls Growing Up in Late Victorian and Edwardian England*; Gorham, *Victorian Girl and the Feminine Ideal*; and Rowbotham, *Good Girls*, which offer interesting comparisons to the young women in this study. Recently, both American and European historians have evinced more interest in girlhood. See Nelson and Vallone, eds., *Girl's Own*; and Maynes, Søland, and Benninghaus, eds., *Secret Gardens, Satanic Mills*. Identity formation in adolescence—particularly in relation to girls' relationships with their mothers—has garnered more attention. See, for example, Theriot, *Mothers and Daughters in Nineteenth-Century America*; and the essays in Kelley, ed., *Woman's Being, Woman's Place*, especially O'Brien, "Tomboyism and Adolescent Conflict." An interesting unpublished study of southern girls' adolescence as represented in antebellum literature is Nix, "Exuberant Flow of Spirits." To date, however, the only published study of girlhood and adolescence in the Old South is Stowe, "Growing Up Female." For other, broader treatments of female adolescence in the United States, see Brumberg, *Body Project*; Rishoi, *From Girl to Woman*; and White, *Growing Up Female*.

11 Avary, ed., *Virginia Girl in the Civil War*, 7–8.

12 For mixed-sex schools, see Ella Anderson Clark Reminiscences, Clark Papers, Emory; for same-sex schools, see Mary Withers Kirkland, "Reminiscences of Childhood," Withers Papers, SCHS. Margaret Walker Weber recalled that she and her brother initially attended school together, starting at age five; after "some years," her brother transferred to an all-boys school and Weber transferred to an all-girls school. See Margaret Isabella Walker Weber Reminiscences, SHC. On boys' and girls' play with each other, see Ella Anderson Clark Reminiscences, Clark

Papers, Emory; Margaret Isabella Walker Weber Reminiscences, SHC; Avary, ed., *Virginia Girl in the Civil War*, 14; Cross and Cross, eds., *Child of Glencoe*, 50, 101; Scarborough, "So It Was When Her Life Began," 430–31; and Loula Kendall Rogers Journal, June 28, July 5, 1855, Rogers Collection, Emory.

On childhood in the Old South, see, for example, Censer, *North Carolina Planters*, 43; and Daniel Blake Smith, *Inside the Great House*, chaps. 1 and 3. British historians note a similar lack of marked gender distinctions prior to puberty. See Gorham, *Victorian Girl*, chap. 4; and Rowbotham, *Good Girls*, chap. 2, especially p. 110.

Although my subjects do not specifically mention playing with black children, studies of slave youth, based on oral histories with former slaves, suggest that interracial play was commonplace. In addition, like their white counterparts, African American boys and girls played together. However, such play as often reinforced racial inequality as it subverted it. See King, *Stolen Childhood*, 44–45, 50–55; and Schwartz, *Born in Bondage*, 93–94.

13 Gay Robertson Blackford Reminiscences, ca. 1820–70, VHS; for other references to this game, see Anna Rosalie Quitman Journal, February 13, 1852, Quitman Family Papers, SHC microfilm; and Cross and Cross, eds., *Child of Glencoe*, 50.

14 Anna Rosalie Quitman Journal, January 26, 27, 28, 29, 1852, Quitman Family Papers, SHC microfilm.

15 Ella Anderson Clark Reminiscences, Clark Papers, Emory. My description of girls' clothing is taken from Ripley, *Social Life in Old New Orleans*, 5; Gay Robertson Blackford Reminiscences, VHS; and Scarborough, "So It Was When Her Life Began," 437.

16 Loula Kendall Rogers Journal, June 29, July 5, Rogers Collection, Emory. See also Mary Withers Kirkland, "Reminiscences of Childhood," Withers Papers, SCHS; Gay Robertson Blackford Reminiscences, VHS; Anna Rosalie Quitman Journal, January 26, February 5, 14, 18, 23, March 2, April 3, July 26, 1852, Quitman Family Papers, SHC microfilm; Morrill, ed., *My Confederate Girlhood*, 16; Cross and Cross, eds., *Child of Glencoe*, 21, 37, 71; Scarborough, "So It Was When Her Life Began," 435, 439; and Myra Inman Diary, April 15, 1861, SHC.

For boys' preference for vigorous outdoor play, see Rotundo, *American Manhood*, chap. 2. Slave children's play was more often unstructured, requiring little in the way of a material culture (dolls, books, samplers). Moreover, when elite girls engaged in these types of activities, they appear to have excluded their slave playmates. See King, *Stolen Childhood*, 46, 51, 56.

17 Rose P. Ravenel Reminiscences, ca. 1920, Ravenel Papers, SCHS; Anna Rosalie Quitman Journal, February 4, 1852, Quitman Family Papers, SHC.

18 For examples of doll play, see Cross and Cross, eds., *Child of Glencoe*, 21, 71 (first quotation); Anna Rosalie Quitman Journal, January 26, April 3, 1852, Quitman Family Papers, SHC; and Gay Robertson Blackford Reminiscences, VHS. On "the politics of dollhood in nineteenth-century America," see Formanek-Brunell, *Made to Play House*, chap. 1. For second quotation, see Rose P. Ravenel Reminiscences, ca. 1920, Ravenel Papers, SCHS.

19 "All My Dolls Names," n.d., [1851], and "All my dolls letters," n.d., [1851], Anna Rosalie Quitman Journal, Quitman Family Papers, SHC.

20 Anna Rosalie Quitman Journal, February 24, 25, 31, March 15, 16, 1852, Quitman Family Papers, SHC; Morrill, *My Confederate Girlhood*, 16–17.

21 Ella Anderson Clark Reminiscences, Clark Papers, Emory. See also Margaret Isabella Walker Weber Reminiscences, SHC.

22 On mumblety-peg, see Avary, ed., *Virginia Girl in the Civil War*, 14. On girls' household tasks and their mother's instructions, see Anna Rosalie Quitman Journal, February 4, 22, March 1, 4, May 28, June 24, October 2, 1852, Quitman Family Papers, SHC; Cross and Cross, eds., *Child of Glencoe*, 21, 92, 98; Rose P. Ravenel Reminiscences, Ravenel Papers, SCHS; Margaret Isabella Walker Weber Reminiscences, SHC; and Scarborough, "So It Was When Her Life Began," 436. On supervising slave attendants (at the age of eight!), see Eppes, *Through Some Eventful Years*, 47, 53. For an introduction to the extensive literature on nineteenth-century American domesticity, see Boydston, *Home and Work*; Cott, *Bonds of Womanhood*; Sklar, *Catharine Beecher*, and Matthews, "*Just a Housewife.*"

23 Ripley, *Social Life in Old New Orleans*, 37; Margaret Isabella Walker Weber Reminiscences, SHC; Cross and Cross, eds., *Child of Glencoe*, 31, 38; Gay Robertson Blackford Reminiscences, VHS; Myra Inman Diary, July 25 and 26, 1861, SHC; Ripley, *Social Life in Old New Orleans*, 37. On the importance of textile production in the Old South, see Clinton, *Plantation Mistress*, 24; and Fox-Genovese, *Within the Plantation Household*, 120–28.

24 Margaret Isabella Walker Weber Reminiscences, SHC; Loula Kendall Rogers Journal, June 28, 1855 (recalling 1848); June 29, 1855 (recalling 1850); and July 5, 1855 (recalling 1852), Rogers Collection, Emory. For other accounts of household activities, see Anna Rosalie Quitman Journal, January 24, 31, February 6, 10, March 11, 1852, Quitman Family Papers, SHC; Rose P. Ravenel Reminiscences, Ravenel Papers, SCHS; Gay Robertson Blackford Reminiscences, VHS; Cross and Cross, eds., *Child of Glencoe*, 31, 50–51; Scarborough, "So It Was When Her Life Began," 432; Myra Inman Diary, January 21, 1861, SHC; and Eppes, *Through Some Eventful Years*, 100–101.

25 Sally Elmore Taylor Memoir, Elmore Papers, SHC microfilm; Ripley, *Social Life in Old New Orleans*, 5.

26 Anna Rosalie Quitman Journal, September 11, 1855, Quitman Family Papers, SHC.

27 Minnie Bacot to [Jane Allston], n.d., 1866, Allston Family Papers, SCHS; Jennie Johnson to Martha Johnson, May 7, 1859, Johnson Papers, Duke; C. P. Spencer to Alice Kerr, September 2, 1872, Kerr Papers, SHC. See also Myra Inman Diary, January 18, March 15, 1861, SHC; and Mary Fries Patterson Diary, August 31, 1863, SHC.

28 An exception was North Carolinian Emily Bland Southall, whose cousin (and future husband) Julian Moore referred to her twenty-first birthday as the day that she attained "the age of discretion." See Julian Moore to Emily Bland Southall, July 19, 1864, Southall-Bowen Family Papers, SHC. The lack of clarity on the age of (female) adulthood characterized the national context as well. See Hunter, *How Young Ladies Became Girls*, 130. See also Chudacoff, "Life Course of Women."

29 Alice's Mother to Belle Price, November 20, 1859, Simrall Papers, SHC; and C. P. Spencer to Alice Kerr, September 2, 1872, Kerr Papers, SHC. Although the latter reference comes from the postbellum era, Madame de Saussure's writings date

to the antebellum years. Spencer may have been referring either to the original (French) commentaries on Madame de Stael or to the English reprint by southern educator Almira Phelps. See Phelps, *Fireside Friend*.

30 Maria Catherine Wiestling Diary, March 19, [1838], Emory.

31 Susan McDowall Diary, April 10, 1856, Duke.

32 Kett, *Rites of Passage*.

33 Smith-Rosenberg, "Puberty to Menopause" and "Hysterical Woman"; see also Brumberg, *Body Project*, 7–11; and Hunter, *How Young Ladies Became Girls*, 130–40. For British views of puberty, see Gorham, *Victorian Girl*, chap. 5.

34 On family and health concerns in the Old South, see, for instance, Blake, "Ties of Intimacy," and Stowe, *Doctoring the South*. On the fear of consumption, see William Wirt to Elizabeth Wirt, August 19, 1828; William Wirt to Elizabeth G. Wirt, April 25, 1829; and Rosa Wirt to Catharine Gamble, February 18, 1831, Wirt Papers, MHS.

35 Mary Whitfield to Mother, October 16, November 2, December 4, 1839, March 11, 1843; Mary Whitfield to Father, January 14, 1841, February 18, 1843, July 17, 1844, Whitfield Family Papers, Auburn. I am indebted to Dwayne Cox for sharing this wonderful collection with me.

36 W. M. Green to Nathan Whitfield, February 17, 1830; John E. Jacobson to Nathan Whitfield, January 3, 1840, n.d., May 12, 1842, July 18, [1844?]; Rachel Whitfield to Betsy Whitfield, September 26, December 10, 1839, February 5, 1840; Betsy Whitfield to Mary Whitfield, February 3, 1844, Whitfield Family Papers, Auburn.

37 Jabour, "'Grown Girls'"; Jabour, "'It Will Never Do for Me to Be Married,'" 219–22; Jabour, *Marriage in the Early Republic*.

38 For examples of concern in postbellum correspondence, see the letters of Deborah Warren to her daughter Julia in the Edward J. Warren Papers, SHC. On April 7, 1867, she wrote: "Every day I am more and more impressed with the necessity of girls taking better care of themselves." By the 1880s, Rebecca Collins knew that she could use ill health as an excuse to avoid her studies; "you must not expect anything of a report from me for you know I can not study when I have neuralgia & I get the teachers to excuse me which they all do & of course I dont get any marks," she explained. See Rebecca Collins to Anne Collins, May 8, 1880, and other letters in the Collins Papers, SHC. See also the letters of Martha Faison to Winifred Faison in 1889–90 in Faison Papers, SHC, and the letters of Belle Simrall to Josephine Simrall, 1890–99, Simrall Papers, SHC.

Illuminating the antebellum attitude, writing in 1844, one southern mother even suggested that schoolwork, far from being the cause of illness, was a cure. "Nancy is at school," Mary Pettigrew wrote to her husband, William, of their daughter, who had been in delicate health for nearly two years, "and I do not think any one would perceive that she is not perfectly well. Going to school is, I think, the very best think [sic] for her, for while at home her mind is constantly fixed on herself and that causes her to be melancholy" (Mary Pettigrew to William Pettigrew, June 19, 1844, Pettigrew Family Papers, SHC). See also William Bryan to Ebenezer Pettigrew, August 27, 1842; and Ann Pettigrew to Ebenezer Pettigrew, October 17, November 16, 1842, with postscript by John Bryan, Pettigrew Family Papers, SHC.

The turning point, in terms of a new concern for young women that drew a connection between academic rigor and poor health, may have roughly coincided with the Civil War; in 1861, Jennie Munford confided to a relative that her sister Lizzie had "a very bad cold," which prevented her from reading. See Jennie Munford to Charles Ellis Munford, February 9, 1861, Munford-Ellis Family Papers, Duke.

39 Mary Frances Gray to George Gray, [1870], Gray Family Papers, SHC. For discussions of puberty in the nineteenth century, see Brumberg, *Body Project*, chap. 1; Kett, *Rites of Passage*, 133–43; and Smith-Rosenberg, "Puberty to Menopause."

40 Elizabeth Wirt to William Wirt, January 9, 1831 (quotation); Catharine G. Wirt to Catharine Gamble, July 17, 1830; Rosa Wirt to Elizabeth Wirt, August 16, 1830; William Wirt to Elizabeth Wirt, August 20, 1830, Wirt Papers, MHS.

41 Elizabeth Wirt to Laura Wirt, August n.d., 1826, Wirt Papers, MHS. Elizabeth wrote in response to a postscript that Laura appended to a letter by her father, which has been scribbled out and is illegible; see William Wirt to Elizabeth Wirt, August 24, 1826, Wirt Papers, MHS. See also Brumberg, *Body Project*, 11–16, 29–55.

42 On cramps, see Laura Wirt Randall to Elizabeth and William Wirt, November 26, 1827; Catharine G. Wirt to Catharine Gamble, July 17, 1830; Elizabeth Wirt to Catharine Gamble, July 26, 1830; and Elizabeth Wirt to William Wirt, postscript to Ellen Wirt to William Wirt, January 9, 1831, Wirt Papers, MHS. On acne, see Elizabeth Wirt to William Wirt, November 17, December 30, 1824; William Wirt to Elizabeth Wirt, August 26, October 20, 1825, July 29, 31, 1826; Elizabeth G. Wirt to Elizabeth Wirt, April 29, 1829; and Rosa Wirt to Elizabeth and William Wirt, July 21, 1831, Wirt Papers, MHS. For other Victorian parents' and physicians' interpretations of adolescent acne, see Brumberg, *Body Project*, 59–66.

43 William Wirt to Elizabeth Wirt, November 29, 1828, Wirt Papers, MHS.

44 Edith Elmer Diary, May 15, 1884, Duke; M. A. T. Crowder to Bettie Crowder, February 28, 1870, Crowder-Miller Family Papers, SHC; Eloise Whitaker to Liz, January 19, 1896, Whitaker Papers, SHC. Southerners shared this reticence with other Americans. See Hunter, *How Young Ladies Became Girls*, 131–36.

45 For quotations, see Ann Steele to John Steele, February 11, 1801, Steele Papers, SHC; William Wirt to Elizabeth Wirt, December 19, 1825, Wirt Papers, MHS; and St. Mary's School Notebook, SHC. See also William Polk to Mary Polk, December 11, 1822, and Sarah Polk to Mary Polk, March 11, 1823, Polk, Badger, and McGehee Family Papers, SHC; and "Dress," Mary Jefferson Randolph Commonplace Book, 1826, VHS. On fashion magazines, see Anna Rosalie Quitman Diary, March 10, 12, 1852, Quitman Family Papers, SHC; and Scarborough, "So It Was When Her Life Began," 439. For the costs of clothing, see, for instance, Elizabeth Early to Mary Elizabeth Early, April 10, 1841, Early Family Papers, VHS; Mary Elizabeth Whitfield to Betsy Whitfield, May 12, 17, 1835, April 8, 1840; account of Mary Whitfield to John C. Jacobson, 1840; and account of Mary Whitfield, June 28, 1843, all in Whitfield Family Papers, Auburn; Elizabeth Wirt to William Wirt, October 14, 1823, Wirt Papers, MHS; and Emma Shannon to Levina Shannon, March 16, April 16, 1858, Crutcher-Shannon Papers, CAH; and for friends' exchanges of fashion news, see Nell to Elizabeth W. Allston, n.d., Allston Family Papers, SCHS; Laura Wirt to Catharine Wirt, August 22, 1826, Wirt Papers, MHS; and Mary Shannon to Emma

and Ann Shannon, May 12, 1858, Crutcher-Shannon Papers, CAH. On cultural anxieties surrounding fashion, see Halttunen, *Confidence Men and Painted Women*, chap. 3.

46 Eliza Lavalette Barksdale Diary, June 9, 10, August 19, 21, 1836, VHS.

47 "Dress," Mary Jefferson Randolph Commonplace Book, 1826, VHS; William Polk to Mary Polk, December 11, 1822; Sarah Polk to Mary Polk, March 11, 1823, Polk, Badger, and McGehee Family Papers, SHC. See also Kate Landing, "What Makes a True Lady," May 7, 1872; and "Fashion," May 28, 1872, Smith Papers, Duke.

48 Julia Turner to Caroline Turner, August 3, 1847, Harnett County Papers, SHC. For other references to adopting longer skirts, see Mary Whitfield to Betsy Whitfield, August 20, 1841, Whitfield Family Papers, Auburn; A. H. Brown to [Jane Allston], July 3, 1866, Allston Family Papers, SCHS; and Mother to Mary Belle Porcher, August 16, 1859, Porcher Family Papers, SCHS. "Short" skirts fell to the lower calf and were short enough to show the ankle-length pantalettes that girls wore beneath them. On age and skirt length, see also Hunter, *How Young Ladies Became Girls*, 140–45.

49 Scarborough, "So It Was When Her Life Began," 437.

50 For references to beginning to wear stays or corsets, see Rebecca Collins to Anne Collins, October 9, 1879, Collins Papers, SHC; Mary E. Whitfield to Parents, August 19, 1840, Whitfield Family Papers, Auburn; Laura Wirt to William Wirt, November 19, 23, 1819; Elizabeth Wirt to William Wirt, July 29, 1826; William Wirt to Elizabeth Wirt, July 31, 1826, August 15, 1830, Wirt Papers, MHS; Mary Withers Kirkland, "Reminiscences of Childhood," n.d., Withers Papers, SCHS; and Emma Shannon to Levina Shannon, March 16, 1858, Crutcher-Shannon Papers, CAH. See also Hunter, *How Young Ladies Became Girls*, 142–43. On hoopskirts, see Cross and Cross, eds., *Child of Glencoe*, 62; and Mary Fries Patterson Diary, November 25, 1863, SHC. With the exception of the brief enthusiasm for the "classical" draperies of the early nineteenth century, corsets characterized all the different fashions popularized in antebellum America. See Halttunen, *Confidence Men and Painted Women*, 74.

51 Indeed, the custom of lacing made even sedentary activities uncomfortable. Laura Wirt complained that the "jolting" of a carriage caused her "corset bone" to "hurt her very much." See William Wirt to Elizabeth Wirt, August 15, 1830, Wirt Papers, MHS. See also Laura Wirt to Elizabeth Wirt, April 28, 1820, ibid. For northern girls' reflections on the transformation, see Hunter, *How Young Ladies Became Girls*, 143, 145. For a discussion of the cultural significance of hoopskirts, see Faust, *Mothers of Invention*, 223.

52 See, for example, Kate Landing to Thomas Smith, May 31, June 8, 20, 1872, Smith Papers, SHC; William Wirt to Laura Wirt, May 3, 1818; Laura Wirt to Elizabeth Wirt, May 1, 1820; Laura Wirt to Elizabeth Wirt, postscript to William Wirt to Elizabeth Wirt, August 5, 1825, Wirt Papers, MHS; and Minnie [Bacot] to [Jane Allston], May 27, 1866, Allston Family Papers, SCHS. For preteen hairstyles, see Murray, *My Mother Used to Say*, 63–64; and Ripley, *Social Life in Old New Orleans*, 5. This discussion draws from Louisa May Alcott's fictional description in *Little Women*. See also Dyhouse, *Feminism and the Family in England*, 22; and Hunter, *How Young Ladies Became Girls*, 141.

53   Halttunen, *Confidence Men and Painted Women*, chap. 3; Charlene Boyer Lewis, *Ladies and Gentlemen on Display*, 164–65; quotation from Ripley, *Social Life in Old New Orleans*, 5.

54   See, for example, Ann Steele to John Steele, February 11, 1801, Steele Papers, SHC. References include Gil Blas, Pope, and Dr. Bennett's *Letters to a Young Lady*. For discussions of such advice for girls in Victorian England, see Gorham, *Victorian Girl*, chap. 6.

55   Janet Henderson Randolph, "A Perfect Woman," April 11, 1862, Randolph Family Papers, VHS.

56   Fannie Page Hume Diary, January 18, 1862, SHC.

57   For quotation, see Ann Steele to John Steele, February 11, 1801, Steele Papers, SHC. For examples of discussions of ladylike behavior, see Richard Trapier Brumby to Ann Eliza Brumby, April 3, 1858, Brumby Paper, SHC; Mary Jefferson Randolph Commonplace Book, VHS; Judith McGuire to Mary Anna McGuire, August 22, n.d., Claiborne Family Papers, VHS; Kate Landing, "What Makes a True Lady," May 7, 1872, Smith Papers, SHC; Janet Henderson Randolph, "A Perfect Woman," April 11, 1862, Randolph Family Papers, VHS; Father to Rachel Mordecai, July 3, 1798, and Father to Rachel and Ellen Mordecai, March 18, 1799, Mordecai Family Papers, SHC; William Polk to Mary Polk, March 18, 1822, and Leonidas Polk to Mary Polk, January 12, 1823, Polk, Badger, and McGehee Family Papers, SHC; and Cary Whitaker to Anna Whitaker, August 1, 1831, Wills Papers, SHC.

58   John Jacobson to Mr. Bryan, January 3, 1840, Whitfield Family Papers, Auburn; Susanna McDowell to Susan McDowell, January 2, n.d., and n.d., McDowell Family Papers, VHS; Mary Jefferson Randolph Commonplace Book, 1826, VHS; Father to Rachel Mordecai, July 3, 1798, Mordecai Family Papers, SHC. See also J. Price to Isabella Price, May 29, 1853, Simrall Papers, SHC.

59   On boy's and girls' different "emotional cultures" and the importance of suppressing anger for girls, see Stearns, "Girls, Boys, and Emotions," 37–43.

60   Father to Rachel Mordecai, July 3, 1798, Mordecai Family Papers, SHC; Mary R. Kenan to Mary Kenan, September 2, 1839, Kenan Family Papers, SHC; see also Hunter, *How Young Ladies Became Girls*, 98–103.

61   "Our Rules for This Summer," [1852], Anna Rosalie Quitman Journal, Quitman Family Papers, SHC.

62   Rose P. Ravenel Reminiscences, SCHS.

63   James Ramsay to Margaret Ramsay, February 13, 1865, James Graham Ramsay Papers, VHS.

64   See also Hunter, *How Young Ladies Became Girls*, 98–103.

65   Sarah Harriet Apphia Hunter Diary, February 26, 1835, Hunter Family Papers, VHS.

66   Alice L. to Belle Price, March 7, 1858, Simrall Papers, SHC.

67   Susanna McDowell to Susan McDowell, April 15, 1847, November 23, 30, 1848, McDowell Family Papers, VHS.

68   For quotations, see [illegible] to Mary Whitfield, November 9, 1844, Whitfield Family Papers, Auburn; and Elvira Boswell to Martha Hunter, October 2, 1831, Hunter Family Papers, VHS. On parents' encouragement of youthful conversion, see, for example, Isabella Miller to Jane Constance Miller, October 2, 1840, Hinton

Papers, SHC; and George Badger to Sally Badger, February 23, 1848, Polk, Badger, and McGehee Family Papers, SHC.

69   For an introduction to antebellum Americans' ideas about religion and femininity, see especially Cott, *Bonds of Womanhood*; Douglas, *Feminization of American Culture*; and Welter, "Cult of True Womanhood." On evangelical religion in the South, see Heyrman, *Southern Cross*. For quotations, see Hunter, *How Young Ladies Became Girls*, 145–48.

    The South was predominantly Protestant, with the chief denominations being Baptist, Methodist, and Presbyterian. One account of a Jewish girl is Ashkenazi, ed., *Civil War Diary of Clara Solomon*.

70   James Graham Ramsay to Margaret F. Ramsay, February 13, 1865, James Graham Ramsay Papers, SHC.

71   Hunter, *How Young Ladies Became Girls*, 147.

72   Emily to Mary Whitfield, November 9, 1844, Whitfield Family Papers, Auburn. See also Mary Virginia Early to Elizabeth Early, October 14, 1841, Early Family Papers, VHS; Mary R. Kenan to Mary Kenan, September 2, 1839, SHC; Margaret Whitaker to Cary Whitaker, May 12, 1852, February 21, 1853, Wills Papers, SHC; Olin Davis to R. Bale Davis, June 10, 1859, Beale-Davis Family Papers, SHC; Mamie Normal to Mrs. J. E. Hunter, April 3, 1887, Littleton College Memorabilia, SHC; [illegible] to Mary Whitfield, November 9, 1844, Whitfield Family Papers, Auburn; C. Alice Ready Diary, April 20, June 10, 1860, SHC; Maria Catherine Wiestling Diary, February 28, [1838], Emory; and Stoops, *Heritage*, 35–36.

73   Mary Anderson to Ella Noland, August 7, 1849, MacKenzie Papers, SHC.

74   C. Alice Ready Diary, June 10, 1860, SHC. See also Hunter, *How Young Ladies Became Girls*, 146–47.

75   Lizzie Kimberly to John Kimberly, March 29, 1858, Kimberly Papers, SHC. For examples of such diaries, see Jane Hunter Diary, Hunter Family Papers, VHS; Catharine G. Wirt Diary, Wirt Papers, MHS; Catharine Wiestling Diary, Emory; and Julia M. Southall Sabbath Journal, Southall-Bowen Family Papers, SHC. For discussions of southern girls' and women's religious diary-keeping, see especially Hobgood-Oster, *She Glanceth from Earth to Heaven*, chap. 2; Hobgood-Oster, *Sabbath Journal of Judith Lomax*; and Gillespie, "'Clear Leadings of Providence.'" See also Hunter, *How Young Ladies Became Girls*, 146–47.

76   Maria Catherine Wiestling Diary, February 27, 1838, January 6, 1839, Emory; Mary Anderson to Ella Noland, August 7, 1849, MacKenzie Papers, SHC. I am indebted to Katherine Beckley for interpreting Wiestling's cramped handwriting and transcribing her often repetitious diary.

77   For quotations, see Ann Webster Gordon Christian Diary, January 7, 1860, VHS; and Mary Page to Lucy McGuire, April 18, n.d., Byrd Family Papers, VHS. On southern women and religion, see especially Friedman, *Enclosed Garden*; Heyrman, *Southern Cross*, chap. 4; Kierner, "Martha Hancock Wheat"; and Lyerly, *Methodism and the Southern Mind*, chap. 5. On conversion specifically, see Jabour, "Resisting the Altar," and Gillespie, "1795." On young women (including southern girls) and religious conversion, see Hunter, *How Young Ladies Became Girls*, 146–49.

78   Richard Trapier Brumby to Ann Eliza Brumby, April 3, 1858, Brumby Paper, SHC.

79 Elizabeth Lindsay to Apphia Rouzee, October 16, 1811, Hunter Family Papers, VHS.

80 J. Price to Belle Price, May 29, 1853, Simrall Papers, SHC.

81 Martha Rowena Munroe to Mr. and Mrs. Hendly Varner, June 22, 1843, Kell Papers, Duke.

82 Father to Rachel Mordecai, July 3, 1798, Mordecai Family Papers, SHC; Elizabeth Noland to Ella Noland, April 1844, MacKenzie Papers, SHC; Cary Whitaker to Anna Whitaker, March 10, 1831, Wills Papers, SHC; William Polk to Mary Polk, March 18, 1822, Polk, Badger, and McGehee Family Papers, SHC; J. McPherson to Elizabeth McPherson, [April 1837], Ferebee, Gregory, and McPherson Family Papers, SHC.

83 Loula Kendall Rogers Journal, June 27, 1855, Rogers Collection, Emory. I am indebted to Katherine Beckley for her assistance in transcribing Rogers's extensive personal writings.

84 Kate Landing, "What Makes a True Lady," May 7, 1872, Smith Papers, Duke. While this essay dates from the postbellum era, its sentiments accord closely with the dictates of antebellum femininity, as demonstrated above.

CHAPTER TWO

1 S. Anthony to William Graham, September 15, 1841; W. H. Ellison to William Graham, February 1, 1842, Graham Papers, SHC.

2 Margaret Graham to William Graham, October 29, 1842; Margaret Graham to Mother, November 5, 1843, December 20, 1843, ibid.

3 Margaret Graham to William Graham, October 29, 1842; Margaret Graham to Mother, November 5, 1842, ibid.

4 W. H. Ellison to William Graham, February 1, 1842; Margaret Graham to William Graham, October 29, 1842; Margaret Graham to Mother, November 5, 1843, December 20, 1843, ibid.

5 For a case study of the resistance bred at school, see Stowe, "Growing Up Female." For quotation, see Pope, "Preparation for Pedestals."

6 For quotation, see M. Green to Nathan Whitfield, October 20, 1840, Whitfield Family Papers, Auburn. For the national scene, see especially Kerber, *Women of the Republic*, chap. 7; and Norton, *Liberty's Daughters*, chap. 9. See also Kelley, "'Vindicating the Equality of Female Intellect'"; Anne Firor Scott, "Ever-Widening Circle"; Sklar, "Schooling of Girls"; and Vinovskis and Bernard, "Beyond Catharine Beecher." On southern women's education, see Farnham, *Education of the Southern Belle*, and Stowe, "Not-So-Cloistered Academy." See also Berry, "History of Women's Higher Education"; Kilbride, "Philadelphia and the Southern Elite," chap. 5; McDaniel, "'Let the Daughters Be Educated'"; Nguyen, "Value of Learning"; and Pizzano, "Education of Women." For case studies of southern academies and southern educators, see Hanft, "Mordecai's Female Academy"; Johanna Miller Lewis, "Social and Architectural History"; Anne Firor Scott, "Almira Lincoln Phelps"; Spalding, ed., *Higher Education for Women*; and Stoops, *Heritage*.

7 William Polk to Mary Polk, March 18, 1822, Polk, Badger, and McGehee Family Papers, SHC.

8 For other treatments of higher education and student life, see Horowitz, *Campus*

Life; Hunter, *How Young Ladies Became Girls*, chap. 7; and Pace, *Halls of Honor*. For the connections between higher education, independent identity, and feminist consciousness, see Lerner, *Creation of Feminist Consciousness*, 224, 226–27, 233; and Vicinus, *Independent Women*, 7. See also Palmieri, *In Adamless Eden*.

9   Sarah Wheeler to Mother, April 10, [1833], Southall-Bowen Family Papers, SHC; Elizabeth Alexander to A. F. Alexander, December 15, 1852, A. F. Alexander Papers, SHC. For other examples of this phrasing, see Mary Whitfield to Nathan Whitfield, October 7, 1839, February 13, April 29, September 5, 1841, February 18, 1843, July 8, 17, 1844, Whitfield Family Papers, Auburn.

10 Mary Elizabeth Whitfield to Elizabeth Whitfield, March 11, 1843, Whitfield Family Papers, Auburn; Mrs. Sallie S. Cotton, Alumnae Address, May 25, 1897, Duke.

11 Cary Whitaker to Anna Whitaker, May 24, 1829, March 10, 1831, Wills Papers, SHC; William Polk to Mary Polk, March 18, May 28, 1822, Polk, Badger, and McGehee Family Papers, SHC; Mother to Elizabeth Amis, [August 3, 1851], Blanchard Papers, SHC.

12 For quotations, see Richard Trapier Brumby to Ann Eliza Brumby, April 3, 1858, Brumby Paper, SHC; and J. McPherson to Elizabeth McPherson, [April 1837], Ferebee, Gregory, and McPherson Family Papers, SHC. For broader discussions of the conflicting messages inherent in female education in the nineteenth-century United States, see also Antler, *Educated Woman and Professionalization*; Antler and Biklen, eds., *Changing Education*; Frankfort, *Collegiate Women*; Rosenberg, *Beyond Separate Spheres*; and Solomon, *In the Company of Educated Women*. For the international scene, see Hunt, ed., *Lessons for Life*; Jordan, "'Making Good Wives and Mothers'"; Pederson, "Life's Lessons"; Rogers, "Boarding Schools, Women Teachers, and Domesticity"; and Rogers, "Competing Visions of Girls' Secondary Education."

13 Marcus C. Stephens to Mary Ann Primrose, November 7, 1841, Stephens Letters, SHC.

14 John Steele to Ann Steele, December 27, 1860, Steele Papers, SHC.

15 For examples of parents' emphasis on the "ornamental" aspects of education and on the importance of epistolary and conversational abilities, see John Steele to Ann Steele, December 27, 1800, Steele Papers, SHC; James Ramsay to Margaret Ramsay, February 6, 1865, James Graham Ramsay Papers, SHC; William Polk to Mary Polk, July 27, 1822, April 13, 1823, Polk, Badger, and McGehee Papers, SHC; Mother to Elizabeth Amis, July 15, 1851, Blanchard Papers, SHC; R. E. Emmet to Caroline Gordon, n.d., 1843, and Sarah H. Brown to Caroline Gordon, December 17, 1843, Gordon and Hackett Family Papers, SHC; Margaret Mordecai to Ellen Mordecai, October 16, 1837, Devereux Papers, SHC; William Wirt to Catharine Wirt, May 1, 1825, May 28, 1826, and William Wirt to Agnes Wirt, May 23, 1826, Wirt Papers, MHS; and Anne Davis Bedinger to William Lucas, September 11, 1859, Lucas Family Papers, VHS.

16 For quotation, see Jason Gordon to Caroline Gordon, August 6, 1843, Gordon and Hackett Family Papers, SHC. For southern girls' schools' curricula, see Farnham, *Education of the Southern Belle*, chap. 3.

17 See, for example, Patricia Mercer Diary, 1840, CAH; St. Mary's School Grade Reports, July 1858, Crutcher-Shannon Family Papers, CAH; Monthly Reports of St.

Mary's School, January 1860, Kimberly Papers, SHC; Report for Georgia Female College, April 1, 1843, Graham Papers, SHC; Report for Wesleyan Female College, March 31, 1857, Rogers Collection, Emory; Report for South Carolina Female Collegiate Institute, October 1854, Porcher Family Papers, SCHS; and F. Palmer to Nathan Whitfield, March 22, 1845; Mary Whitfield to Betsy Whitfield, March 14, 1839, August 20, 1841; Rachel Whitfield to Betsy Whitfield, September 26, 1839; Mary Whitfield to Brother, October 7, 1839; Mary Whitfield to Nathan Whitfield, November 2, 1839, July 27, 1841, January 14, 1842; Mary Whitfield to Parents, August 19, [October 3], 1840; Rachel Whitfield to Nathan Whitfield, October 23, 1839; Mary Whitfield to Rachel Whitfield, January 21, 1841; and Circular for Masonic Institute (formerly Dayton Female Seminary), 1849, Whitfield Family Papers, Auburn.

This analysis contrasts with that offered by Jane Hunter, who argues that public coeducational schools offered more intellectual rigor than private single-sex schools. See *How Young Ladies Became Girls*, 192–201. Also on the academic breadth of southern girls' schools, see Tolley, "Science for Ladies."

18 Marcus C. Stephens to Mary Ann Primrose, November 7, 1841, Stephens Letters, SHC.

19 William Wirt to Laura, Catharine, and Elizabeth G. Wirt, May 23, 1829, Wirt Papers, MHS.

20 By contrast, Jane Hunter argues that southern girls' schools were less rigorous than their northern coeducational counterparts. On academic competition in coeducational (mostly northern) schools, see Hunter, *How Young Ladies Became Girls*, 203–9.

21 See, for example, the monthly reports for Lizzie and Emma Kimberly from St. Mary's School, January 1860, Kimberly Papers (quotation), SHC; Margaret Graham's report from Georgia Female College for the quarter ending April 1, 1843, Graham Papers, SHC; Mary Faison's report from the Charlotte Female Institute for the month ending December 15, 1869, Faison Papers, SHC; Kate Landing's letter-report to Thomas Smith, August 29, 1871, Smith Papers, Duke; Rebecca Collins's report for the second month of classes at St. Mary's School in 1878, Collins Papers, SHC; and Winifred Faison's report for September and October 1889 from August Female Seminary, Faison Papers, SHC. Also on grade reports, see Farnham, *Education of the Southern Belle*, 88–89.

22 Emma Kimberly to John Kimberly, March 7, 1857, Kimberly Papers, SHC (see also ibid., March 7, 1856, March 14 and April 7, 1857); Millie Birckhead to Edward Birckhead, April 7, 1861, Birckhead Papers, Duke. See also the correspondence between Kate Landing and her uncle, Thomas Smith, in the 1870s in Smith Papers, Duke.

23 Patricia Mercer Diary, October 13, November 10, 1840, CAH.

24 Emma Shannon to Mother, June 5, 1858, Crutcher-Shannon Family Papers, CAH; Olin Davis to Brother, January 16, [1858; misdated 1857], Beale-Davis Family Papers, SHC. On "reading out" grades, see Patricia Mercer Diary, October 14, 1840, CAH; Francis Moody to Marcus Moody, August 10, 1863, Sims Family Papers, SHC; and Rebecca Collins to Anne Collins, March 1, 1878, Collins Papers, SHC.

25 For a similar description of youth peer culture, see Charlene Boyer Lewis, *Ladies and Gentlemen on Display*, 142.

26 Kate Landing, "The Morning of Life," November 14, 1871, Smith Papers, Duke. For comments on compositions and their topics, see Til to Jennie, March 25, 1857, Emory; Mary Wiley Diary, October 16, 1894, Wiley Papers, SHC; St. Mary's School Notebook, ca. 1850s, SHC; Lucy McIver, "Home Influence," [November 23, 1857], McIver Papers, SHC; "The Advantages of an Education," enclosed in Julia M. Southall Journal, Southall-Bowen Family Papers, SHC; Mary Elizabeth Whitfield to Mother, March 11, 1843, Whitfield Family Papers, Auburn; Kate Landing, "What Makes a True Lady," May 7, 1872; "Fashion," May 28, 1872; "Homesickness," November 12, 1872; and "Labor," n.d., Smith Papers, Duke; and Mary Jefferson Randolph Commonplace Book, 1826, VHS, containing essays on, among other topics, "the effects of patience and perseverance in acquiring a good education" and "the deportment principles and manners that constitute a lady." Patricia Mercer's composition topics are more interesting than most; she wrote essays on her home state of Texas, on Indians, on slavery, and on such questions as whether politics were "consistent with morality." See Patricia Mercer Diary, CAH.

27 Olin Davis to R. Beale Davis, March 12, 1859, Beale-Davis Family Papers, SHC; Julie Warren to Deborah Warren, February 10, 1866, Warren Papers, SHC.

28 Mary Virginia Early to Elizabeth Early, January 30, 1839, Early Family Papers, VHS; Patricia Mercer Diary, November 2, 1840, CAH.

29 Patricia Mercer Diary, October 19, 20, 21, November 2, 1840, CAH. See also Farnham, *Education of the Southern Belle*, 89–90; and Harwell, ed., "Louisiana Burge," 154, 156–57. On male commencement examinations, see Pace, *Halls of Honor*, 28–33.

30 Winifred Faison to Martha Faison, May 2, 1891 (quotation), Faison Papers, SHC. For examples of schoolgirls' comments on examinations, see, for example, Penelope Skinner to Joseph Skinner, [October 3, 1832] and [December 22, 1832], Skinner Family Papers, SHC; Martha Turner to Carolina Turner, April 24, 1846, Harnett County Papers, SHC; Margaret Whitaker to Cary Whitaker, May 26, 1853, Wills Papers, SHC; Olin Davis to Brother, January 16, [1858; misdated 1857], Beale-Davis Family Papers, SHC; Winifred Faison to Martha Faison, January 22, 1890, Faison Papers, SHC; Mary Elizabeth Whitfield to Elizabeth Whitfield, February 14, April 8, 1840; Mary Elizabeth Whitfield to Nathan Whitfield, February 13, 1841; Mary Elizabeth Whitfield to Needham Whitfield, April 29, 1841, Whitfield Family Papers, Auburn. For less common parental notice of examinations, see, for example, W. McPherson to Elizabeth McPherson, May 30, 1835, Ferebee, Gregory, and McPherson Family Papers; and Cary Whitaker to Anna Whitaker, May 24, 1829, Wills Papers, SHC.

31 Mary Elizabeth Whitfield to Nathan Whitfield, Whitfield Family Papers, Auburn; Margaret Graham to William Graham, October 29, 1842, Graham Papers, SHC; Emma Shannon to Levina Shannon, March 16, 1858, Crutcher-Shannon Family Papers, CAH. See also Farnham, *Education of the Southern Belle*, 89–90.

32 Francis Moody to Marcus Moody, August 10, 1863, Sims Family Papers, SHC; Martha Turner to Caroline Turner, November 6, 1846, Harnett County Papers, SHC; Mary Virginia Early to Elizabeth Early, August 11, 1840, Early Family Papers, VHS. See also Mary Whitfield to Mother, May 17, 1835, April 8, August 20, 1840, May 22,

1843; and "Frank" to Mary Whitfield, March 10, 1845, Whitfield Family Papers, Auburn.

33 Mamie Normal to Mrs. J. E. Hunter, April 3, 1887, Littleton College Memorabilia, SHC; Winifred Whitfield to Nathan Whitfield, December 19, 1826, Whitfield Family Papers, Auburn; Penelope Skinner to Tristrim Skinner, [December 22, 1832], Skinner Family Papers, SHC. See also Patricia Mercer Diary, October 14, 1840, CAH.

34 Martha Rowena Munroe to Mr. and Mrs. Hendly Varner, June 22, 1843, Kell Papers, Duke.

35 Nancy Green, "Female Education and School Competition"; Jabour, "'Grown Girls,'" 51–52.

36 For quotation, see Emma Kimberly to John Kimberly, April 7, 1857, Kimberly Papers, SHC. The dominant presence of women teachers is indicated by Sallie Faison's observations at the Charlotte Female Institute (North Carolina), run by Mr. and Mrs. Burwell. Sallie Faison observed, "Mr Burwell has very little to do with the school." See Sallie Faison to Martha Faison, October 2, 1869, Faison Papers, SHC. For similar relationships at St. Mary's School in North Carolina, see Stoops, *Heritage*, 46.

37 Unlike the women's community described by Charlene Boyer Lewis at the Virginia Springs, the one created within the world of the female academy was an *exclusively* same-sex society. See Charlene Boyer Lewis, *Ladies and Gentlemen on Display*, 134–38.

38 William Polk to Mary Polk, December 11, 1862, Polk, Badger, and McGehee Family Papers, SHC; James M. Garnett to Peter Hagner, February 1, 1823, Hagner Papers, SHC.

39 Elizabeth Noland to Ella Noland, April n.d., 1844, December 25, 1846, MacKenzie Papers, SHC; A. M. Baker to Daughters, n.d., Wills Papers, SHC.

40 Mary Virginia Early to Elizabeth Early, October 26, 1839, Early Family Papers, VHS. See also Francis E. Moody to Marcus Moody, July 31, 1863, Sims Family Papers, SHC; and Sallie Faison to Martha Faison, October 2, 1869, Faison Papers, SHC.

41 For quotation, see Hunter, *How Young Ladies Became Girls*, 188. On faculty-student relations and teachers' role as mentors at Wellesley College, see Palmieri, *In Adamless Eden*, chap. 11, especially pp. 186–88 and 191–95. For similar relationships at St. Mary's School in North Carolina, see Stoops, *Heritage*, 46.

42 Lizzie Kimberly to John Kimberly, March 5, 1859, and March 29, [1859], Kimberly Papers, SHC. On female faculty friendships, see Palmieri, *In Adamless Eden*, chap. 8.

43 Margaret Mordecai to Ellen Mordecai, October 16, 1837, Devereux Papers, SHC. The lone crush on a male teacher was recorded by Margaret Anne Ulmer, an Alabama student who attended Tuskegee Female Academy in 1858. See Margaret Anne Ulmer Diary, SHC microfilm.

44 Anna Cameron Diary, November 19, 20, 21, December 2, 3, 8, 1863, Cameron Papers, SHC.

45 In addition to Carroll Smith-Rosenberg's classic essay on female friendship, "Female World of Love and Ritual," see Lasser, "'Let Us Be Sisters Forever,'" and Stowe, "'The Thing, Not Its Vision.'" On female friendship in southern schools,

see Farnham, *Education of the Southern Belle*, chap. 7; and Stowe, "Not-So-Cloistered Academy." On peer culture and romantic friendships in northern schools, see Hunter, *How Young Ladies Became Girls*, 176–88.

On school rules, see, for example, Woody, *History of Women's Education*, 1:434–41; Farnham, *Education of the Southern Belle*, 130–39; and Stoops, *Heritage*, 41–52. On physical design, see Horowitz, *Alma Mater*. On male colleges in the South, see Pace, *Halls of Honor*, 37.

46 Margaret Whitaker to Cary Whitaker, May 26, 1853, Wills Papers, SCHS; Ann Shannon to Mary Shannon, May 14, 1858, Crutcher-Shannon Family Papers, CAH.

47 Ella Anderson Clark Reminiscences, Clark Papers, Emory. See also Mary Belle Porcher to Father, February 26, 1857, Porcher Family Papers, SCHS.

48 Ella Anderson Clark Reminiscences, Clark Papers, Emory.

49 Lucy Warren to Deborah Warren, October 14, 1865, Warren Papers, SHC; "Plan of our dormitory," Fannie Patton to Charlotte Kern, January 24, [1862], Patton Papers, SHC; Julie Turner to Caroline Turner, [ca. 1846], Harnett County Papers, SHC. On sleeping arrangements in southern schools, see also Farnham, *Education of the Southern Belle*, 163; and Johanna Miller Lewis, "Social and Architectural History," 137.

50 Susan McDowall Diary, January 4, 11, 16, 18, April 9, 27, May 4, 8, 1856, Duke. See also Francis Moody to Marcus Moody, July 31, August 10, 1863, Sims Family Papers, SHC; Josephine Simrall to Belle Simrall, [Spring 1892], Simrall Papers, SHC; Meta [Craig] to Jennie Webb, August 7, 1897, Webb Family Papers, SHC; Mary Whitfield to Mother, September 21, 1839, Whitfield Family Papers, Auburn; Loula Kendall Rogers Journal, July 9, November 29, 1855, Rogers Collection, Emory; and Harwell, ed., "Louisiana Burge," 151–52.

51 Mary Elizabeth Whitfield to Nathan Whitfield, April 20, 1844, Whitfield Family Papers, Auburn.

52 [Mary Belle Porcher] to Father, February 26, 1857, Porcher Family Papers, SCHS; Martha Turner to Henry Turner, February 3, 1847, Harnett County Papers, SHC.

53 [Mary Belle Porcher] to Father, February 26, 1857, Porcher Family Papers, SCHS; Ella Anderson Clark Reminiscences, Clark Papers, Emory. See also Stoops, *Heritage*, 46–47, 62, 92.

54 Sarah Wheeler to Mother, April 21, 1833, Southall-Bowen Family Papers, SHC; Sally Lucas to William Lucas, May 22, 1850, Lucas Family Papers, VHS. See also Lucy Warren to Deborah Warren, October 14, 1865, Warren Papers, SHC; and Stoops, *Heritage*, 41–48. Unlike the parents of young people who visited the Virginia Springs, schoolgirls' parents do not seem to have sanctioned even a temporary relaxation of the rules of proper conduct. On the Springs, see Charlene Boyer Lewis, *Ladies and Gentlemen on Display*, 142–51.

55 Lucy Warren to Deborah Warren, October 14, 1865, Warren Papers, SHC; Julia Frances Lilly to Minerva Ewing, December 20, 1859, Turner Papers, SHC; Stoops, *Heritage*, 48. See also Farnham, *Education of the Southern Belle*, 136, 138–39.

56 Marion Richardson Album, Duke.

57 On southern male student life, see Coulter, *College Life in the Old South*; Glover, " 'Let Us Manufacture Men' "; and Pace, *Halls of Honor*, chaps. 3 and 4.

58 The literature on same-sex relationships in nineteenth-century America is vast. See especially Smith-Rosenberg, "Female World of Love and Ritual." On same-sex friendships in the South, see Stowe, "'The Thing, Not Its Vision.'" For an overview of changing ideas about female sexuality, see Cott, "Passionlessness"; Faderman, *Odd Girls and Twilight Lovers, Surpassing the Love of Men,* and *To Believe in Women;* and Smith-Rosenberg, "New Woman as Androgyne."

59 For quotation, see Stoops, *Heritage,* 53. On men's pursuit of women, see Pace, *Halls of Honor,* 73–81.

60 Daisy L. to Belle Price, December 25, 1857, Simrall Papers, SHC.

61 Susan McDowall Diary, January 2, 1856, Duke. On assigned partners, see Mary Elizabeth Whitfield to Rachel Whitfield, January 21, 1841, and Mary Elizabeth Whitfield to Nathan Whitfield, October 28, 1843, Whitfield Family Papers, Auburn.

62 Aunt Em to Winifred Faison, September 16, 1889, Faison Papers, SHC; Lucy Warren to Deborah Warren, October 14, 1865, Warren Papers, SHC; Emma Kimberly to John Kimberly, March 12, 1859, Kimberly Papers, SHC; Susan McDowall Diary, April 11, 1856, Duke.

63 Susan McDowall Diary, January 2, 3, 4 (quotation), 8, 9, 10 (quotation), 11, 16, 26 (quotation), April 6, 9, 11 (quotation), 12, 18, 27, Duke.

64 Laura Wirt Randall to Louisa Cabell Carrington, March 26, 1828, Randall Papers, VHS. Also on the "heart," see Cott, *Bonds of Womanhood,* 161–68. Cott explains: "The identification of women with the heart also implied that they would find truly reciprocal interpersonal relationships only with other women" (168).

65 Loula Kendall Rogers Diary, July 9, 1855 (recalling 1853 and 1854), Rogers Collection, Emory.

66 Ibid., July 11, 18, 21, August 24, 28, 1855.

67 For changing scientific and social views of same-sex intimacy, see Smith-Rosenberg, "New Woman as Androgyne," and Faderman, *To Believe in Women,* chaps. 9, 13, and 17. For southern schoolgirls' descriptions of physical contact, see Sallie to Ella Noland, May 2, 1852, MacKenzie Papers, SHC. For quotation, see Lizzie G. M., September 26, 1861, Eliza Anna Goodwin Album, 1857–63, Miscellaneous Albums, vol. 6, SHC. See also Farnham, *Education of the Southern Belle,* 155–60.

68 Addie to Anna Louise Norman, April 24, [1861?], Wills Papers, SHC.

69 Mary Louisa Read to Mary V. Carrington, May 28, 1829, Carrington Family Papers, VHS. I am grateful to Mary Carroll Johansen for alerting me to this collection. See also Mary Belle Porcher to Mother, [December 1857], Porcher Family Papers, SCHS.

70 Sallie to Millie Birckhead, April 23, 1864, Birckhead Papers, Duke. See also Susan McDowall Diary, April 12, 1856, Duke; and Loula Kendall Rogers Journal, July 6, 21, August 24, 1855, Rogers Collection, Emory.

71 Nannie Nottingham to Olin Davis, August 13, 1858, Beale-Davis Family Papers, SHC. See also Henrietta Collins to Anne Collins, September 18, 1887, Collins Papers, SHC.

72 Til to Jennie, March 25, 1857, Harris Family Papers, Emory. See also Loula Kendall Rogers Journal, July 9, 1855, Rogers Collection, Emory; and Harwell, ed., "Louisiana Burge," 151.

73　Mary Elizabeth Whitfield to Nathan Whitfield, October 28, 1843, Whitfield Family Papers, Auburn; Harwell, ed., "Louisiana Burge," 151–52. See also Lucy Warren to Deborah Warren, October 14, 1865, Warren Papers, SHC; Susan McDowall Diary, January 11, April 9, and May 4, 1856, Duke; and Farnham, *Education of the Southern Belle*, 163.

74　Susan McDowall Diary, January 11, April 9, May 4, 1856, Duke; Sallie Collinson to Anna Louisa Norman, May 14, 1860, Wills Papers, SHC; M. Love to Jennie Johnson, February 14, 1859, Johnson Papers, Duke.

75　Sallie Collinson to Anna Louisa Norman, [ca. 1860], Wills Papers, SHC. See also Sallie Collinson to Anna Louisa Norman, [May 14, 1860], July 7, 1860; and Nellie Morgan to Anna Louisa Norman, December 8, 1860, Wills Papers, SHC; and Farnham, *Education of the Southern Belle*, 159–60.

76　Nannie Nottingham to Olin Davis, August 13, 1858, Beale-Davis Family Papers, SHC; Sallie Collinson to Anna Louisa Norman, n.d. [1860], Wills Papers, SHC; Susan McDowall Diary, January 3, 1856, Duke.

77　Sallie to Ella Noland, May 2, 1852, MacKenzie Papers, SHC; Jessie Ferguson, "To My Friend Miss Ida A. Southworth," July 8, 1859, Ida Ann Southworth Album, 1859–63, Miscellaneous Albums, vol. 1, SHC. For helping to shape my ideas about a female self-in-relation, I am indebted to conversations with Barbara Andrew, as well as Gilligan, *In a Different Voice*.

78　Elizabeth Nelson to Mary Carrington, March 15, 1831, Carrington Family Papers, VHS. Age seventeen was the most common end date for schooling, although some girls ended their schooling a year earlier or later. See, for example, Loula Kendall Rogers Journal, January 10, October 14, 1856, and May 25 and July 3, 1857, Rogers Collection, Emory; Jennie Johnson to Martha Johnson, May 7, 1859, Johnson Papers, Duke; Lizzie Kimberly to John Kimberly, August 5, 1859, Kimberly Papers, SHC; and Martha Faison to Winifred Faison, February 18, 1891, Faison Papers, SHC.

79　Susan McDowall Diary, January 8, 1856, Duke.

80　Mary Virginia Early to Elizabeth Early, October 14, 1841, Early Family Papers, VHS; Ella to Olin Davis, January 27, 1860, Beale-Davis Family Papers, SHC.

81　For a mass-produced "album of affection," see Ellen Temple Hill Minor Album, 1856–75, VHS. See also Farnham, *Education of the Southern Belle*, 148. For a more extended discussion of autograph albums, see Jabour, "Albums of Affection."

82　"School-Days Remembered" and "My Last Day at School," Mary Jane Patterson Album, 1840–54, VHS.

83　S. Emma Graves, 1861, Harriet L. Scollay Autograph Album, 1857–1863, VHS.

84　Eliza Anna Goodwin Album, 1857–63, Miscellaneous Albums, vol. 6, SHC.

85　"Your True friend S.," February 1, 1840, Mary Virginia Early Brown Autograph Album, 1840–45, Early Family Papers, VHS.

86　S. A. Brown, "Dear Matt," December 2, 1859, Martha Ann Kirkpatrick Album, Miscellaneous Albums, vol. 9, SHC.

87　Hollie to Olin Davis, June 15, 1860, Beale-Davis Family Papers, SHC.

88　Daisy L. to Belle Price, December 25, 1857, Simrall Papers, SHC.

89 Loula Kendall Rogers Journal, January 10, 1856, and July 3, 1857, Rogers Collection, Emory.

90 Jennie Johnson to Martha Johnson, May 7, 1859, Johnson Papers, Duke; Mary Page to Lucy McGuire, June 2, n.d., Byrd Family Papers, VHS; Olin Davis to R. Beale Davis, May 6, June 10, 1859, Beale-Davis Family Papers, SHC.

91 For descriptions of commencement ceremonies and addresses, see Eschbach, *Higher Education of Women*, 141; Harwell, ed., "Louisiana Burge," 157; and Susan Davis Nye Hutchinson Journals, May 9, 1814, SHC. See also Annie Collins to Anne Collins, May 22, 1880, Collins Papers, SHC; Frances Josephine Southall, "Certificates of Proficiency," July 12, 1871, Southall-Bowen Family Papers, SHC; and Winifred Faison to Martha Faison, May 2, 1891, Faison Papers, SHC.

92 [Josephine Southall,] "Chronicles of the Wesleyan," Southall-Bowen Family Papers, SHC.

93 See also Hunter, *How Young Ladies Became Girls*, chap. 9.

CHAPTER THREE

1 Laura Wirt to Louisa Cabell Carrington, May 3, 1819, June 13, 1826, Randall Papers, VHS; William Wirt to Dabney Carr, December 21, 1809, Wirt Papers, MHS. See also Jabour, "'It Will Never Do for Me to Be Married.'"

2 William Wirt to Dabney Carr, June 8, 1804, in William Wirt Letters to Dabney Carr, 1803–31, Virginia State Library and Archives, Richmond, Virginia; Laura Wirt to William Wirt, June 15, 1810, Wirt Papers, MHS.

3 William Wirt to Elizabeth Wirt, September 22, 1809, September 9, 1810; William Wirt to Laura Wirt, May 23, 1820, Wirt Papers, MHS.

4 Elizabeth Wirt to Laura Wirt, May 26, 1820, Wirt Papers, MHS; Laura Wirt to Catharine Gamble, May 24, 1818, Wirt Papers, MHS; Laura Wirt to Louisa Cabell, May 3, 1819, Randall Papers, VHS; Elizabeth Wirt to William Wirt, November 22, 1824, Wirt Papers, MHS.

5 Laura Wirt to Louisa Cabell, November 4, 1819, Randall Papers, VHS.

6 Jabour, "'It Will Never Do for Me to Be Married,'" 212–13.

7 Elizabeth Wirt to William Wirt, May 6, 1825; William Wirt to Elizabeth Wirt, May 20, 1825, Wirt Papers, MHS.

8 William Wirt to Laura Wirt, December 22, 1824, ibid.

9 Lizzie C. to Margaret L. Beall, February 10, 1857, John Andrew Ramsay Papers, SHC; Grace Elmore Diary, December 14, 1861, SHC microfilm; Elizabeth Ruffin Diary, July–September 1827, Cocke Papers, SHC; Mary Hawes to Virginia Pearl, November 7, 1851, Terhune Papers, Duke. See also Lizzie Kimberly to John Kimberly, April 20, 1858, Kimberly Papers, SHC; and Martha Faison to Winifred Faison, October 23, 1889, Faison Papers, SHC.

For the U.S. context, see Hunter, *How Young Ladies Became Girls*, 333–41. For information on this stage of life in Great Britain, see Gorham, *Victorian Girl*, chap. 3.

10 Elizabeth M. Nelson to Mary V. Carrington, March 15, 1831, Carrington Family Papers, VHS. See also Elizabeth M. P. Nelson Commonplace Book, VHS.

11 See, for example, Mary Pettigrew to Johnston Pettigrew, April 30, [1846], Pettigrew Family Papers, SHC; and Mary L. Berkely to Ella Noland, March 25, 1851, MacKenzie Papers, SHC.

12 Burr, ed., *Secret Eye*, 94; Bleser, ed., *Tokens of Affection*, 20–21. On southern women's isolation more generally, see Clinton, *Plantation Mistress*, chap. 9.

13 Brady, ed., *George Washington's Beautiful Nelly*, 24; Mary L. Berkely to Ella Noland, March 25, 1851, MacKenzie Papers, SHC.

14 Frances Higginbotham to Anna Higginbotham Hoskins, December 20, 1834, Higginbotham Family Papers, VHS.

15 Ellen Louise Power Diary, January 1, 2, 6, 18, 27, February 5, 1862, SHC microfilm. As discussed in Chapter 8, most southern women found that the Civil War offered a respite from boredom and loneliness, but this early in the conflict and from the vantage point of rural Louisiana, Power's diary continued to reflect antebellum trends.

16 Elizabeth Ruffin Diary, July–September 1827, Cocke Papers, SHC. See also Michael O'Brien, ed., *Evening When Alone*, 57–58, 60, 64, 65, 69, 72, 73.

17 Mary Page to Lucy McGuire, April 2 and 18, n.d., Byrd Family Papers, VHS; Amanda Jane Cooley Roberts Diary, June 30, 1850, VHS. On romantic love in Victorian America, see especially Lystra, *Searching the Heart*. On this ideal in the southern context, see Jabour, *Marriage in the Early Republic*, and Jan Lewis, *Pursuit of Happiness*.

18 H. B., "Woman," n.d., Sophia Coutts Album, VHS; A. H. B., "On Friendship," September 3, 1832, Mary Ann Caruthers Album, VHS; Unidentified to Eliza Cornelia Grantham, October 28, n.d., Larue Family Papers, VHS.

19 "What is going on tonight" and "Home at last," Lizzie G. Davis Composition Book, 1859, Duke.

20 For "marriage trauma," see Cott, *Bonds of Womanhood*, 80–83. For discussions of northern girls' ambivalence about marriage, see Hunter, *How Young Ladies Became Girls*, 342–50; and in the southern context, see Cashin, "'Decidedly Opposed to the Union.'" On the overwhelming significance of marriage for southern women, see Clinton, *Plantation Mistress*, chap. 4. For numbers, see Clinton, *Plantation Mistress*, Appendix A, p. 223; and Pease and Pease, *Ladies, Women, and Wenches*, 10–11. On married women's property rights in the North and South, see Basch, *In the Eyes of the Law*, and Salmon, *Women and the Law of Property*; and on domestic feminism, see Daniel Scott Smith, "Family Limitation, Sexual Control," and Sklar, "Victorian Women and Domestic Life." For a more extended discussion of southern wives' legal status, see Chapter 6; for more on domestic feminism and birth control, see Chapter 7.

21 For northern reformers' and feminists' responses to male vice, see Hessinger, *Seduced, Abandoned, and Reborn*, and Smith-Rosenberg, "Beauty, the Beast, and the Militant Woman."

22 Amanda Virginia Edmonds Journals, April 11, July 8, 1861, Chappelear Papers, VHS; see also ibid., January 9, March 12, 20, 21, June 24, July 27, 1864; and Ann Eliza Wight to Mary Carrington, April 24, 1837, Carrington Family Papers, VHS. On the culture of honor and the practice of heavy drinking, see Wyatt-Brown,

Southern Honor, and Rosengarten, *Tombee*. On domestic abuse in the Old South, see Baptist, "'My Mind Is to Drown You'"; Cole, "Keeping the Peace"; Cashin, ed., *Our Common Affairs*, 13; and Woodward and Muhlenfeld, eds., *Private Mary Chesnut*, 18.

23 Lizzie Neblett Diary, May 12, 1852, in Murr, ed., *Rebel Wife in Texas*, 47. On the South's sexual double standard, see Clinton, *Plantation Mistress*, chaps. 5 and 6. On interracial sexual liaisons in the Old South, see Joshua D. Rothman, *Notorious in the Neighborhood*, especially chap. 5. On the North, see Hessinger, *Seduced, Abandoned, and Reborn*, quotations pp. 23, 148.

24 Woodward and Muhlenfeld, eds., *Private Mary Chesnut*, 42.

25 J. McPherson to Elizabeth McPherson, December 22, 1836; see also Courtney McPherson Wilson to Elizabeth McPherson, February 9, 1837, both in Ferebee, Gregory, and McPherson Family Papers, SHC. On married women and the law, see Basch, *In the Eyes of the Law*, and Hartog, *Man and Wife in America*, chap. 4. On Hammond's strategies for economic advancement, see Faust, *James Henry Hammond*, chap. 4.

26 Murr, ed., *Rebel Wife in Texas*, 45.

27 Willie to Mary Virginia Early, August 19, 1844, Early Family Papers, VHS.

28 Cashin, "'Decidedly Opposed to the Union,'" 751; Ann Eliza Wight to Mary Carrington, April 24, 1837, Carrington Family Papers, VHS. On the North, see Smith-Rosenberg, "Female World of Love and Ritual."

29 Mary Virginia Hawes to Virginia Pearl, September 13, [1849], Terhune Papers, Duke.

30 For quotations, see Laas, *Love and Power*, 10; Michael O'Brien, ed., *Evening When Alone*, 67; Chambers-Schiller, *Liberty, a Better Husband*, 13; and Sally to Emma Nicholson, January 20, 1858, Emma Pauline Nicholson Alexander Papers, SHC. For comparisons to the British context, see also Freeman and Klaus, "Blessed or Not"; Watkins, "Spinsters"; and Vicinus, *Independent Women*.

31 Laura Margaret Cole Smith Diary, October 1, 1833, Brumby and Smith Family Papers, SHC microfilm (this "diary" was written in the form of letters to female friends and relatives). For other discussions of young women's conceptions of "single blessedness" in the South see Cashin, "'Decidedly Opposed to the Union'"; Jabour, "'It Will Never Do for Me to Be Married'"; and Stowe, "The Thing, Not Its Vision.'"

32 Clinton, *Plantation Mistress*, 85; Amanda Virginia Edmonds Journals, February 15, 1859, Chappelear Papers, VHS; Caroline Brooks Lilly Books, vol. 1, April 14, 1837, SHC. For more on the unflattering stereotypes of southern spinsters, see Carvill, "Stereotype of Spinsters in Southern Fiction."

For a contrasting interpretation, see Broussard, "Female Solitaires." Broussard argues that in the Old South, the "servant ideal"—a life in service to the larger patriarchal order—superseded the domestic ideal of marriage and motherhood and provided single women with a respectable role in southern life. Susan Bradford Eppes's comments affirm Broussard's contention; she wrote that single women were welcomed into southern households: "An old maid relative was looked upon as a gift direct from Heaven, a blessed boon to add to the comfort and pleasure of home." See Eppes, *Through Some Eventful Years*, 116. For comparisons of rates of singlehood in northern and southern cities, see Pease and Pease, *Ladies, Women, and Wenches*, 10–11.

33 On single women in southern cities, see Carter, *Southern Single Blessedness*. See also Broussard, "Female Solitaires," and Clinton, *Plantation Mistress*, 85–86. A published diary of a southern single woman is Hobgood-Oster, ed., *Sabbath Journal of Judith Lomax*; see also Michael O'Brien, ed., *Evening When Alone*. A typical unpublished diary of a single woman is the Angelina Selden Edrington Diary, Edrington Family Papers, VHS. See also Mary McPhail to Mary Carrington, January 30, 1832, Carrington Family Papers, VHS.

34 Mary Pettigrew to William Pettigrew, June 23, 1843, Pettigrew Family Papers, SHC; Tariffa Cocke Witherspone to Juliana Cocke, November 5, 1860, Cocke Papers, SHC; Lou Hill to Anna Lee Hill, December 10, [1888?], Hill Family Papers, VHS.

35 Sarah Lois Wadley Diary, SHC microfilm; Burr, ed., *Secret Eye*, 108. See also Mary Pettigrew to William Pettigrew, September 6, [1843], and June 23, 1843, Pettigrew Family Papers, SHC.

36 Brady, ed., *George Washington's Beautiful Nelly*, 32; Jane Garland to Sarah Garland, April 20, 1819, and n.d. [May 1819], Garland Family Papers, VHS; M. L. Berkely to Ella Noland, October 23, 1849, MacKenzie Papers, SHC; Jinnie to Ella Noland, April 12, 1850, MacKenzie Papers, SHC; Susan McDowall Diary, May 13, 1857, Duke; Mary Brown to Margaret Steele, April 16, [1807], Steele Papers, SHC. For other examples, see Sarah Lois Wadley Diary, April 16, 1860, SHC microfilm; Mary Hawes to Virginia Dance, July 21, [1846], Terhune Papers, Duke; William H. Cabell to Elizabeth Wirt, June 28, 1824, Wirt Papers, MHS; Emma Shannon to Levina Shannon, March 16, 1858; Emma Shannon to Alice Shannon, March 29, 1858; and Emma Shannon to Marmaduke Shannon, April 12, 1858, Crutcher-Shannon Family Papers, CAH.

37 Ann Eliza Wight to Mary Carrington, August 22, n.d., Carrington Family Papers, VHS. See also Judith McGuire to Mary Anna McGuire Claiborne, February 20, 1845, Claiborne Family Papers, VHS. On southern women's housekeeping responsibilities, see, for example, Clinton, *Plantation Mistress*, chap. 2.

38 Amanda Jane Cooley Roberts Diary, 1842–54, and Elizabeth Ann Cooley McClure Diary, 1842–47, VHS; Burr, ed., *Secret Eye*, 108.

39 Emily Bland Southall to Julia Southall, September 24, 1862, Southall-Bowen Family Papers, SHC (see also Emily Bland Southall Diary, January 2, 14, 1862, ibid.); Mary Hawes to Virginia Dance, July 21, [1846], Terhune Papers, Duke.

40 For quotation, see Mary Hawes to Virginia Pearl, June 24, 1848, Terhune Papers, Duke; see also M. L. Berkely to Ella Noland, October 23, 1849, and Jinnie to Ella Noland, April 12, 1850, MacKenzie Papers, SHC; and Ann Eliza Wight to Mary Carrington, August 22, n.d., Carrington Family Papers, VHS.

41 Susan Cornwall Diary, 1857–66, SHC microfilm.

42 Sarah Lois Wadley Diary, October 18, 1860, SHC microfilm.

43 M. L. Berkeley to Ella Noland, October 23, 1849, MacKenzie Papers, SHC.

44 Mary Pettigrew to Charles Pettigrew, August 14, 1844, Pettigrew Family Papers, SHC; Brady, ed., *George Washington's Beautiful Nelly*, 19; C. Carr to Ella Noland, Au-

gust 3, 1849, MacKenzie Papers, SHC; Susan McDowall Diary and Scrapbook, n.d., Duke.

45 Ellen to Jane Miller, February 7, 1844, Hinton Papers, SHC.

46 Jabour, "'Grown Girls,'" 62.

47 Mary Brown to Margaret Steele, April 16, [1807], Steele Papers, SHC.

48 Caroline Elliott to Lucy McIver, August 12, [1859], McIver Papers, SHC.

49 Sallie S. Manson to Emma Nicholson, June 16, 1866, Emma Pauline Nicholson Alexander Papers, SHC.

50 On "the business of benevolence," see Ginzberg, *Women and the Work of Benevolence*. For women's organizations in the antebellum South, see especially Lebsock, *Free Women of Petersburg*, chap. 7; and Bellows, *Benevolence Among Slaveholders*, 40–50, 115. On the role of single women in such groups, see Carter, "Indispensable Spinsters."

51 Mary McPhail to Mary Carrington, January 30, 1832, Carrington Family Papers, VHS.

52 On Catharine Wirt and her sisters, see Jabour, "'Grown Girls,'" 58–60 (quotation).

53 Jabour, "'Grown Girls,'" 59–60; Sarah to Mary Carrington, December 10, 1828, Carrington Family Papers, VHS.

54 On the Grimké sisters, see Lerner, *Grimké Sisters from South Carolina*; on the limitations on southern women's activism, see Varon, *We Mean to Be Counted*.

55 For quotation, see Caroline Brooks Lilly Books, vol. 1, April 7, 1837, SHC. On teaching in the North, see, for example, Perlmann, Siddali, and Whitescarver, "Literacy, Schooling, and Teaching."

56 Julia Southall Daily Diary, January 2, October 4, 1868; Julia Southall to Emily Bland Southall, October 31, 1862; Julia Southall Weekly Diary, January 1, 1869; Julia Southall to Emily Bland Southall, May 1, 1863; Julia Southall to Josephine Southall, January 11, 1873, Southall-Bowen Family Papers, SHC.

57 Sarah Varick Cozens Morrison Diary, September 15, 1834, SHC; L. M. Atkinson to Mary Whitfield, [1845?], Whitfield Family Papers, Auburn.

58 Susan A. Webb Diary, January 4, 1864, Webb Family Papers, SHC; Caroline Brooks Lilly Books, vol. 1, April 3 and 7, 1837, SHC.

59 Susan A. Webb Diary, February 17, 1859, Webb Family Papers, SHC; Julia Southall to Emily Bland Southall, October 3, 1861, Southall-Bowen Family Papers, SHC.

60 Amanda Jane Cooley Roberts Diary, March 27, April 10 and 16, 1842, VHS.

61 Elizabeth Ann Cooley McClure Diary, November 20, 1842; Amanda Jane Cooley Roberts Diary, September 15, 1844, VHS.

62 Mary Virginia Early to Elizabeth Early, February 4, n.d. [ca. 1842], Early Family Papers, VHS; Sarah Lois Wadley Diary, February 21, 1861, and January 11, 1862, SHC microfilm; Burr, ed., *Secret Eye*, 71.

63 Agnes L. Miller, "Womanhood," n.d., in author's possession, courtesy of Tammy H. Whitlock. For northern girls, see Hunter, *How Young Ladies Became Girls*, 154–62.

64 Loula Kendall Rogers Diary, January 9, 1858, Rogers Collection, Emory.

65 Elizabeth Ann Cooley McClure Diary, November 20, 1842, VHS.

66 Mary Virginia Early, "Woman's Destiny," June 13, 1842, Early Family Papers, VHS.

67 Mary Hawes to Virginia Pearl, November 7, 1851, Terhune Papers, Duke.

68 Loula Kendall Rogers Journal, July 3, 1857, Rogers Collection, Emory.

69 Michael O'Brien, ed., *Evening When Alone*, 60.

70 Mary Hawes to Virginia Pearl, November 7, 1851, Terhune Papers, Duke.

71 Grace Elmore Diary, August 16, 1862, November 19, 1863, SHC microfilm.

72 Ibid., December 14, 20, 1861, September 13, 1862.

73 Ibid., November 23, 1861.

74 Penelope Skinner to Tristrim Skinner, February 26, 1840, Skinner Family Papers, SHC.

CHAPTER FOUR

1 Undated poem by Ella Noland, ca. 1850–51; Elizabeth Noland to Sally Gibson, March 20, 1851, MacKenzie Papers, SHC.

2 Ella Noland to Elizabeth Noland, February 6, [1851], MacKenzie Papers, SHC.

3 Ibid.

4 Carrie Sage to Ella Noland, November 28, 1850, MacKenzie Papers, SHC.

5 C. Carr to Ella Noland, August 3, 1849; Mary L. Berkeley to Ella Noland, March 23, October 23, 1849; Carrie Sage to Ella Noland, November 28, 1850; Elizabeth Noland to Sally Gibson, March 20, 1851; Marion to Ella Noland, November 2, [1851], MacKenzie Papers, SHC.

6 Carrie Sage to Ella Noland, November 28, 1850; Marion to Ella Noland, July 18, 1851; Elizabeth Noland to Ella Noland, November 6, 1851, MacKenzie Papers, SHC.

7 Marion to Ella Noland MacKenzie, March 15, [1854]; see also Mary to Ella Noland, March 3, 1852, MacKenzie Papers, SHC.

8 Mary Isabella Walker Weber Reminiscences, SHC; Mary Elizabeth McPhail to Mary Carrington, September 30, 1831, Carrington Family Papers, VHS. See also Catharine G. Wirt to William Wirt, January 1, 1827, Wirt Papers, MHS; and Catharine G. Wirt Diary, November 14, 1827, Wirt Papers, MHS. For the phrase "coming out" and for a contrasting interpretation of the southern belle, see Roberts, *Confederate Belle*, 15.

9 Roberts, *Confederate Belle*, 15; Mary Miller to Etheldred Miller, April 14, 1846, Davis Papers, Duke.

10 For quotations, see Catharine G. Wirt Diary, November 14, 1827, Miscellaneous Papers of Catharine G. Wirt, Wirt Papers, MHS; Roberts, *Confederate Belle*, 16; and Jabour, "It Will Never Do for Me to Be Married," 215. For the Wirt family, seventeen seems to have been regarded as the ideal age for a debut; the three eldest daughters made their debuts at age seventeen, and William Wirt once stated that his expectation was that Laura would "enter the world" at age seventeen and be married by the age of twenty. See William Wirt to Dabney Carr, December 21, 1809, Wirt Papers, MHS. For examples of the pattern of birth-order marriages and debuts, see Jabour, *Marriage in the Early Republic*, 113; for a discussion of the significance of this pattern and of exceptions to it in the antebellum South, see Censer, *North Carolina Planters*, 90–91.

11 For "turned-out young lady," see Sallie S. Manson to Emma Nicholson, June 16, 1866, Emma Pauline Nicholson Alexander Papers, SHC; Caroline Kean Hill Davis Diary, October 22, 1860, VHS; and Jabour, "It Will Never Do for Me to Be Mar-

ried," 215. For "belle," see Mary Isabella Walker Weber Reminiscences, SHC; Sarah Woolfolk Clay and Mary R. Combs to Eliza Spragins, September 22, 1842, Spragins Family Papers, VHS; Elizabeth Noland to Sally Gibson, March 20, 1851, MacKenzie Papers, SHC; and Laas, *Love and Power*, 23.

12 The best overview of debuts in America is Marling, *Debutante*, especially chaps. 1–3. Other popular treatments of nineteenth-century debuts and their contemporary counterparts include Best, *Prom Night*; and Vida, *Girls on the Verge*. On debuts in Victorian New York, see Montgomery, *Displaying Women*, 20–21 and 46–52. For the post–Civil War South, see Rambuss, "Spenser and Milton at Mardi Gras." For comments on southern women's power in courtship, see Censer, *North Carolina Planters*, 78; Clinton, *Plantation Mistress*, 61–62; and Charlene Boyer Lewis, *Ladies and Gentlemen on Display*, 180. The most extended discussion of the antebellum southern belle regards her as a showpiece for her family's honor and a tool to enhance their reputation; see Roberts, *Confederate Belle*, chap. 1. For a case study of one postwar southern belle, see Laas, *Love and Power*, chap. 2. On the importance southerners attached to ritual more generally, see Stowe, *Intimacy and Power in the Old South*.

13 See, for example, Jabour, *Marriage in the Early Republic*, 112–13; and Pease and Pease, *Family of Women*, 60–62. See also Roberts, *Confederate Belle*, 16.

14 Catharine G. Wirt to William Wirt, January 1, 1827, Wirt Papers, MHS; see also Elizabeth Wirt to William Wirt, January 1, 1827, ibid.

15 Catharine G. Wirt Diary, November 14, 1827, Wirt Papers, MHS. For more on Catharine Wirt, see Jabour, "Resisting the Altar."

16 On the European convention of being presented at court and Americans' adoption of this practice, see Marling, *Debutante*, chap. 1. Although most studies focus on the Anglo-American context, this practice was widespread among the European aristocracy. See Rundquist, "Presentation at Court." On aristocratic distinctions in the American capitol, see Allgor, *Parlor Politics*, especially chap. 2. On the Wirt family, see Jabour, *Marriage in the Early Republic*. Marling's discussion seems to indicate that, prior to the Civil War, northern girls usually "came out" at private tea parties hosted by their mothers. After the Civil War, northern girls were frequently presented at the British royal court. See Marling, *Debutante*, chap. 2 and pp. 23–28.

17 On the importance of purity in antebellum America generally, see, for example, Welter, "Cult of True Womanhood." On the particular emphasis laid on this ideal in the Old South, see especially Clinton, *Plantation Mistress*, 87–89, 121–22. On white dresses, see Jabour, *Marriage in the Early Republic*, 122; Ella Noland to Elizabeth Noland, February 6, [1851], MacKenzie Papers, SHC; Margaret Isabella Walker Weber Reminiscences, SHC; and Virginia Campbell Shelton Diary, April 21, 1835, VHS. On traveling to cities for debuts, see Jane Garland to Sarah Garland, February 19, 1819, Garland Family Papers, VHS; Jeanie to Tariffa Cocke, January 21, 1852, Cocke Papers, SHC; and Carrie Sage to Ella Noland, November 28, 1850, MacKenzie Papers, SHC. On dancing and debuts, see Marling, *Debutante*, chap. 3.

18 "Bubbles," Lizzie G. Davis Composition Book, Duke.

19 Clay-Clopton, *Belle of the Fifties*, 11; Burr, ed., *Secret Eye*, 118.

20 Brady, ed., *George Washington's Beautiful Nelly*, 25 n. 23; Jane Garland Cobbs to Sarah Garland, May 9, 1819, Garland Family Papers, VHS; Unknown to Emma Nichol-

son, January 25, 1866, Emma Pauline Nicholson Alexander Papers, SHC. It's not clear if young women themselves, or the adults around them, initiated this practice. However, in the case of Lizzie Kimberly, who is profiled in Chapter 1, Lizzie definitely took the initiative in calling herself "Lilly" at roughly the same time that adults began to refer to her as "Miss Kimberly," suggesting that Lizzie encouraged adults to acknowledge her new status.

21 Fannie Hatcher to Mary Eugenia Bennett, February 10, 1856, Bennett and Hill Family Papers, SHC; Samuel Garland to Sarah Garland, January 4, 1821, Garland Family Papers, VHS; Mary Louisa Read to Mary V. Carrington, Carrington Family Papers, VHS. Other means of announcing one's social availability included joining one's mother on social calls or hosting tea at one's home. See Marling, *Debutante*, chap. 2.

22 William Wirt to Dabney Carr, December 21, 1809; Robert Wirt to Elizabeth Wirt, February 26, 1821, Wirt Papers, MHS.

23 Penelope Skinner to Tristrim Skinner, March 12, April 5, 22, 1839, Skinner Family Papers, SHC. Also on the debut as an announcement of a young woman's availability for marriage, see Bossard and Boll, "Rite of Passage."

24 Jane Garland to Sarah Garland, February 19, 1819, Garland Family Papers, VHS; Mary Virginia Early to Virginia Burton, May 25, 1840, Early Family Papers, VHS. See also Bleser, ed., *Tokens of Affection*, 39–40; Jabour, " 'It Will Never Do for Me to Be Married,' " 221; and Jabour, "Hearts Divided," 245.

25 Margaret Steele to Mary Steele, January 1, 27, 1807; Margaret Steele to John Steele, February 19, 1807, Steele Papers, SHC.

26 Mary Brown to Margaret Steele, September 4, 1807, Steele Papers, SHC; Mollie to Margaret L. Beall, January 7, 1857, John Andrew Ramsay Papers, SHC.

27 M. L. Berkely to Ella Noland, March 23, 1849; Ella Noland to Elizabeth Noland, February 6, [1851]; Marion to Sally Gibson, April 11, [1851], MacKenzie Papers, SHC. See also Laas, *Love and Power*, 10; Clay-Clopton, *Belle of the Fifties*, 1; Margaret Isabella Walker Weber Reminiscences, SHC; Penelope Skinner to Tristrim Skinner, [October 30, 1839], Skinner Family Papers, SHC; and Lucy Anne Pope to Delia Hayes, April 9, 1813, Claiborne Family Papers, VHS. Winter seasons usually began in October or November and continued into March or April. In the summertime, the southern elite could mingle at the fashionable Virginia Springs, but these do not seem to have been favored spots for official debuts. See Charlene Boyer Lewis, *Ladies and Gentlemen on Display*.

28 Sarah Woolfolk Clay and Mary R. Combs to Eliza Spragins, September 22, 1842, Spragins Family Papers, VHS; C. Alice Ready Diary, July 15, 1861, SHC; Margaret Mordecai to Ellen Mordecai, December 2, 1840, Devereux Papers, SHC. Philadelphia was a popular destination for well-to-do southerners to showcase their wealth and establish themselves as a regional elite. See Kilbride, "Philadelphia and the Southern Elite."

29 Sarah Woolfolk Clay and Mary R. Combs to Eliza Spragins, September 22, 1842, Spragins Family Papers, VHS.

30 Jane Garland Cobbs to Sarah Garland, May 9, 1819, Garland Family Papers, VHS; Laura Margaret Cole Smith Diary, 1833–34, Brumby and Smith Family Papers, SHC; M. L. Berkeley to Ella Noland, March 23, 1849, and June 11, [1849], MacKen-

zie Papers, SHC; Pollie to Emma Nicholson, September 19, 1862, Emma Pauline Nicholson Alexander Papers, SHC.

31 Mary L. Berkeley to Ella Noland, March 25, 1851, MacKenzie Papers, SHC ("sober"); Margaret Mordecai to Ellen Mordecai, December 2, 1840, Devereux Papers, SHC ("gay"); William Wirt to Elizabeth Wirt, May 20, 1825, Wirt Papers, MHS ("rusticate"); Mary Telfair (Savannah) to Mary Few, October 28, 1814, in Cashin, ed., *Our Common Affairs*, 86 ("adamantine").

32 Laura Wirt to Robert Wirt, January 12, 1826, Wirt Papers, MHS; Mary Elizabeth McPhail to Mary Carrington, September 30, 1831, Carrington Family Papers, VHS; Mary Cooke to Martha Hunter, February 1, 1841, Hunter Family Papers, VHS.

33 Mary Brown to Margaret Steele, Steele Papers, SHC; Laura Wirt to Robert Wirt, January 12, February 3, 1823, Wirt Papers, MHS.

34 H. L. T. to Emily Conrad, August 2, 1854, Hunt Papers, Duke; Ann Steele to Aunt [Nessfield], March 12, 1802, Steele Papers, SHC. See also Gillespie, "Mary Briscoe Baldwin," 72.

35 Virginia Campbell Shelton Diary, January 12, April 21, June 10, November 28, 1835; July 19, 1836, VHS.

36 Catharine G. Wirt Diary, November 14, 21, 1827; November 1, 1829, Wirt Papers, MHS.

37 William Wirt to Elizabeth Wirt, May 20, 1825, Wirt Papers, MHS; [Maria Roy] to Delia Hayes, August 2, 1809, Claiborne Family Papers, VHS; Catharine G. Wirt Diary, January 1, 1834, February 19, 1835, "Texts of Scripture going to prove the equality & immortality of women," July 1835, Wirt Papers, MHS.

38 Ann Eliza Wight to Mary Carrington, August 22, n.d., Carrington Family Papers, VHS.

39 Mary Telfair (Savannah) to Mary Few, October 28, 1814, in Cashin, ed., *Our Common Affairs*, 86; Mary Hawes to Virginia Pearl, September 18, 1848, Terhune Papers, Duke.

40 Fannie S. Hatcher to Mary Eugenia Bennett, August 27, 1857, Bennett and Hill Family Papers, SHC.

41 Sarah F. Brown to Sarah Garland, February 21, 1819, Garland Family Papers, VHS.

42 Laura Margaret Cole Smith Diary, Brumby and Smith Family Papers, SHC (this "diary" was written in the form of letters to female friends and relatives); Ellen Finley to [Matilda Abernathy], July 26, 1859, Dickson Papers, SHC. For other examples of this behavior, see Laas, *Love and Power*, 9.

43 Margaret Steele to Mary Steele, January 27, 1807, Steele Papers, SHC.

44 Ann Steele to Mary Steele, November 13, 1801, Steele Papers, SHC; Mary Page to Lucy McGuire, March 14, n.d., Byrd Family Papers, VHS; Elvira Boswell to Martha Hunter, February 13, 1832, Hunter Family Papers, VHS; Mary Cooke to Martha Hunter, January 19, 1840, Hunter Family Papers, VHS; Willie to Mary Virginia Early, August 19, 1844, Early Family Papers, VHS; Fannie S. Hatcher to Mary Eugenia Bennett, Bennett and Hill Family Papers, SHC; Mary Hawes to Virginia Pearl, September 18, 1848, Terhune Papers, Duke.

45 Susan McDowall Diary, January 15, 1857, Duke; Cashin, ed., *Our Common Affairs*, 163.

46　Mary Brown to Margaret Steele, March 10, 1810, Steele Papers, SHC; Elizabeth Ruffin Cocke to Tariffa Cocke, March 25, 1848, Cocke Papers, SHC. On age differences in the Old South, see Clinton, *Plantation Mistress*, 60 and Appendix A, table 3, p. 233.

47　Mary McPhail to Mary Carrington, March 4, 1835; Anne Eliza Wight to Mary Carrington, April 24, 1837, Carrington Family Papers, VHS.

48　Bettie to Eliza Cocke, July 13, 1862, Cocke Papers, SHC; Bleser, ed., *Tokens of Affection*, 39–40.

49　Sally B. to Eliza Spragins, n.d., Spragins Family Papers, VHS; Eliza Lavalette Barksdale Diary, VHS; Maria Roy to Delia Hayes, December 5, 1813, Claiborne Family Papers, VHS; Mary Hawes to Virginia Pearl, September 18, 1848, Terhune Papers, Duke. See also Censer, *North Carolina Planters*, 76–78.

50　Penelope Skinner to Tristrim Skinner, September 4, 1837, March 12, 1839, January 15, 1840, Skinner Family Papers, SHC.

51　Laas, *Love and Power*, 16, 22; Kate Rose to Ella Noland, February 29, 1848, MacKenzie Papers, SHC. See also Bleser, ed., *Tokens of Affection*, 18. For a discussion of adults' attitudes toward flirtation, see Charlene Boyer Lewis, *Ladies and Gentlemen on Display*, 181–82.

52　Laura Wirt to Louisa Cabell Carrington, July 10, 1824, Randall Papers, VHS; Mary Francis Page Cook to Lucy Carter, March 13, n.d., Byrd Family Papers, VHS; Laas, *Love and Power*, 10.

53　Mary Brown to Margaret Steele, September 4, 1807, Steele Papers, SHC; Ellen to [Matilda Abernathy], November 12, 1859, Dickson Papers, SHC.

54　Elizabeth Noland to Sally Gibson, March 20, 1851, MacKenzie Papers, SHC; Anne Eliza Wight to Mary Carrington, April 24, 1837, Carrington Family Papers, VHS.

55　Virginia Taylor to Lydia Russell, n.d., Jones Family Papers, VHS; Fannie S. Hatcher to Mary Eugenia Bennett, Bennett and Hill Family Papers, SHC; Laura Wirt to Louisa Cabell Carrington, July 10, 1824, Randall Papers, VHS.

56　Marion to Ella Noland, November 2, [1851], MacKenzie Papers, SHC; Mary Brown to Margaret Steele, April 16, [1807], Steele Papers, SHC; Mary Page to Lucy McGuire, June 27, 1867, Byrd Family Papers, VHS. See also Margaret Steele to Mary Steele, January 27, 1807, July 1, 1808, Steele Papers, SHC; Julia Southall Personal Journal, 1871–76, Southall-Bowen Family Papers, SHC; and Woodward and Muhlenfeld, eds., *Private Mary Chesnut*, 21.

57　Mary Francis Page to Lucy Carter, June 27, 1867, and March 13, n.d., Byrd Family Papers, VHS; Julia Southall to Blannie Southall Moore, November 22, 1865, Southall-Bowen Family Papers, SHC. See also Murr, ed., *Rebel Wife in Texas*, 45; and Mary Hawes to Virginia Pearl, August 26, 1850, Terhune Papers, Duke. The phrase "civil death" is taken from Flexnor, *Century of Struggle*, 7.

58　Mary Hawes to Virginia Pearl, August 26, 1850, Terhune Papers, Duke.

59　Leavitt, "Under the Shadow of Maternity," 133; see also Dye, "History of Childbirth in America." On southern women and motherhood, see McMillen, *Motherhood in the Old South*, statistics p. 81.

60　Laura Wirt to Louisa Cabell Carrington, November 20, 1822, Randall Papers, VHS. See also Cornelia Grantham to Mother, December 19, n.d., Larue Family Papers, VHS; Fannie Hatcher to Mary Eugenia Bennett, August 27, 1857, Bennett and Hill

Family Papers, SHC; and Anne to Elizabeth Spragins, n.d., Spragins Family Papers, VHS.

61 Julia Southall to Blannie Southall Moore, November 22, 1865, Southall-Bowen Family Papers, SHC. See also Mary Brown to Margaret Steele, July 1, 1808, Steele Papers, SHC; and Fannie Hatcher to Mary Eugenia Bennett, August 30, 1856, Bennett and Hill Family Papers, SHC.

62 O'Brien, ed., *Evening When Alone*, 67; Elizabeth Alexander to A. F. Alexander, December 15, 1852, A. F. Alexander Papers, SHC; Fannie Hatcher to Mary Eugenia, June 7, 1856, Bennett and Hill Family Papers, SHC; Jane Garland to Sarah Garland, February 19, 1819, Garland Family Papers, VHS.

63 Pollie S. to Emma Nicholson, September 19, 1862, Emma Pauline Nicholson Alexander Papers, SHC; Lizzie Cochran to Margaret Beall, March 9, 1857, John Andrew Ramsay Papers, SHC.

64 Harriet to Julia Conrad, October 23, 1840, Jones Family Papers, SHC; Ellen to Jane Constance Miller, January 17, 1844, Hinton Papers, SHC.

65 John Devereux to Ellen Mordecai, July 28, 1841, Devereux Papers, SHC. For courtship on the national stage, see Lystra, *Searching the Heart*; Ellen K. Rothman, *Hands and Hearts*; and Daniel Scott Smith, "Parental Power and Marriage Patterns." For courtship in the South, see Censer, *North Carolina Planters*, chap. 4; Clinton, *Plantation Mistress*, 59–65; Charlene Boyer Lewis, *Ladies and Gentlemen on Display*, 175–87; and Stowe, *Intimacy and Power in the Old South*, chap. 2. For case studies of courtship and the cultural contexts informing it, see Blauvelt, "Women, Words, and Men"; Gelles, "Gossip"; McMahon, "'While Our Souls Together Blend'"; MacMullen, *Sarah's Choice*; and Minkema, "Hannah and Her Sisters." For less common case studies from the nineteenth-century South, see especially Friend, "Belles, Benefactors"; Stowe, "'The Thing, Not Its Vision'"; and Wates, "Precursor to the Victorian Age."

66 See, for example, Caroline Brooks Lilly Books, May 10, 1838, SHC; Waddy Butler to Lucy Wood, May 22, 1859, and May 16, 1860, Lucy Wood Butler Papers, SHC; and G. H. S. to Jane Allston, September 20, 1869, Allston Family Papers, SCHS. See also Guion G. Johnson, "Courtship and Marriage Customs"; and Charlene Boyer Lewis, *Ladies and Gentlemen on Display*, 145.

67 Eliza Lavalette Barksdale Diary, May 25, 1836, VHS (quotations); see also ibid., June 9, 10, August 19, 20, 21, and October 21, 1836.

68 For quotations, see John Price to Belle Price, October 27, 1859, Simrall Papers, SHC; and David S. Garland to Sarah and Mary Garland, n.d., and Jane Garland to Sarah and Mary Garland, February 4, 1819, Garland Family Papers, VHS; see also Sally Gibson to Ella Noland, June 20, 1851, MacKenzie Papers, SHC; Anne E. Davis to William Lucas, June 13, 1850, Lucas Family Papers, VHS; Minnie Bacot to [Jane Allston], August 10, 1866, Allston Family Papers, SCHS; and William Wirt to Elizabeth Wirt, May 9, 1824; Laura Wirt to William Wirt, May 11, 1824; William Wirt to Laura Wirt, May 13, 1824; Elizabeth Wirt to William Wirt, October 22, 28, 1824, Wirt Papers, MHS. See also Censer, *North Carolina Planters*, 65–68, 78–95; and Charlene Boyer Lewis, *Ladies and Gentlemen on Display*, 145–50. Lewis points out that at the comparatively relaxed social setting of the Virginia Springs, it was up

to women to maintain the rules of social interaction. While men engaged in illicit activities, including sex with prostitutes, women maintained the rules of respectability.

69 Cary Whitaker to Anna Whitaker, August 1, 1831, Wills Papers, SHC; Elizabeth Ruffin Cocke to Tariffa Cocke, January 24, [1848?], Cocke Papers, SHC; Elizabeth Noland to Ella Noland, December 25, 1846, MacKenzie Papers, SHC. On female purity and the sexual and racial double standard in the Old South, see Clinton, *Plantation Mistress*, chap. 5; and Pease and Pease, *Ladies, Women, and Wenches*, 140–43. Escaped North Carolina slave Harriet Jacobs drew a sharp contrast between the sexual protection of white girls and the sexual exploitation of black ones, explaining, "That which commands admiration in the white woman only hastens the degradation of the female slave." This was particularly true in adolescence. "I once saw two beautiful children playing together," Jacobs wrote in "The Trials of Girlhood." "One was a fair white child; the other was her slave, and also her sister. . . . The fair child grew up to be a still fairer woman. From childhood to womanhood her pathway was blooming with flowers, and overarched by a sunny sky. Scarcely one day of her life had been clouded when the sun rose on her happy bridal morning. How had those years dealt with her slave sister, the little playmate of her childhood? She, also, was very beautiful; but the flowers and sunshine of love were not for her. She drank the cup of sin, and shame, and misery, whereof her persecuted race are compelled to drink" (*Incidents*, 28–29; see also pp. 13, 27, and 31).

70 Isabella Miller to Jane Constance Miller, August 23, 1840, Hinton Papers, SHC.

71 Clay-Clopton, *Belle of the Fifties*, 13–14; Elizabeth Ruffin Diary, February 6, 11, 1827, Cocke Papers, SHC. See also Virginia Campbell Shelton Diary, July 29, 1837, VHS; and Friend, "Belles, Benefactors," 102.

72 H. L. T. to Emily Conrad, August 2, 1854, Hunt Papers, Duke. See also Halttunen, *Confidence Men and Painted Ladies*, 56–58.

73 For a similarly negative assessment of courtship from the man's perspective, see Friend, "Belles, Benefactors."

74 Caroline Brooks Lilly Books, September 23, November 17, 26, and December 2, 8, and 17, 1838, SHC.

75 Erastus Hopkins to Sarah Bennett, May 18, 1835, Hopkins Correspondence, SCHS. For other descriptions of such types of courtship, see Elizabeth Wirt to William Wirt, November 20, 22, 1820, May 6, 10, 11, 24, 26, 27, 29, 1828, Wirt Papers, MHS.

76 For examples of such occasions, see Elizabeth Ann Cooley McClure Diary, September 28, November 9, 1845, VHS; and Jabour, *Marriage in the Early Republic*, 17. For a discussion of the etiquette of courtship correspondence, see Stowe, *Intimacy and Power in the Old South*, 58–67.

77 John LaBruce to Jane Allston, n.d., Allston Family Papers, SCHS; Elizabeth Cooley Diary, January 4, 1846, VHS; Carrie Sage to Ella Noland, November 28, 1850, MacKenzie Papers, SHC.

78 For quotations, see Wyatt Patterson to Lottie Dye, September 14, 1863, Patterson-Dye Correspondence, SCHS; and Richard Johnson to Isabella Mackay, April 16 and June 14, 1863, Johnson Family Papers, SCHS. On the importance of privacy, see Wyatt Patterson to Lottie Dye, May 10, 1863, and January [14], 1864, Patterson-Dye

Correspondence, SCHS. For an excellent example of this evolution, see the court-ship letters of Emma Shannon and William Crutcher, 1859–60, Crutcher-Shannon Family Papers, CAH.

79 Mary Miller to Charles Davis, September 17, 1848, Davis Papers, Duke.

80 Joseph Blount Skinner to Maria Lowther, [n.d., 1803], Skinner Family Papers, SHC. The Skinners' son, Tristrim, likewise found that his courtship of his young ward and onetime student, Eliza Harwood, was complicated by the need for propriety. See Harwood-Skinner correspondence, 1840–48, Skinner Family Papers, SHC.

81 Sarah Satterlee to Mary Hudson Ellett, May 1 and June 5, 1855, Ellett–St. Catherine's Alumnae Association Papers, VHS; Nannie Hoskins Williams Diary, August 21, 1869, SHC. For more examples of cousinly courtships, see Emma Sue Gordon Diary, Perkins Family Papers, SHC; and Emily Bland Southall Diary, Southall-Bowen Family Papers, SHC. On cousin marriage, see Censer, *North Carolina Planters*, 84–87, and Clinton, *Plantation Mistress*, 57–58 and Appendix A, table 2, p. 233.

82 Emma Sue Gordon Diary, May 15 and 19, 1863, Perkins Family Papers, SHC. In her study of New England courtships, Ellen K. Rothman finds much more evidence of sexual expression, although women's responsibility to set the limits of sexual con-tact was consistent with the behavior described here. See "Sex and Self-Control." In her study of southern courtships, Charlene Boyer Lewis indicates that while elite men sometimes engaged in premarital sex (with slaves and prostitutes, not with their courting partners), well-to-do women did not. See *Ladies and Gentlemen on Display*, 146, 148.

83 Emma Sue Gordon Diary, June 18, 1863, Perkins Family Papers, SHC.

84 Cornelia McIver to Lucy McIver, January 3, 1857, McIver Papers, SHC; Cuthbert to Elizabeth Lucas, June 27, 1851, Cuthbert Letters, SCHS; Elizabeth Ann Cooley Mc-Clure Diary, March 15, 1846, VHS; William Henry Wills to Anna Whitaker, [January 1, 1835], Wills Papers, SHC. For examples of unchaperoned visits, see Mary Fries Patterson Diary, 1863–64, SHC; and Nathalie E. Baylies to Mary Hudson Ellett, August 12, 1856, Ellett–St. Catherine's Alumnae Association Papers, VHS. For examples of secret engagements, see Penelope Skinner to Tristrim Skinner, February 26, 1840; Tristrim Skinner to Eliza Harwood, November 28, 1848, Skinner Family Papers, SHC; Cornelia McIver to Lucy McIver, January 3, 1857, McIver Papers, SHC; Bettie to Margaret L. Beall, November 8, 1857, John Andrew Ramsay Papers, SHC; Elizabeth Higginbotham to Anna Higginbotham, January 30, 1829, Higginbotham Family Papers, VHS; Judith C. Nelson to Maria Lowther Skinner, March 6, 1805, Skinner Family Papers, SHC; Unknown to Jane Allston, October 29, 1869, Allston Family Papers, SCHS; and Wyatt Patterson to Lottie Dye, Septem-ber 26, 1863, Patterson-Dye Correspondence, SCHS. On erotic dreams (always re-lated by men), see Emma Sue Gordon Diary, May 19, 1863, Perkins Family Papers, SHC; and Wyatt Patterson to Lottie Dye, November 17, 1863, Patterson-Dye Cor-respondence, SCHS.

85 Cuthbert to Elizabeth Lucas, June 27, 1851, Cuthbert Letters, SCHS; Wyatt Patter-son to Lois Dye, September 26, 1863, Patterson-Dye Correspondence, SCHS; Mary Francis Page to Lucy Page Carter, December 17, 1861, Byrd Family Papers, VHS; Waddy Butler to Lucy Wood, February 20, 1861, Lucy Wood Butler Papers, SHC.

86 Cuthbert to Elizabeth Lucas, June 27, 1851, Cuthbert Letters, SCHS; Anna Hendree to Thomas Norwood, August 3, 1850, Norwood Family Papers, VHS.

87 Sarah Bennett to Erastus Hopkins, April 6, June 1, 1835, Hopkins Correspondence, SCHS.

CHAPTER FIVE

1 Lizzie Neblett Diary, "Introduction," March 16, 1852, quoted in Murr, ed., *Rebel Wife*, 23. Original held in the Elizabeth Scott Neblett Papers, CAH.

2 March 17, 20, April 10, 1852, ibid., 24, 25, 32. See also pp. 26, 69.

3 March 20, April 3, 19, 29, May 3, 9, 10, 1852, ibid., 27, 29, 38, 42, 43, 45–46. An avid reader, Lizzie also quoted frequently from the Bible (both the Old and the New Testaments), from eighteenth-century English authors (especially Milton and Pope), and from nineteenth-century sentimental novels. See 27 n. 9; 28 n. 11; 30 nn. 16, 17; 31 nn. 19, 20; 31 nn. 22, 23; 33 nn. 27, 28; 34 nn. 29, 30, 31; 35 nn. 32, 33; 36 n. 35; 37 nn. 37, 38; 38 n. 42; 39 n. 43; 42 n. 48, 49, 50; 47 n. 55.

4 April 3, 10, 12, 19, 22, ibid., 29, 30, 31, 33, 34, 38, 39. Lizzie said that she felt "sad," "despairing," and "indifferent" and was unable to concentrate on or find pleasure in any activity. See pp. 25, 39, 41, 42.

5 May 3, 1852, ibid., 43. On women's legal status, see, for example, Basch, *In the Eyes of the Law*, and Salmon, *Women and the Law of Property*.

6 Lizzie Neblett Diary, April 14, 22, May 3, 15, 24, 1852, quoted in Murr, ed., *Rebel Wife*, 35–36, 40, 43, 48, 49.

7 April 10, 12, 14, 22, May 5, 7, 1852, ibid., 30, 33–35, 35, 40, 44.

8 March 20, April 10, 19, May 7, 1852, ibid., 26, 30, 38, 44.

9 Nannie Hoskins Williams Diary, August 21, 1869, SHC.

10 Amanda Virginia Edmonds Journals, January 27 and 28, 1859, Chappelear Papers, VHS; Mary Shannon to Emma and Ann Shannon, February 7, 1858, Crutcher-Shannon Papers, CAH.

11 Elizabeth Ann Cooley McClure Diary, January 1, 1845, VHS.

12 Elizabeth Ruffin Diary, July–September 1827, Cocke Papers, SHC. For an introduction to the extensive literature on domesticity, see Cott, *Bonds of Womanhood*; Matthews, *"Just a Housewife"*; Sklar, *Catharine Beecher*; and Welter, "Cult of True Womanhood." On the idealization of "home," see Clark, *American Family Home*; McDannell, *Christian Home in Victorian America*; Nylander, *Our Own Snug Fireside*; and Van de Wetering, "Popular Concept of 'Home.'"

13 John Steele to Ann Steele, April 18, 1801, Steele Papers, SHC; Lizzie Scott Neblett Diary, May 10, 1852, quoted in Murr, ed., *Rebel Wife*, 46. The phrase "haven in a heartless world" comes from Lasch, *Haven in a Heartless World*.

14 Sarah Satterlee to Mary Hudson Ellett, June 5, 1855, Ellett–St. Catherine's Alumnae Association Papers, VHS.

15 Unknown to [Matilda Abernathy], February n.d., 1860, Dickson Papers, SHC. Chambers-Schiller suggests that "single blessedness" was limited to northern women in *Liberty, a Better Husband*, introduction. Although Jacobson Carter indicates otherwise, her scope is limited to women in the coastal urban centers of

Savannah, Georgia, and Charleston, South Carolina. See *Southern Single Blessedness*.

16 Elizabeth Neblett Diary, April 10, 1852, in Murr, ed., *Rebel Wife*, 30, 45; see also May 10, 1852, quoted in ibid.; Mary Miller to Charles Davis, September 17, 1848, Mary Miller Davis Papers, Duke; Eliza Harwood to Tristrim Skinner, April 7, 1846, Skinner Family Papers, SHC.

17 Emma Sue Gordon Diary, April 19 and May 15, 1863, Perkins Family Papers, SHC.

18 Caroline Kean Hill Davis Diary, October 22, 1860, VHS.

19 On romantic love and the companionate ideal, see especially Jabour, *Marriage in the Early Republic*, and Lystra, *Searching the Heart*. For contrasting interpretations of northern and southern women's "sphere," see Cott, *Bonds of Womanhood*, and Fox-Genovese, *Within the Plantation Household*.

20 J. B. Solomon to Emily Conrad, January 10, 1855, Hunt Papers, Duke. Most women emphasized their desire to make sure that their prospective husbands loved them, rather than the reverse; for an example of a woman who questioned the depths of her own affection, rather than her fiancé's, see Josephine Southall to Neil Bowen, December 11, [1865], Southall-Bowen Family Papers, SHC.

21 Bazil Kiger to Caroline Kiger, January 1, 1852, Kiger Family Papers, CAH. See also Censer, *North Carolina Planters*, 65–67; and Clinton, *Plantation Mistress*, 59–60.

22 Unidentified to Eliza Cornelia Grantham, October 28, n.d., Larue Family Papers, VHS. See also Mary Brown to Margaret Steele, July 4, 1807, Steele Papers, SHC.

23 "To bind herself to one for whom she feels no affection, such a union could be productive of nothing but misery, and that for life," Ready pronounced (C. Alice Ready Diary, April 20, 1860, SHC); Mary Shannon to Emma and Ann Shannon, February 7, 1858, Crutcher-Shannon Family Papers, CAH; Caroline Brooks Lilly Books, November 21, 1838, SHC.

24 Sally Elmore to Rosine della Torre, July n.d., 1848, Elmore Papers, SHC microfilm, reel 24.

25 Mary Brown to Margaret Steele, July 4, 1807, Steele Papers, SHC. Similarly, Laura Margaret Cole vowed: "I will not give away my heart, and am afraid to exchange it, lest I should not get one in return equally valuable" (Laura Margaret Cole Smith Diary, 1833–34, Brumby and Smith Family Papers, SHC).

26 Elizabeth Ann Cooley McClure Diary, April 23, 1843, VHS.

27 On engagements elsewhere in the country, see Cogan, *All-American Girl*, chap. 5; and Rothman, *Hands and Hearts*, 68–75, 157–64. For quotation, see Clinton, *Plantation Mistress*, 59.

28 Sarah Satterlee to Mary Ellett, [February 15, 1858], Ellett–St. Catherine's Alumnae Association Papers, VHS.

29 Mary Page to Lucy McGuire, June 27, 1867, Byrd Family Papers, VHS; Waddy Butler to Lucy Wood, September 29, 1860 (quotation), February 20, 1861, Lucy Wood Butler Diary, July 3, 1861, Lucy Wood Butler Papers, SHC; Loula Kendall Rogers Journal, December 25, 1861, January 1, 20, 1862, and Loula Kendall to James Henry Rogers, January 5, 22, May 7, 1862, Rogers Collection, Emory; Bettie Bernard to Frances Bernard Capps and Mary Jane Bernard, April 7 [9?], 1859, Bernard Family Papers, VHS. For other examples of anxious bridegrooms and reluctant brides,

see Richard Johnson to Isabella Mackay, August 27, September 24, October 30, November 10, 1863, February 17, [1864], Johnson Family Papers, SCHS; Neil Bowen to Josephine Southall, March 19, 1877, and Julian Moore to Blannie Southall, August 28, 1864, Southall-Bowen Family Papers, SHC; and William H. Wills to Anna Whitaker, [January 1, 1835], Wills Papers, SHC. This pattern also held true in the antebellum North. See Rothman, *Hands and Hearts*, 68–72, 157.

30 Kate Rose to Ella Noland, February 29, 1848, MacKenzie Papers, SHC. See also Mary Page to Lucy McGuire, June 2, n.d., Byrd Family Papers, VHS.

31 Elizabeth Ann Cooley McClure Diary, December 28, 1845, VHS.

32 Lucy Randolph Page Carter to Lucy Carter McGuire, January 23, 1867, Byrd Family Papers, VHS.

33 Elizabeth Ann Cooley McClure Diary, November 9, 1845, VHS. For other accounts of engagement, see, for example, Cornelia McIver to Lucy McIver, January 3, 1857, McIver Papers, SHC; and unknown to Emma Nicholson, January 25, 1866, Emma Pauline Nicholson Alexander Papers, SHC.

34 For quotation, see Tristrim Skinner to Eliza Harwood, November 28, 1848, Skinner Family Papers, SHC. On parental approval, see, for example, Penelope Skinner to Tristrim Skinner, February 26, 1840, ibid.; J. McPherson to Elizabeth McPherson, December 22, 1836, Ferebee, Gregory, and McPherson Family Papers, SHC; Julian Moore to Blannie Southall, August 28, 1864, Southall-Bowen Family Papers, SHC; Nannie Hoskins Williams Diary, November 1, 1869, SHC; Nathalie E. Baylies to Mary Hudson Ellett, August 12, 1856, Ellett–St. Catherine's Alumnae Association Papers, VHS; Elizabeth Higginbotham to Anna Higginbotham, February 18, 1829 [misdated 1828], Higginbotham Family Papers, VHS; and Mary Cooke to Martha Hunter, January 11, 1842, Hunter Family Papers, VHS. Men, as well as women, desired parental approval. See, for example, James Sims to Francis Moody, August 10, September 13, 1868, Sims Family Papers, SHC. On friends' blessings, see, for instance, J. McPherson to Elizabeth McPherson, December 22, 1836, and Courtney McPherson Wilson to Elizabeth McPherson, February 9, 1837, Ferebee, Gregory, and McPherson Family Papers, SHC; and Bettie Bernard to Frances Bernard Capps and Mary Jane Bernard, April 7 [9?], 1859, Bernard Family Papers, VHS. See also Censer, *North Carolina Planters*, 79–81.

35 [Josephine Southall Paper], March 1877, Southall-Bowen Family Papers, SHC; Mary Page to Lucy McGuire, June 27, 1867, Byrd Family Papers, VHS; Jane A. Dowell to Lydia Russell, March 4, 1850, Jones Family Papers, VHS; Mary Fries Patterson Diary, 1863–64, SHC. The term "marriage trauma" comes from Cott, *Bonds of Womanhood*, 80–83.

36 Mary Hawes to Virginia Pearl, April 17, [1852], Terhune Papers, Duke. See also Bettie to Margaret L. Beall, November 8, 1857, John Andrew Ramsay Papers, SHC.

37 Mary Fries Patterson Diary, 1863–64, SHC; Caroline Brooks Lilly Books, December 22, 1838, SHC; Mary Polk to Sarah Blount, October 26, 1826, Polk, Badger, and McGehee Papers, SHC; Nannie Hoskins Williams Diary, January 31, 1870, SHC (emphasis added).

38 Southern legislators and judges were more likely to grant divorce *a mensa e thoro*— divorce of bed and board, or legal separation, under which a woman's property re-

mained her husband's. Even when they granted an absolute divorce, they generally prohibited remarriage. On married women's legal status in antebellum America, see Basch, *In the Eyes of the Law*, and Salmon, *Women and the Law of Property*. On divorce law and practice, see Riley, *Divorce*. On divorce and separation in the antebellum South, see Censer, "'Smiling Through Her Tears,'" and Salmon, *Women and the Law of Property*, 72–73, 80.

39 Nannie Hoskins Williams Diary, July 31, 1870, SHC; Caroline Brooks Lilly Books, November 26, 1838, SHC; Penelope Skinner to Tristrim Skinner, February 26, 1840, Skinner Family Papers, SHC; Emma Sue Gordon Diary, January 26, October 19, 1863, Perkins Family Papers, SHC. See also Emily McEwen to Mary Polk, February 15, 1825, Polk, Badger, and McGehee Family Papers, SHC; and Willie to Mary Virginia Early, August 19, 1844, Early Family Papers, VHS.

40 Anna Hendree to Thomas Norwood, October 15, 1851, Norwood Family Papers, VHS. For southern girls' relative inexperience with household matters, see Fox-Genovese, *Within the Plantation Household*, 112–14. For the connection between wifely duty and husbandly affection, see, for example, Lizzie Scott Neblett, "A Review of the past eight years," January 22, 1860, in Murr, ed., *Rebel Wife*, 74–75.

41 Bettie Bernard to Frances Bernard Capps and Mary Jane Bernard, April 7 [9?], 1859, Bernard Family Papers, VHS.

42 Elizabeth Fischer to Anna Higginbotham, March 26, 1830, Higginbotham Family Papers, VHS.

43 Mary Page to Lucy McGuire, n.d., Byrd Family Papers, VHS; Nannie Hoskins Williams Diary, October 2 [4?], 1870, SHC; Mary Hawes to Virginia Pearl, August 16, 1856, Terhune Papers, Duke.

44 Mary Page to Lucy McGuire, n.d., Byrd Family Papers, VHS. For the shift "from patriarchy to companionship," see Griswold, *Family and Divorce in California*, chap. 1. For other discussions of the political economy of marriage and the importance of romantic love, see Lebsock, *Free Women of Petersburg*, chap. 2; and Lystra, *Searching the Heart*, chap. 6. A companionate marriage was not necessarily an equal relationship, however; see Jabour, *Marriage in the Early Republic*.

45 Mary Cooke to Martha Hunter, January 11, 1842, Hunter Family Papers, VHS; Emma Sue Gordon Diary, June 18, 1863, Perkins Family Papers, SHC.

46 Bettie Maney Kimberly to Annie Maney, January 23, 1860, Kimberly Papers, SHC.

47 Ann Eliza Wright to Mary Carrington, January 23, n.d., Carrington Family Papers, VHS; Anna Hendree to Thomas Norwood, January 14, 1851, Norwood Family Papers, VHS. On migration, see Censer, "Southwestern Migration," and Cashin, *Family Venture*.

48 Lucy Wood to Waddy Butler, August 11, 1860, Lucy Wood Butler Papers, SHC; Anna Hendree to Thomas Norwood, August 12, 1851, Norwood Family Papers, VHS.

49 Anna Hendree to Thomas Norwood, June 8, 1852, Norwood Family Papers, VHS. For an analysis of such novels (many written by southern authors), see Tracey, *Plots and Proposals*; for another real-life example of this pattern, see Jabour, *Marriage in the Early Republic*, 15–17.

50 Anna Hendree to Thomas Norwood, October 15, 1851, Norwood Family Papers, VHS.

51 Mary Francis Page to Lucy Page Carter, March 13, n.d.; Mary Page to Lucy McGuire, March 14, n.d., June 27, 1867, Byrd Family Papers, VHS.

52 Mary Francis Page to Lucy Carter, March 13, n.d.; Mary Page to Lucy McGuire, June 27, 1867, Byrd Family Papers, VHS; Anna Hendree to Thomas Norwood, August 20, 1851, Norwood Family Papers, VHS; Emma Shannon Crutcher to Will Crutcher, January 6, 1861, Crutcher-Shannon Papers, CAH; Burr, " 'Woman Made to Suffer,' " 218.

53 Cuthbert to Elizabeth Lucas, June 27, 1851, Cuthbert Letters, SCHS.

54 Erastus Hopkins to Sarah Bennett, May 18, 1835, Hopkins Correspondence, SCHS.

55 Richard Johnson to Isabella Mackay, June 5, August 27, September 24, October 30, November 10, 1863, Johnson Family Papers, SCHS.

56 Tristrim Skinner to Eliza Harwood, October 14, 1848, Skinner Family Papers, SHC.

57 Loula Kendall to Henry Rogers, September 4, 1862, Rogers Collection, Emory; Burr, ed., *Secret Eye*, 109.

58 For case studies of romantic love and male dominance in nineteenth-century southern marriages, see Bleser, "Perrys of Greenville"; Bleser and Heath, "Clays of Alabama"; Burr, " 'Woman Made to Suffer' "; and Jabour, *Marriage in the Early Republic*. See also Drew Gilpin Faust's epilogue to Bleser, ed., *In Joy and in Sorrow*, 253–59.

59 Tristrim Skinner to Eliza Harwood, February 8, 1849, Skinner Family Papers, SHC; William Henry Wills to Anna Whitaker, [March 23, 1835], Wills Papers, SHC; Nannie Hoskins Williams Diary, October 2 [4?], 1870, SHC.

60 Tristrim Skinner to Eliza Harwood, October 14, 1848, February 8, 1849, Skinner Family Papers, SHC; Julian Moore to Blannie Southall, May 5, 1863, Southall-Bowen Family Papers, SHC; Waddy Butler to Lucy Wood, July 4, 1860, Lucy Wood Butler Papers, SHC.

61 Jabour, " 'It Will Never Do for Me to Be Married,' " 214, 228–29; Burr, ed., *Secret Eye*, 108. See also Nannie Hoskins Williams Diary, June 13, 1870, SHC.

62 Nannie Hoskins William Diary, August 21, 1869, SHC. For other examples, see Julian Moore to Blannie Southall, August 5, 1864, Southall-Bowen Family Papers, SHC; Ellen Shackelford to George Washington Gift, July 29, 1863, Gift Papers, SHC microfilm; and Loula Kendall to Henry Rogers, [July 8, 1862], Rogers Collection, Emory.

63 Sarah Bennett to Erastus Hopkins, June 1, 1835, Hopkins Correspondence, SCHS; Lucy Wood to Waddy Butler, August 11, 1860, and Waddy Butler to Lucy Wood, September 8, 1860, Lucy Wood Butler Papers, SHC. See also Richard Johnson to Isabella Mackay, January 2, [1863], Johnson Family Papers, SCHS.

64 The case of migration, discussed below, also indicates the limits of southern female influence. For an example of an urban, professional southern couple, see Jabour, *Marriage in the Early Republic*.

65 Anna Hendree to Thomas Norwood, March 15, 1851, Norwood Family Papers, VHS; Mary Miller to Charles Davis, October 22, 1848, Davis Papers, Duke.

66 Lucy Wood to Waddy Butler, October 12, 1860, Lucy Wood Butler Papers, SHC; Bettie Bernard to Frances Bernard Capps, July 4, 1859, Bernard Family Papers, VHS.

67 For quotation, see Jabour, " 'Privations & Hardships.' " On the lure of the Old Southwest and the consequences for women, see Cashin, *Family Venture*, especially

chap. 2. Also on migration, see Censer, "Southwestern Migration"; and on kinship networks, see Cashin, "Structure of Antebellum Planter Families."

68 Mary Massenburg to Emma Nicholson, November 10, 1866, Emma Pauline Nicholson Alexander Papers, SHC; Mary E. Moor to Matilda Abernathy, November 30, 1857, Dickson Papers, SHC.

69 Laura Wirt Randall to Louisa Cabell Carrington, July 16, 1827, Randall Papers, VHS.

70 Mary E. Moor to Matilda Abernathy, November 30, 1857, Dickson Papers, SHC; Mary Virginia Hawes to Virginia Pearl, March 21, 1851, Terhune Papers, Duke.

71 Laura Wirt to Louisa Cabell Carrington, October 8, 1826, Randall Papers, VHS.

72 Nannie Hoskins Williams Diary, August 21, 1869, SHC; Bettie Bernard to Frances Bernard Capps and Mary Jane Bernard, April 7 [9?], 1859, Bernard Family Papers, SHC.

73 Cornelia Taylor to Ella Noland, April 8, 1852, and Richard Noland to Ella Noland, March 20, [1852], MacKenzie Papers, SHC.

74 Mary Page to Lucy McGuire, June 27, 1867, Byrd Family Papers, VHS.

CHAPTER SIX

1 Loula Kendall Rogers Journal, March n.d., September 10, 1860; December 27, 1862; January 14, 1863, Rogers Collection, Emory. See also entries for June 29, 1855; May 25, 1857; October 23, 1858; March 1, 7, December 18, 1859; December 25, 1860; November 12, 1861; January 18, 20, 1862.

2 Ibid., September 28, 1860; December 25, 1861; January 7, 18, 1862.

3 Ibid., January 18, 20, May 19, August 18, September 1, December 21, 1862.

4 Ibid., December 9, 1862; January 6, 19, 24, March 8, 1863.

5 Ibid., March 8, April 2, 13, 1863; May 19, December 31, 1864; January 6, 1865.

6 Anne Eliza Pleasants Gordon Diary, June 22, 1857, VHS.

7 Anna Hendree to Thomas Norwood, n.d. [Spring 1853], Norwood Family Papers, VHS.

8 Mary Fries Patterson Diary, June 14, 1864, SHC; Elizabeth Ann Cooley McClure Diary, March 15, 1846, VHS; Ellie Hunter Journal, June 12, 1858, SHC; Mary Polk Badger to Lucius Polk, December 13, 1826, Polk, Badger, and McGehee Family Papers, SHC.

9 For quotation, see Mary Polk to Lucius Polk, June 30, 1826, Polk, Badger, and McGehee Family Papers, SHC. On wedding preparations, see Amanda Jane Cooley Roberts Diary, February 22, 1845, VHS; Elizabeth Ann Cooley McClure Diary, March 15, 1846, VHS; Mary Fries Patterson Diary, June 1, 4, 7, 8, 9, 11, 13, 1864, SHC; and Emma Sue Gordon Diary, October 3, 20, 1864, Perkins Family Papers, SHC. Wedding dresses were usually white, but they were relatively simple; brides generally devoted only a line or two to descriptions of them. See, for example, Emily McEwen to Mary Polk, February 15, 1825, Polk, Badger, and McGehee Family Papers, SHC. For examples of delays, see Kate Corbin to Sally Munford, December 27, [1863], Munford-Ellis Family Papers, Duke; and Mary Polk to Sarah Blount, October 26, 1826, Polk, Badger, and McGehee Family Papers, SHC.

10 For quotations, see Elizabeth Ann Cooley McClure Diary, March 15, 1846, VHS;

Gay Robertson Blackford Reminiscences, n.d., VHS; Emily McEwen to Mary Polk, February 15, 1825, Polk, Badger, and McGehee Family Papers, SHC; and J. McPherson to Elizabeth McPherson, December 22, 1836, Ferebee, Gregory, and McPherson Family Papers, SHC. For other descriptions of weddings, see Mary Virginia Early Brown Diary, January 8, 1852, Early Family Papers, VHS; Anne Eliza Pleasants Gordon Diary, June 22, 1857, VHS; Samuella Hart Curd Diary, May 3, 1860, VHS; Mary Fries Patterson Diary, June 14, 1864, SHC; Emily McEwen to Mary Polk, February 15, 1825, and Mary Polk to Sarah Blount, October 26, 1826, Polk, Badger, and McGehee Family Papers, SHC; and Eliza Lavalette Barksdale Diary, June 9, 1836, VHS.

11 Rosina Ursula Young Mordecai Commonplace Book, 1830–35, VHS. For another example of a wedding album, see Mary Jane Patterson Album, VHS.

12 M.T.S., [untitled], [March 5, 1835], Rosina Ursula Young Mordecai Commonplace Book, VHS.

13 Pauline, [untitled], March 5, 1835, and Pauline, "To Rosina on her Bridal-day," March 5, [1835], Rosina Ursula Young Mordecai Commonplace Book, VHS.

14 Mary Jane Patterson Album, VHS; Rebecca, "Woman's Love," n.d., and "Woman," n.d., Sophia Coutts Album, VHS.

15 Mahaly Pleasants, March 5, 1835, Rosina Ursula Young Mordecai Commonplace Book, VHS.

16 Jane, [untitled], n.d., Rosina Ursula Young Mordecai Commonplace Book, VHS.

17 Loula Kendall Rogers Journal, January 24, 1863, Rogers Collection, Emory; Mary Massenburg to Emma Nicholson, November 10, 1866, Emma Pauline Nicholson Alexander Papers, SHC; Lucy Taylor to Elizabeth Kane, January 8, [1847], Wickham Family Papers, VHS. See also Mary Fries Patterson Diary, June 3, 1864, SHC; Emily McEwen to Mary Polk, February 15, 1825, Polk, Badger, and McGehee Family Papers, SHC; and Samuella Hart Curd Diary, May 3–15, 1860, VHS.

18 Rosina Ursula Young Mordecai Commonplace Books, VHS; Loula Kendall Rogers Journal, December 14, 1862, Rogers Collection, Emory; Elizabeth Ann Cooley McClure Diary, March 15, 1846, VHS; Tristrim Skinner to Eliza Harwood, February 8, 1849, Skinner Family Papers, SHC; Mary Virginia Early Brown Diary, January 8, 1852, Early Family Papers, VHS; Lucy Taylor Wickham to Elizabeth Kane, February 2, 1847, Wickham Family Papers, VHS; Blannie Southall Moore to Julia Southall, Southall-Bowen Family Papers, SHC. See also Julia Southall to Blannie Southall Moore, November 22, 1865, Southall-Bowen Family Papers, SHC; and Fox-Genovese, "Family and Female Identity."

19 Loula Kendall Rogers Journal, January 6, 14, 1863, Rogers Collection, Emory; Samuella Hart Curd Diary, May 15, 1860, VHS; Caroline Brooks Lilly Books, December 31, 1839, SHC; Mary Fries Patterson Diary, June 14, 1864, SHC.

20 Emma Sue Gordon Diary, August 20, 1863, Perkins Family Papers, SHC.

21 Loula Kendall Rogers Journal, December 24, 1860; September 1, December 5, 1862; January 5, 1863, Rogers Collection, Emory.

22 Samuella Hart Curd Diary, May 3–15, 1860, VHS. Interestingly, Curd and her female attendants took advantage of the opportunity to attend a women's rights convention, but Curd, offended at the presence of African Americans at the event, pro-

nounced herself disgusted by the proceedings, and she and her entourage left early to go shopping for new hats. See, for other examples, Kimberly Papers, SHC; Anne Eliza Pleasants Gordon Diary, 1857, VHS; Penelope Skinner to Tristrim Skinner, February 26, 1840, Skinner Family Papers, SHC; Mary Harper Beall to Mrs. C. E. Harper, November 19, 1858, Mary Harper Beall Letter, SHC; and Loula Kendall Rogers Journal, December 5, 1862, Rogers Collection, Emory.

23 Anne Eliza Pleasants Gordon Diary, June 22, 1857, VHS; Samuella Hart Curd Diary, May 3–15, 1860, VHS.

24 Caroline Brooks Lilly Books, January 2, 1839, SHC. See also Emily McEwen to Mary Polk, February 15, 1825, Polk, Badger, and McGehee Family Papers, SHC; Caroline Brooks Lilly Books, January 2, 1839, SHC; and Eliza Harwood Skinner to Mrs. Galt, February 23, 1849, Skinner Family Papers, SHC.

25 Samuella Hart Curd Diary, May 15, 1860, VHS.

26 Elizabeth Ann Cooley McClure Diary, March 15, 29, 1846, VHS.

27 Penelope Eliza Howard Alderman Diary, January 11, 1851, SHC.

28 Eliza Harwood Skinner to Mrs. Galt, February 23, 1849, Skinner Family Papers, SHC.

29 Ibid.

30 Margaret Mordecai Devereux to Ann Mordecai, November 24, [1842], Devereux Papers, SHC.

31 For other accounts containing these elements, see, for example, Elizabeth Higginbotham Fischer to Sisters, October 17, 1829, Higginbotham Family Papers, VHS; Anne Eliza Pleasants Gordon Diary, June 22, 1857, SHC; Lucy Taylor Wickham to Elizabeth Kane, February 2, 1847, Wickham Family Papers, VHS; Emma Sue Gordon Diary, October 22, 1863, Perkins Family Papers, SHC; Kate Landing to Fannie Smith, March 25, 1878, Smith Papers, Duke; and Laura Wirt Randall to Elizabeth Wirt, February 9–16, 1828, Wirt Papers, MHS.

32 Eliza Steele MacNamara to John and Mary Steele, January 12, 1815, Steele Papers, SHC. On household production and slave labor in the Old South, see Clinton, *Plantation Mistress*, chap. 2; and Fox-Genovese, *Within the Plantation Household*, 120–28 and 137–39. On household production in a southern city, see Jabour, *Marriage in the Early Republic*, 31–33. For appearances of the phrase "going to housekeeping" and variations on it, see Margaret Steele to Mary Steele, October 9, 1814, and Eliza Steele MacNamara to Mary Steele, November 14, 1814, Steele Papers, SHC; Sallie Emory to Ella Noland MacKenzie, November [1855]; and Carrie Sage to Ella Noland MacKenzie, December 9, 1853, MacKenzie Papers, SHC; and Sarah Satterlee to Mary Ellett, August 1, n.d., and October 24, n.d., Ellett–St. Catherine's Alumnae Association Papers, VHS.

33 Carrie Sage to Ella Noland MacKenzie, February 17, 1854, MacKenzie Papers, SHC; Caroline Brooks Lilly Books, February 6, 1839, SHC.

34 Sarah Satterlee to Mary Ellett, October 24, [1859?], Ellett–St. Catherine's Alumnae Association Papers, VHS; Carrie Sage to Ella Noland MacKenzie, September 28, [1854], MacKenzie Papers, SHC.

35 Mary Miller Davis to Elizabeth Miller, January 7, 1849, and Mat and Elizabeth Miller to Mary Miller Davis, April 25, 1849, Davis Papers, Duke.

36 Elizabeth Lindsay Gordon to Apphia Rouzee, September n.d., Hunter Family Papers, VHS; John and Margaret Devereux to Ellen Mordecai, December 17, 1842, Devereux Papers, SHC. For an in-depth discussion of one southern wife's household management, see Jabour, *Marriage in the Early Republic*, 31–34 and passim. On the difficulties of managing household help, see Jabour, *Marriage in the Early Republic*, 102–6 and passim. On mistress-slave and mistress-servant relations, see also Cole, "Servants and Slaves"; Fox-Genovese, *Within the Plantation Household*, 22–23, 97, 207; and Jabour, "Between Mistress and Slave."

37 Margaret Mordecai Devereux to Ellen Mordecai, June 18, 1842, Devereux Papers, SHC; Eliza Steele MacNamara to John and Mary Steele, January 12, 1815, Steele Papers, SHC; Caroline Brooks Lilly Books, January 2, 5, 7, and 19, 1860, SHC.

38 Harriet V. Payne Turner to Mary Carrington, February 3, 1838, Carrington Family Papers, VHS. On boardinghouses, see, for example, Bettie Maney Kimberly to Annie Maney, January 20, [1861; misdated 1860], Kimberly Papers, SHC; Penelope Skinner Warren to Mrs. Dr. William C. Warren, September 11, 1840, Skinner Family Papers, SHC; Mary Miller Davis to Elizabeth Miller, January 7, 1849, Davis Papers, Duke; and Mary McPhail Smith to Mary Carrington, February 3, [1837], Carrington Family Papers, VHS. Brides usually moved to the homes of their in-laws. For an example of a young wife who resided with her own mother, however, see Sarah Satterlee to Mary Ellett, October 24, n.d., Ellett–St. Catherine's Alumnae Association Papers, VHS. Laura Wirt Randall lived first in a boardinghouse and then with her relatives; see Laura Wirt Randall to William Wirt, September 30, 1827, and Laura Wirt Randall to Elizabeth Wirt, October 28, 1827, Wirt Papers, MHS.

39 Sally Elmore Taylor Memoir, Elmore Papers, SHC microfilm, reel 24; Martha A. Harrison to Eliza Spragins, March 14, 1843, Spragins Family Papers, VHS.

40 Bettie Maney Kimberly to Annie Maney, January 13, [1861], Kimberly Papers, SHC. See also Frances Stuart Anderson to Frances Baldwin Stuart, October 31, n.d., Stuart Family Papers, VHS. For examples of diaries, see Samuella Hart Curd Diary, August 23, 24, 1860, VHS; and Caroline Brooks Lilly Books, January 2, 5, 7, and 19, 1860, SHC.

41 Bettie Maney Kimberly to Annie Maney, January 20, [1861; misdated 1860], Kimberly Papers, SHC; Mary Polk Badger to Lucius Polk, December 13, 1826, Polk, Badger, and McGehee Family Papers, SHC. For other examples, see Martha A. Harrison to Eliza Spragins, March 14, 1843, Spragins Family Papers, VHS; Eliza Steele MacNamara to John and Mary Steele, January 12, 1815, Steele Papers, SHC; Emma Sue Gordon Diary, October 22, 1863, Perkins Family Papers, SHC; and Penelope Skinner Warren to Tristrim Warren, [April 14, 1840], Skinner Family Papers, SHC.

42 Margaret Steele to Mary Steele, [November 21, 1814], Steele Papers, SHC; Elizabeth Wirt to Laura Wirt Randall, April 11, 1828, Wirt Papers, MHS. See also Emily Bland Southall Diary, January 16, 1862, Southall-Bowen Family Papers, SHC.

43 Eliza Steele MacNamara to Mary Steele, May 17, 1815, Steele Papers, SHC.

44 Margaret Mordecai Devereux to Ellen Mordecai, [1842], and John and Margaret Devereux to Ellen Mordecai, November 27, 1842, Devereux Papers, SHC.

45 Nathalie E. Baylies to Mary Hudson Ellett, June 1, 1855, Ellett–St. Catherine's

Alumnae Association Papers, VHS. See also Margaret Mordecai Devereux to Ellen Mordecai, June 18, 1842, Devereux Papers, SHC; and Margaret Devereux to Jane Miller, February 4, 1844, Hinton Papers, SHC.

46 Eliza Lucinda Garnett to Martha Hunter, n.d., and Florentina Morena Garnett to Martha Hunter, March 9, 1854, Hunter Family Papers, VHS; Gay Robertson Blackford Reminiscences, VHS. See also the correspondence of (friends) Sarah Thompson Anderson Guerrant and Emilia Eugenia Monteiro, Guerrant Family Papers, VHS; and the correspondence of (sisters) Elizabeth Higginbotham and Ann Higginbotham Hoskins, Higginbotham Family Papers, VHS.

47 Eliza Steele MacNamara to Mary Steele, November 14, 1814, Steele Papers, SHC; Margaret Mordecai Devereux to Ellen Mordecai, [1842], Devereux Papers, SHC; Judith McGuire to Mary Anna McGuire Claiborne, February 20 and December 31, 1846, Claiborne Family Papers, VHS; Jabour, "'Privations & Hardships,'" 267–69.

48 Mary McPhail Smith to Mary Carrington, February 3, [1837], Carrington Family Papers, VHS. Unfortunately, southern linguistic conventions often make it difficult to ascertain the status and race of "servants." It is reasonably safe to assume that the majority of people in this category were slaves, however. On slave and free labor in urban households, see especially Cole, "Servants and Slaves." On plantation mistresses' dependence on slave labor, see Fox-Genovese, *Within the Plantation Household*, 116–19.

49 Caroline Brooks Lilly Books, January 7, 1839, SHC; Judith McGuire to Mary Anna McGuire Claiborne, February 20, 1845, Claiborne Family Papers, VHS; Bettie Maney Kimberly to Annie Maney, [January 1861], Kimberly Papers, SHC; Eliza MacNamara Steele to Mary Steele, December 13, 1814, Steele Papers, SHC; Caroline Brooks Lilly Books, July [27], 1839, SHC.

50 Margaret Mordecai Devereux to Ellen Mordecai, with postscript by John Devereux, [1842], and John and Margaret Devereux to Ellen Mordecai, November 27, 1842, Devereux Papers, SHC.

51 Margaret Mordecai Devereux to Ellen Mordecai, [1842], Devereux Papers, SHC.

52 Margaret Mordecai Devereux to Ellen Mordecai, February 3, 1844, Devereux Papers, SHC; see also John and Margaret Devereux to Ellen Mordecai, December 17, 1842, ibid.

53 Drew Faust also calls attention to this paradox in her study of southern women during the Civil War. See *Mothers of Invention*, xiii. For quotation, see Elizabeth Wirt to Laura Wirt Randall, October 12, 18, 1826, Wirt Papers, MHS.

54 Caroline Brooks Lilly Books, January 5, 1839, SHC. See also Cott, *Bonds of Womanhood*, chap. 2.

55 Mary Virginia Early Brown Diary, September 30, 1852, Early Family Papers, VHS; Carrie Sage to Ella Noland MacKenzie, September 28, [1854], MacKenzie Papers, SHC. See also Martha A. Harrison to Eliza Spragins, March 14, 1843, Spragins Family Papers, VHS; and Mary Stuart McGuire to Frances Baldwin Stuart, February 6, n.d., Stuart Family Papers, VHS.

56 Martha Hunter Hitchcock to Martha Hunter, August 5, 1842, December 14, 1841, and November n.d., 1845, Hunter Family Papers, VHS.

57 Lucy Taylor Wickham to Elizabeth Kane, February 2, 1847, Wickham Family Papers,

VHS. For a similar description of quietly reading together, see Margaret Mordecai Devereux to Ellen Mordecai, [1842], Devereux Papers, SHC.

58 Penelope Skinner Warren to Thomas Warren, August 28, [1840], Skinner Family Papers, SHC; Caroline Brooks Lilly Books, June 1, 1839, SHC; Emma Sue Gordon Diary, October 22, 1863, Perkins Family Papers, SHC.

59 Mary McPhail Smith to Mary Carrington, March 22, 1837, Carrington Family Papers, VHS; Martha A. Harrison to Eliza Spragins, March 14, 1843, Spragins Family Papers, VHS (note: This letter is in very bad condition and editorial insertions are reasonable surmise); Mary to [Matilda Abernathy], November 1, 1859, Dickson Papers, SHC.

60 Laura Wirt Randall to Louisa Cabell Carrington, n.d., [1827–28], March 6, 1828, May 27, 1829, May 23, 1831, Randall Papers, VHS. See also Jabour, " 'Privations and Hardships.' "

61 Lizzie Scott Neblett, "A Review of the past eight years," January 22, 1860, in Murr, ed., *Rebel Wife*, 74–75.

62 Martha Hunter Hitchcock to Sarah Hunter, July 22, n.d., March 8 and December 14, 1841, and Martha Hunter Hitchcock to Martha Hunter, January 28, 1840, Hunter Family Papers, VHS.

63 Murr, ed., *Rebel Wife*, 352, 362, 372.

64 Ibid., 26.

65 Martha Hunter Hitchcock said that her husband was "so necessary to [her] happiness" that every hour of separation found her "wretched." See Martha Hunter Hitchcock to Martha Hunter, August 5, 1842, Hunter Family Papers, VHS.

66 Margaret Lea Graves to Charles Graves [January 24, 1863], Graves Papers, SHC microfilm. On marriage in the Old South, see especially Jabour, *Marriage in the Early Republic*. Other case studies of southern marriages include Bleser, "Perrys of Greenville," and Laas, *Love and Power*.

67 Elvira Fowler to Martha Hunter, November 8, 1835, Hunter Family Papers, VHS.

68 Elizabeth Ann Cooley McClure Diary, April 18, 1846, VHS; Sarah Satterlee to Mary Ellett, October 24, n.d., Ellett–St. Catherine's Alumnae Association Papers, VHS.

69 Elizabeth Gordon to Apphia Rouzee, November 5, 1816, Hunter Family Papers, VHS; Margaret Lea Graves to Charles Graves, February 16, [1863], Graves Papers, SHC microfilm; Anna Whitaker Wills to William Henry Wills, September 22, 1835, Wills Papers, SHC.

70 Martha Hitchcock to Martha Hunter, June 18, 1841, Hunter Family Papers, VHS.

71 Penelope Skinner Warren to Thomas Warren, August 9 and 22, 1840, Skinner Family Papers, SHC; Mary Polk Badger to George Badger, February 12, 1827, Polk, Badger, and McGehee Family Papers, SHC.

72 Sarah Harrison to Edward Harrison, September 25, 1849, Harrison Family Papers, VHS; Margaret Lea Graves to Charles Graves, May 28, 1863, Charles Graves Papers, SHC microfilm; Carrie to Ella Noland MacKenzie, August 2, 1853, MacKenzie Papers, SHC.

73 Penelope Skinner Warren to Thomas Warren, September 13, 1840, Skinner Family Papers, SHC; Mary Polk Badger to George Badger, February 12, 1827, Polk, Badger, and McGehee Family Papers, SHC.

74 Penelope Skinner Warren to Thomas Warren, August 8, 1840, Skinner Family Papers, SHC.

75 Emma Crutcher to Will Crutcher, January 6, 1861, Crutcher-Shannon Family Papers, CAH.

76 Mary Virginia Early Brown Diary, May 19, 1850, June 8, January 2, 1852, Early Family Papers, VHS; Elizabeth Wirt to William Wirt, October [6; misdated October 7], 1827, Wirt Papers, MHS.

77 Samuella Hart Curd Diary, May 15, 1860, VHS; Eliza MacNamara to Mary Steele, January 24, 1815, Steele Papers, SHC; Louisa R. Livingston to Mary Hudson Ellett, March 15, [1855], Ellett–St. Catherine's Alumnae Association Papers, SHC.

78 Mary Stuart McGuire to Frances Baldwin Stuart, February 6, n.d., Stuart Family Papers, VHS; Mary Virginia Early Brown Diary, June 25, 1852, Early Family Papers, VHS.

79 Elizabeth Wirt to Laura Wirt Randall, September 9, October 12, 18, 1827, Wirt Papers, MHS.

80 Loula Kendall to James Henry Rogers, May 7, June 24, 1862, Rogers Collection, Emory.

CHAPTER SEVEN

1 Martha Hunter Hitchcock to Martha Hunter, January 28, 1840, Hunter Family Papers, VHS.

2 Ibid., March 28, 1840.

3 Ibid., September 20, 1840.

4 Ibid., September 20, 1840; April 27, 1843; February 12, 1845.

5 Ibid., February 12, November n.d., 1845; June 25, 1846.

6 Ibid., February 12, 1845; June 25, 1846.

7 See Lystra, Searching the Heart, introduction.

8 William Wirt to Elizabeth Wirt, October 16, 1802, and Elizabeth Wirt to William Wirt, November 1, 1808, Wirt Papers, MHS. See, for other examples, Margaret Lea Graves to Charles Graves [January 24, 1863], Graves Papers, SHC microfilm; and Lottie Dye Patterson to Wyatt Patterson, December 24, 1864, Patterson-Dye Family Correspondence, SCHS.

9 Ellen Shackelford Gift to George Gift, June 25, 1864, Graves Papers, SHC microfilm; see also ibid., September 30, 1864.

10 Some southern women cooperated with their husbands in practicing abstinence to limit and space their pregnancies, but there is no evidence that any of the women in this study did so. See Lewis and Lockridge, "'Sally Has Been Sick.'" On the decline in birthrates in the nineteenth century, see Daniel Scott Smith, "Family Limitation." On continued high birthrates in the antebellum South, see McMillen, Motherhood in the Old South, 32–33; and Anne Firor Scott, "Women's Perspective," 178–79.

11 Elizabeth Higginbotham Fischer to Sisters, October 17, 1829, and Elizabeth Higginbotham Fischer to Anna Higginbotham, March 26, 1830, Higginbotham Family Papers, VHS; Elizabeth Noland to Ella Noland, November 4, 1849, MacKen-

zie Papers, SHC. See also Mary Page to Lucy McGuire, June 27, 1867, Byrd Family Papers, VHS; George Badger to Sally Badger McGehee, August 26, 1856, Polk, Badger, and McGehee Family Papers, SHC; and Lottie Dye Patterson to Wyatt Patterson, December 24, 1864, and Wyatt Patterson to Lottie Dye Patterson, February 4, 1865, Patterson-Dye Correspondence, SCHS.

12 Jinnie to Ella Noland, April 12, 1850, MacKenzie Papers, SHC; Leavitt, "Under the Shadow of Maternity," 133; see also Dye, "History of Childbirth in America," 100.

13 Samuella Hard Curd Diary, August 15, 16, September 10, November 6, 1860; January 19, March 28, April 11, June 3, 1861, VHS.

14 Sarah Satterlee to Mary Ellett, [May 16, 1860], Ellett–St. Catherine's Alumnae Association Papers, VHS; Elizabeth Fischer to Anna Hoskins, March 10, 1842, Higginbotham Family Papers, VHS.

15 Carrie Sage to Ella Noland MacKenzie, January 6, 1856, MacKenzie Papers, SHC; Sarah Satterlee to Mary Ellett, [May 16, 1860], Ellett–St. Catherine's Alumnae Association Papers, VHS. See also McMillen, *Motherhood in the Old South*, 107–8.

16 Murr, ed., *Rebel Wife*, 202, 362–63. On contraception and abortion in Victorian America, see Brodie, *Contraception and Abortion*; Degler, *At Odds*, chaps. 8–10 (quotation); D'Emilio and Freedman, *Intimate Matters*; and Mohr, *Abortion in America*.

17 Murr, ed., *Rebel Wife*, 39, 416. For more on Lizzie Neblett, see Faust, "'Trying to Do a Man's Business,'" and Jabour, "Marriage and Family."

18 Elizabeth Fischer to Anna Higginbotham Hoskins, January n.d., 1831, Higginbotham Family Papers, VHS.

19 Richard Johnson to Isabella Johnson, June 26, 1864, Johnson Family Papers, SCHS; Elizabeth Noland to Ella Noland MacKenzie, October 11, 1853, MacKenzie Papers, SHC; Ellen Shackelford Gift to George Gift, October 20, 1864, SHC microfilm; Mary Polk Badger to George Badger, March 8, 1827, Polk, Badger, and McGehee Family Papers, SHC; John and Margaret.Mordecai Devereux to Ellen Mordecai, [1842], Devereux Papers, SHC. See also Elizabeth Fischer to Anna Higginbotham, March 26, 1830, Higginbotham Family Papers, VHS; Lottie Dye Patterson to Wyatt Patterson, December 24 and 29, 1864, Patterson-Dye Correspondence, SCHS; and McMillen, *Motherhood in the Old South*, 31–34.

20 Caroline Brooks Lilly Books, April 22, 1839, SHC; Judith McGuire to Mary Anna McGuire Claiborne, August [1845], Claiborne Family Papers, VHS. See, for other examples of illness/pregnancy, Margaret Lea Graves to Charles Graves, May 28, 1863, Graves Papers, SHC microfilm; Sarah Satterlee to Mary Ellett, [May 16, 1860], Ellett–St. Catherine's Alumnae Association Papers, VHS; Elizabeth Fischer to Anna Higginbotham, March 26, 1830, Higginbotham Family Papers, VHS; and Sarah Bennett Hopkins to Erastus Hopkins, March 17, 1836, Hopkins Correspondence, SCHS.

21 Frances Stuart Atkinson to Frances Baldwin Stuart, n.d., and Mary Stuart McGuire and Frances Stuart Atkinson to Frances Baldwin Stuart, n.d., Stuart Family Papers, VHS. See also McMillen, *Motherhood in the Old South*, chap. 4.

22 Margaret Lea Graves to Charles Graves, May 28, 1863, Graves Papers, SHC microfilm; Caroline Brooks Lilly Books, September 6, 1839, SHC; Penelope Skinner Warren to Thomas Warren, August 28, [1840], Skinner Family Papers, SHC; Martha

Hunter Hitchcock to Martha Hunter, April 27, 1843, Hunter Family Papers, VHS; Mary Stuart McGuire to Frances Baldwin Stuart, n.d., Stuart Family Papers, VHS. See also Sarah Bennett Hopkins to Erastus Hopkins, March 17, 1836, Hopkins Correspondence, SCHS; and McMillen, *Motherhood in the Old South*, 44–45.

23 Penelope Skinner Warren to Thomas Warren, August 8, 9, 16, 1840, Skinner Family Papers, SHC; Caroline Brooks Lilly Books, August 16, 1839, SHC. See also Elizabeth Fischer to Anna Higginbotham Hoskins, January n.d., 1831, Higginbotham Family Papers, VHS; Sallie Emory to Ella Noland MacKenzie, February 12, 1854, MacKenzie Papers, SHC; Caroline Brooks Lilly Books, July 31, September 6, 1839, SHC; Penelope Skinner Warren to Thomas Warren, August 9, 16, 28, 1840, Skinner Family Papers, SHC; and Sarah Bennett Hopkins to Erasmus Hopkins, March 9, 24, 29, 1836, Hopkins Correspondence, SCHS.

24 Margaret Lea Graves to Charles Graves, May 28, 1863, Graves Papers, SHC microfilm; Sally Emory to Ella Noland MacKenzie, February 12, 1854, MacKenzie Papers, SHC. See also Lottie Dye Patterson to Wyatt Patterson, December 24, 1864, and Wyatt Patterson to Lottie Patterson, February 8, 1865, Patterson-Dye Correspondence, SCHS. The monitoring also reflected the new medical belief that life began at conception, rather than at quickening, which led to a new concern with protecting the life of the fetus and thus increased attention to the expectant mother's daily regimen. See McMillen, *Motherhood in the Old South*, 25, 35–38.

25 Caroline Brooks Lilly Books, July 31, September 6, 1839, SHC.

26 Penelope Skinner Warren to Thomas Warren, August 9, 16, 28, 1840, Skinner Family Papers, SHC. On medical advice, see McMillen, *Motherhood in the Old South*, 35–39, 55.

27 Penelope Skinner Warren to Thomas Warren, August 28, [1840], September 4, 1840, and Tristrim Skinner to Eliza Harwood, March 20, 1841, Skinner Family Papers, SHC.

28 McMillen, *Motherhood in the Old South*, 81; Caroline Brooks Lilly Books, August 8 and 12, 1839, SHC. See also Maria Louisa C. Marshall to Eliza C. Gould, April 12, 1827, in Cashin, ed., *Our Common Affairs*, 90–91; and Murr, ed., *Rebel Wife*, 74–75. McMillen, *Motherhood in the Old South*, confirms that expectant mothers' fears focused on their own health, rather than that of the fetuses they carried. See pp. 54–55.

29 Elizabeth Fischer to Anna Hoskins, March 24, April 2, 1831; March 10, 1842, Higginbotham Family Papers, VHS; Murr, ed. *Rebel Wife*, 67–68.

30 Carrie Sage to Ella Noland MacKenzie, December 9, 1853, and Sallie Emory to Ella Noland MacKenzie, February 12, 1854, MacKenzie Papers, SHC. On twilight sleep, see Leavitt, *Brought to Bed*, 128–41.

31 Murr, ed., *Rebel Wife*, 355–56; Sallie Emory to Ella Noland MacKenzie, February 12, 1854, MacKenzie Papers, SHC; Caroline Brooks Lilly Books, August 4, September 14, 1839, SHC.

32 Elizabeth Fischer to Anna Hoskins, March 10, 1842, Higginbotham Family Papers, VHS; Carrie Sage to Ella Noland MacKenzie, February 17, 1854, MacKenzie Papers, SHC; Murr, ed., *Rebel Wife*, 74–75.

33 Murr, ed., *Rebel Wife*, 68, 70, 75.

34 Carrie Sage to Ella Noland MacKenzie, February 17, 1854, MacKenzie Papers, SHC.

35 Sarah Bennett Hopkins to Erastus Hopkins, March 9, 24, [1836], Hopkins Correspondence, SCHS; Penelope Skinner Warren to Thomas Warren, August 16, 1840, Skinner Family Papers, SHC.

36 Caroline Brooks Lilly Books, August 29, 1839, SHC.

37 Elizabeth Fischer to Anna Hoskins, March 10, 1842, Higginbotham Family Papers, VHS; Caroline Brooks Lilly Books, September 29, 1839, SHC; see also Sallie Emory to Ella Noland MacKenzie, February 12, 1854, MacKenzie Papers, SHC; Frances Stuart McGuire and Frances Stuart Atkinson to Frances Baldwin Stuart, n.d., Stuart Family Papers, VHS; Gay Robertson Blackford Reminiscences, VHS; Samuella Hart Curd Diary, November 6, 1860; April 11, August 24, 1861, VHS; Margaret Lea Graves to Charles Graves, March 2, 1864, Graves Papers, SHC microfilm; Loula Kendall Rogers Journal, August 31, 1864, Rogers Collection, Emory; and McMillen, *Motherhood in the Old South*, chap. 3. On men's presence and assistance in the early nineteenth century, see Johansen, "Before the Waiting Room."

38 On the national trend, see Leavitt, *Brought to Bed*; Scholten, *Childbearing in American Society*; and Wertz and Wertz, *Lying-In*. Especially critical analyses of this shift include English and Ehrenreich, *Witches, Midwives, and Nurses*; Smith-Rosenberg, "Abortion Movement and the AMA"; and Ulrich, *Midwife's Tale*. On the incursions of male accoucheurs in the South, see McMillen, *Motherhood in the Old South*, 68–71.

39 Leavitt, *Brought to Bed*; Scholten, *Childbearing in American Society*; Ulrich, *Midwife's Tale*.

40 Sarah Bennett Hopkins to Erastus Hopkins, March 9, [1836], Hopkins Correspondence, SCHS.

41 Samuella Hart Curd Diary, August 24, 1864, VHS.

42 Margaret Lea Graves to Charles Graves, March 2, 1864, Graves Papers, SHC microfilm; Caroline Brooks Lilly Books, September 26, 30, October 18, November 6, 27, December 4, 1839, SHC.

43 For quotation, see Murr, ed., *Rebel Wife*, 275. For an introduction to the vast literature on child rearing and motherhood in this era, see Kuhn, *Mother's Role in Childhood Education*; Jan Lewis, "Motherhood and the Construction of the Male Citizen"; MacLeod, *Moral Tale*; Reinier, *From Virtue to Character*; and Wishy, *Child and the Republic*.

44 Aunt and Mother to Sarah Bennett Hopkins, May 15, 1836, Hopkins Correspondence, SCHS.

45 Lucy Wickham to Elizabeth Kane, September 29, 1850, Wickham Family Papers, VHS; Mary Virginia Early Brown Diary, July 9, 1850, Early Family Papers, VHS; Elizabeth Fischer to Anna Hoskins, June 1, 1839, Higginbotham Family Papers, VHS. See also Samuella Hart Curd Diary, March 13, 1862, VHS.

46 McMillen, *Motherhood in the Old South*, chaps. 5 and 6.

47 Loula Kendall Rogers Journal, August 31, September 13, November 16, 1864; Loula Kendall Rogers to James Henry Rogers, November 9, [1864], Rogers Collection, Emory.

48 McMillen, *Motherhood in the Old South*, chap. 5.

49 Sarah Bennett Hopkins to Erastus Hopkins, May 20, June 8, 1836, Hopkins Correspondence, SCHS. On puerperal fever, see McMillen, *Motherhood in the Old South*, 95, 101–2, 105.

50 Laura Wirt Randall to Elizabeth Wirt, July 18, 26, August 10, 1828, Wirt Papers,

MHS; Mary Virginia Early Brown Diary, January 2, 1852, Early Family Papers, VHS; Samuella Hart Curd Diary, August 26–31, September 18, 23, October 1, 6, 12, 26, 1861, VHS. See also Lucy Wickham to Elizabeth Kane, September 29, 1850, Wickham Family Papers, VHS; Kate Corbin Pendleton to Sally Munford, December 17, 1864, Munford-Ellis Family Papers, Duke; and Murr, ed., *Rebel Wife*, 67.

51   Caroline Brooks Lilly Books, September 30, 1839, SHC; Samuella Hart Curd Diary, August 26–31, September 18, 23, October 1, 1861, VHS.

52   Laura Wirt Randall to Elizabeth Wirt, July 18, 26, August 10, 1828, Wirt Papers, MHS; Bettie Maney Kimberly to Annie Maney, January 13, [1861, misfiled 1859], Kimberly Papers, SHC; Samuella Hart Curd Diary, October 1, 1861, VHS.

53   Caroline Brooks Lilly Books, November 6, 16, December 24, 31, 1839, SHC. On the placement of children's cradles, see Lucy Wickham to Elizabeth Kane, September 29, 1850, Wickham Family Papers, VHS; Kate Corbin Pendleton to Sally Munford, December 17, 1864, Munford-Ellis Family Papers, Duke; and Elizabeth Wirt to William Wirt, December [13?], 1812, Wirt Papers, MHS. For more on breast-feeding patterns in one southern family, see Jabour, *Marriage in the Early Republic*, 36, 38, 40–41, 44, 77.

54   For examples of these and other ailments, see Murr, ed., *Rebel Wife*, 68; Martha Hitchcock to Martha Hunter, February 12, November n.d., 1845, June 25, 1846, Hunter Family Papers, VHS; and Samuella Hart Curd Diary, October 1, 1861, March 16, 1862, VHS. For more on southern mothers' care for ill children, see McMillen, *Motherhood in the Old South*, chap. 6.

55   Carrie Sage to Ella Noland MacKenzie, September 28, [1854], Mackenzie Papers, SHC.

56   Elizabeth Fischer to Anna Hoskins, January n.d., June 1, 1839, Higginbotham Family Papers, VHS; Mary Virginia Early Brown Diary, January 2, 1852, Early Family Papers, VHS; Martha Hunter Hitchcock to Martha Hunter, November n.d., 1845, Hunter Family Papers, VHS. This raises interesting questions regarding women who did not (or could not) bear children. None of the women in my study falls into this category. However, the Civil War diarist Mary Chesnut, who never bore children, was also one of the most vocal critics of both slavery and patriarchy, bearing out my assertion that maternity ended resistance. See Woodward and Muhlenfeld, eds., *Private Mary Chesnut*. For an extended discussion on the meanings of childlessness in a child-centered society, see May, *Barren in the Promised Land*.

57   Murr, ed., *Rebel Wife*, 64; Sarah Satterlee to Mary Ellett [May 16, 1860], Ellett-St. Catherine's Alumnae Association Papers, VHS; Loula Kendall Rogers to James Henry Rogers, February 9, [1864], Rogers Collection, Emory.

58   Bettie Maney Kimberly to Annie Maney, February 24, 1861, Kimberly Papers, SHC; Lucy Wickham to Elizabeth Kane, May 14, 1849, Wickham Family Papers, VHS; Laura Wirt Randall to Elizabeth Wirt, September 18, 1828, Wirt Papers, MHS.

59   Carrie Sage to Ella Noland MacKenzie, December 9, 1853, January 6, 1856, MacKenzie Papers, SHC; Loula Kendall Rogers to James Henry Rogers, November 9, [1864], Rogers Collection, Emory; Samuella Hart Curd Diary, October 12, 26, 1861, VHS.

60   Loula Kendall Rogers to James Henry Rogers, November 9, [1864], Rogers Collec-

tion, Emory; Margaret Mordecai Devereux to Ellen Mordecai, April 16, 1847, Devereux Papers, SHC; Elizabeth Fischer to Anna Hoskins, February 1, 1834, Higginbotham Family Papers, VHS. See also Bettie Maney Kimberly to Annie Maney, February 24, March 3, 1861, Kimberly Family Papers, SHC; and Nathalie E. Baylies to Mary Hudson Ellett, March 11, 1859, Ellett–St. Catherine's Alumnae Association Papers, VHS.

61 Judith C. Nelson to Maria Lowther Skinner, March 6, 1804, Skinner Family Papers, SHC; Caroline Brooks Lilly Books, November 27, 1839, SHC; Mary Virginia Early Brown Diary, January 2, 1852, Early Family Papers, VHS; Murr, ed., *Rebel Wife*, 276.

CHAPTER EIGHT

1 East, ed., *Sarah Morgan*, introduction, 5. Also on Morgan, see Juncker, "Behind Confederate Lines."

2 East, ed., *Sarah Morgan*, xix–xx, xxiii, 25. See also ibid., 611. The phrase "reluctant Confederate" is Daniel Crofts's. See Crofts, *Reluctant Confederates*.

3 East, ed., *Sarah Morgan*, 51, 68–69.

4 Ibid., 73–74, 76, 122, 609.

5 Ibid., 65, 122–23, 607.

6 Ibid., 64, 88, 139, 256–57; see also 410–11.

7 Ibid., 65.

8 Ibid., 77, 123–24, 166; see also 410–11, 491, 504.

9 Ibid., 65, 141.

10 Ibid., 167, 546.

11 Ibid., 40–41, 59, 141, 175, 548; see also 5, 35–36, 61–63, 80–82, 125, 542, 550–51.

12 Ibid., 153, 217, 582, 605.

13 Ibid., 103, 550–51.

14 Ibid., 564, 579–80.

15 For other treatments of young women in the Civil War South, see Ott, "When the Flower Blooms in Winter," and Roberts, *Confederate Belle*. On the importance of studying the Civil War era from a generational perspective, see also Censer, *Reconstruction of White Southern Womanhood*, 5–6.

16 Lucy Wood to Waddy Butler, January 21, 1861, "Letters and Diary of a Civil War Bride," Lomax Family Papers, VHS.

17 For recent treatments of southern women's political interests, see Allgor, *Parlor*; Kierner, *Women's Place*; and Varon, *We Mean to Be Counted*. For an older view, see Genovese, "Toward a Kinder and Gentler America." On southern women's thoughts on secession, see Cashin, ed., *Our Common Affairs*, 255–301. On Civil War–era children as "little politicians," see Marten, *Children's Civil War*, 24–26. The discussion that follows centers on women living in the secessionist states who evinced Confederate sentiments. Perhaps because their views did not accord with the mythology of the Lost Cause developed in the postwar years, there are few extant diaries for women from border states or with Union sympathies. For an exception to this rule, see Smith and Cooper, eds., *Window on the War*.

18 Morrill, ed., *My Confederate Girlhood*, 1; Clift, ed., *Private War*, 1, 4; C. Alice Ready Diary, July 15, 1861, SHC.

19 Cashin, ed., *Our Common Affairs*, 275; Bonner, ed., *Journal of a Milledgeville Girl*, 9–10; Sutherland, ed., *Very Violent Rebel*, 24; Morrill, ed., *My Confederate Girlhood*, 25; Sally Munford to Jennie Munford, April 24, 1862, and Sally Munford to Lizzie Munford, April 30, 1862, Munford-Ellis Family Papers, Duke; Sarah Lois Wadley Diary, June 1, 1862, SHC microfilm. For other examples, see Baer, ed., *Shadows on My Heart*, 27, 57, 60, 70, 195, 319; Cashin, ed., *Our Common Affairs*, 270–71, 283–86, 296–98; Eppes, *Through Some Eventful Years*, 125, 139–46, 154, Wright, *Southern Girl in '61*, 187; Robertson, ed., *Lucy Breckinridge*, 189, 198; Anderson, ed., *Brokenburn*, 94; Sarah Lois Wadley Diary, October 24, 1860, April 18, 20, 1861, SHC microfilm; Sallie Munford to Jennie Munford, June 1, 1862, Munford-Ellis Family Papers, Duke; Malinda B. Ray Diary, Friday, July 19, 1861, Ray Papers, SHC; Robertson, ed., *Confederate Lady Comes of Age*, 15, 21, 35, 70; Miers, ed., *When the World Ended*, 19; Underwood, "War Seen Through a Teen-ager's Eyes," 179–80, 183, 187; Yeatman, ed., "'What an Awful and Grand Spectacle It Is!,'" 41–43; Sutherland, ed., *Very Violent Rebel*, 3, 20, 38, 42; Lander, ed., "Confederate Girl Visits Pennsylvania," 116; and C. Alice Ready Diary, March 9, 1862, SHC. On "the politicization of the southern belle," see Ott, "When the Flower Blooms in Winter," chap. 3.

20 Barrows, "History of Lucy Cobb Institute," 19, 57; Marszalek, ed., *Diary of Miss Emma Holmes*, 264; Kemper, "Civil War Reminiscences," 315. See also Sally E. J. Broyles Dilworth Diary, May 7, 1865, Cocke Papers, Duke. By contrast, James Marten argues that at least some southern schoolgirls "managed to ignore . . . the war entirely." See *Children's Civil War*, 118.

21 Wright, *Southern Girl in '61*, 57; Sophia Haskell Cheves, "A Schoolgirl's Recollection of Fort Sumter," Sophia Lovell Haskell Cheves Papers, SCHS.

22 Anderson, ed., *Brokenburn*, 13. For an example of a young woman who took no notice of the war until 1862, see Ellen Louise Power Diary, February 24, 1862, SHC microfilm.

23 Kate Corbin to Sally Munford, January 17, 1861, Munford-Ellis Family Papers, Duke.

24 Elizabeth Collier Diary, April 11, 1862, SHC; Sutherland, ed., *Very Violent Rebel*, 13, 25.

25 Smith and Cooper, eds., *Window on the War*, 7, 28; Marszalek, ed., *Diary of Miss Emma Holmes*, 1; Cotton, ed., *From the Pen of a She-Rebel*, 45. On southern women in the Civil War era, see especially the classic, Scott, *Southern Lady*; for a more recent assessment, see Faust, *Mothers of Invention*. Faust does not distinguish between girls, young women, and mature women, although she uses many of the same sources used in this study. See also Rable, *Civil Wars*. On the war's effects on children more generally, see Marten, *Children's Civil War*.

26 Lois Charlotte Dye to Wyatt Patterson, Patterson-Dye Correspondence, SCHS; Baer, ed., *Shadows on My Heart*, 40; Anderson, ed., *Brokenburn*, 19. See also Baer, ed., *Shadows on My Heart*, 9, 39; Elizabeth Collier Diary, August 28, 1861, SHC; Sarah Lois Wadley Diary, April 18, 1861, SHC; Patty Vest to Sally Munford, Munford-Ellis

Family Papers, Duke; and Sally E. J. Broyles Dilworth Diary, April 15, 1865, Cocke Papers, Duke. An exception to the frenzy of Confederate nationalism was Frances Peter, a Unionist in Lexington, Kentucky. See Smith and Cooper, eds., *Window on the War*. Confederate Tennessee resident Amanda McDowell, a particularly religious and thoughtful young woman, was a different kind of exception. She regarded the war as "unjust and unholy" and described "Secession" (not Lincoln) as "the greatest tyrent that ever reigned over this country." See Cashin, ed., *Our Common Affairs*, 286, 303–4. For border residents' views on the war, see Lady, "Five Tri-State Women." See also Revels, *Grander in Her Daughters*, chap. 5.

27 Stoops, *Heritage*, 57, 62–63, 66, 83; Sophia Haskell Cheves, "A Schoolgirl's Recollection of Fort Sumter," Sophia Lovell Haskell Cheves Papers, SCHS. Schoolgirls who did not share the dominant sentiment were ostracized. See Recollections of Letitia Dabney Miller of Mississippi in Cashin, ed., *Our Common Affairs*, 288. For more on schoolgirls and southern loyalty, see Doyle, "Nurseries of Treason."

28 Loula Kendall Journal, February 22, 1861, Rogers Collection, Emory. See also Eppes, *Through Some Eventful Years*, 125, 154.

29 East, ed., *Sarah Morgan*, 64–65, 67; Marten, *Children's Civil War*, 150. For other examples of Confederate dress, see Clift, ed., *Private War*, 4; Baer, ed., *Shadows on My Heart*, 129; Wright, *Southern Girl in '61*, 119; Marten, *Children's Civil War*, 149; and East, ed., *Sarah Morgan*, 64. Young southern women took particular notice of the Confederate flag, sometimes drawing it in their journals. See, for example, Marszalek, ed., *Diary of Miss Emma Holmes*, 13, 100; and Wright, *Southern Girl in '61*, 59.

30 Andrews, *War-Time Journal*, 172, 312–13. For another example of a young woman who supported the Confederacy despite her father's lack of enthusiasm for secession, see Morrill, ed., *My Confederate Girlhood*, x, 25. One young woman who clearly echoed her father's views was Susan Bradford Eppes, whose father took her to witness the secession convention. See Eppes, *Through Some Eventful Years*, 139–46.

31 Lucy Wood Diary, May 24, 1861, Lomax Family Papers, VHS.

32 For quotations, see Marszalek, ed., *Diary of Miss Emma Holmes*, 484; and [Harrison], "Virginia Girl," 608. For explorations of this ideal, see Faust, "Altars of Sacrifice," and Whites, *Civil War as a Crisis in Gender*.

33 Clift, ed., *Private War*, 18; Marszalek, ed., *Diary of Miss Emma Holmes*, 2; Emma Shannon Crutcher to Will Crutcher, January 6, 1861, Crutcher-Shannon Family Papers, CAH. For additional examples of women's organized war work, see Andrews, *War-Time Journal*, 83; Clift, ed., *Private War*, 28–29; *Confederate Scrap-Book*, 44; Eppes, *Through Some Eventful Years*, 179; 262; Marszalek, ed., *Diary of Miss Emma Holmes*, 65, 101; Baer, ed., *Shadows on My Heart*, 264; Murray, *My Mother Used to Say*, 101; Anderson, ed., *Brokenburn*, 39; Lucy Wood Diary, May 2, 1861, "Letters and Diary of a Civil War Bride," Lomax Family Papers, VHS; Sarah Wadley Diary, July 9, August 21, 28, September 6, 1861, SHC; Margaret Lea Graves Reminiscences, Graves Papers, SHC microfilm; Lucy Munford to Jennie Munford, June 14, 1862, and Mother to Jennie Munford, June 27, 1862, Munford-Ellis Family Papers, Duke; Miers, ed., *When the World Ended*, 12; Cross and Cross, eds., *Child of Glencoe*, 62–63; Marten, *Children's Civil War*, 178; and Milton Maxcy Leverett to Fred Leverett, February 20, 1863, and

Mary Bull Leverett to Milton Maxcy Leverett, May 30, 1864, in Taylor, Matthews, and Power, eds., *Leverett Letters*, 200, 314. Schoolgirls held their own events and formed their own societies. See, for example, Bonner, ed., *Journal of a Milledgeville Girl*, 15; Marszalek, ed., *Diary of Miss Emma Holmes*, 2; and Barrows, "History of Lucy Cobb Institute," 19. Of course, young women also engaged in these activities as individuals and on behalf of their own family members. Even then, however, they often combined forces with friends and neighbors. See, for example, Ellen Louise Power Diary, June 4, August 8, October 20, and November 11, 1862, SHC microfilm; Kate Munford to Sally Munford, May 25, 1861, Munford-Ellis Family Papers, Duke; and Milton Maxcy Leverett to Mary Maxcy Leverett, May 10, 1862; Anne Leverett DeSaussure to Fred Leverett, June 22, 1862; Milton Maxcy Leverett to Mary Bull Leverett, August 8, 1862; Milton Maxcy Leverett to Julia Leverett, August 8, 1862; and Milton Maxcy Leverett to Anne Leverett DeSaussure, June 20, 1862, in Taylor, Matthews, and Power, eds., *Leverett Letters*, 127, 139, 144, 160, 162. Frances Peter, a Kentucky Unionist, engaged in similar activities, although her efforts were directed for the benefit of Union soldiers. See Smith and Cooper, eds., *Window on the War*, 18. Also on southern women's organized war work, see Faust, *Mothers of Invention*, 23–29; and Revels, *Grander in Her Daughters*, chap. 2.

34 Eppes, *Through Some Eventful Years*, 151. For examples of young women's sewing, see Bonner, ed., *Journal of a Milledgeville Girl*, 67; Anderson, ed., *Brokenburn*, 39, 47; and Lucy Wood to Waddy Butler, May 2, 1861, "Letters and Diary of a Civil War Bride," Lomax Family Papers, VHS.

35 Emily Voss to Sally Munford, November 1, 1861, Munford-Ellis Family Papers, Duke; Clift, ed., *Private War*, 19; *Confederate Scrap-Book*, 253–54; Lucy Wood Diary, May 24, 1861, Lomax Family Papers, VHS.

36 Baer, ed., *Shadows on My Heart*, 291; Sutherland, ed., *Very Violent Rebel*, 17; see also 12, 13, 16, 22, 31, 49–50, 55, 65, 103.

37 Lois Charlotte Dye to Wyatt Patterson, December 6, 1861, Patterson-Dye Correspondence, SCHS; Sarah Lois Wadley Diary, August 21, 1861, SHC microfilm.

38 Marszalek, ed., *Diary of Miss Emma Holmes*, 74, 77, 91; Clift, ed., *Private War*, 28; Sarah Lois Wadley Diary, September 15, 1861, SHC microfilm; Robertson, ed., *Lucy Breckinridge*, 74; Patty Vest to Sally Munford, September 26, 1861, Munford-Ellis Family Papers, Duke. Also on knitting, see Anderson, ed., *Brokenburn*, 47; Bonner, ed., *Journal of a Milledgeville Girl*, 66; Eppes, *Through Some Eventful Years*, 155; Macon, *Reminiscences*, 10; and Kate Corbin to Sally Munford, August 23, 1861, and Emily Voss to Sally Munford, November 1, 1861, Munford-Ellis Family Papers, Duke.

39 Rose P. Ravenel Reminiscences, Ravenel Papers, SCHS; Anderson, ed., *Brokenburn*, 312; Marszalek, ed., *Diary of Miss Emma Holmes*, 101; see also 344.

40 [Harrison], "Virginia Girl," 612; Wright, *Southern Girl in '61*, 53; Alice Lucas to Brother, June 2, 1864 (quotation), Lucas-Ashley Family Papers, Duke. On northern women's work as nurses, see, for example, Ross, "Arranging a Doll's House." On southern girls' desire to work as nurses and on social restrictions (usually enforced by mothers but sometimes by fathers or husbands), see Grace Elmore Diary, December 3, 1861, SHC microfilm; Kate Corbin to Sally Munford, August 23,

1861, Munford-Ellis Family Papers, Duke; Loula Kendall to James Henry Rogers, March 5, 1862, Rogers Collection, Emory; and East, ed., *Sarah Morgan*, 123–24. For other examples of girls' work as nurses, see Baer, ed., *Shadows on My Heart*, 88; and Lucy Wood Diary, July 19, 23, August 28, 1861, "Letters and Diary of a Civil War Bride," Lomax Family Papers, VHS.

41 Wright, *Southern Girl in '61*, 151; Emma Shannon Crutcher to Will Crutcher, January 14, 1861, Crutcher-Shannon Family Papers, CAH.

42 Baer, ed., *Shadows on My Heart*, 291.

43 Sutherland, ed., *Very Violent Rebel*, 4, 5, 13, 25, 43, 108, 113; see also 117, 119.

44 Ibid., 85, 90, 113, 118, 123.

45 Ibid., 38; see also 123.

46 Leslie, "Myth of the Southern Lady."

47 For quotation, see [Harrison], "Virginia Girl," 608. On adult southern women and the Civil War, see Faust, "Altars of Sacrifice"; Faust, "War Story for Confederate Women," 165; and Faust, *Mothers of Invention*, 16–23, 135, 159, 168–78. For southern girls' comments on *Macaria*, see Sarah E. J. Broyles Dilworth Diary, January 6, 1865, Cocke Papers, Duke. For examples of southern mothers' "very proper" deportment and counsels to their wayward daughters, see Baer, ed., *Shadows on My Heart*, 62; and Sutherland, ed., *Very Violent Rebel*, 113.

48 Anderson, ed., *Brokenburn*, 17.

49 Sarah Lois Wadley Diary, April 21, 1861, SHC microfilm; Elizabeth Collier Diary, August 28, 1861, SHC; Marszalek, ed., *Diary of Miss Emma Holmes*, 235, 236; Maggie Munford to Mother, June 9, 1862, Munford-Ellis Family Papers, Duke; Anderson, ed., *Brokenburn*, 24. For similar complaints, see Sally E. Broyles Diary, January 6, 1865, Cocke Papers, Duke.

50 Virginia Wilson Hankins Diary, n.d., June 12, 1863, Hankins Family Papers, VHS.

51 Cotton, ed., *From the Pen of a She-Rebel*, 61; Andrews, *War-Time Journal*, 32.

52 Baer, ed., *Shadows on My Heart*, 43; Robertson, ed., *Lucy Breckinridge*, 140–41; C. Alice Ready Diary, March 11, 1862, SHC.

53 Underwood, "War Seen Through a Teen-ager's Eyes," 181; Baer, ed., *Shadows on My Heart*, 62, 77, 109; Miers, ed., *When the World Ended*, 55.

54 C. Alice Ready Diary, April 8, 15, 19, 1862, SHC.

55 Sarah Lois Wadley Diary, April 21, September 29, 1861, SHC microfilm; Lucy Wood Diary, February 27, 1862, "Letters and Diary of a Civil War Bride," Lomax Family Papers, VHS. Similarly, Emma LeConte demanded: "Why does not the President call out the women if there are [not] enough men?" See Miers, ed., *When the World Ended*, 90. Drew Faust (*Mothers of Invention*, 231) writes: "Nearly every female Confederate diarist at some point expressed the desire to be a man." See also Eppes, *Through Some Eventful Years*, 150.

56 Sarah Lois Wadley Diary, March 2, 1862, SHC microfilm; C. Alice Ready Diary, March 20, April 15, 21, 1862, SHC. A few southern women did cross-dress and fight in the Confederate army. See Faust, *Mothers of Invention*, 202–3.

57 On southern women's spiritual crisis, see Rable, *Civil Wars*, chap. 10. Drew Gilpin Faust speculates: "It may well have been because of its women that the South lost the Civil War." See "Altars of Sacrifice," 199.

58   Loula Kendall Rogers to James Henry Rogers, September 17, 1863; Loula Kendall
      Rogers Journal, December 31, 1864, Rogers Collection, Emory.

59   Sarah E. Broyles Diary, May 1, 1865, Cocke Papers, Duke; Elizabeth Collier Diary,
      April 25, 1865, SHC; Revels, *Grander in Her Daughters*, 136. For another example, see
      Miers, ed., *When the World Ended*, 4.

60   Quoted in Leslie, "Myth of the Southern Lady," 42.

61   East, ed., *Sarah Morgan*, 141.

62   By contrast, Roberts (*Confederate Belle*) contends that young women whose upbring-
      ings had "prepared [them] for a world that would soon be lost forever" stubbornly
      refused to "reconstruct the Southern feminine ideal." "Instead they lamented their
      existences and used their diaries to recall the glorious past" (34, 179). For quota-
      tions, see Baer, ed., *Shadows on My Heart*, 241; Imogene Hoyle to Amaryllis Bomar,
      June 25, September 28, 1864, Bomar Family Papers, Emory; and Andrews, *War-
      Time Journal*, 84. For examples of occupation and invasion, see Baer, ed., *Shadows
      on My Heart*; Cotton, ed., *From the Pen of a She-Rebel*, 7, 10, 16; Macon, *Reminiscences*,
      12–14, 64–66, 105, 110–12; Sutherland, ed., *Very Violent Rebel*; Yeatman, ed., "What
      an Awful and Grand Spectacle It Is," 41–43; Myra Inman Diary, SHC; Alice Wil-
      liamson Diary, Duke; Ellen Louise Power Diary, June 23, 1863, SHC microfilm; and
      Nannie [Ruffin?] to Eliza Cocke, May 6, 1863, Cocke Papers, SHC. For examples of
      refugeeing, see Andrews, *War-Time Journal*; East, ed., *Sarah Morgan*; Anderson, ed.,
      Brokenburn; Frances James La Rue Dorsey Diary, VHS; Elizabeth Collier Diary, SHC;
      Fannie Page Hume Diary, July 1862, SHC; Emily Bland Southall Diary, Southall-
      Bowen Family Papers, SHC; Munford-Ellis Family Papers, Duke; and Lucas-Ashley
      Family Papers, Duke.

63   Andrews, *War-Time Journal*, 21; Anderson, ed., *Brokenburn*, 224; E. Munford to Jennie
      Munford, May 13, 1862, Munford-Ellis Family Papers, Duke; see also Sallie Mun-
      ford to Jennie Munford, June 1, 1862, and Sally Munford to Jennie Munford, Sep-
      tember 2, 1863, Munford-Ellis Family Papers, Duke.

64   [Harrison], "Virginia Girl," 607; Sallie Munford to Jennie Munford, June 1, 1862,
      Munford-Ellis Family Papers, Duke; Andrews, *War-Time Journal*, 21. For other ex-
      amples of this pattern of divided families, see Frances James La Rue Dorsey Diary,
      VHS; Fannie Page Hume Diary, SHC; Mary Lucas to Anne Virginia Lucas, Decem-
      ber 20, [1862], Lucas-Ashley Family Papers, Duke; Mary Maxcy Leverett to Milton
      Maxcy Leverett, February 24, 1864, in Taylor, Matthews, and Power, eds., *Leverett
      Letters*, 384; and "Civil War Reminiscences of Sophia Haskell Cheves," Sophia Has-
      kell Cheves Papers, SCHS. Also on girls traveling without male companions, see
      Avary, ed., *Virginia Girl*, 43–46; East, ed., *Sarah Morgan*, 101; Robertson, ed., *Confed-
      erate Lady Comes of Age*, 36–37; Wright, *Southern Girl in '61*, 179–80; and "Civil War
      Reminiscences of Sophia Haskell Cheves," Sophia Haskell Cheves Papers, SCHS.

65   Stowell, "'Family of Women and Children'"; Marszalek, ed., *Diary of Miss Emma
      Holmes*, 338; Robertson, ed., *Confederate Lady Comes of Age*, 6, 28; Lou Wilkinson
      to Jane Allston, July 9, 1864, Allston Family Papers, SCHS. For other examples,
      see Anderson, ed., *Brokenburn*; Kate Corbin to Sally Munford, May 25, 1861, and
      Kate Corbin to Sally Munford, February 16, 1863, Munford-Ellis Family Papers,
      Duke; Amanda Virginia Edmonds Journals, September 1, 1861, Chappelear Papers,

VHS; and Imogene Hoyle to Amaryllis Bomar, September 28, 1864, Bomar Family Papers, Emory. See also Faust, *Mothers of Invention*, chap. 2.

66   Kate Corbin to Sally Munford, August 1, 1861, November 19, 1862, Munford-Ellis Family Papers, Duke.

67   Sally Munford to Jennie Munford, September 2, 1863; compare to Lucy Munford to Jennie Munford, June 14 and 29, 1862, all in Munford-Ellis Family Papers, Duke.

68   Kate Corbin to Sally Munford, November 19, 1862, Munford-Ellis Family Papers, Duke; Marszalek, ed., *Diary of Miss Emma Holmes*, 471. For other comments on servants' departure and the necessity of undertaking household tasks, see Ruth to Elizabeth Allston, December 3, 1865, Allston Family Papers, SCHS; Bettie to Eliza Cocke, July 28, 1865, Cocke Papers, SHC; Baer, ed., *Shadows on My Heart*, 208, 210; Cotton, ed., *From the Pen of a She-Rebel*, 42; Eppes, *Through Some Eventful Years*, 309; Macon, *Reminiscences*, 57–58; Miers, ed., *When the World Ended*, 54; and Lady, "Five Tri-State Women," 215.

69   Marszalek, ed., *Diary of Miss Emma Holmes*, 289, 445; Anderson, ed., *Brokenburn*, 146; Cotton, ed., *From the Pen of a She-Rebel*, 42; Cross and Cross, eds., *Child of Glencoe*, 93.

70   Andrews, *War-Time Journal*, 373.

71   Kate Corbin to Sally Munford, November 19, 1862, Munford-Ellis Family Papers, Duke; Baer, ed., *Shadows on My Heart*, 102.

72   Avary, ed., *Virginia Girl*, 307–8; Baer, ed., *Shadows on My Heart*, 214.

73   Kate Corbin to Sally Munford, November 19, 1862, Munford-Ellis Family Papers, Duke.

74   Andrews, *War-Time Journal*, 374–75; Marszalek, ed., *Diary of Miss Emma Holmes*, 456. Joyce Broussard describes this phenomenon as "class anguish." See "Female Solitaires," 348–50 (quotation).

75   Cotton, ed., *From the Pen of a She-Rebel*, 42; Sarah Bull Barnwell to Mary Maxcy Leverett, February 21, 1866, in Taylor, Matthews, and Power, eds., *Leverett Letters*, 407.

76   Smedes, *Memorials of a Southern Planter*, 224–25; Kate Corbin to Sally Munford, November 19, 1862, Munford-Ellis Family Papers, Duke.

77   Avary, ed., *Virginia Girl*, 350; Marszalek, ed., *Diary of Miss Emma Holmes*, 461; Anderson, ed., *Brokenburn*, 373. See also Marszalek, ed., *Diary of Miss Emma Holmes*, 454; and Baer, ed., *Shadows on My Heart*, 210.

78   Patty Vest to Sally Munford, September 26, 1861, and Kate Corbin to Sally Munford, August 23, 1861, Munford-Ellis Family Papers, Duke.

79   Ardella Brown to Cynthia Blair, May 20, 1863, Blair Papers, Duke. All misspellings in original. For the standard interpretation of Confederate women's marriage prospects, see Faust, *Mothers of Invention*, 139–41 and 145–51; Rable, *Civil Wars*, 51–54; and Roberts, *Confederate Belle*, 87–93. Joyce Linda Broussard echoes this theme in her recent study, writing that young women in the Civil War era were "the spinsters of the post-war era" because the Civil War produced a shortage of potential husbands. See "Female Solitaires," 151. Victoria Ott offers a twist on the usual storyline, arguing that while "the absence of potential suitors on the homefront forced many to reconsider their prospects," "many young women willingly postponed marriage until after the war," instead enjoying the relative freedom from constraint of wartime courtships. However, Ott finds no lasting changes in young

women's attitudes toward or roles in marriage in the postwar period. See "When the Flower Blooms in Winter," 16–17 and chap. 4.

80 Andrews, *War-Time Journal*, 61; C. Alice Ready Diary, February 13, 1862, SHC; Mary Lucas to Emma Lucas, February 28, [1864], Lucas-Ashley Family Papers, Duke; Kate Corbin to Sally Munford, July 3, 1861, Munford-Ellis Family Papers, Duke; Nancy Royall to Cynthia Blair, December 1, 1863, Blair Papers, Duke. See also Marszalek, ed., *Diary of Miss Emma Holmes*, 169.

81 Marszalek, ed., *Diary of Miss Emma Holmes*, 266; Wright, *Southern Girl in '61*, 135 (quotation), 241; Lou Wilkinson to Jane Allston, July 9, 1864, Allston Family Papers, SCHS; Underwood, "War Seen Through a Teen-ager's Eyes," 183; Andrews, *War-Time Journal*, 8.

82 Jule Moore to Blannie Southall, May 5, 1863, quoting Julia Southall to Jule Moore, Southall-Bowen Family Papers, SHC; Macon, *Reminiscences*, 6, 11, 85, 91. In Richmond, the capital of the Confederacy, there was actually a surplus of marriageable white men. See Barber, "'White Wings of Eros.'" See also Broussard, "Female Solitaires," 322–23, 326–27.

83 East, ed., *Sarah Morgan*, 35; Andrews, *War-Time Journal*, 76; Minnie Bacot to Jane Allston, December 3, 1865, Allston Family Papers, SCHS; Wright, *Southern Girl in '61*, 194. This was also true of Unionist areas of the South. In May 1863, Lexingtonian General Orlando Willcox held a "hop," a festive ball that featured twenty-four dances. See Smith and Cooper, eds., *Window on the War*, 29. For other Confederate examples, see Anderson, ed., *Brokenburn*, 101; C. Alice Ready Diary, March 3, 1862, SHC; Marszalek, ed., *Diary of Miss Emma Holmes*, 22, 25; Sophia Haskell Cheves, "A Schoolgirl's Recollection of Fort Sumter," Sophia Lovell Haskell Cheves Papers, SCHS; Lucy Wood Diary, April 17, 1861, "Letters and Diary of a Civil War Bride," Lomax Family Papers, VHS; and Wright, *Southern Girl in '61*, 136. For some young women, watching troops drill became a new source of amusement. See, for example, Amanda Virginia Edmonds Journal, June 13, 1863, Chappelear Papers, VHS; Malinda B. Ray Diary, July 19, 1861, Ray Papers, SHC; Mary Maxcy Leverett to Milton Maxcy Leverett, February 24, 1862, in Taylor, Matthews, and Power, eds., *Leverett Letters*, 107; and Kemper, "Civil War Reminiscences," 317.

84 Amanda Virginia Edmonds Journal, September 6, 1862, September 13, October 15, 1863, Chappelear Papers, VHS.

85 "Civil War Reminiscences of Sophia Haskell Cheves," Sophia Haskell Cheves Papers, SCHS; Anderson, ed., *Brokenburn*, 345; Sallie Bowcock to Millie Birckhead, June 17, 1861, Birckhead Papers, Duke. While men were eager to marry during the war, women were more reluctant. For example, see Waddy Butler to Lucy Wood, September 29, 1860; and Lucy Wood to Waddy Butler, October 12, 1860, February 11, 1861, "Letters and Diary of a Civil War Bride," Lomax Family Papers, VHS; Kate Corbin to Sally Munford, August 11, October 20, December 27, 1863, Munford-Ellis Family Papers, Duke; and Wyatt Patterson to Lottie Dye, January [14], 1864, Patterson-Dye Correspondence, SCHS.

86 Clift, ed., *Private War*, 19.

87 Bonner, ed., *Journal of a Milledgeville Girl*, 116, 118; Andrews, *War-Time Journal*, 256. At St. Mary's School, the students engaged in midnight fortune-telling to assess

their marital prospects and the safety of their sweethearts. See Stoops, *Heritage*, 74. Kate Stone's friend Missie Morris still held out hope for marriage in 1864. See Anderson, ed., *Brokenburn*, 301.

88 Barber, "'White Wings of Eros,'" 119; Kate Corbin to Sally Munford, March 7, 1863, Munford-Ellis Family Papers, Duke; Marszalek, ed., *Diary of Miss Emma Holmes*, 225, 471; see also 16, 123. For an example of "rather a hurried up affair" at the end of the war, see Minnie Bacot to Jane Allston, n.d., 1866, Allston Family Papers, SCHS.

89 Baer, ed., *Shadows on My Heart*, 322; Taylor, Matthews, and Power, eds., *Leverett Letters*, 455; Mother to Maggie Munford, August 13, [1862]; Kate Corbin to Sally Munford, July 3, 1861, Munford-Ellis Family Papers, Duke; East, ed., *Sarah Morgan*, 550.

90 E. J. Julian to Cynthia Blair, January 19, 1861, Blair Papers, Duke; Lucy Wood to Waddy Butler, October 12, 1860, "Letters and Diary of a Civil War Bride," VHS. On young women's awareness of the possibility that soldier-husbands might never return home, see Mary Lucas to Emma Lucas, February 28, May 8, [1864], Lucas-Ashley Family Papers, Duke; Robertson, ed., *Lucy Breckinridge*, 36; and Marszalek, ed., *Diary of Miss Emma Holmes*, 356.

Some women canceled their engagements entirely. According to Texas refugee Kate Stone, the war made for increased flirtations and engagements—but not marriages. Both women and men understood that relationships between soldiers and civilians were "just a piece of amusement on both sides," she noted, even when young women made "partial engagements" that they had no intention of honoring. Stone referred to the Civil War years as "the days of lightly-won and lightly-held hearts." See Anderson, ed., *Brokenburn*, 345, 354. A letter to Floride Clemson from her mother in 1863 regarding a broken engagement in the neighborhood suggests that Stone may have been right in her assessment that the war encouraged flirtation more than commitment. See Lander, ed., "Confederate Girl Visits Pennsylvania," 121.

91 Kate Corbin to Sally Munford, March 28, undated [May/June], August 26, October 21, December 27, 1863, Munford-Ellis Family Papers, Duke.

92 East, ed., *Sarah Morgan*, 550; Grace Elmore Diary, September 13, 1862, SHC microfilm; Julia M. Southall Personal Journal, 1871–76; Julia M. Southall Personal Journal, n.d.; Julia M. Southall Journal and Commonplace Book, n.d.; and Julia M. Southall to Jule Moore, January 1, 1864, Southall-Bowen Family Papers, SHC.

93 Robertson, ed., *Confederate Lady Comes of Age*, 19, 83; see also 7, 46, 49, 41, 53, 55, 58, 71, 72, 84.

94 Quotations repeated from preceding discussion and from the opening cameo.

95 Anderson, ed., *Brokenburn*, 355. For more on Stone's negative assessments of men and marriage, see ibid., 369, 376, 379, 336, 338, 206, 176, 163.

96 On *Macaria* and singlehood, see Faust, *Mothers of Invention*, 168–78; see also Tracey, *Plots and Proposals*, chap. 2. Faust notes that "nearly every Confederate woman who discussed her reading in a diary or in her correspondence mentioned *Macaria*" (*Mothers of Invention*, 175).

97 Andrews, *War-Time Journal*, 1.

98 Imogene Hoyle to Amaryllis Bomar, June 25, 1864, Bomar Family Papers, Emory;

Marszalek, ed., *Diary of Miss Emma Holmes*, 325. On elite women's activities in the postwar years, see, for example, Edwards, *Scarlett Doesn't Live Here Anymore*, chap. 9; Edwards, *Gendered Strife and Confusion*; Faust, *Mothers of Invention*, 248–54; Gilmore, *Gender and Jim Crow*; and Whites, *Civil War as a Crisis in Gender*, chaps. 5 and 6. In her study of women's changing role in the late-nineteenth-century South, Jane Turner Censer (*Reconstruction of White Southern Womanhood*, 6) credits the "younger generations" with the "reconstruction of white southern womanhood." Indeed, Censer suggests that many of Anne Firor Scott's claims about the emergence of a "new" southern woman are most applicable to young women. See Scott's *Southern Lady*, chap. 4 and pt. 2.

99 Grace Elmore Diary, September 21, 1865, SHC microfilm; Miers, ed., *When the World Ended*, 22. For other examples, see Andrews, *War-Time Journal*, 186.

100 Marszalek, ed., *Diary of Miss Emma Holmes*, 461, 469; Mary Bull Leverett to Milton Maxcy Leverett, July 30, 1868, in Taylor, Matthews, and Power, eds., *Leverett Letters*, 448; Cross and Cross, eds., *Child of Glencoe*, 64.

101 Marszalek, ed., *Diary of Miss Emma Holmes*, 461; Julia Southall Daily Diary, January 2, 1868, Southall-Bowen Family Papers, SHC. For examples of Civil War and Reconstruction teachers, see Mary Lucas to Anne Virginia Lucas, December 20, [1862], Lucas-Ashley Family Papers, Duke; Caroline Kean Hill Davis Diary, VHS; Julia Southall to Emily Bland Southall, October 3, 1861, October 31, 1862, May 1, 1863; Julia Southall to Jule Moore, January 1, 1864; and Julia Southall Daily Diary, 1868, Southall-Bowen Family Papers, SHC; Sutherland, ed., *Very Violent Rebel*, 6; and Mary Maxcy Leverett to Anne Leverett DeSaussure, February 18, 1867, in Taylor, Matthews, and Power, eds., *Leverett Letters*, 414. On North Carolina's teaching gender ratio, see Stoops, *Heritage*, 86.

102 Miers, ed., *When the World Ended*, 28, 68, 72, 105; see also 75, 109.

103 For quotations, see Marszalek, ed., *Diary of Miss Emma Holmes*, 172, 251, 325; see also 186–87, 314–15, 378.

104 Sally E. Broyles Diary, May 7, 1865, Cocke Papers, Duke.

EPILOGUE

1 See Cita Cook, "Women's Role"; Cox, *Dixie's Daughters*; and Parrott, "'Love Makes Memory Eternal.'"

2 See especially Edwards, *Gendered Strife and Confusion*; Faust, *Mothers of Invention*; and Whites, *Civil War as a Crisis in Gender*. See also Edwards, *Scarlett Doesn't Live Here Anymore*, and Gilmore, *Gender and Jim Crow*.

3 For quotations, see Gilmore, *Gender and Jim Crow*, xix, and Faust, *Mothers of Invention*, 256. See also Scott, *Southern Lady*.

4 On southern women and progressive reform, see, for example, Bordin, *Woman and Temperance*, 52–88; Elna Green, *Southern Strategies*; Hall, *Revolt Against Chivalry*; Janiewski, *Sisterhood Denied*; Joan Marie Johnson, *Southern Ladies*; McArthur, *Creating the New Woman*; McDowell, *Social Gospel*; Sims, *Power of Femininity*; Turner, *Women, Culture, and Community*; Wedell, *Elite Women*; and Wheeler, *New Women of the New South*. For a synthetic treatment and broad interpretation of these and other

changes in white women's role in the South, see Censer, *Reconstruction of White Southern Womanhood*.

5 This interpretation meshes with Jane Turner Censer's in *The Reconstruction of White Southern Womanhood*, 5–6, which proposes a generational model for social change in the New South, and conflicts with Giselle Roberts's *Confederate Belle*, which is thus far the only study of southern women to use age as a category of analysis. For a northern analysis of life cycles among women, see Boylan, "Timid Girls." See also Florence Elliott Cook, "Growing Up White, Genteel, and Female."

BIBLIOGRAPHY

ARCHIVAL COLLECTIONS

Auburn University, Auburn, Alabama
  Whitfield Family Papers
Center for American History, University of Texas at Austin, Austin, Texas
  Crutcher-Shannon Family Papers
  Kiger Family Papers
  Patricia Mercer Diary
Duke University Special Collections, Durham, North Carolina
  Sarah E. R. Ballowe Album
  Edward F. Birckhead Papers
  Cynthia and Mildred Blair Papers
  Ignatius W. Brock Papers
  Annie Burnham Autograph Album
  Campbell Family Papers
  William Johnson Cocke Papers
      Sarah E. J. Broyles Dilworth Diary
  Lizzie G. Davis Composition Book
  Mary Miller Davis Papers
  Edith Elmer Diary
  Nathan G. Hunt Papers
  George W. Johnson Papers
  John McIntosh Kell Papers
  John Knight Papers
  Lucas-Ashley Family Papers
  Sarah Magill Papers
  Susan McDowall Diary and Scrapbook
  Munford-Ellis Family Papers
  Frank Lewis Reid Papers
  Marion Morgan Richardson Autograph Album
  Scarborough Family Papers
  Thomas M. Smith Papers
  James Southgate Papers
  Mary Virginia Hawes Terhune Papers

George W. West Papers

Alice Williamson Diary

Emory University Libraries, Robert W. Woodruff Library, Atlanta, Georgia

Bomar Family Papers

Warren A. Candler Papers

James Osgood Andrew Clark Papers

Ella Anderson Clark Reminiscences

Harris Family Papers

Robert Watkins Lovett Papers

Sue Richardson Diary

Loula Kendall Rogers Collection

Loula Kendall Rogers Journal

Maria Catherine Wiestling Diary

Maryland Historical Society, Baltimore, Maryland

William Wirt Papers (also available on microfilm at Fondren Library, Rice University, Houston, Texas)

Catharine G. Wirt Diary

South Carolina Historical Society, Charleston, South Carolina

Sophia Lovell Haskell Cheves Papers

"Civil War Reminiscences of Sophia Haskell Cheves"

"A Schoolgirl's Recollection of Fort Sumter"

Lise Ravenel Childs Letters

Cuthbert Letters to Miss Elizabeth O. A. Lucas

Jacob Deveaux Guerard Letter to Alice Screven

Erastus Hopkins Correspondence

Johnson Family Papers

Thomas Jefferson Withers Papers

Mary Withers Kirkland, "Reminiscences of Childhood"

Patterson-Dye Correspondence

Porcher Family Papers

Rose P. Ravenel Papers

Rose P. Ravenel Reminiscences ("My Youth")

Withers Letters

Southern Historical Collection, University of North Carolina, Chapel Hill, North Carolina

Penelope Eliza Howard Alderman Papers

A. F. Alexander Papers

Emma Pauline Nicholson Alexander Papers

Beale-Davis Family Papers

Mary Harper Beall Letter

Bennett and Hill Family Papers

Elizabeth Blanchard Papers

Sarah P. Brame Album (miscellaneous albums)

Catherine Brown Album (miscellaneous albums)

Ann Eliza Brumby Paper

Brumby and Smith Family Papers
    Laura Margaret Cole Smith Diary
Lucy Wood Butler Papers
Sarah Rebecca Cameron Papers
    Ann Cameron Diary
Cameron Family Papers
Hope Summerell Chamberlain Papers
Henry Harrison Cocke Papers
    Elizabeth Ruffin Diary
Elizabeth Collier Diary
Anne Cameron Collins Papers
Emma Lee Hutchison Cosby Papers
Frances Leard Creighton Album (miscellaneous albums)
Crowder-Miller Family Papers
Margaret Mordecai Devereux Papers
William G. Dickson Papers
Dobson Family Papers
Henry William Faison Papers
Ferebee, Gregory, and McPherson Family Papers
Foxhall Family Papers
Galloway Family Papers
Eliza Anna Goodwin Album (miscellaneous albums)
Gordon and Hackett Family Papers
William P. Graham Papers
Gray Family Papers
Peter Hagner Papers
Harnett County (North Carolina) Papers
Harris Family Papers
Laurens Hinton Papers
John De Berniere Hooper Papers
Julia E. Horner Papers
Fannie Page Hume Diaries
Ellie Hunter Journal
Susan Davis Nye Hutchinson Journals
Myra Inman Diary
Calvin Jones Papers
Jones Family Papers
Joyner Family Papers
Kenan Family Papers
Alice Spencer Kerr Papers
John Kimberly Papers
Martha Ann Kirkpatrick Album (miscellaneous albums)
Caroline Brooks Lilly Books
Joseph Adolph Linn Papers
Littleton College Memorabilia

Thomas M. Logal Papers
 Kate Virginia Cox Diary
Ella Noland MacKenzie Papers
Lucy E. McIver Papers
Miscellaneous albums
Mordecai Family Papers
Sarah Varick Cozens Morrison Diary
Lillian Moseley Album (miscellaneous albums)
Nisbet and Marye Family Papers
Mollie A. Parham Diary
Mary Fries Patterson Diary
James W. Patton Papers
Perkins Family Papers
 Emma Sue Gordon Diary
Pettigrew Family Papers
Polk, Badger, and McGehee Family Papers
Quitman Family Papers
 Anna Rosalie Quitman Journal
James Graham Ramsay Papers
John Andrew Ramsay Papers
David A. Ray Papers
 Malinda B. Ray Diary
C. Alice Ready Diary
St. Mary's School Notebook
Elizabeth Hairston Seawall Papers
Charles B. Simrall Papers
Sims Family Papers
Skinner Family Papers
Southall-Bowen Family Papers
 Emily Bland Southall Diary
 Julia M. Southall Diary and Journals
  Sabbath Journal (1862–65)
  Vacation Diary (1864)
  Daily Diary (1868)
  Weekly Diary (1869–71)
  Personal Journal (1871–76)
  Diary and Journal (September 1873)
  Diary (1873–74)
  Personal Journal (undated)
  Journal and Commonplace Book (undated)
Ida Ann Southworth Album (miscellaneous albums)
Steed and Phipps Family Papers
 Elizabeth Lundie Phipps Diary
John Steele Papers
Marcus Cicero Stephens Letters

Preston H. Turner Paper

Edward J. Warren Papers

Webb Family Papers

    Susan A. Webb Diary

Margaret Isabella Walker Weber Reminiscences

Eloise Whitaker Papers

Cora E. White Papers

Calvin Henderson Wiley Papers

Nannie Hoskins Williams Diary

William Henry Wills Papers

Southern Historical Collection, University of North Carolina, Chapel Hill, North Carolina, Microfilm

    Susan Cornwall Diary

    Franklin Elmore Papers

        Sally Elmore Taylor Memoirs

    Grace Elmore Diary

    Ellen Shackelford Gift Papers

    Charles Graves Papers

    Margaret Lea Letters

    Ellen Louise Power Diary

    Margaret Anne Ulmer Diary

    Sarah Lois Wadley Diary

    Mary Susannah Winans Album

Virginia Historical Society, Richmond, Virginia

    Theron Hervey Bakewell Papers

    Eliza Lavalette Barksdale Diary

    Bernard Family Papers

    Fannie Rebecca Black Album

    Gay Robertson Blackford Reminiscences

    Byrd Family Papers

    Carrington Family Papers

    Mary Ann Caruthers Album

    Frances Douglas Chancellor Album

    Penelope Abbett Chancellor Album

    Amanda Virginia Edmonds Chappelear Papers

        Amanda Virginia Edmonds Journals

    Ann Webster Gordon Christian Diary

    Claiborne Family Papers

    Nannie Cottrell Album

    Sophia Coutts Album

    Samuella Hart Curd Diary

    Daniel Family Papers

    Caroline Kean Hill Davis Diary

    Julia C. V. C. Smith Davis Album

    Dearing Family Papers

Frances James La Rue Dorsey Diary

Sarah Dandridge Cooke Duval Papers

Early Family Papers

 Mary Virginia Early Brown Diary

Edrington Family Papers

 Angelina Selden Edrington Diary

Ellett–St. Catherine's Alumnae Association Papers

Martha Beaston Tyler Floyd Commonplace Book

Mary Ella Fourqurean Fry Commonplace Book

Garland Family Papers

Anne Eliza Pleasants Gordon Diary

Minnie Cox Graham Diary

Grove Family Papers

Guerrant Family Papers

Gwathmey Family Papers

 Mary Atwood Gwathmey Album

Hankins Family Papers

 Virginia Wilson Hankins Diary

Harrison Family Papers

Higginbotham Family Papers

Hill Family Papers

Hughes Family Papers

Hunter Family Papers

Mary Walker Lupton Irish Autograph Album

Jones Family Papers

Larue Family Papers

Frances James La Rue Diary

Linkous Family Papers

Anna Clayton Logan Memoirs

Lomax Family Papers

 "Letters and Diary of a Civil War Bride" (typescript)

Ida Spooner Lownes Commonplace Book

Lucas Family Papers

Anna Lee Blanton McCluer Memoir

Elizabeth Ann Cooley McClure Diary

McDowell Family Papers

Miller Family Papers

Ellen Temple Hill Minor Album

Rosina Ursula Young Mordecai Commonplace Book

Elizabeth M. P. Nelson Commonplace Book

Norwood Family Papers

Winifred Blount Hill Norwood Commonplace Book

Margaret J. Palmer Commonplace Book

Mary Jane Patterson Album

Mary Baskerville Carrington Rachal Autograph Album

Laura Wirt Randall Papers
Mary Jefferson Randolph Commonplace Book
Randolph Family Papers
Ridley Family Papers
Amanda Jane Cooley Roberts Diary
Annie Kelly Saunders Papers
    Annie Kelly Saunders Page Diary
Harriet L. Scollay Autograph Album
Virginia Campbell Shelton Diary
Spragins Family Papers
Stuart Family Papers
Tennant Family Papers
    Janet Bruce Williams Diary
Thomas Family Papers
Julia Gardiner Tyler Papers
Wickham Family Papers
Judith Gates Winfree Memoirs
Jeannette Young Album

PUBLISHED LETTERS, DIARIES, AND MEMOIRS

Anderson, John Q., ed. *Brokenburn: The Journal of Kate Stone, 1861–1868.* Baton Rouge: Louisiana State University Press, 1995.

Andrews, Eliza Frances. *War-Time Journal of a Georgia Girl, 1864–1865.* Edited by Spencer Bidwell King Jr. Macon, Ga.: Ardivan Press, 1960.

Ashkenazi, Elliott, ed. *The Civil War Diary of Clara Solomon: Growing Up in New Orleans, 1861–1862.* Baton Rouge: Louisiana State University Press, 1995.

Avary, Myrta Lockett, ed. *A Virginia Girl in the Civil War, 1861–1865: Being a Record of the Actual Experiences of the Wife of a Confederate Officer.* New York: D. Appleton and Company, 1903, 1915.

Baer, Elizabeth R., ed. *Shadows on My Heart: The Civil War Diary of Lucy Rebecca Buck of Virginia.* Athens, Ga.: University of Georgia Press, 1997.

Bleser, Carol, ed. *Tokens of Affection: The Letters of a Planter's Daughter in the Old South.* Athens: University of Georgia Press, 1996.

Bonner, James C., ed. *The Journal of a Milledgeville Girl, 1861–1867.* Athens: University of Georgia Press, 1964.

Brady, Patricia, ed., *George Washington's Beautiful Nelly: The Letters of Eleanor Parke Custis Lewis to Elizabeth Bordley Gibson.* Columbia: University of South Carolina Press, 1991.

Burr, Virginia Ingraham, ed. *The Secret Eye: The Journal of Ella Gertrude Clanton Thomas, 1848–1889.* Chapel Hill: University of North Carolina Press, 1990.

Cashin, Joan E., ed. *Our Common Affairs: Texts from Women in the Old South.* Baltimore: Johns Hopkins University Press, 1996.

Clay-Clopton, Virginia. *A Belle of the Fifties: Memoirs of Mrs. Clay of Alabama.* Edited by Leah Rawles Atkins, Joseph H. Harrison Jr., and Sara A. Hudson. 1905. Reprint, Tuscaloosa: University of Alabama Press, 1999.

Confederate Scrap-Book. [Composed by Lizzie Cary Daniel]. Richmond: J. L. Hill Publishing Company, 1893.

Clift, G. Glenn, ed. *The Private War of Lizzie Hardin*. Frankfort: Kentucky Historical Society, 1963.

Cotton, Gordon A., ed. *From the Pen of a She-Rebel: The Civil War Diary of Emilie Riley McKinley*. Columbia: University of South Carolina Press, 2001.

Cross, Eleanor P., and Charles B. Cross Jr., eds. *Child of Glencoe: Civil War Journal of Katie Darling Wallace*. Chesapeake, Va.: Norfolk County Historical Society, 1983.

DuBois, Ellen Carol, ed. *Elizabeth Cady Stanton–Susan B. Anthony Reader: Correspondence, Writings, Speeches*. Rev. ed. Boston: Northeastern University Press, 1992.

East, Charles, ed. *Sarah Morgan: The Civil War Diary of a Southern Woman*. Athens: University of Georgia Press, 1991.

Eppes, Susan Bradford. *Through Some Eventful Years*. 1926. Reprint, Gainesville: University of Florida Press, 1968.

[Harrison, Constance Cary.] "A Virginia Girl in the First Year of the War." *Century Magazine* 30 (1885): 606–14.

Harwell, Richard B., ed. "Louisiana Burge: The Diary of a Confederate College Girl." *Georgia Historical Quarterly* 36 (June 1952): 144–63.

Kemper, Mary Lee. "Civil War Reminiscences at Danville Female Academy." *Missouri Historical Review* 62 (April 1968): 314–20.

Lady, Claudia Lynn. "Five Tri-State Women during the Civil War: Day-to-Day Life." *West Virginia History* 43 (Spring 1982): 206–13.

———. "Five Tri-State Women During the Civil War: Views on the War." *West Virginia History* 43 (Summer 1982): 303–21.

Lander, Ernest M., Jr., ed. "A Confederate Girl Visits Pennsylvania, July–September 1863." *Western Pennsylvania Historical Magazine* 59 (1966): 116–26.

Macon, Emma Cassandra Rieley. *Reminiscences of the Civil War*. Cedar Rapids, Iowa: Torch Press, 1911.

Marszalek, John F., ed. *The Diary of Miss Emma Holmes, 1861–1866*. Baton Rouge: Louisiana State University Press, 1979, 1994.

Miers, Earl Schenck, ed. *When the World Ended: The Diary of Emma LeConte*. New York: Oxford University Press, 1957.

Morrill, Lily Logan, ed. *My Confederate Girlhood: The Memoirs of Kate Virginia Cox Logan*. Richmond: Garrett & Massie, 1932.

Murr, Erika L., ed. *A Rebel Wife in Texas: The Diary and Letters of Elizabeth Scott Neblett, 1852–1864*. Baton Rouge: Louisiana State University Press, 2001.

Murray, Elizabeth Dunbar. *My Mother Used to Say: A Natchez Belle of the Sixties*. Boston: Christopher Publishing House, 1959.

Norse, Clifford C. "School Life of Amanda Worthington of Washington County, 1857–1862." *Journal of Mississippi History* 34 (May 1972): 107–17.

O'Brien, Michael, ed. *An Evening When Alone: Four Journals of Single Women in the South, 1827–1867*. Charlottesville: University Press of Virginia, 1993.

Phelps, Mrs. Lincoln. *The Fireside Friend, or Female Student: Being Advice to Young Ladies on the Important Subject of Education. With an Appendix, on Moral and Religious Education, from the French of Madame de Saussure*. Boston: Marsh, Capen, Lyon, and Webb, 1840.

Ripley, Eliza. *Social Life in Old New Orleans: Being Recollections of my Girlhood.* New York: D. Appleton and Company, 1912.

Robertson, Mary D., ed. *A Confederate Lady Comes of Age: The Journal of Pauline DeCaradeuc Heyward, 1863–1888.* Columbia: University of South Carolina Press, 1992.

———. *Lucy Breckinridge of Grove Hill: The Journal of a Virginia Girl, 1862–1864.* Columbia: University of South Carolina Press, 1994.

Rowland, Kate Mason, and Mrs. Morris L. Croxall, eds. *The Journal of Julia LeGrand: New Orleans, 1862–1863.* Richmond: Everett Waddey, 1911.

Scarborough, Lucy Paxton. "So It Was When Her Life Began: Reminiscences of a Louisiana Girlhood." *Louisiana Historical Quarterly* 13 (July 1930): 428–44.

Smedes, Susan Dabney. *Memorials of a Southern Planter.* Edited by Fletcher M. Green. Jackson: University Press of Mississippi, 1981.

Smith, John David, and William Cooper Jr., eds. *Window on the War: Frances Dallam Peter's Lexington Civil War Diary.* Lexington, Ky.: Lexington-Fayette Historical Commission, 1976.

Sutherland, Daniel E., ed. *A Very Violent Rebel: The Civil War Diary of Ellen Renshaw House.* Knoxville: University of Tennessee Press, 1996.

Taylor, Frances Wallace, Catherine Taylor Matthews, and J. Tracy Power, eds. *The Leverett Letters: Correspondence of a South Carolina Family, 1851–1868.* Columbia: University of South Carolina Press, 2000.

Underwood, Betsy Swint. "War Seen Through a Teenager's Eyes." *Tennessee Historical Quarterly* 20 (June 1961): 177–87.

Woodward, C. Vann, and Elisabeth Muhlenfeld, eds. *The Private Mary Chesnut: The Unpublished Civil War Diaries.* New York: Oxford University Press, 1984.

Wright, Mrs. D. Giraud [Louise Wigfall Wright]. *A Southern Girl in '61: The War-Time Memories of a Confederate Senator's Daughter.* New York: Doubleday, 1905.

Yeatman, Ted, ed. "'What an Awful and Grand Spectacle It Is!' Fear in the Heart of North Carolina." *Civil War Times Illustrated* 22 (1984): 41–43.

MONOGRAPHS AND ANTHOLOGIES

Allgor, Catherine. *Parlor Politics: In Which the Ladies of Washington Help Build a City and a Government.* Charlottesville: University Press of Virginia, 2000.

Antler, Joyce. *The Educated Woman and Professionalization: The Struggle for a New Feminine Identity, 1890–1920.* New York: Garland Publishing, Inc., 1987.

Antler, Joyce, and Sari Knopp Biklen, eds. *Changing Education: Women as Radicals and Conservators.* New York: State University of New York Press, 1990.

Appleton, Thomas, and Angela Boswell, eds. *Searching for Their Places: Women in the South Across Four Centuries.* Columbia: University of Missouri Press, 2003.

Ayers, Edward, and John C. Willis, eds. *The Edge of the South: Life in Nineteenth-Century Virginia.* Charlottesville: University Press of Virginia, 1991.

Bardaglio, Peter. *Reconstructing the Household: Families, Sex, and the Law in the Nineteenth-Century South.* Chapel Hill: University of North Carolina Press, 1995.

Basch, Norma. *Framing American Divorce: From the Revolutionary Generation to the Victorians.* Berkeley: University of California Press, 1999.

————. *In the Eyes of the Law: Women, Marriage, and Property in Nineteenth-Century New York.* Ithaca: Cornell University Press, 1982.

Bellows, Barbara L. *Benevolence Among Slaveholders: Assisting the Poor in Charleston, 1670–1860.* Baton Rouge: Louisiana State University Press, 1993.

Best, Amy L. *Prom Night: Youth, Schools and Popular Culture.* New York: Routledge, 2000.

Blassingame, John. *The Slave Community: Plantation Life in the Antebellum South.* New York: Oxford University Press, 1972.

Bleser, Carol, ed. *In Joy and in Sorrow: Women, Family and Marriage in the Victorian South.* New York: Oxford University Press, 1991.

Bordin, Ruth. *Woman and Temperance: The Quest for Power and Liberty, 1873–1900.* Philadelphia: Temple University Press, 1981.

Boydston, Jeanne. *Home and Work: Housework, Wages, and the Ideology of Labor in the Early Republic.* New York: Oxford University Press, 1990.

Brodie, Janet. *Contraception and Abortion in Nineteenth-Century America.* Ithaca: Cornell University Press, 1994.

Brumberg, Joan Jacobs. *The Body Project: An Intimate History of American Girls.* New York: Random House, 1997.

Campbell, Edward D. C., Jr., and Kym S. Rice, eds. *A Woman's War: Southern Women, Civil War, and the Confederate Legacy.* Charlottesville: University Press of Virginia, 1996.

Carter, Christine Jacobson. *Southern Single Blessedness: Unmarried Women in the Urban South, 1800–1865.* Urbana: University of Illinois Press, 2006.

Cashin, Joan E. *Family Venture: Men and Women on the Southern Frontier.* New York: Oxford University Press, 1991.

————, ed. *Our Common Affairs: Texts from Women in the Old South.* Baltimore: Johns Hopkins University Press, 1996.

Censer, Jane Turner. *North Carolina Planters and Their Children, 1800–1860.* Baton Rouge: Louisiana State University Press, 1984.

————. *The Reconstruction of White Southern Womanhood, 1865–1895.* Baton Rouge: Louisiana State University Press, 2003.

Chambers-Schiller, Lee Virginia. *Liberty, a Better Husband: Single Women in America: The Generations of 1780 to 1840.* New Haven: Yale University Press, 1984.

Clark, Clifford Edward, Jr. *The American Family Home, 1800–1960.* Chapel Hill: University of North Carolina Press, 1986.

Clayton, Bruce L., and John A. Salmond, eds. *"Lives Full of Struggle and Triumph": Southern Women, Their Institutions, and Their Communities.* Gainesville: University Press of Florida, 2003.

Clinton, Catherine. *The Plantation Mistress: Woman's World in the Old South.* New York: Pantheon Books, 1982.

————. *Tara Revisited: Women, War, and the Plantation Legend.* New York: Abbeville Press, 1995.

————, ed. *Southern Families at War: Loyalty and Conflict in the Civil War South.* New York: Oxford University Press, 2000.

Clinton, Catherine, and Nina Silber, eds. *Divided Houses: Gender and the Civil War.* New York: Oxford University Press, 1992.

Cogan, Frances B. *All-American Girl: The Ideal of Real Womanhood in Mid-Nineteenth-Century America*. Athens: University of Georgia Press, 1989.

Coryell, Janet, Thomas H. Appleton Jr., Anastatia Sims, and Sandra Gioia Treadway, eds. *Negotiating Boundaries of Southern Womanhood: Dealing with the Powers that Be*. Columbia: University of Missouri Press, 2000.

Cott, Nancy F. *The Bonds of Womanhood: "Woman's Sphere" in New England, 1785–1835*. New Haven: Yale University Press, 1977.

———. *Public Vows: A History of Marriage and the Nation*. Cambridge: Harvard University Press, 2000.

Coulter, E. Merton. *College Life in the Old South*. Athens: University of Georgia Press, 1951.

Cox, Karen L. *Dixie's Daughters: The United Daughters of the Confederacy and the Preservation of Confederate Culture*. Gainesville: University Press of Florida, 2003.

Crofts, Daniel. *Reluctant Confederates: Upper South Unionists in the Secession Crisis*. Chapel Hill: University of North Carolina Press, 1993.

Daniels, Christine, and Michael V. Kennedy, eds. *Over the Threshold: Intimate Violence in Early America*. New York: Routledge, 1999.

Degler, Carl. *At Odds: Women and the Family in America from the Revolution to the Present*. New York: Oxford University Press, 1980.

D'Emilio, John, and Estelle B. Freedman. *Intimate Matters: A History of Sexuality in America*. New York: Harper and Row, 1988.

Douglas, Ann. *The Feminization of American Culture*. New York: Knopf, 1977.

Dyhouse, Carol. *Feminism and the Family in England, 1880–1939*. Oxford: Basil Blackwell, 1989.

———. *Girls Growing Up in Late Victorian and Edwardian England*. London: Routledge & Kegan Paul, 1981.

Edwards, Laura F. *Gendered Strife and Confusion: The Political Culture of Reconstruction*. Urbana: University of Illinois Press, 1997.

———. *Scarlett Doesn't Live Here Anymore: Southern Women in the Civil War Era*. Urbana: University of Illinois Press, 2000.

Egerton, Douglas R. *Gabriel's Rebellion: The Virginia Slave Conspiracies of 1800 and 1802*. Chapel Hill: University of North Carolina Press, 1993.

———. *He Shall Go Out Free: The Lives of Denmark Vesey*. Madison, Wis.: Madison House, 1999.

———. *Rebels, Reformers, and Revolutionaries: Collected Essays and Second Thoughts*. New York: Routledge, 2002.

English, Deirdre, and Barbara Ehrenreich. *Witches, Midwives, and Nurses: A History of Women Healers*. London: Compendium Press, 1974.

Eschbach, Elizabeth Seymour. *The Higher Education of Women in England and America, 1865–1920*. New York: Garland Publishing, Inc., 1993.

Faderman, Lillian. *Odd Girls and Twilight Lovers: A History of Lesbian Life in Twentieth-Century America*. New York: Columbia University Press, 1991.

———. *Surpassing the Love of Men: Romantic Friendship and Love Between Women from the Renaissance to the Present*. New York: Morrow, 1981.

————. *To Believe in Women: What Lesbians Have Done for America—A History.* Boston: Houghton Mifflin, 1999.

Farnham, Christie Anne. *The Education of the Southern Belle: Higher Education and Student Socialization in the Antebellum South.* New York: New York University Press, 1994.

Faust, Drew Gilpin. *James Henry Hammond and the Old South: A Design for Mastery.* Baton Rouge: Louisiana State University Press, 1982.

————. *Mothers of Invention: Women of the Slaveholding South in the American Civil War.* Chapel Hil: University of North Carolina Press, 1996.

————. *Southern Stories: Slaveholders in Peace and War.* Columbia: University of Missouri Press, 1992.

Flexnor, Eleanor. *Century of Struggle: The Women's Rights Movement in the United States.* Cambridge: Harvard University Press, 1959.

Formanek-Brunell, Miriam. *Made to Play House: Dolls and the Commercialization of American Girlhood, 1830–1930.* New Haven: Yale University Press, 1993.

Fox-Genovese, Elizabeth. *Within the Plantation Household: Black and White Women of the Old South.* Chapel Hill: University of North Carolina Press, 1989.

Frankfort, Roberta. *Collegiate Women: Domesticity and Career in Turn-of-the-Century America.* New York: New York University Press, 1977.

Fraser, Walter J., Jr., R. Frank Saunders Jr., and Jon L. Wakelyn, eds. *The Web of Southern Social Relations: Women, Family, and Education.* Athens: University of Georgia Press, 1985.

Friedman, Jean E. *The Enclosed Garden: Women and Community in the Evangelical South, 1830–1900.* Chapel Hill: University of North Carolina Press, 1985.

Friend, Craig Thompson, and Lorri Glover, eds. *Southern Manhood: Perspectives on Masculinity in the Old South.* Athens: University of Georgia Press, 2004.

Genovese, Eugene D. *Roll, Jordan, Roll: The World the Slaves Made.* New York: Pantheon Books, 1974.

Gilligan, Carol. *In a Different Voice: Psychological Theory and Women's Development.* Cambridge, Mass.: Harvard University Press, 1982.

Gilmore, Glenda Elizabeth. *Gender and Jim Crow: Women and the Politics of White Supremacy in North Carolina, 1896–1920.* Chapel Hill: University of North Carolina Press, 1996.

Ginzberg, Lori. *Women and the Work of Benevolence: Morality, Politics, and Class in the Nineteenth-Century United States.* New Haven: Yale University Press, 1990.

Gorham, Deborah. *The Victorian Girl and the Feminine Ideal.* Bloomington: Indiana University Press, 1982.

Green, Elna C. *Southern Strategies: Southern Women and the Woman Suffrage Question.* Chapel Hill: University of North Carolina Press, 1997.

Griswold, Robert. *Family and Divorce in California, 1850–1900: Victorian Illusions and Everyday Realities.* Albany: State University of New York Press, 1982.

Gutman, Herbert. *The Black Family in Slavery and Freedom, 1750–1925.* New York: Pantheon Books, 1976.

Hall, Jacquelyn Dowd. *Revolt Against Chivalry: Jessie Daniel Ames and the Women's Campaign Against Lynching.* New York: Columbia University Press, 1979.

Halttunen, Karen. *Confidence Men and Painted Women: A Study of Middle-class Culture in America, 1830–1870.* New Haven: Yale University Press, 1982.

Hartog, Hendrik. *Man and Wife in America: A History.* Cambridge: Harvard University Press, 2000.

Hessinger, Rodney. *Seduced, Abandoned, and Reborn: Visions of Youth in Middle-Class America, 1780–1850.* Philadelphia: University of Pennsylvania Press, 2005.

Heyrman, Christine Leigh. *Southern Cross: The Beginnings of the Bible Belt.* New York: Knopf, 1997.

Hobgood-Oster, Laura. *She Glanceth from Earth to Heaven: The Phenomenon of Love Mysticism Among Women in Antebellum Virginia and Maryland.* New Orleans: University Press of the South, 1991.

———, ed. *The Sabbath Journal of Judith Lomax (1774–1828).* Atlanta: Scholars Press, 1999.

Horowitz, Helen Lefkowitz. *Alma Mater: Design and Experience in the Women's Colleges from Their Nineteenth-Century Beginnings to the 1930s.* Amherst: University of Massachusetts Press, 1993.

———. *Campus Life: Undergraduate Cultures from the End of the Eighteenth Century to the Present.* New York: Knopf, 1987.

Hunt, Felicity, ed. *Lessons for Life: The Schooling of Girls and Women, 1850–1950.* London: Basil Blackwell, 1987.

Hunter, Jane N. *How Young Ladies Became Girls: The Victorian Origins of American Girlhood.* New Haven: Yale University Press, 2002.

Jabour, Anya. *Marriage in the Early Republic: Elizabeth and William Wirt and the Companionate Ideal.* Baltimore: Johns Hopkins University Press, 1998.

Janiewski, Dolores E. *Sisterhood Denied: Race, Gender, and Class in a New South Community.* Philadelphia: Temple University Press, 1985.

Johnson, Joan Marie. *Southern Ladies, New Women: Race, Region, and Clubwomen in South Carolina, 1890–1930.* Gainesville: University Press of Florida, 2004.

Kelley, Mary, ed. *Woman's Being, Woman's Place: Female Identity and Vocation in American History.* Boston: G. K. Hall & Co., 1979.

Kerber, Linda K. *Women of the Republic: Intellect and Ideology in Revolutionary America.* Chapel Hill: University of North Carolina Press, 1980.

Kett, Joseph F. *Rites of Passage: Adolescence in America, 1790 to the Present.* New York: Basic Books, 1977.

Kierner, Cynthia. *Women's Place in the Early South: Gender and the Public Sphere, 1700–1835.* Cornell: Cornell University Press, 1998.

King, Wilma. *Stolen Childhood: Slave Youth in Nineteenth-Century America.* Bloomington: Indiana University Press, 1995.

Kuhn, Anne L. *The Mother's Role in Childhood Education: New England Concepts, 1830–1860.* New Haven: Yale University Press, 1947.

Laas, Virginia Jeans. *Love and Power in the Nineteenth Century: The Marriage of Violet Blair.* Fayetteville: University of Arkansas Press, 1998.

Lasch, Christopher. *Haven in a Heartless World: The Family Besieged.* New York: Basic Books, 1977.

Leavitt, Judith Walzer. *Brought to Bed: Childbearing in America, 1750–1950.* New York: Oxford University Press, 1986.

Lebsock, Suzanne. *The Free Women of Petersburg: Status and Culture in a Southern Town, 1784–1860.* New York: W. W. Norton, 1984.

Lerner, Gerda. *The Creation of Feminist Consciousness: From the Middle Ages to Eighteen-seventy.* New York: Oxford University Press, 1993.

———. *The Grimké Sisters from South Carolina: Pioneers for Woman's Rights and Abolition.* New York: Oxford University Press, 1998.

Levine, George, ed. *Constructions of the Self.* New Brunswick: Rutgers University Press, 1992.

Lewis, Charlene M. Boyer. *Ladies and Gentlemen on Display: Planter Society at the Virginia Springs, 1790–1860.* Charlottesville: University Press of Virginia, 2001.

Lewis, Jan. *The Pursuit of Happiness: Family and Values in Jefferson's Virginia.* New York: Cambridge University Press, 1983.

Lyerly, Cynthia Lynn. *Methodism and the Southern Mind, 1770–1810.* New York: Oxford University Press, 1998.

Lystra, Karen. *Searching the Heart: Women, Men, and Romantic Love in Nineteenth-Century America.* New York: Oxford University Press, 1989.

MacLeod, Anne Scott. *A Moral Tale: Children's Fiction and American Culture, 1820–1860.* Hamden, Conn.: Archon Books, 1975.

MacMullen, Ramsay. *Sarah's Choice, 1828–1832.* New Haven: Past Times Press, 2001.

Marling, Karal Ann. *Debutante: Rites and Regalia of American Debdom.* Lawrence: University Press of Kansas, 2004.

Marten, James. *The Children's Civil War.* Chapel Hill: University of North Carolina Press, 1998.

Matthews, Glenna. *"Just a Housewife": The Rise and Fall of Domesticity in America.* New York: Oxford University Press, 1987.

May, Elaine Tyler. *Barren in the Promised Land: Childless Americans and the Pursuit of Happiness.* Cambridge: Harvard University Press, 1995.

Maynes, Mary Jo, Birgitte Søland, and Christina Benninghaus, eds. *Secret Gardens, Satanic Mills: Placing Girls in European History, 1750–1960.* Bloomington: Indiana University Press, 2005.

McArthur, Judith N. *Creating the New Woman: The Rise of Southern Women's Progressive Culture in Texas, 1893–1918.* Tuscaloosa: University of Alabama Press, 1999.

McDannell, Colleen. *The Christian Home in Victorian America, 1840–1900.* Bloomington: Indiana University Press, 1986.

McDowell, John Patrick. *The Social Gospel in the South: The Woman's Home Mission Movement in the Methodist Episcopal Church South, 1886–1939.* Baton Rouge: Louisiana State University Press, 1982.

McMillen, Sally G. *Motherhood in the Old South: Pregnancy, Childbirth, and Infant Rearing.* Baton Rouge: Louisiana State University Press, 1990.

Mohr, James. *Abortion in America: The Origins and Evolutions of National Policy, 1800–1900.* New York: Oxford University Press, 1978.

Montgomery, Maureen E. *Displaying Women: Spectacles of Leisure in Edith Wharton's New York.* New York: Routledge, 1998.

Nelson, Claudia, and Lynne Vallone, eds. *The Girl's Own: Cultural Histories of the Anglo-American Girl, 1830–1915*. Athens: University of Georgia Press, 1994.

Norton, Mary Beth. *Liberty's Daughters: The Revolutionary Experience of American Women, 1750–1800*. Boston: Little, Brown, 1980.

Nylander, Jane C. *Our Own Snug Fireside: Images of the New England Home, 1760–1860*. New Haven: Yale University Press, 1993.

Pace, Robert F. *Halls of Honor: College Men in the Old South*. Baton Rouge: Louisiana State University Press, 2004.

Palmieri, Patricia Ann. *In Adamless Eden: The Community of Women Faculty at Wellesley*. New Haven: Yale University Press, 1995.

Pease, Jane H., and William H. Pease. *Ladies, Women, and Wenches: Choice and Constraint in Antebellum Charleston and Boston*. Chapel Hill: University of North Carolina Press, 1990.

———. *A Family of Women: The Carolina Petigrus in Peace and War*. Chapel Hill: University of North Carolina Press, 1999.

Phillips, Ulrich Bonnell. *American Negro Slavery*. 1918. Reprint, Baton Rouge: Louisiana State University Press, 1966.

Rable, George C. *Civil Wars: Women and the Crisis of Southern Nationalism*. Urbana: University of Illinois Press, 1989.

Raboteau, Albert J. *Slave Religion: The "Invisible Institution" in the Antebellum South*. New York: Oxford University Press, 1978.

Reinier, Jacqueline S. *From Virtue to Character: American Childhood, 1775–1850*. New York: Twayne Publishers, 1996.

Revels, Tracy J. *Grander in Her Daughters: Florida's Women during the Civil War*. Columbia: University of South Carolina Press, 2004.

Riley, Glenda. *Divorce: An American Tradition*. New York: Oxford University Press, 1991.

Rishoi, Christie. *From Girl to Woman: American Women's Coming-of-Age Narratives*. Albany: State University of New York Press, 2003.

Roberts, Giselle. *The Confederate Belle*. Columbia: University of Missouri Press, 2003.

Rosenberg, Rosalind. *Beyond Separate Spheres: Intellectual Roots of Modern Feminism*. New Haven: Yale University Press, 1982.

Rosengarten, Theodore, ed. *Tombee: Portrait of a Cotton Planter*. New York: McGraw Hill, 1988.

Rothman, Ellen K. *Hands and Hearts: A History of Courtship in America*. New York: Basic Books, 1984.

Rothman, Joshua D. *Notorious in the Neighborhood: Sex and Families across the Color Line in Virginia, 1787–1861*. Chapel Hill: University of North Carolina Press, 2003.

Rotundo, E. Anthony. *American Manhood: Transformations in Masculinity from the Revolution to the Modern Era*. New York: BasicBooks, 1993.

Rowbotham, Judith. *Good Girls Make Good Wives: Guidance for Girls in Victorian Fiction*. Oxford: Basil Blackwell, 1989.

Ryan, Mary P. *Cradle of the Middle Class: The Family in Oneida County, New York, 1790–1865*. New York: Cambridge University Press, 1981.

Salmon, Marylynn. *Women and the Law of Property in Early America*. Chapel Hill: University of North Carolina Press, 1986.

Scholten, Catherine M. *Childbearing in American Society, 1650–1850*. New York: New York
University Press, 1985.

Schwartz, Marie Jenkins. *Born in Bondage: Growing Up Enslaved in the Antebellum South*.
Cambridge, Mass.: Harvard University Press, 2000.

Scott, Anne Firor. *Making the Invisible Woman Visible*. Urbana: University of Chicago
Press, 1984.

———. *The Southern Lady: From Pedestal to Politics, 1830–1890*. Chicago: University of
Chicago Press, 1970.

Scott, James C. *Domination and the Arts of Resistance: Hidden Transcripts*. New Haven: Yale
University Press, 1990.

———. *Weapons of the Weak: Everyday Forms of Peasant Resistance*. New Haven: Yale
University Press, 1985.

Sims, Anastatia. *The Power of Femininity in the New South: Women's Organizations and
Politics in North Carolina, 1880–1930*. Columbia: University of South Carolina Press,
1997.

Sklar, Kathryn Kish. *Catharine Beecher: A Study in American Domesticity*. New York: Yale
University Press, 1973.

———. *Women's Rights Emerges from the Antislavery Movement: A Brief History with
Documents*. Boston: Bedford/St. Martin's, 2000.

Smith-Rosenberg, Carroll. *Disorderly Conduct: Visions of Gender in Victorian America*. New
York: Oxford University Press, 1985.

Smith, Daniel Blake. *Inside the Great House: Planter Family Life in Eighteenth-Century
Chesapeake Society*. Ithaca: Cornell University Press, 1980.

Solomon, Barbara Miller. *In the Company of Educated Women: A History of Women and
Higher Education in America*. New Haven: Yale University Press, 1985.

Spalding, Phinizy, ed. *Higher Education for Women in the South: A History of Lucy Cobb
Institute, 1858–1994*. Athens: Georgia Southern Press, 1994.

Stampp, Kenneth M. *The Peculiar Institution: Slavery in the Ante-Bellum South*. New York:
Knopf, 1956.

Stoops, Martha. *The Heritage: The Education of Women at St. Mary's College, Raleigh, North
Carolina, 1842–1982*. Raleigh, N.C.: St. Mary's College, 1984.

Stowe, Steven M. *Doctoring the South: Southern Physicians and Everyday Medicine in the
Mid-Nineteenth Century*. Chapel Hill: University of North Carolina Press, 2004.

———. *Intimacy and Power in the Old South: Ritual in the Lives of the Planters*. Baltimore:
Johns Hopkins University Press, 1987.

Sugg, Redd S., Jr. *Motherteacher: The Feminization of American Education*. Charlottesville:
University Press of Virginia, 1978.

Theriot, Nancy M. *Mothers and Daughters in Nineteenth-Century America: The Biosocial
Construction of Femininity*. Lexington: University Press of Kentucky, 1996.

Tracey, Karen. *Plots and Proposals: American Women's Fiction, 1850–1890*. Urbana:
University of Illinois Press, 2000.

Turner, Elizabeth Hayes. *Women, Culture, and Community: Religion and Reform in Galveston,
1880–1920*. New York: Oxford University Press, 1997.

Ulrich, Laurel Thatcher. *A Midwife's Tale: The Life of Martha Ballard, Based on Her Diary,
1785–1812*. New York: Vintage Books, 1991.

Varon, Elizabeth R. *We Mean to Be Counted: White Women and Politics in Antebellum Virginia.* Chapel Hill: University of North Carolina Press, 1998.

Vicinus, Martha. *Independent Women: Work and Community for Single Women, 1850–1920.* Chicago: University of Chicago Press, 1985.

Vida, Vendela. *Girls on the Verge: Debutante Dips, Gang Drive-Bys, and Other Initiations.* New York: St. Martin's Press, 1999.

Wedell, Marsha. *Elite Women and the Reform Impulse in Memphis, 1875–1915.* Knoxville: University of Tennessee Press, 1991.

Wertz, Richard, and Dorothy Wertz. *Lying-In: A History of Childbirth in America.* New York: Schocken Books, 1979.

Wheeler, Marjorie Spruill. *New Women of the New South: The Leaders of the Woman Suffrage Movement in the Southern States.* New York: Oxford University Press, 1993.

White, Barbara A. *Growing Up Female: Adolescent Girlhood in American Fiction.* Westport, Conn.: Greenwood Press, 1985.

Whites, LeeAnn. *The Civil War as a Crisis in Gender: Augusta, Georgia, 1860–1890.* Athens: University of Georgia Press, 1995.

Wiener, Marli F. *Mistresses and Slaves: Plantation Women in south Carolina, 1830–1880.* Urbana: University of Illinois Press, 1997.

Wishy, Bernard. *The Child and the Republic: The Dawn of Modern American Child Nurture.* Philadelphia: University of Pennsylvania Press, 1968.

Wood, Kirsten E. *Masterful Women: Slaveholding Widows from the American Revolution through the Civil War.* Chapel Hill: University of North Carolina, 2004.

Woody, Thomas. *A History of Women's Education in the United States.* 2 vols. New York: Octagon Books, 1929.

Wyatt-Brown, Bertram. *Southern Honor: Ethics and Behavior in the Old South.* New York: Oxford University Press, 1983.

ARTICLES AND ESSAYS

Allmendinger, David F., Jr. "Mount Holyoke Students Encounter the Need for Life-Planning, 1837–1850." *History of Education Quarterly* 19 (Spring 1979): 27–46.

Baptist, Edward E. " 'My Mind Is to Drown You and Leave You Behind': 'Omie Wise,' Intimate Violence, and Masculinity." In *Over the Threshold: Intimate Violence in Early America,* edited by Christine Daniels and Michael V. Kennedy, 94–110. New York: Routledge, 1999.

Barber, E. Susan. " 'The White Wings of Eros': Courtship and Marriage in Confederate Richmond." In *Southern Families at War: Loyalty and Conflict in the Civil War South,* edited by Catherine Clinton, 119–32. New York: Oxford University Press, 2000.

Barrows, Phyllis Jenkins. "History of Lucy Cobb Institute, 1858–1950." In *Higher Education for Women in the South: A History of Lucy Cobb Institute, 1858–1994,* edited by Phinizy Spalding, 5–83. Athens: University of Georgia Press, 1994.

Berry, Trey. "A History of Women's Higher Education in Mississippi, 1819–1882." *Journal of Mississippi History* 53 (November 1991): 303-20.

Blauvelt, Martha Tomhave. "Women, Words, and Men: Excerpts from the Diary of Mary Guion." *Journal of Women's History* 2 (Fall 1990): 177–84.

Bleser, Carol K. "The Perrys of Greenville: A Nineteenth-Century Marriage." In *The Web of Southern Social Relations: Women, Family, and Education*, edited by Walter J. Fraser Jr., R. Frank Saunders Jr., and Jon L. Wakelyn, 72–89. Athens: University of Georgia Press, 1985.

Bleser, Carol K., and Frederick Heath. "The Clays of Alabama: The Impact of the Civil War on a Southern Marriage." In *In Joy and in Sorrow: Women, Family, and Marriage in the Victorian South, 1830–1900*, 135–53. New York: Oxford University Press, 1991.

Blight, David W. "No Desperate Hero: Manhood and Freedom in a Union Soldier's Experience." In *Divided Houses: Gender and the Civil War*, edited by Catherine Clinton and Nina Silber, 55–75. New York: Oxford University Press, 1992.

Bossard, James H. S., and Eleanor S. Boll. "Rite of Passage—A Contemporary Study." *Social Forces* 26, no. 3 (March 1948): 247–55.

Boylan, Anne M. "Timid Girls, Venerable Widows and Dignified Matrons: Life Cycle Pattern Among Organized Women in New York and Boston, 1797–1840." *American Quarterly* 38 (Winter 1986): 779–97.

Burr, Virginia I. "'A Woman Made to Suffer and Be Strong': Ella Gertrude Clanton Thomas, 1834–1907." In *In Joy and in Sorrow: Women, Family and Marriage in the Victorian South*, edited by Carol Bleser, 215–32. New York: Oxford University Press, 1991.

Carter, Christine Jacobson. "Indispensable Spinsters: Maiden Aunts in the Elite Families of Savannah and Charleston." In *Negotiating Boundaries of Southern Womanhood: Dealing with the Powers that Be*, edited by Janet Coryell, Thomas H. Appleton Jr., Anastatia Sims, and Sandra Gioia Treadway, 110–34. Columbia: University of Missouri Press, 2000.

Cashin, Joan E. "Culture of Resignation." In *Our Common Affairs: Texts from Women in the Old South*, edited by Joan E. Cashin, 1–41. Baltimore: Johns Hopkins University Press, 1996.

———. "'Decidedly Opposed to the Union': Women's Culture, Marriage, and Politics in Antebellum South Carolina." *Georgia Historical Quarterly* 78 (Winter 1994): 735–59.

———. "Into the Trackless Wilderness: The Refugee Experience in the Civil War." In *A Woman's War: Southern Women, Civil War, and the Confederate Legacy*, edited by Edward D. C. Campbell Jr. and Kym S. Rice, 29–53. Charlottesville: University Press of Virginia, 1996.

———. "The Structure of Antebellum Planter Families: 'The Ties that Bound Us Was Strong.'" *Journal of Southern History* 56 (February 1990): 55–70.

Censer, Jane Turner. "'Smiling Through Her Tears': Ante-Bellum Southern Women and Divorce." *American Journal of Legal History* 25 (January 1982): 114–34.

———. "Southwestern Migration Among North Carolina Planter Families: 'The Disposition to Emigrate.'" *Journal of Southern History* 57 (August 1991): 407–26.

Chudacoff, Howard P. "The Life Course of Women: Age and Age Consciousness, 1865–1915." *Journal of Family History* 5 (Fall 1980): 274–92.

Cole, Stephanie. "Keeping the Peace: Domestic Assault and Private Prosecution in

Antebellum Baltimore." In *Over the Threshold: Intimate Violence in Early America*, edited by Christine Daniels and Michael V. Kennedy, 148–69. New York: Routledge, 1999.

Cook, Cita. "Women's Role in the Transformation of Winnie Davis into the Daughter of the Confederacy." In *Searching for Their Places: Women in the South Across Four Centuries*, edited by Thomas Appleton and Angela Boswell, 144–60. Columbia: University of Missouri Press, 2003.

Cott, Nancy F. "Passionlessness: An Interpretation of Victorian Sexual Ideology, 179–1850." In *A Heritage of Her Own: Toward a New Social History of American Women*, edited by Nancy F. Cott and Elizabeth H. Pleck, 162–81. New York: Simon and Schuster, 1979.

Cullen, Jim. "'I's a Man Now': Gender and African American Men." In *Divided Houses: Gender and the Civil War*, edited by Catherine Clinton and Nina Silber, 76–91. New York: Oxford University Press, 1992.

Doyle, Elisabeth Joan. "Nurseries of Treason: Schools in Occupied New Orleans." *Journal of Southern History* 26 (May 1960): 161–79.

Dye, Nancy Schrom. "History of Childbirth in America." *Signs* 6 (Autumn 1980): 97–108.

Faust, Drew Gilpin. "Altars of Sacrifice: Confederate Women and the Narratives of War." *Journal of American History* 76 (March 1990): 1200–1228.

———. "'Trying to Do a Man's Business': Gender, Violence, and Slave Management in Civil War Texas." *Gender and History* 4 (Summer 1992): 197–214.

———. "A War Story for Confederate Women: Augusta Jane Evans's *Macaria*." In *Southern Stories: Slaveholders in Peace and War*, 160–73. Columbia: University of Missouri Press, 1992.

Faust, Drew Gilpin, et al. "Coming to Terms with Scarlett." *Southern Cultures* 5 (1999): 1–48.

Fox-Genovese, Elizabeth. "Family and Female Identity in the Antebellum South: Sarah Gayle and Her Family." In *In Joy and in Sorrow: Women, Family, and Marriage in the Victorian South*, edited by Carol Bleser, 15–31. New York: Oxford University Press, 1991.

———. "Scarlett O'Hara: The Southern Lady as New Woman." *American Quarterly* 33 (Fall 1981): 391–411.

Freeman, Ruth, and Patricia Klaus. "Blessed or Not? The New Spinster in England and the United States in the Late Nineteenth and Early Twentieth Centuries." *Journal of Family History* 9 (Winter 1984): 394–414.

Friend, Craig Thompson. "Belles, Benefactors, and the Blacksmith's Son: Cyrus Stuart and the Enigma of Southern Gentlemanliness." In *Southern Manhood: Perspectives on Masculinity in the Old South*, edited by Craig Thompson Friend and Lorri Glover, 92–112. Athens: University of Georgia Press, 2004.

Gelles, Edith B. "Gossip: An Eighteenth-Century Case." *Journal of Social History* 22 (Summer 1989): 667–83.

Genovese, Eugene. "Toward a Kinder and Gentler America: The Southern Lady in the Greening of the Politics of the Old South." In *In Joy and in Sorrow: Women, Family, and Marriage in the Victorian South*, edited by Carol Bleser, 125–34. New York: Oxford University Press, 1991.

Gillespie, Joanna Bowen. "'The Clear Leadings of Providence': Pious Memoirs and the Problems of Self-Realization for Women in the Early Nineteenth Century." *Journal of the Early Republic* 5 (Summer 1985): 197–221.

———. "Mary Briscoe Baldwin (1811–1877), Single Woman Missionary and 'Very Much My Own Mistress.'" *Anglican and Episcopal History* 57, no. 1 (1988): 63–92.

———. "1795: Martha Laurens Ramsay's 'Dark Night of the Soul.'" *William and Mary Quarterly* 48 (January 1991): 68–92.

Glover, Lorri. "'Let Us Manufacture Men': Educating Elite Boys in the Early National South." In *Southern Manhood: Perspectives on Masculinity in the Old South*, edited by Craig Thompson Friend and Lorri Glover, 22–48. Athens: University of Georgia Press, 2004.

Green, Nancy. "Female Education and School Competition: 1820–1850." In *Woman's Being, Woman's Place: Female Identity and Vocation in American History*, edited by Mary Kelly, 127–41. Boston: Hall, 1979.

Hanft, Sheldon. "Mordecai's Female Academy." *American Jewish History* 79 (Autumn 1989): 72–93.

Hawes, Joseph M. "The Strange History of Female Adolescence in the United States." *Journal of Psychohistory* 13 (Summer 1985): 51–63.

Hunter, Jane. "Inscribing the Self in the Heart of the Family: Diaries and Girlhood in Late-Victorian America." *American Quarterly* 44 (March 1992): 51–81.

Jabour, Anya. "Albums of Affection: Female Friendship and Coming of Age in Antebellum Virginia." *Virginia Magazine of History and Biography* 107 (Spring 1999): 125–58.

———. "Between Mistress and Slave: Elizabeth Wirt's White Housekeepers, 1808–1825." In *Beyond Image and Convention: Explorations in Southern Women's History*, edited by Janet L. Coryell, Martha H. Swain, Sandra Gioia Treadway, and Elizabeth Hayes Turner, 28–52. Columbia: University of Missouri Press, 1998.

———. "'College Girls': The Female Academy and Female Identity in the Old South." In *"Lives Full of Struggle and Triumph": Southern Women, Their Institutions, and Their Communities*, edited by Bruce L. Clayton and John A. Salmond, 74–92. Gainesville: University Press of Florida, 2003.

———. "'Grown Girls, Highly Cultivated': Female Education in an Antebellum Southern Family." *Journal of Southern History* 64 (February 1998): 23–64.

———. "'It Will Never Do for Me to Be Married': The Life of Laura Wirt Randall, 1803–1834." *Journal of the Early Republic* 17 (Summer 1997): 193–236.

———. "Marriage and Family in the Nineteenth-Century South." In *Major Problems in the History of American Families and Children*, edited by Anya Jabour, 121–30. Boston: Houghton Mifflin, 2005.

———. "'The Privations & Hardships of a New Country': Southern Women and Southern Hospitality on the Florida Frontier." *Florida Historical Quarterly* 75 (Winter 1997): 259–75.

———. "Resisting the Altar: A Case Study of Conversion and Courtship in the Antebellum South." *Maryland Historical Magazine* 96 (Spring 2001): 29–51.

Johansen, Shawn. "Before the Waiting Room: Northern Middle-Class Men,

Pregnancy, and Birth in Antebellum America." *Gender and History* 7 (August 1995): 183–200.

Johnson, Guion G. "Courtship and Marriage Customs in Antebellum North Carolina." *North Carolina Historical Review* 8 (1931): 384–402.

Jordan, Ellen. "'Making Good Wives and Mothers'? The Transformation of Middle-Class Girls' Education in Nineteenth-Century Britain." *History of Education Quarterly* 21 (Winter 1991): 439–62.

Juncker, Clara. "Behind Confederate Lines: Sarah Morgan Dawson." *Southern Quarterly* 30 (Fall 1991): 7–17.

Kelley, Mary. "'Vindicating the Equality of Female Intellect': Women and Authority in the Early Republic." *Prospects* 17 (1993): 1–27.

Kierner, Cynthia. "Martha Hancock Wheat: Piety within Patriarchy." *Virginia Magazine of History and Biography* 50 (1992): 78–98.

Lasser, Carol. "'Let Us Be Sisters Forever': The Sororal Model of Nineteenth-Century Female Friendship." *Signs* 14 (August 1988): 158–81.

Leavitt, Judith Walzer. "Under the Shadow of Maternity: American Women's Responses to Death and Debility Fears in Nineteenth-Century Childbirth." *Feminist Studies* 12 (Spring 1986): 129–54.

Leslie, Kent Anderson. "A Myth of the Southern Lady: Antebellum Proslavery Rhetoric and the Proper Place of Woman." *Sociological Spectrum* 6 (1986): 31–49.

Lewis, Jan. "Motherhood and the Construction of the Male Citizen in the United States, 1750–1850." In *Constructions of the Self*, edited by George Levine, 143–63. New Brunswick, N.J.: Rutgers University Press, 1992.

Lewis, Jan, and Kenneth L. Lockridge. "'Sally Has Been Sick': Pregnancy and Family Limitation Among Virginia Gentry Women, 1780–1830." *Journal of Social History* 22 (Fall 1988): 5–19.

Lewis, Johanna Miller. "A Social and Architectural History of the Girls' Boarding School Building at Salem, North Carolina." *North Carolina Historical Review* 66 (April 1989): 125–48.

McMahon, Lucia. "'While Our Souls Together Blend': Narrating a Romantic Readership in the Early Republic." In *An Emotional History of the United States*, edited by Peter N. Stearns and Jan Lewis, 66–90. New York: New York University Press, 1988.

Minkema, Kenneth P. "Hannah and Her Sisters: Sisterhood, Courtship, and Marriage in the Edwards Family in the Early Eighteenth Century." *New England Historical and Genealogical Register* 146 (January 1992): 35–56.

Mitchell, Reid. "Soldiering, Manhood, and Coming of Age: A Northern Volunteer." In *Divided Houses: Gender and the Civil War*, edited by Catherine Clinton and Nina Silber, 43–54. New York: Oxford University Press, 1992.

Nguyen, Julia Huston. "The Value of Learning: Education and Class in Antebellum Natchez." *Journal of Mississippi History* 61, no. 3, 237–63.

O'Brien, Sharon. "Tomboyism and Adolescent Conflict: Three Nineteenth-Century Case Studies." In *Woman's Being, Woman's Place: Female Identity and Vocation in American History*, edited by Mary Kelly, 351–72. Boston: G. K. Hall & Co., 1979.

Parrott, Angie. "'Love Makes Memory Eternal': The United Daughters of the Confederacy in Richmond, Virginia, 1897–1920." In *The Edge of the South: Life in Nineteenth-Century Virginia*, edited by Edward Ayers and John C. Willis, 219–38. Charlottesville: University Press of Virginia, 1991.

Pederson, Joyce Senders. "Life's Lessons: Liberal Feminist Ideals of Family, School, and Community in Victorian England." In *The Girl's Own: Cultural Histories of the Anglo-American Girl, 1830–1915*, edited by Claudia Nelson and Lynne Vallone, 195–214. Athens: University of Georgia Press, 1994.

Perlmann, Joel, Silvana R. Siddali, and Keith Whitescarver. "Literacy, Schooling, and Teaching among New England Women, 1730–1820." *History of Education Quarterly* 37 (Summer 1997): 117–39.

Rambuss, Richard. "Spenser and Milton at Mardi Gras: English Literature, American Cultural Capital." *Boundary* 27, no. 2 (Summer 2000): 45–72.

Roberts, Giselle. "The New Andromeda: Sarah Morgan and the Post–Civil War Domestic Ideal." In *"Lives Full of Struggle and Triumph": Southern Women, Their Institutions, and Their Communities*, edited by Bruce L. Clayton and John A. Salmond, 38–56. Gainesville: University Press of Florida, 2003.

Rogers, Rebecca. "Boarding Schools, Women Teachers, and Domesticity: Reforming Girls' Secondary Education in the First Half of the Nineteenth Century." *French Historical Studies* 19 (Spring 1995): 153–81.

———. "Competing Visions of Girls' Secondary Education in Post-Revolutionary France." *History of Education Quarterly* 34 (Summer 1994): 147–70.

Ross, Kristie. "Arranging a Doll's House: Refined Women as Union Nurses." In *Divided Houses: Gender and the Civil War*, edited by Catherine Clinton and Nina Silber, 97–113. New York: Oxford University Press, 1992.

Rothman, Ellen K. "Sex and Self-Control: Middle-Class Courtship in America, 1770–1870." *Journal of Social History* 15 (Spring 1982): 409–25.

Rundquist, Angela. "Presentation at Court: A Corporate Female Ritual of Transition in Sweden, 1850–1962." *Anthropology Today* 3, no. 6 (1987): 2–6.

Scott, Anne Firor. "Almira Lincoln Phelps: The Self-Made Woman in the Nineteenth Century." *Maryland Historical Magazine* 75 (September 1980): 203–17.

———. "The Ever-Widening Circle: The Diffusion of Feminist Values from the Troy Female Seminary, 1822–1872." *History of Education Quarterly* 19 (Spring 1979): 3–25.

———. "Women's Perspective on the Patriarchy in the 1850s." In *Making the Invisible Woman Visible*, 175–89. Urbana and Chicago: University Press of Chicago, 1984.

Sklar, Kathryn Kish. "The Schooling of Girls and Changing Community Values in Massachusetts Towns, 1750–1820." *History of Education Quarterly* 33 (Winter 1993): 512–42.

———. "Victorian Women and Domestic Life: Mary Todd Lincoln, Elizabeth Cady Stanton, and Harriet Beecher Stowe." In *Women and Power in American History*, 2d ed., vol. 1, To 1880, 225–39. Upper Saddle River, N.J.: Prentice Hall, 2002.

Smith, Daniel Scott. "Family Limitation, Sexual Control, and Domestic Feminism in Victorian America." In *A Heritage of Her Own: Toward a New Social History of American Women*, edited by Nancy F. Cott and Elizabeth H. Pleck, 222–45. New York: Simon and Schuster, 1979.

———. "Parental Power and Marriage Patterns: An Analysis of Historical Trends in Hingham, Massachusetts." *Journal of Marriage and the Family* 35 (1973): 419–28.

Smith-Rosenberg, Carroll. "The Abortion Movement and the AMA, 1850–1880." In *Disorderly Conduct: Visions of Gender in Victorian America*, 217–44. New York: Oxford University Press, 1985.

———. "Beauty, the Beast, and the Militant Woman: A Case Study in Sex Roles and Social Stress in Jacksonian America." In *Disorderly Conduct: Visions of Gender in Victorian America*, 109–28. New York: Oxford University Press, 1985.

———. "The Female World of Love and Ritual: Relations Between Women in Nineteenth-Century America." In *Disorderly Conduct: Visions of Gender in Victorian America*, 53–76. New York: Oxford University Press, 1985.

———. "The Hysterical Woman: Sex Roles and Role Conflict in Nineteenth-Century America." In *Disorderly Conduct: Visions of Gender in Victorian America*, 197–216. New York: Oxford University Press, 1985.

———. "The New Woman as Androgyne: Social Disorder and Gender Crisis, 1870–1936." In *Disorderly Conduct: Visions of Gender in Victorian America*, 245–96. New York: Oxford University Press, 1985.

———. "Puberty to Menopause: The Cycle of Femininity in Nineteenth-Century America." In *Disorderly Conduct: Visions of Gender in Victorian America*, 182–96. New York: Oxford University Press, 1985.

Stearns, Peter N. "Girls, Boys, and Emotions: Redefinitions and Historical Change." *Journal of American History* 80 (June 1993): 36–74.

Stowe, Steven M. "Growing Up Female in the Planter Class." *Helicon Nine* 17 (1987): 194–205.

———. "The Not-So-Cloistered Academy: Elite Women's Education and Family Feeling in the Old South." In *The Web of Southern Social Relations: Women, Family, and Education*, edited by Walter J. Fraser Jr., R. Frank Saunders Jr., and Jon L. Wakelyn, 90–106. Athens: University of Georgia Press, 1985.

———. "The Rhetoric of Authority: The Making of Social Values in Planter Family Correspondence." *Journal of American History* 73 (March 1987): 916–33.

———. "Singleton's Tooth: Thoughts on the Form and Meaning of Antebellum Southern Family Correspondence." *Southern Review* 25 (Spring 1989): 323–33.

———. "'The Thing, Not Its Vision': A Woman's Courtship and Her Sphere in the Southern Planter Class." *Feminist Studies* 9 (Spring 1983): 113–30.

Stowell, Daniel W. "'A Family of Women and Children': The Fains of East Tennessee during Wartime." In *Southern Families at War: Loyalty and Conflict in the Civil War South*, edited by Catherine Clinton, 155–74. New York: Oxford University Press, 2000.

Tolley, Kim. "Science for Ladies, Classics for Gentlemen: A Comparative Analysis of Scientific Subjects in the Curricula of Boys' and Girls' Secondary Schools in the United States, 1794–1850." *History of Education Quarterly* 36 (Summer 1996): 129–54.

Van de Wetering, Maxine. "The Popular Concept of 'Home' in Nineteenth-Century America." *Journal of American Studies* 18 (April 1984): 5–28.

Vinovskis, Maris, and Richard M. Bernard. "Beyond Catharine Beecher: Female Education in the Antebellum Period." *Signs* 3 (Summer 1978): 856–69.

Wates, Wylma. "Precursor to the Victorian Age: The Concept of Marriage and Family as Revealed in the Correspondence of the Izard Family of South Carolina." In *In Joy and in Sorrow: Women, Family, and Marriage in the Victorian South, 1830–1900*, edited by Carol Bleser, 3–14. New York: Oxford University Press, 1991.

Watkins, Susan Cotts. "Spinsters." *Journal of Family History* 9 (Winter 1984): 310–25.

Welter, Barbara. "The Cult of True Womanhood, 1820–1860." *American Quarterly* 17 (Summer 1966): 151–74.

UNPUBLISHED DISSERTATIONS, THESES, AND PAPERS

Blake, Russell Lindley. "Ties of Intimacy: Social Values and Personal Relationships of Antebellum Slaveholders." Ph.D. diss., University of Michigan, 1978.

Broussard, Joyce Linda. "Female Solitaires: Women Alone in the Lifeworld of Mid-Century Natchez, Mississippi, 1850–1880." Ph.D. diss., University of Southern California, 1998.

Carvill, Caroline. "The Stereotype of Spinsters in Southern Fiction." Ph.D. diss., University of Arkansas, 1989.

Cole, Stephanie. "Servants and Slaves: Domestic Service in the Border Cities, 1800–1850." Ph.D. diss., University of Florida, 1994.

Cook, Florence Elliott. "Growing Up White, Genteel, and Female in a Changing South, 1865 to 1915." Ph.D. diss., University of California at Berkeley, 1992.

Gay, Dorothy Ann. "The Tangled Skein of Romanticism and Violence in the Old South: The Southern Response to Abolitionism and Feminism, 1830–1861." Ph.D. diss., University of North Carolina, 1975.

Jabour, Anya. "Hearts Divided: The Marriage and Family of Elizabeth and William Wirt, 1802–1834." Ph.D. diss., Rice University, 1995.

Kilbride, Dan. "Philadelphia and the Southern Elite: Class, Kinship, and Culture in Antebellum America." Ph.D. diss., University of Florida, 1997.

McDaniel, Mareva Layne. "'Let the Daughters Be Educated': Legal and Literary Discourse about White South Carolina Women's Education, 1840–1900." Ph.D. diss., Emory University, 1997.

Nix, Elizabeth Morrow. "An Exuberant Flow of Spirits: Antebellum Adolescent Girls in the Writing of Southern Women." Ph.D. diss., Boston University, 1996.

Ott, Victoria. "When the Flower Blooms in Winter: Young Women Coming of Age in the Confederacy." Ph.D. diss., University of Tennessee, 2003.

Pizzano, Jacqueline Marie. "The Education of Women in the New Orleans Area." Ed.D. diss., George Peabody College for Teachers, 1978.

Pope, Christie Farnham. "Preparation for Pedestals: North Carolina Antebellum Female Seminaries." Ph.D. diss., University of Chicago, 1977.

INDEX

Abortion, 221. *See also* Birth control

Adolescence, 1–3, 28

—female, 2–3, 4 (ill.), 5; in antebellum South, 3–5, 8–9, 13, 39–40, 45; in Civil War South, 6, 14–15

—male, 1–2

Academies, female, 17, 28, 41–42, 45, 47, 49, 61; in antebellum South, 14, 49–51; in Civil War South, 247–48, 249–50. *See also* Education, female; Schoolgirl culture and identity

Age and age-consciousness, 2; in antebellum South, 17–19, 25–27, 39–40; in Civil War South, 250, 258, 282–83. *See also* Adolescence; Birthdays; Resignation: and age; Resistance: and youth; Schoolgirl culture and identity

Albums, 7, 69, 70 (ill.), 76, 77, 186 (ill.), 186–88

Alcoholism, 89, 91

Anger, 38–39. *See also* Manners and morals; Southern lady, myth of the

Antislavery activity, 102; and organized feminism, 11–12, 104

Autograph albums. *See* Albums

Baptism, 42–43. *See also* Confirmation; Conversion

Belles: in antebellum South, 113, 115–16, 117–18, 120–34, 171–172; in Civil War South, 271–72. *See also* Courtship; Debut

Birth control, 218, 220–21

Birthdays, 19, 25, 27, 39–40, 108, 109

Boarding school. *See* Academies, female; Romantic friendship; Roommates; Schoolgirl culture and identity

Breastfeeding, 231–34

Brooks, Caroline. *See* Lilly, Caroline Brooks

Brown, Mary Virginia Early: at school, 59, 62, 77, 79; and single life, 92–93; on "woman's destiny," 107–8; courtship of, 122, wedding of, 189; on duties of married life, 203, 212–13; on motherhood, 231, 234

Cashin, Joan E., 10

Censer, Jane Turner, 6, 282

Chaperonage: in antebellum South, 87, 138, 140, 142; in Civil War South, 264

Charity work, 102, 128. *See also* Antislavery activity; Feminism; Reform activity

Childbirth, 225–30. *See also* Mortality; Pregnancy

Child care, 216–17, 230–34; slaves' role in, 231, 233–34. *See also* Breastfeeding; Motherhood

Civil War: and coming-of-age, 5–6, 9–10, 14–15, 237, 245, 277, 280; and politicization of southern girls, 245–49; girls' and women's support for, 251–56, 265 (ill.); and gender roles, 251–63; and domestic responsibilities, 265–70; and paid work, 277–80.

Roberts, Amanda Jane Cooley: on marriage, 89; housekeeping responsibilities of, 97; and teaching, 105–6

Rogers, Loula Kendall, 6; girlhood of, 23, 25; adolescence of, 45; and romantic friendship, 73; on commencement, 80–81; on single life, 95 (ill.), 107; on romantic love, 160 (ill.); engagement of, 162, 172; marriage of, 181–84, 183 (ill.); and motherhood, 232, 236; and Confederate nationalism, 250, 262

Romantic friendship, 70–76. *See also* Friendship; Roommates

Romantic love, 89, 157–61, 178–79; as form of emotional leverage, 92, 149, 154, 158–61, 167–70, 178–80, 208, 214; and sentimental novels, 157–58, 169, 181; and male dominance, 170–73, 187, 208–14. *See also* Companionate ideal; Courtship; Engagement; Marriage; Romantic friendship

Roommates, 66–68, 66 (ill.), 72, 75. *See also* Academies, female; Friendship; Romantic friendship; Schoolgirl culture and identity

Rules, 64–65, 65 (ill.), 68–70, 70 (ill.). *See also* Schoolgirl culture and identity

Ruffin, Elizabeth: on single life and "single blessedness," 88, 94, 108–9, 155–56; on courtship, 141

Schoolgirl culture and identity: in antebellum South, 49–51, 80–82; and academic achievement, 51, 55–61; and female friendship, 51, 64–76, 77–80; and student-teacher relations, 61–64; in Civil War South, 247–48, 249–50. *See also* Academies; Curriculum; Education, female; Friendship

Scott, Anne Firor, 2, 11, 281

Scott, Elizabeth (Lizzie). *See* Neblett, Lizzie Scott

Scott, James, 10, 13

Sewing, 23, 96, 97, 181, 204; for slaves, 198, 199–200; during Civil War, 241, 251, 253–55, 279

Sexual behavior, 217–18; same-sex, 73–74, 75; extramarital, 91–92, 207; premarital, 140–41, 146–47; marital, 218, 221. *See also* Sexual double standard; Sexuality

Sexual double standard, 91. *See also* Sexual behavior; Sexuality

Sexuality: female, 70–71, 73–74, 140; male, 71, 91–92. *See also* Sexual behavior; Sexual double standard

"Single blessedness." *See* Single life

Single life: in antebellum South, 85–88, 94–96, 95 (ill.), 106–11, 155–56; statistics on, 90; in Civil War South, 244–45, 270–77

Skinner, Penelope. *See* Warren, Penelope Skinner

Slavery: and female adolescence, 8–9; and myth of the southern lady, 11, 258; girls' attitudes toward, 269. *See also* Antislavery activity; Domestic responsibilities: in slaveholding society; Proslavery arguments

Southall, Julia: on teaching, 104–5, 279; on marriage, 137; on Civil War courtship, 271; on "single blessedness," 275–76

Southern belles, image of, 1–2. *See also* Belles; Courtship; Debut; Southern lady, myth of the

Southern lady, myth of the, 2, 211; and slavery, 11; and Confederate nationalism, 239–43, 248, 251, 256–63; and proslavery arguments, 257–58. *See also* Manners and morals; Southern belles, image of

Teachers: in antebellum South, 61–64. *See also* Teaching

Teaching: as form of resistance, 64; feminization of, 104; and single life, 104–6, 275; during Civil War, 244–45, 275, 279–80